Customer Service

SKILLS AND CONCEPTS FOR SUCCESS

Second Edition

Glencoe
McGraw-Hill

New York, New York   Columbus, Ohio   Woodland Hills, California   Peoria, Illinois

Library of Congress Cataloging-in-Publication Data

Lucas, Robert W.
    Customer service: skills and concepts for success/Robert W. Lucas p. cm.
2nd ed.
Rev. ed. of: Customer service: skills and concepts for success/Robert W. Lucas. ©1996.
Includes bibliographical references and index.
ISBN 0-07-822633-3
    1. Customer services. I. Lucas, Robert W. Customer service. II. Title.

HF5415.5 .L83 2000
658.8'12--dc21

                                                                                00-059614

Glencoe/McGraw-Hill

Send all inquiries to:
Glencoe/McGraw-Hill
21600 Oxnard Street, Suite 500
Woodland Hills, CA 91367

ISBN 0-07-822633-3

3 4 5 6 7 8   079   05 04 03 02

CONTENTS

Welcome to an exciting journey through the wonderful world of customer service into the twenty-first century. The last century was challenging, but hold onto your hats, because, as Dorothy said in *The Wizard of Oz*, "Toto, I don't think we're in Kansas anymore."

The business world, society, and the worldwide demographics have changed dramatically in recent decades. The pace of these changes is greatly accelerating and more changes will come. Further, with advances in technology, change is happening in the business world at a phenomenal pace.

So let's explore the dynamics occurring at every level of every organization in every industry and organization as we examine the people, practices, and events that make the world of customer service what it is today and will be tomorrow.

As you read this book, you will discover that it provides a thorough introduction to a crucial skill set for anyone working in business today—people skills, or the skills to better understand and relate to others.

Our intention is to raise your awareness, prompt your thinking, give you many step-by-step suggestions for improvement, and provide you with a valuable reference for information on how you and your organization can deliver service excellence. The information contained herein will benefit you whether you are new to dealing with others in a business setting or are more experienced with internal customers (e.g., coworkers or other employees) and external customers (e.g., consumers, vendors, or other end users of products).

Although the terms *customer service professional* and *customer service organization* are used throughout the book, they are not meant to be exclusive. Everyone in business or industry today has internal and/or external customers to whom they must provide products, services, information, or other deliverables.

The skills, strategies, and techniques outlined in this book are valid in any industry because they are directed toward identifying customer needs and, then satisfying those needs.

Student Text Features

Customer Service: Skills and Concepts for Success uses a wide variety of text, margin features, and activities to gain and hold your interest while providing insights into the concepts and skills related to customer service.

The text begins with an overview of what customer service involves, then focuses on specific skills and related topics, and finally provides insights into future customer service trends and issues.

The book contains 15 chapters divided into 5 parts. The parts focus on different aspects of customer service: Part 1, "The Profession," Part 2, "Skills for Success," Part 3, "Self-Help Skills," Part 4, "Enhancing Customer Relationships," and Part 5, "Customer Service for the Twenty-First Century." Along with the valuable ideas, guidance, and perspectives offered in this book, you will encounter real-world cases about experts in today's business world, as well as activities to challenge your thinking on the topics discussed.

As you move through each chapter, you will find many helpful tools to enhance your learning experience and assist you in transferring your new knowledge to the workplace.

Each chapter starts with a quote from a famous person—to prompt your thinking related to the chapter topic and focus.

Then behavioral-based **Objectives,** the main concepts that a learner should know or be able to put into use by the end of a chapter, appear. The **Objectives** direct your focus and give you a way to measure your success in grasping the chapter concepts, once you have completed the chapter.

Before you begin each chapter, you will do a self-assessment of your current skills and knowledge levels. This is the **Quick ✔ Preview,** which is a list of brief questions related to providing customer service that you answer and score yourself. Your incorrect answers help you focus on chapters and parts of chapters as you read the book; your correct answers help you determine which chapters and part of chapters you should turn to for reinforcement.

Worksheets are provided in all chapters to give you an opportunity to act immediately on what you have learned. In some cases, you will create samples based on information provided in the chapter, and in others you will develop an action plan or a list of valuable information for future use on the job.

Work It Out activities, also provided in all chapters, challenge your knowledge and provide an opportunity for individual and/or small group work on a specific topic or issue.

The end-of-chapter features begin with a **Summary** that brings together the key concepts and issues.

Chapter Review Questions are given at the end of each chapter to stimulate thinking on how certain situations might be handled using information gained in the chapter. They also can be used as a discussion vehicle to share ideas with others.

Search It Out activities give you an opportunity to expand your knowledge of customer service and your research skills on the Internet. In each chapter, you will be asked to explore the Internet to obtain a variety of customer service facts, figures, and related information that you will use in group activities, presentations, or discussions. You will also have an opportunity to participate in **Collaborative Learning** activities, in which you and one or more of your peers can work through a customer service problem to practice your skills and find answers to your questions.

Face to Face exercises are customer service scenarios in which you assume the role of an employee and use the information provided to determine how you would solve a customer service problem.

From the Frontline features end most chapters. They provide insights into customer service in a variety of businesses, industries, and organizations. Told in the words of experts in the fields, these candid snapshots describe what it is like to provide service in an ever-changing world.

The Appendixes offer a Personal Action Plan, to help you get organized, and a Reader's Customer Service Survey, to help the author—by providing your own feedback on how you view this book. In addition to filling out an actual customer survey to tell us what you liked and did not like, you will also receive a gift for completing and returning the form.

A Glossary, Bibliography, and Index follow the Appendixes.

Basis for Content

This book draws from my 29 years of management, human resources, and service experience. Some research and theoretical material appear in the book, but much of the information is derived from personal experience, research, and the reflections of other people who have experienced customer service encounters.

Whether you are new to business and wish to expand your knowledge of customer service or are more experienced and are able to describe your efforts in dealing with people through customer service, customer relations, or customer encounters, your goal in using this text should be to improve your knowledge and skills. This can lead to total customer satisfaction.

I'm confident that this book will help you reach your goals.

Robert William Lucas

ACKNOWLEDGMENTS

Throughout the years my wife, friend, and life partner M.J. and my mother Rosie have sacrificed much as I have dedicated time and effort to developing this text and others. Their support and love have been an invaluable asset in helping me reach my goals and are much appreciated.

I also thank my publishing team at Glencoe/McGraw-Hill for the many hours of patient expertise they have spent making this text package a tremendous asset for you.

Special thanks also go to the educators who have contributed significantly to the development of this text with their reviews and valuable comments. We thank them for their input.

Arnold G. Abrams
ECPI College of Technology
Hampton, Virginia

John Fulton
Franklin University
Columbus, Ohio

Elizabeth Kerbey
San Jacinto College Central
Pasadena, Texas

Harriet Strickland
Duff's Business Institute
Pittsburgh, Pennsylvania

Dan Vanconcellos
ECPI College of Technology
Roanoke, Virginia

J. M. Vulgan
ECPI Technical College
Roanoke, Virginia

William Wray
ECPI Technical College
Roanoke, Virginia

Doris Youngman
Florida Joint Replacement Center
New Port Richey, Florida

The Profession

Chapter 1

What Is Customer Service?

OBJECTIVES

After completing this chapter, you will be able to:

- *Define customer service.*

- *Identify the socioeconomic and demographic changes that have influenced customer service.*

- *Recognize the factors responsible for a shift to a service culture.*

- *List the six major components of a customer-focused environment.*

"Concentrate your strength against your competitor's relative weakness."
Bruce Henderson

CEO, Boston Consulting Group, Inc.

Before reviewing the content of the chapter, respond to the following statements by placing a "T" for true or an "F" for false on the rules. Use any questions you miss as a checklist of material to which you will pay particular attention as you read through the chapter. For those you get right, congratulate yourself, but review the sections they address in order to learn additional details about the topics.

_____ 1. The concept of customer service evolved from the practice of selling wares in small general stores, off the back of wagons, or out of the home.

_____ 2. The migration from other occupations to the service industry is a recent trend and started in the late 1970s.

_____ 3. One of the reasons for the shift from manufacturing to customer service is that society has changed.

_____ 4. As more women have entered the workforce, the demand for personal services has increased.

_____ 5. Advances in technology have created a need for more employees in manufacturing businesses.

_____ 6. Workers in the United States have more disposable income now than at any other time in history.

_____ 7. As a result of deregulation in a variety of industries, competition has slowed.

_____ 8. Six key components can be identified in a customer service environment.

_____ 9. An organization's "culture" is what the customer experiences.

_____ 10. Quality customer service organizations recruit, select, and train qualified people.

_____ 11. Customers are happy when they receive quality and quantity as promised.

_____ 12. To determine whether delivery needs are being met, organizations must examine industry standards, customer expectations, capabilities, costs, and current and projected requirements.

1. T
2. F
3. T
4. T
5. F
6. T
7. F
8. T
9. T
10. T
11. T
12. T

1 DEFINING CUSTOMER SERVICE

CONCEPT: Customer-focused organizations determine and meet the needs of their internal customers. Their focus is to treat everyone with respect and as if they were special.

Many attempts have been made to define the term *customer service*. However, depending on an organization's focus, such as retailing, industry, manufacturing, or service, the goals of providing customer service may vary. In fact, we often use the term **service industry** as if it were a separate occupational field unto itself; in reality, most organizations provide some degree of customer service. For the purposes of this text, **customer service** is defined as the ability of knowledgeable, capable, and enthusiastic employees to deliver products and services to their internal and external customers in a manner that satisfies identified and unidentified needs and ultimately results in positive word-of-mouth publicity and return business.

Many companies specialize in providing only services. Examples of this type of company are banks and credit unions, consulting firms, Internet service providers, utility companies, call centers, brokerage firms, laundries, plumbing and electrical companies, transportation companies, and medical facilities. Some organizations provide both products and services. Examples are businesses such as car dealerships, retail stores, and manufacturers that have support services for their products, supermarkets, theaters, and restaurants.

The term *service sector* as used by the Census Bureau and the Bureau of Labor Statistics in their reports and projections typically includes:

Transportation, communication, and utilities

Wholesale trade

Retail trade

Finance, insurance, and real estate

Other services (including businesses such as legal firms, barbershops and beauty salons, personal services, housekeeping, and accounting)

Federal government

State and local governments

In addition, there are people who are self-employed and provide various types of services to their customers and clients.

Customer-Focused Organizations

Some common characteristics for **customer-focused organizations** are described below.

They have internal customers (for example, peers, coworkers, bosses, subordinates, people from other areas of their organization) and/or external customers (for example, vendors, suppliers, various telephone callers, others not from within the organization).

Their focus is on determining and meeting the needs of customers while treating everyone with respect and as if they were special. Information, products, and services are easily accessible by customers. Policies are in place to allow employees to make decisions in order to better serve customers.

Management and systems support and appropriately reward employee efforts to serve customers.

Reevaluation of the way business is conducted is ongoing and results in necessary changes and upgrades to deliver timely, quality service to the customer.

Before distribution systems were modernized, peddlers went from house to house, particularly in rural areas, to deliver merchandise or services. Doctors often went to the sick person's home and made house visits. How do these methods of delivery differ from those used today? Do you think the ones used today are better? Why or why not?

The Concept of Customer Service

The concept or practice of customer service is not new. Over the years it has evolved from a meager beginning into a multibillion-dollar endeavor. In the past, when many people worked on farms, small artisans and business owners provided customer service to their neighbors. No multinational chain stores existed. Many small towns and villages had their own blacksmith, general store, boardinghouse, restaurant, tavern, barbershop, and similar service-oriented establishments owned and operated by people living in the town (often the place of business was also the residence of the owner). For people living in more rural areas, peddlers of kitchenware, medicine, and other goods made their way from one location to another to serve their customers and distribute various products. Further, to supplement their income, many people made and sold or bartered products from their homes in what came to be known as *cottage industries*. As trains, covered wagons, and stagecoaches began to cross the country, they carried vendors and supplies as well as provided transportation. During that whole era, customer service differed from what it is today by the fact that the owners and chief executive officers (CEOs) were also motivated frontline employees working face-to-face with their customers. They had a vested interest in providing good service and in succeeding.

When industry, manufacturing, and larger cities started to grow, the service industry really started to gain ground. In the late 1800s, as the mail services matured, companies such as Montgomery Ward and Sears Roebuck introduced the mail-order catalog to address the needs of customers. In rural areas, the population grew and expanded westward, and service providers followed.

Post–World War II Service

Following World War II, there was a continuing rise in the number of people in the United States in service occupations. According to an article published by the Bureau of Labor Statistics, "At the conclusion of the war in 1945, the service industry accounted for only 10 percent of nonfarm employment, compared to 38 percent for manufacturing. In 1982 services surpassed manufacturing as the largest employer among major industry groups. By 1996 the service industry accounted for 29 percent of nonfarm employment, and manufacturing, at 15 percent, was actually somewhat smaller than retail trade."

From an economic impact standpoint, service industries continue to add to the gross domestic product (GDP), of the United States. The *GDP* is a combination of the output of goods and services produced. Just after World War II, the service industry accounted for only 9 percent of GDP, but in 1994 that number had risen to more than 19 percent. During the same period, the contribution by manufacturing fell to 17 percent, down from the previous figure of about 30 percent.[1] See Figure 1-1.

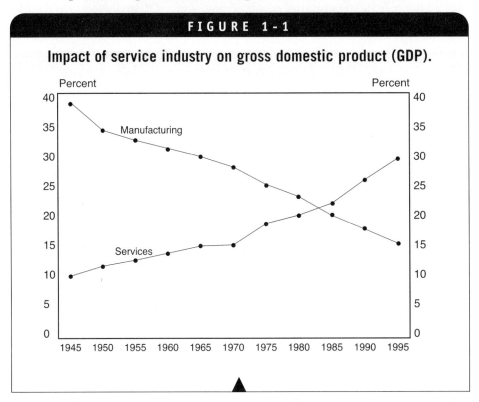

FIGURE 1-1

Impact of service industry on gross domestic product (GDP).

The Shift to Service

Today, businesses have changed dramatically as the economy has shifted from a dependence on manufacturing to a focus on providing timely, quality service. The age of the **service economy** has been alive and strong for some time now. Tied to this trend has been the development of international quality standards by which effectiveness is measured in many multinational organizations.

To highlight the importance of customer service, in 1992, after lobbying by the International Customer Service Association (ICSA), the U.S. Congress proclaimed that the first full week of October each year would be celebrated as National Customer Service Week.

[1] J.R. Meisenheimer II, "The services industry in the 'good' versus 'bad' job debate," *Monthly Labor Review*, U.S. Department of Labor, Bureau of Labor statistics, Washington D.C., February 1998, p.22.

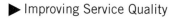

Work It Out
1-1

▶ Improving Service Quality

Take a moment to list some of the changes you have personally witnessed in the business world during your lifetime. Are these changes for better or worse? With these changes in mind, what do you—or would you—do to improve service quality as a customer service professional in your chosen industry or position?

As shown in Figure 1-2, since the end of World War II, people have moved from other occupations to join the rapidly growing ranks of service professionals.

FIGURE 1-2

Migration to the service industry.

Typical Former Occupations	Typical Service Occupations
Farmer	Salesperson
Ranch worker	Insurance agent
Machinist	Food server
Engineer	Administrative assistant
Steelworker	Flight attendant
Homemaker	Call center representative
Factory worker	Repair person
Miner	Travel professional
Tradesperson (for example, watchmaker)	Child care provider
Railroad worker	Security guard

---

2 GROWTH OF THE SERVICE SECTOR

▶ **CONCEPT:** Technology has affected jobs in the following ways: quantity of jobs created, distribution of jobs, and the quality of jobs. The service sector is projected to have the largest job growth.

The Bureau of Labor Statistics has released labor figure projections covering the years 1996–2006 that estimate a rise in the supply of workers by over 15 million people, from 134 million to 149 million people. During that period, service occupations are expected to add 3.9 million new jobs to the economy. Further, during the same period, nine of the top ten industries with the fastest employment growth and eight of the top ten occupations with the largest job growth are projected to be in the service sector.[2] See Figures 1-3 and 1-4.

---

[2] H.N. Fullerton, Jr., "Labor Force 2006: Slowing down and changing composition," *Monthly Labor Review*, U.S. Department of Labor, Bureau of Labor statistics, Washington D.C., November 1997, p.1.

FIGURE 1-3

Top ten industries with the fastest employment growth (1996–2006).

Source: U.S. Department of Labor, Bureau of Labor Statistics.

Numbers in thousands of jobs				
Industry description	Employment		Change, 1996–2006	
	1996	2006	Number	Percent
Computer and data processing services	1,208	2,509	1,301	108
Health services	1,172	1,968	796	68
Management and public relations	873	1,400	527	60
Miscellaneous transportation services	204	327	123	60
Residential care	672	1,070	398	59
Personnel supply services	2,646	4,039	1,393	53
Water and sanitation	231	349	118	51
Individual and miscellaneous social services	846	1,266	420	50
Offices of health practitioners	2,751	4,046	1,295	47
Amusement and recreation services, nec.	1,109	1,565	456	41

FIGURE 1-4

Top ten occupations with the largest job growth 1996–2006).

Source: U.S. Department of Labor, Bureau of Labor Statistics.

Numbers in thousands of jobs				
Industry description	Employment		Change, 1996–2006	
	1996	2006	Number	Percent
Cashiers	3,146	3,677	531	17
Systems analysts	506	1,025	519	103
General managers and top executives	3,210	3,677	467	15
Registered nurses	1,971	2,382	411	21
Salespersons, retail	4,072	4,481	409	10
Truck drivers, light and heavy	2,719	3,123	404	15
Home health aides	495	873	378	76
Teacher aides and education assistants	981	1,352	371	38
Nursing aides, orderlies, and attendants	1,312	1,645	333	25
Receptionists and information clerks	1,074	1,392	318	30

In addition, as technology replaces many production line workers, increasing numbers of service jobs are created. This comes about because, as greater numbers and greater varieties of goods are produced, more service people, salespeople, managers, and other professionals are needed to design and market service delivery systems that support those products. Technology-related service jobs such as those of database administrators, computer support specialists, computer scientists, computer engineers, and systems analysts are expected to continue to grow at a rapid pace.

Impact of the Economy

According to leading economists, today's economy is affecting jobs in three ways: (1) overall quantity of jobs created; (2) the distribution of jobs among industries, occupations, geographic areas, and organizations of different sizes; and (3) the quality of jobs, measured by wages, job security, and opportunities for development.[3]

Quantity of Jobs Being Created

A variety of factors including prevailing interest rates and consumer demand typically cause companies to evaluate how many people they need and which jobs will be established or maintained. In addition, the advent of technology has brought with it the need for many new technical skills in the areas of computer hardware and software operation and maintenance. At the same time, technology has created an opportunity for organizations to transfer tasks previously performed by employees to machines, thus eliminating the need for staff and in many cases leading to *downsizing* (that is, the laying off or dismissal of employees).

Distribution of Jobs

Two parallel trends in job development are occurring. The first comes about from the need for employees to be able to have regular access to personal and professional networks and to engage in collaborative exchanges. This trend means that more jobs are likely to develop in major metropolitan areas, where ease of interaction with peers and suppliers, high customer density, and access to the most current business practices exist. Training and technology resources are also available in these areas. Access to technology resources helps ensure continued learning and growth of employees and also aids organizations in achieving their goals and objectives. Most major growth is projected on the East and West Coasts and in urban areas in the southern and western areas of the country. According to Department of Labor Statistics, the areas with the highest growth of service-related jobs between January 1999 and January 2000 were Texas, South Carolina, Georgia, Florida, California, Nevada, New Hampshire, Maine, and Rhode Island with 4.0 percent and over. Nebraska had the lowest growth with less than 0.0 percent. (See Figure 1-5.)

---

[3]A.P. Carnevale, L. Gainer, and A. Meltzer. *Workplace Basics: The Skills Employers Want* (Washington D.C.: U.S. Department of Labor and American Society for Training and Development, 1989), p.81.

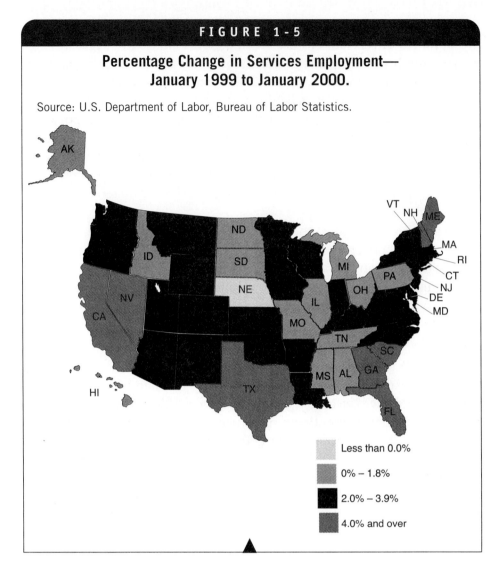

FIGURE 1-5

Percentage Change in Services Employment— January 1999 to January 2000.

Source: U.S. Department of Labor, Bureau of Labor Statistics.

Less than 0.0%

0% – 1.8%

2.0% – 3.9%

4.0% and over

Today, many employees work from their homes all or part of the time. Telecommuting, as this is called, is used frequently by companies in large cities, such as Los Angeles, to decrease travel time. Do you think you would need different skills or abilities to telecommute? Why or why not?

The second trend in job development arises from the ease of transmission and exchange of information by means of technology. It is called telecommuting. Employees can now work from their homes or satellite office location. Government agencies, technology-focused organizations, and many companies with large staffs in major metropolitan areas that experience traffic congestion (for example, Los Angeles, Boston, and Washington, D. C.) often use **telecommuting** to eliminate the need for employees to travel to work each day. The telephone and computer fax modem, make it possible to provide services from almost any remote location. For example, telephone sales and product support services can easily be handled from an employee's home if the right equipment is used. To do this, a customer calls a designated 800 number and a switching device at the company dispatches the call to an employee working at home. This is seamless to the customer, who receives the service needed and has no idea where it originated. You will learn more about technology in customer service in Chapter 7.

Quality of Service Jobs

From an individual standpoint, anyone contemplating a move to a job, whether it is service or otherwise, should consider the quality of that position. Quality can be measured in a variety of ways, and each person values some things more than others do. However, some typical evaluating factors are level of compensation (pay), employee benefits, job security, opportunity for personal and professional growth, required amount of travel, quality of the work environment, structure of the job (that is, responsibilities, reporting hierarchy), and occupational safety. Safety is especially important when machinery and equipment are involved in daily task performance and in light of the rising trend of workplace violence.

The late 1990s was witness to almost incredible economic growth, low interest rates, and new job opportunities. Unemployment rates reached a historic low. However, as the social and workplace demographics continue to shift and people move around in our mobile society, job security will be affected and it is likely that competition for desired jobs will become much more intense. Employees who obtain and maintain the better customer service jobs that provide good working conditions, security, and benefits will be better educated, trained, and prepared. They will also be the ones who understand and have tapped into the concept of professional networking. *Networking* is the active process of building relationships inside and outside the organization through meetings, interactions, and activities that lead to sound interpersonal relationships and sharing of resources. Practices such as joining and becoming actively involved in committees and boards of governors or Directors will prove to be invaluable. Many good books have been published on the subject. The Internet (for example, Amazon.com, Barnes&Noble.com, and Border.com) can lead to such resources.

3 | ADDRESSING THE CHANGES

▶ Concept: All customer-based organizations must provide excellence in service and an environment in which customer needs are identified and satisfied.

Developing strategies for providing premium service that will capture and hold loyal customers has become a priority for most organizations. All customer-based organizations have one focus in common—they must provide service excellence and an environment in which customer needs are identified and satisfied—or perish.

To this end, organizations must become **learning organizations,** a term made popular by the author Peter Senge in his book *The Fifth Discipline.* Basically, a learning organization is one that uses knowledge as a basis for competitive advantage. This means providing ongoing training and development opportunities to employees so that they can gain and maintain cutting-edge skills and knowledge while projecting a positive can-do customer-focused attitude. A learning organization also ensures that there are systems that can adequately compensate and reward employees based on their performance. In such an organization, systems and processes are continuously examined and updated. Learning from mistakes, and adapting accordingly, is crucial. In the past, organizations took a reactive approach to service by waiting for customers to ask for something or by trying to recover after a service breakdown. Often, a small customer service staff dealt with customer dissatisfaction or attempted to fix problems after they occurred. In today's economy, a proactive approach of anticipating customer needs is necessary and becoming common. To excel, organizations must train *all* employees to spot problems and deal with them before the customer becomes aware that they exist. If a service breakdown does occur, managers in truly customer-focused organizations should empower employees at all levels to do whatever is necessary to satisfy the customer. For this to happen, management must educate and train staff members on the techniques and policies available to help serve the customer. They must then give employees the authority to act without asking first for management intervention in order to resolve customer issues. This concept, known as **service recovery**, is described in detail in Part IV, "Enhancing Customer Relationships."

4 SOCIETAL FACTORS AFFECTING CUSTOMER SERVICE

CONCEPT: Many factors caused the economic shift from manufacturing to service. Increased technology, globalization of the economy, deregulation, and many government programs are a few factors. You will read about these and others in the following paragraphs.

You may wonder what, exactly, caused the economic shift from manufacturing to service. Some of the more important factors are discussed in the following sections.

Increased Efficiency in Technology

The development and increased sophistication of machines and computers have caused an increase in production and quality. Two side effects have been an increased need for service organizations to take care of the technology and a decrease in manufacturing and blue-collar jobs.

A major advantage of this change is that machines can work 24 hours, 7–days–a–week with few lapses in quality, no need for breaks, and without increases in salary and benefits. This makes them extremely attractive to profit-minded business and corporate shareholders. Although technology can lead to the loss of some jobs, technological advances in the computer and telecommunications industry alone have created hundreds of service opportunities for people who monitor and run the machines and automated services. Everything from 800 numbers and telemarketing to shopping and service via the Internet, television, and telephone has evolved and continues to expand.

Globalization of the Economy

Beginning in the 1960s, when worldwide trade barriers started to come down, a variety of factors have contributed to expanded international cooperation and competition. This trend has been termed **globalization**. Since the 1960s, advances in technology, communication, and transportation have opened new markets and allowed decentralized worldwide access for production, sales, and service. To survive and hold onto current market share while opening new gateways, U.S. firms need to hone the service skills of their employees, strengthen their quality, and look for new ways of demonstrating that they cannot only deliver but exceed the expectations of customers. All of this means more competition and the evolution of new rules and procedures that they have not been able to obtain in the past. Sometimes the deciding factor for the customer, on whether to purchase a foreign or domestic product, will be the service you provide.

Work It Out 1-2. Personal Exposure to the Global Trend

▶ To help you recognize the impact this global trend has on you and your family as consumers, think about all the products you own (for example, car, microwave oven, television, computer, fax machine). List five major products along with their country of origin (you can find this on the warranty plate along with the product's serial number, usually on the back or bottom of the product).

Product	Origin
_____	_____
_____	_____
_____	_____
_____	_____
_____	_____
_____	_____
_____	_____
_____	_____

Deregulation of Many Industries

Over the years, we have witnessed the deregulation of a number of industries (airlines and the telephone and the utility industries in the later 1990s to the early 2000s). **Deregulation** is the removal of government restrictions on an industry. The continuing deregulation of major U.S. public services has caused competition to flourish. However, deregulation has also brought major industry shakeups, sometimes leading to breakdowns in service quality in many companies. These events have created opportunities for newly established companies to step in with improvements to close the gaps and better serve customers.

Geopolitical Changes

Events such as oil embargoes, political unrest, and conflicts and wars involving various countries have reduced U.S. business access and competition within some areas of the world (for example, Cuba, Vietnam, Iran, Iraq) while some countries have free access in those areas. These circumstances not only limit access to product, manufacturing, and distribution channels but also reduce the markets to which U.S. businesses can offer products and services. For example, every closed port or country border has a negative effect on travel industry professionals, such as reservationists, air transport and manufacturing employees, and tour guides.

Other positive and negative historical changes have occurred that—like it or not—have affected the way companies do business and will continue to do so into the twenty-first century. The passage of the **North American Free Trade Agreement (NAFTA)** made it possible for many U.S.-based companies to relocate and send jobs across borders in order to find less expensive labor forces, increase profits, and avoid unions. The demise of the Soviet Union and the political and economic chaos that ensued as companies jockeyed to establish business relationships with the Commonwealth of Independent States (CIS) has also had an impact. The unexpected resignation from office on the eve of the new millennium by Russian President Boris Yeltsin, and the successor he handpicked to finish his term, added political fuel that will no doubt have longstanding effects. Whether these effects will be positive or negative remains to be seen. Further events, such as trade agreements with China and the thawing of relations with Vietnam, have opened new political doors. The severance of relations with Iran and Iraq and several other nations as the result of human rights violations, violence, terrorism, and military-related actions have created obstacles to international trade and commerce.

Geopolitical events such as these will lead to more multinational mergers and a need for better understanding of diversity-related issues by employees and managers. With increased ease of transportation and communication, companies cannot afford to ignore international competitors. For years, American firms viewed Japan as their chief economic and business rival. Now other countries are challenging Japan (Taiwan, Korea, Vietnam, China) and are becoming firmly entrenched in the marketplace. An example of this was the introduction of the South Korea–made KIA car line into the U.S. market in the 1990s. Although many Pacific Rim countries experienced severe economic setbacks during the 1990s—from inflation and a variety of political factors—these countries have traditionally been strengthened through adversity.

Increase in the Number of White-Collar Workers

With the movement out of factories and mines, and off the farm, more people find themselves working at a traditional 9 to 5 office job or providing service on a variety of work shifts (telephone and technical support centers). This trend has led to the creation of new types of service occupations: Office workers need to have someone clean their clothes, spruce up their homes (inside and out), care for their children, do their shopping, run their errands, and feed their families. In effect, the service phenomenon has spawned its own service trend.

Socioeconomic Programs

Two programs have begun in the United States that promise to have an impact on the labor force in general and on the service sector in particular. They are the Welfare to Work Partnership and Workforce Investment Act of 1998.

Welfare to Work Partnership

This program, the **Welfare to Work Partnership,** is a national, nonpartisan, not-for-profit organization created to encourage and assist businesses that hire individuals who are formerly on public assistance (welfare). The Welfare to Work Partnership was founded by United Airlines, United Parcel Service (UPS), Burger King, Monsanto, and Sprint and focuses on supporting small, medium, and large businesses that hire former welfare recipients. As of 1999, there were over 10,000 partner organizations employing some 400,000 people.

According to the Welfare to Work Partnership, the impact on the labor force is potentially significant because there is a huge labor pool in the welfare ranks. One estimate is that over 4 million women, who are statistically the primary breadwinners on assistance, have on average over four years of experience. If these people can successfully gain access to the labor force, there will be a major effect on the service sector. This conclusion is substantiated in part by a 1998 Welfare to Work membership survey conducted by Wirthlin Worldwide. The study found that, in general, the positions offered to welfare recipients are most likely to be in the service arena—clerical (37 percent), custodial or janitorial (13 percent), service work (32 percent), and general labor (49 percent). And, as stated earlier, other service industries are spawned when more people enter the workplace. In the case of welfare recipients, 33 percent need transportation and 30 percent need child care.

Workforce Investment Act of 1998

The **Workforce Investment Act of 1998** was signed into law by President Bill Clinton and started a major initiative to streamline and improve public sector employment and training services. For the most part, the law replaces the old Job Training Partnership Act (JTPA) of 1982. By the year 2000 each state must establish a Workforce Investment Board to help develop a plan for implementing the law.

Basically, centers will be established in each state that will provide job seekers with a wide range of services, from skill assessment and counseling to training and job search assistance. The centers will help people new to the job market develop work-readiness skills and find employment, and will also provide ongoing support. The impact of both the Welfare to Work Partnership and the Workforce Investment Act is that businesses will have access to larger labor pools, training, and funding that can assist making them more competitive. They will also be able to staff and maintain a workforce that is up to the task of facing a global challenge.

More Women Entering the Workforce

The fact that more women are in the workplace means that many of their traditional roles in society have shifted, out of necessity or convenience, to service providers such as cleaners, cooks, and child care providers. The tasks previously handled by the stay-at-home wife and mother are now being handled by the employees of various service companies. And, with these numbers continuing to grow each year, the need for more and better service providers will increase proportionately as workers search for someone to handle chores once delegated to the traditional homemaker.

As a matter of fact, the Department of Labor has published statistics showing that the number of women in the workplace, in all age groups, continues to grow more rapidly than the number of men. As a result, women's share of the workplace is projected to increase from about 46 percent in 1997 to approximately 47 percent in 2006.[4]

A More Diverse Population Is Entering the Workforce

As with the entrance of women into the workforce, the increase in numbers of people of color entering the workforce will have a profound impact on the business environment. Not only are the members of this expanded worker category bringing with them new ideas, values, expectations, needs, and levels of knowledge, experience, and ability, but as consumers themselves, they bring a better understanding of the needs of the various groups that they represent. During the period 1996–2006, projections are that Hispanics will enter the workforce at a faster pace than in the past until their numbers equal those of the African–American population. During the same period, white non-Hispanic workers will see their numbers drop from 75 to 73 percent of the labor force. Asians and other people of color will account for 5 percent of workers. These figures are up from the 1986–1996 period.[5] (Figure 1-6.)

You will explore these trends, and other diversity factors, further in Chapter 10.

More Older Workers Entering the Workforce

Think about the last time you went to a fast-food restaurant or a retail store like McDonald's, Wendy's, Burger King, Wal-Mart, Big K Mart, or Target. Did you notice the number of people serving and assisting you who seemed

[4]H.N. Fullerton, Jr., "Labor Force 2006: Slowing down and changing composition," Monthly Labor Review, U.S.Department of Labor, Bureau of Labor Statistics, Washington D.C., November 1997, p. 1.

[5]Ibid.

to be older than people you usually see in those roles? This relatively new phenomenon is the result of a variety of social factors. The most significant factor is that the median age of people in the United States is rising because of the aging of the "baby boom" generation (those born between 1946 and 1964).[6] For example, according to an *Orlando Sentinel* newspaper article of January 1, 2000, the average age of a resident in Orlando, Florida, is 36. And, from a workplace perspective, this means that more of the people in this age group will stay in the workplace or return once they leave. This may be caused by pure economic necessity, since many people may have not prepared adequately for retirement and cannot be certain that the Social Security system will support them. Some people return to the workplace for social reasons—they miss the work and/or the opportunity to interact with others and feel useful. Whatever the reason for the desire or willingness of older workers to reenter the workflow, many organizations have realized that they often have an admirable work ethic. Also, since there are not enough entry-level people in the traditional pool of younger workers (because of smaller birthrates during the 1970s), companies are actively recruiting older workers.

FIGURE 1-6

Entrants into the labor force by gender, race, and Hispanic origin (totals based on workers who stay in the workplace).

Source: U.S. Department of Labor, Bureau of Labor Statistics (1996–2006 projections).

Entrants to workforce by sex, race, and Hispanic origin
(Totals based on workers who stay in the workplace

Group	1986	1996	2006
Total	117,834	133,944	148,847
Men	65,422	72,087	78,226
Women	52,412	61,857	70,620
White non-Hispanic	94,026	100,915	108,166
Men	52,442	54,451	56,856
Women	41,583	46,464	51,310
Black non-Hispanic	12,483	14,795	15,983
Men	6,279	7,091	7,347
Women	6,204	7,704	8,636
Hispanic origin	8,076	12,774	17,401
Men	4,948	7,646	10,235
Women	3,128	5,128	7,166
Asian & other non-Hispanic	3,249	5,459	7,296
Men	1,753	2,899	3,788
Women	1,496	2,561	3,508
Share (percent)	100	100	100
Men	55.5	53.8	52.6
Women	44.5	46.2	47.4

---

[6]According to U.S. Department of Labor Statistics, the baby boom generation (people born between 1946 and 1964) is one of the largest population groups in the country.

Desire for Better Use of Leisure Time

Nowadays, Americans and workers of other developed nations are enjoying increasing amounts of leisure time. In the United States, workers now have more disposable income and as a whole are growing older. These factors have heightened a desire to relax, enjoy children and grandchildren, and do other things that they value—people want to use their free time in more personally satisfying ways. To accomplish this, they now rely more heavily on service organizations to maintain their desired lifestyle. Examples of some of the services tapped by the members of today's society are personal grocery shopping services, lawn services, dog walkers, laundry pickup and delivery, and executive book summaries that condense current business publications to a three- or four-page synopsis of key points.

Expectation of Quality Service

Most customers expect that if they pay a fair dollar, in return they will receive a quality product or service. If their expectations are not met, customers simply call or visit a competing company where they can receive what they think they paid for. A classic example of the power of the consumer was the spending of billions of dollars by the U.S. government and businesses to ensure that the so-called **Y2K** bug did not debilitate computer systems at the stroke of midnight on December 31, 1999. Had preventive measures not been taken to fix a programming oversight made decades ago, there would have been a monumental consumer outcry as services shut down across the country and world.

The expectation of quality service that most consumers have also creates a need for better-trained and better-educated customer service professionals. Not only do these professionals need up-to-date product information, but they also need to be abreast of current organizational policies and procedures, what the competition offers, and the latest techniques in customer service and satisfaction.

Better-Educated Customers

Customers today are not only more highly educated than in the past, they are also well informed about the price, quality, and value of products and services. This has occurred in part through the advertising and publicity by companies competing for market share and by the activities of consumer information and advocacy groups that have surfaced. As Syms, a discount-clothing store, used to tout in its advertising, "An informed consumer is our best customer." That advertising campaign was based on the belief that if you shop around and compare quality and costs, you will come back to Syms. This type of strategy sends a message that "we have nothing to hide" and invites customer confidence.

Armed with knowledge about what they should receive for their money, consumers make it extremely difficult for less than reputable businesspeople to prosper or survive. With consumers now on the defensive and ready to fight back, all business owners find that they have to continually prove the worth of their products and services. They must provide customer satisfaction or face losing customers to competitors.

Growth of E-Commerce

The last decade of the twentieth century was witness to unimagined use of the personal computer and the Internet by the average person. Almost any product is available at the click of a mouse or keyboard, or voice command. Consumers regularly "surf the net" for values in products and services without ever leaving their homes or offices. This new way of accessing goods and services through technology has been termed **e-commerce.**

Armed with a password, site addresses, and credit cards, shoppers use this virtual marketplace to satisfy needs that they likely did not know they had before logging onto their computer and connecting with the Internet. And, with so many options available for just a small investment of time, they can comparison shop simply by changing screens. No wonder the twentieth century saw the establishment of more millionaires and billionaires than any of its predecessors. The creators and owners of the most innovative sites and products can provide products and services worldwide without ever physically coming into contact with a customer, and yet can amass huge reserves of money. Examples of these success stories are e-Bay (an on-line auction service) and Amazon.com (an on-line book and product seller and auction line), which have become household names and are used by millions of shoppers yearly.

WORKSHEET 1-1

Your Perceptions

Take time to reflect on the factors you just read about and what they mean to customers. Answer these questions.

1. In what ways have you observed customers becoming more educated in recent years? _____

_____

_____

2. Has the trend by organizations to provide a wider variety of services and products by more varied means affected your life? If so, in what ways? _____

_____

_____

3. Have you witnessed an impact of more women and people of color entering the workforce? If so, how? _____

_____

_____

_____

Your Perceptions

4. In what ways have you benefited from services resulting from technological improvements? _____

_____

_____

5. What services do you use that regularly save time for other activities? _____

_____

_____

6. In what industries have you seen service personnel added during the past five years? What roles are these employees playing? _____

_____

_____

7. What examples of breakdowns in service have you heard about or experienced in your own geographic area that have led to the development or expansion of new industries or companies? _____

_____

_____

8. How many major purchases have you or your family made in the past five years of goods manufactured in the United States? Goods manufactured overseas? _____

_____

_____

5 THE CUSTOMER SERVICE ENVIRONMENT

▶ **CONCEPT:** In this section the six components that make up a service environment and contribute to customer service delivery are discussed. Use these factors to ensure that a viable customer service environment is the responsibility of every employee of the organization—not just the customer service representatives.

Let's take time to examine the six key components of a customer service environment, which will illustrate many factors that contribute to customer service delivery:

1. The customer

2. Organizational culture

3. Human resources

4. Products/deliverables

5. Delivery systems

6. Service

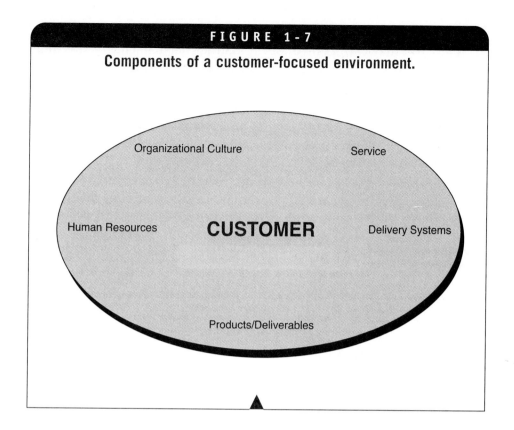

FIGURE 1-7

Components of a customer-focused environment.

Organizational Culture

Service

Human Resources

CUSTOMER

Delivery Systems

Products/Deliverables

What goes into the making of quality customer service? This is discussed in the following sections.

The Customer

As shown in Figure 1-7, the key component in a customer-focused environment is the customer. All aspects of the service organization revolve around the customer. Without the customer, there is no reason for any organization to exist. And, since all employees have customers, either internal or external, there must be a continuing consciousness of the need to provide exceptional, enthusiastic customer service. As Karl Albrecht and Ron Zemke say in their 1990 book *Service America*, "If you're not serving the customer, you'd better be serving someone who is." This is true because if you aren't providing stellar support and service to internal customers, external customers usually suffer.

Internal Customers

Many people in the workplace will tell you that they do not have "customers." They are wrong. Anyone in an organization has customers. They may not be traditional customers who come to buy or use products or services. Instead, they are **internal customers** who are coworkers, employees of other departments or branches, and other people who work within the same organization. They also rely on others in their organization to provide services, information, and/or products that enable them to do their jobs.

Recognizing this formidable group of customers is important and crucial for on-the-job success. That is because, in the internal customer chain, an employee is sometimes a customer and at other times a supplier. At times, you may call a coworker in another department for information. Later that same day, this coworker may call you for a similar reason. For example, suppose you work in the service center of a company that sells automobile parts. The people in the accounting department might provide services to you in the form of a biweekly paycheck or information on customer accounts (supplier). At other times, they may call to request customer information related to an order so that they can ensure accuracy of an invoice (customer). Only when both parties are acutely aware of their role in this customer-supplier relationship can the organization effectively prosper and grow to full potential.

Work It Out
1-3

Work It Out 1-3. Who Are My Internal Customers?

▶ Take a few minutes to think about your current organization or select any organization and create two lists: one of your internal customers and another of your suppliers. Then compare your lists to see which customers also act as suppliers and help you better serve the external customers of your organization.

Customers   **Suppliers**

_____   _____

_____   _____

_____   _____

_____   _____

_____   _____

External Customers

External customers may be current or potential customers or clients. They are the ones who actively seek out, research, and buy, rent, or lease products or services offered by your organization.

Work It Out
1-4

Work It Out 1-4. Types of Service

▶ Take a minute to think about customer service. In what ways do organizations typically provide service to external customers?

Organizational Culture

Without the mechanisms and atmosphere to support frontline service, the other components of the business environment cannot succeed. Put simply, organizational culture is what the customer experiences. This culture is made up of a collection of subcomponents, each of which contributes to the overall service environment. The impact of culture on customer satisfaction is discussed further in Chapter 2.

Perceptions of Culture

Think about a service or retail establishment you frequent (for example, restaurant, bookstore, laundry, department store, library, gas station, convenience store) and then answer the following questions.

1.As a customer, how do you perceive the service culture of that establishment?

_____

_____

_____

_____

2. What are some indicators leading to your perception?

_____

_____

_____

_____

3. If you were in charge of the organization, what would you do to improve service? Keep these ideas for improvement in mind and, if possible, implement them in your own customer service job.

_____

_____

_____

_____

_____

Human Resources

To make the culture work, an organization must take great care in recruiting, selecting, and training qualified people. That's why, when you apply (or applied) for a job as a customer service professional, a thorough screening process will be (or was) used to identify your skills, knowledge, and aptitudes. Without motivated, competent workers, planning, policy, and procedure change or systems adaptation will not make a difference in customer service. Many organizations go to great lengths to obtain and retain the "right" employees. Employees who are skilled, motivated, and enthusiastic about providing service excellence are hard to find and are appreciated by employers and customers. As noted earlier, organizations now rely on all employees to provide service excellence to customers; however, they also maintain specially trained "elite" groups of employees who perform specific customer-related functions. Depending on their organization's focus, these individuals have a variety of titles (for example, a customer service representative in a retail organization might be called a *member counselor* in an association, but these employees often perform similar functions). Some typical titles and functions performed by customer service personnel are described in the next sections.

Customer Service (CS)/Member Support Clerk

This is typically an entry-level position requiring strong organizational ability, an ability to follow instructions, listen, and manage time, and a desire to help. Key functions are clerical support, which includes filing, researching information, typing, and similar assignments.

Customer Service (CS) Representative/Member Counselor

This position is an entry-level position into the customer service field (although many people have years of experience in the job). Since these employees interact directly with customers and potential customers, they need strong interpersonal (communication, conflict management, listening) skills as well as a desire to help others, a fondness for working with people, a knowledge of organizational products and services, and thorough understanding of what a CS representative does. Key functions include interacting face-to-face or over the telephone with customers, receiving and processing orders or requests for information and services, responding to customer inquiries, handling complaints, and performing associated customer contact assignments.

Data Entry/Order Clerk

The data entry/order clerk is an entry-level position requiring knowledge of personal computers and software, ability to work on repetitive tasks for long periods of time, and an eye for accuracy. Key functions include verifying and batching orders received from customer service representatives for input by computer personnel. In organizations that have personal computer systems connected by networks, data entry/order clerks enter data, and generate and maintain reports.

Senior Customer Service (CS) Representative/Member Counselor

This position is usually staffed by personnel with experience as CS representatives. A position like this one requires a person with a sound understanding of basic supervisory skills, since job duties may include providing feedback, training, and support and administering performance appraisals to other representatives or counselors.

Inbound/Outbound Telemarketing Specialist

Customer service representatives may perform some or all of the functions of this job, but often specially hired or trained employees fill the position. In many organizations these employees are full-time or part-time sales personnel whose job is to use the telephone to call customers or potential customers or receive orders or questions from customers. Employees in these positions need strong self-confidence because of the number of rejections to offers and irate calls they receive, sound verbal communication and listening skills, positive attitude, good knowledge of sales techniques, ability to handle people who are upset, and a desire to help others through identification and satisfaction of needs. Key functions include placing and/or receiving calls, responding to inquiries with product and service information, asking for and recording orders, and following up on leads and requests for information.

In addition to these positions, many organizations have supervisor, manager, director, and vice president positions in most of the job areas indicated or in the service area as a whole. The existence of higher-level positions provides opportunities for upward advancement and learning as experience is gained.

Attracting and Training Employees

Work It Out
1-5

▶ Think about organizational strategies aimed at recruiting and training service employees. What are some things you have heard or read about that companies are doing to attract, hire, and keep qualified employees?

_____

_____

_____

_____

_____

_____

_____

_____

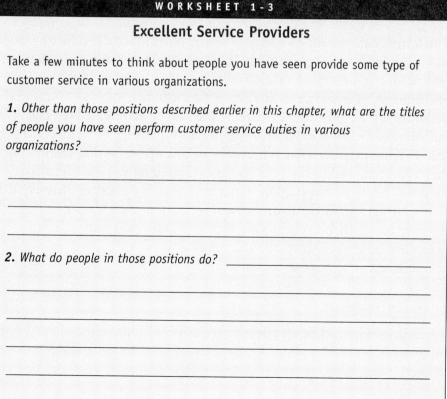

WORKSHEET 1-3

Worksheet ▼
1-3

Excellent Service Providers

Take a few minutes to think about people you have seen provide some type of customer service in various organizations.

*1. Other than those positions described earlier in this chapter, what are the titles of people you have seen perform customer service duties in various organizations?*_____

_____

_____

_____

2. What do people in those positions do? _____

_____

_____

_____

_____

WORKSHEET 1-4

Career Development

Look through your local paper or go to the library and get a copy of *The New York Times*, the *Washington Post*, or a similar paper. Scan the employment section. What type of employees and skills are service companies currently looking for? What salaries are they offering? List the information here.

Type of Employee	Skills Required	Salaries

Use this information to target your own future development and job search.

Products/Deliverables

The fourth component of a service environment is the product or deliverable offered by an organization. The product or deliverable may be a tangible item manufactured or distributed by the company, such as a piece of furniture, or a service available to the customer, such as a pest extermination service. In either case, there are two potential areas of customer satisfaction or dissatisfaction—quality and quantity. If your customers receive what they perceive as a quality product or service to the level that they expected, and in the time frame promised or viewed as acceptable, they will likely be happy. On the other hand, if customers believe that they were sold an inferior product or given an inferior service or one that does not match their expectations, they will likely be dissatisfied and could take their business elsewhere. They may also provide negative word-of-mouth advertising for the organization.

Delivery Systems

The fifth component of an effective service environment is the method(s) by which the product or service is delivered. In deciding the manner of delivery, organizations examine the following factors.

Industry standards: How is the competition currently delivering? Are current organizational delivery standards in line with those of competitors?

Customer expectations: Do customers expect delivery to occur in a certain manner within a specified time frame? Are alternatives acceptable?

Capabilities: Do existing or available systems within the organization and industry allow for a variety of delivery methods?

Costs: Will providing a variety of techniques add real or perceived value at an acceptable cost? If there are additional costs, will consumers be willing to absorb them?

Current and projected requirements: Are existing methods of delivery, such as mail, phone, and face-to-face service meeting the needs of the customer and will they continue to do so in the future?

WORKSHEET 1-5

The Customer Perspective

To get a better understanding of how your customers feel about service and their expectations, put yourself in the customer's place and answer the following question. As a customer, once you make a purchase or sign a lease, what do you expect of a product and the company selling or leasing it? Explain.

_____

_____

Worksheet ▼
1-5

Service

Stated simply, *service* is the manner in which you and other employees treat your customers and each other as you deliver your company's product(s) or other deliverables. Effective use of the techniques and strategies outlined later in this book is required in order to satisfy the needs of your customers.

---

6 | WHY SHOULD ORGANIZATIONS PROVIDE GOOD SERVICE?

CONCEPT: Without high-level customer service, companies lose business. The following chapters will build on the techniques and skills you need to develop and/or sharpen to keep this from happening.

Although the idea may seem almost too simple, the bottom line is that without high-level customer service, companies lose business. The remaining chapters will show you exactly what to do, and what skills to develop and sharpen, to stop this from happening. We'll look at why customers leave, and what can be done to prevent them from leaving.

Summary

Chapter Summary

As many organizations move toward a more quality-oriented, customer-focused environment, developing and fine-tuning policies, procedures, and systems to better identify customer needs and meet their expectations will be crucial. Through a concerted effort to perfect service delivery, organizations will be able to survive and compete in a global economy. More emphasis must be placed on finding out what the consumer expects and going beyond those expectations. Total customer satisfaction is not just a buzz phrase; it is a way of life that companies are adopting in order to gain and maintain market share. As a customer service professional, it will be your job to help foster a customer-oriented service environment.

CHAPTER REVIEW QUESTIONS

Either on your own or in discussion with someone else, review what you have learned in this chapter by responding to the following questions:

1. What is service?

   _____

   _____

   _____

   _____

2. Describe some of the earliest forms of customer service.

   _____

   _____

   _____

   _____

3. What are some of the factors that have facilitated the shift to a service economy?

   _____

   _____

   _____

   _____

4. Why are more organizations developing specially trained customer service personnel?

   _____

   _____

   _____

   _____

5. What have been some of the causes of the changing business environment in recent decades?

_____

_____

_____

_____

6. What are the six key components of a customer service environment?

_____

_____

_____

_____

7. Describe the impact of a company's culture on its success in a customer-focused business environment.

_____

_____

_____

_____

8. What role does the human resources element of the customer service environment play in customer satisfaction?

_____

_____

_____

_____

9. What two factors related to an organization's products or deliverables can lead to customer satisfaction or dissatisfaction?

_____

_____

_____

_____

10. When organizations select a delivery method for products or services, where do they get information on the best approach to take?

_____

_____

_____

_____

Searching the Web for Salary and Related Information

To learn more about the history, background, and components of customer service occupations, select one of the topics below, log on to the Internet, and gather additional research data. One valuable site is the U.S. Department of Labor at <http://stats.bls.gov>.

Report your findings to your work team members, peers, or students depending on the setting in which you are using this book.

- *Research the projected salaries and benefits for customer service providers in your industry or in one that interests you.*
- *Develop a bibliographic listing of books and other publications on topics introduced in this chapter. The resources should be less than five years old.*

You can do this by going to sites such as:

<http://www.Amazon.com>

<http://www.Borders.com>

<http://www.Barnes + Noble.com>

<http://www.glencoe.com/ps>

- *Find the Websites of at least three companies that you believe have adopted a positive customer service attitude and are benefiting as a result.*
- *Select any issue raised in this chapter and research it further.*

FACE-TO-FACE

Getting Ready for New Employee Orientation at PackAll

Background

PackAll is a packing and storage company headquartered in Minneapolis, Minnesota, with franchises located in 21 cities throughout the United States. Since opening its first franchise in Minneapolis in 1987, the company has shown great market potential, ending its first year with a profit and growing every year since.

The primary services of the organization are packaging and preparing nonperishable items for shipment and mailing via parcel post. Air-conditioned spaces for short-term storage of personal items and post office boxes are also available to customers.

To ensure consistency of service at all locations, specific standards for employee training and service delivery have been developed and implemented. Before owners or operators can hang up their PackAll sign, they must sign an agreement to comply with standards and must successfully complete a rigorous eight-week management-training program. The program focuses on the key management and business skills necessary to run a successful business and educates employees on corporate philosophy and culture. In addition management offers tips for guiding employee development. At intervals of three and six months after opening their operation, owners or operators are required to participate in a retreat during which they share best practices, receive additional management training, and have an opportunity to ask questions in a structured setting.

Your Role

Today, you joined a PackAll franchise in Orlando, Florida, as a customer service representative. New-employee orientation will be held tomorrow. At that time, you will learn about the service culture, policies and procedures, techniques for handling customers, and specific job skills and requirements.

Before being hired, you were told that your primary duties would be to service customers, provide information about services offered, write up customer orders, collect payments, and package and label orders.

Critical Thinking Questions

1. What interpersonal skills do you currently have that will allow you to be successful in your new position? _____

   _____

   _____

   _____

2. What general questions about handling customers do you have for your supervisor? _____

   _____

   _____

   _____

3. If a customer asks for a service that PackAll does not provide, how will you handle the situation? Exactly what will you say? _____

   _____

   _____

   _____

   _____

Contributing to the Service Culture

OBJECTIVES

After completing this chapter, you will be able to:

- *Explain the elements of a service culture.*

- *Describe the job responsibilities of a typical service provider.*

- *Realize that service delivery is similar in large and small organizations.*

- *Recognize customer-friendly systems.*

- *Implement strategies for promoting a positive service culture.*

"After you discover what your customers really want, you can turn to establishing your business goals and a strategy to achieve them. Whatever they are, they should be oriented toward the customer."

Jan Carlzon, President, Scandinavian Airlines in his book *Moments of Truth*

Before reviewing the chapter content, respond to the following questions by placing a "T" for true or an "F" for false on the rules. Use any questions you miss as a checklist of material to which you will pay particular attention as you read through the chapter. For those you get right, congratulate yourself, but review the sections they address in order to learn additional details about the topic.

_____ 1. Service cultures include such things as policies and procedures.

_____ 2. To remain competitive, organizations must continually monitor and evaluate their systems.

_____ 3. Advertising, service delivery, and complaint resolution are examples of customer-friendly systems.

_____ 4. To better face daily challenges and opportunities in the workplace, you should strive to increase your knowledge, build your skills, and improve your attitude.

_____ 5. Some of the tools used by organizations to measure service culture include employee focus groups, mystery shoppers, and customer lotteries.

_____ 6. By determining the added value and results for me (AVARFM), you can develop more personal commitment to service excellence.

_____ 7. Use of "they" language when dealing with customers helps demonstrate your commitment to your organization and its culture.

_____ 8. Communicating openly and effectively is one technique for working more closely with customers.

_____ 9. Even though you depend on vendors and suppliers, they are not your customers.

_____ 10. Business etiquette dictates that you should return all telephone calls within four hours.

_____ 11. Your job of servicing a customer should end at the conclusion of a transaction so that you can switch your attention to new customers.

_____ 12. Customers want value for their money and effective, efficient service.

1. T   4. T   7. F   10. F
2. T   5. F   8. T   11. F
3. T   6. T   9. F   12. T

1 | DEFINING A SERVICE CULTURE

CONCEPT: Many elements contribute to a service culture.

What is a **service culture** in an organization? The answer is that it is different for each organization. No two organizations operate in the same manner, have the same focus, or provide management that accomplishes the same results. Among other things, a culture includes the values, beliefs, norms, rituals, and practices of a group or organization. Any policy, procedure,

FIGURE 2-1 •

Elements of a service culture.

Many elements define a successful organization. Some of the more common are shown here.

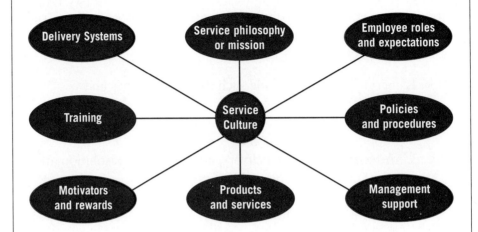

Service philosophy or mission: The direction or vision of an organization that supports day-to-day interactions with the customer.

Employee roles and expectations: The specific communications or measures that indicate what is expected of employees in customer interactions and that define how employee service performance will be evaluated.

Delivery systems: The way an organization delivers its products and services.

Policies and procedures: The guidelines that establish how various situations or transactions will be handled.

Products and services: The materials, products, and services that are state of the art, competitively priced, and meet the needs of customers.

Management support: The availability of management to answer questions and assist front-line employees in customer interactions when necessary. Also, the level of management involvement and enthusiasm in coaching and mentoring professional development.

Motivators and rewards: Monetary rewards, material items, or feedback that prompts employees to continue to deliver service and perform at a high level of effectiveness and efficiency.

Training: Instruction or information provided through a variety of techniques that teach knowledge or skills, or attempt to influence employee attitude toward excellent service delivery.

action, or inaction on the part of your organization contributes to the service culture. Figure 2-1 provides an overview of the typical elements of a service culture. Other elements may be specific to your organization or industry. You play a key role in communicating the culture to your customers. You may communicate through your appearance, your interaction with customers, and your knowledge, skill, and attitude. Culture also encompasses your products and services, and the physical appearance of the organization's facility, equipment, or any other aspect of the organization with which the customer comes into contact.

An organization's service culture is made up of many facets, each of which affects the customer and helps determine the success or failure of customer service initiatives. Too often, organizations overpromise and underdeliver because their cultural and internal systems (*infrastructure*) do not have the ability to support customer service initiatives. For example, suppose that management has the marketing department develop a slick piece of literature describing all the benefits of a new product or service provided by a new corporate partner. Then a special 800 number is set up to handle customer responses, but no additional staff is hired to handle the customer calls. The project is likely doomed to fail.

Service Philosophy or Mission

Generally, an organization's approach to business, or its **philosophy**, is driven from the top of the organization. Upper management, including members of the board of directors, when appropriate, sets the vision or tone and direction of the organization. Without a clearly planned and communicated vision, the service ethic ends at the highest levels. This is often a stumbling block where many organizations falter because of indecision or dissension at the upper echelons.

Leadership, real and perceived, is crucial to service success. In successful organizations, members of upper management make themselves clearly visible to frontline employees and are in tune with customer needs and expectations.

Although it is wonderful when organizations go to the trouble of developing and hanging a nicely framed formal mission or philosophy statement on the wall, if it is not a functional way of life for employees, it serves little purpose. (Figure 2-2 shows some typical philosophy or mission statements.)

FIGURE 2-2

Sample philosophy or mission statements.

Organizations of all sizes and types have mission or philosophy statements, designed to communicate values and purpose to customers and employees.

A.B. Dick: "To provide superior value in print solutions to customers around the world. We are steadfast in our commitment to helping our customers achieve higher-level results—from start to finish."

Yamaha Motor Company: "We create 'Kando'—Touching People's Hearts. We at Yamaha Motor are committed to creating a higher level of customer satisfaction, using our ingenuity and enthusiasm to enrich people's lives."

Procter and Gamble: "We will provide products of superior quality and value that improve the lives of the world's consumers. As a result, consumers will reward us with leadership sales and profit growth, allowing our people, our shareholders, and the communities in which we live and work to prosper."

▼

Creative Presentation Resources, Inc: "Our mission is to partner with clients in order to deliver timely, world-class human resource development interventions and products at a fair, competitive price."

Nissan: "Our first commitment is to customer satisfaction. Through diligent efforts to develop new customers and expand our customer base, we are contributing to the ongoing progress and enrichment of society."

Brunswick Hills Police Department: "It is the mission of the Brunswick Hills Police Department to enforce the laws of the United States of America, the State of Ohio, and the Resolutions of Brunswick Hills Township. Further, it is our mission to enforce the law with impartiality and courtesy, to respect the Constitutional Rights of all people, and to provide services to the citizens of Brunswick Hills Township that will enhance their quality of life."

Juvenile Diabetes Foundation: "To find a cure for diabetes and its complications through the funding of research."

Southwest Airlines: "Dedication to the highest quality of Customer Service delivered with a sense of warmth, friendliness, individual pride, and Company Spirit."

Work It Out 2-1. Organizational Culture

▶ Think about your own organization's service culture or, if you're not actively working as a customer service professional, the culture of an organization with which you are familiar.

1. What do you believe the service philosophy of this organization to be? Why?

_____

_____

_____

_____

2. Are there things that make the organization unique? If so, what are they?

_____

_____

_____

3. What factors (positive or negative) about employee performance in this organization stand out in your mind? _____

_____

_____

_____

4. Are there factors about the culture that detract from effectiveness? If so, what are they? _____

_____

_____

_____

Employee Roles and Expectations

In addition to some of the job responsibilities of service providers described in Chapter 1, many tasks and responsibilities are assigned to frontline service providers. Depending on your job, the size and type of your organization, and the industry involved, the roles and expectations may be similar from one organization to another, and yet they may be performed in a variety of different ways. Such roles and expectations are normally included in your job description and in your performance goals. They are updated as necessary during your tenure on the job. Where goals are concerned, you are typically measured against them during a performance period and subsequently rewarded or not rewarded, depending on your performance and your organization's policy.

RUMBA

For you and your organization to be successful in providing superior service to your external and internal customers, your roles and expectations must be clearly defined and communicated in terms of the following characteristics, sometimes referred to as **RUMBA** (realistic, understandable, measurable, believable, attainable).

Realistic Your behavior and responsibilities must be in line with the reality of your particular workplace and customer base. Although it is possible to transfer a standard of performance from one organization, and even industry, to another, modifications may be necessary to fit your specific situation. For example, is it realistic that all customer calls must be handled within a specified time period? Many managers set specific goals in terms of "talk time" for their customer service representatives. Can every angry customer be calmed and handled in a 2- to 3-minute time frame? If not, then a standard such as this sets up employees for failure.

After a performance goal has been set for you, evaluate it fairly and objectively for a period of time (possibly 30 days). This allows time for a variety of opportunities to apply it. At the end of the specified trial period, if you think the goal is unrealistic, go to your supervisor or team leader and discuss modifying it. In preparation for this discussion, think of at least two viable alternatives to the goals. Also, recognize that performance goals are often driven by organizational goals and those passed down from upper management. Although they might be modified, it may take some time for the change to come about, so be patient. Ultimately, if the goal cannot be modified, do your best to perform within the established standard so that your professional image does not suffer.

Understandable You must have a sound understanding of your performance goals before you can act appropriately and effectively, just the way you need to understand how to do your job or how to communicate with others in the workplace. You should first try to participate in the establishment of your goals and those of your department or team. Once goals are in place, you and everyone else affected must have a clear understanding of them so that you can effectively reach the assigned goal.

As part of the understanding step, you should apply all the skills covered in Chapters 3 to 5 related to giving and receiving information effectively. If you do not understand your goals and responsibilities, ask for clarification.

Measurable   Can your performance be measured? Yes. Typically, factors such as time, productivity, quantifiable results, revenue, or manner of performance (how you accomplish your job tasks in terms of following an established step-by-step formula) are used to determine your accomplishment of goals. In a production environment, or in certain sales environments, performance can be measured by reviewing the number of products made or sales completed. In a purely customer-focused environment, measurement can be in terms of factors such as talk time on the telephone, number of customers effectively served, customer feedback surveys and satisfaction cards, and letters or other written correspondence—or, on the negative side, by customer complaints.

Whatever the measure, it is your responsibility to be sure that you know the acceptable level and do your best to perform to that level. If something inhibits your performance, or if organizational obstacles such as conflicting priorities, overburdening multiple assignments, policies, procedures, equipment, or other employees stand in your way, you should immediately discuss the difficulties with the appropriate authority.

Believable   For any goal to be attained, it must be believable to the people who will strive to reach it and to the supervisors who will monitor it. The biggest issues in developing goals are to make them believable and to ensure that they make sense and tie in directly with the established overall departmental and organizational goals. Too often, employees are given assignments that are contrary to the ultimate purpose or mission of the organization. For example, suppose that your organizational philosophy states in part that your purpose is "to provide quality products at a competitive price in a low-pressure customer atmosphere." Your supervisor establishes a goal that requires you to have "x" number of sales per shift as an outbound sales representative. This number is two more than the typical average for a salesperson during a work shift. You recognize that to achieve this goal, you will have to be more "persuasive" than usual or than you feel comfortable.

The supervisor is putting you in the awkward position of either making your goals or facing punitive actions and losing rewards. Moreover, this practice can violate some basic principles of ethical behavior. This practice also defeats the part of the organizational philosophy that states, "in a low-pressure customer atmosphere." The topic of ethics will be discussed later in this chapter in the section "Twelve Strategies for Promoting a Positive Service Culture."

Attainable   Given the right training, management support, and organizational environment in which the tools, information, assistance, and rewards are provided, you can attain your goals. The determining factor, however, is you and your attitude toward achieving agreed-upon levels.

Managers should always attempt to set up win-win situations in which you, your organization, and ultimately, the customer benefit from any service encounter. However, you should be aware that in the "real world," this does not always happen—systems break down. In such cases, it is up to you to ensure that service continues to be delivered to customers in a seamless fashion. They should not hear about internal problems, and quite honestly, the customers probably do not care about these problems. They should be able to expect that products and services they paid for are delivered when promised, in the manner agreed upon, and without inconvenience to them. Anything less is unacceptable and is poor service.

Roles in Larger Organizations

As customers have matured in their knowledge of service standards and what they expect of providers, they look for certain qualifications in those who serve. They gain knowledge from numerous sources that help them be more savvy in their dealings with businesses (for example, *Consumer Reports* magazine, Internet research, and television shows such as *20/20, Dateline*, and *60 Minutes*). Many times, these customers become sticklers about service and when they do not get the level of service they expect, they take their business elsewhere. In some cases, they might give the organization a second chance by complaining. This benevolent initiative, allowing organizations to "fix themselves," is often done as a test. If you or your peers fail, several things can occur. You may not only lose a customer, but you may also "gain" an onslaught of negative word-of-mouth publicity that can irreparably damage an organization's image as a whole and yours specifically.

Customers expect employees to have the following qualifications and characteristics in both large and small organizations.

- *Broad general knowledge of products and service*
- *Interpersonal communication skills*
- *Technical expertise related to products sold and serviced*
- *Positive, customer-focused, "can-do" attitude*
- *Initiative*
- *Motivation*
- *Integrity*
- *Loyalty (to the organization, to products, and to customers)*
- *Team spirit*
- *Creativity*
- *Ethical behavior*
- *Time management skills*
- *Problem-solving capability*
- *Conflict resolution skills*

Such skills and capabilities are crucial, whether you are operating a cash register, polishing a car, handling a returned item, repairing a sink, coaching an executive or technical manager (for example, a consultant who offers seminars on enhancing interpersonal skills), or dealing with a negative situation (for example, a shoplifter or disgruntled customer). If you fail to possess and/or exhibit any or all of these factors, the end result could be a breakdown in the relationship between you and your customer, with ultimately negative repercussions.

Roles in Smaller Organizations

The growth of small businesses since the early 1990s has skyrocketed, especially women- and minority-owned businesses. Many small business entrepreneurs started out of necessity (because of layoffs or downsizing) or out of frustration caused by limitations within a larger structure (lack of promotion opportunity, low salaries, actual or perceived discrimination, poor management, or continual changes).

With this massive growth of sole proprietorships (one-owner businesses) and small businesses has come more choice for customers. This growth has also created problems for people making the transition from large to small organizations. This is because in addition to having to possess all the qualifications and characteristics listed earlier, employees in small businesses perform greatly varied tasks. Typically, the human resources and technical systems they might call upon for support are limited. If something goes wrong, they cannot "bump the problem upstairs," nor can they obtain immediate, on-site assistance. This often causes customer frustration or anger.

The types of jobs that fall into this struggling category run the gamut of industries. Some examples are:

- *Accountant*
- *Consultant*
- *Automotive mechanic*
- *Computer technician*
- *Salesperson*
- *Caterer*
- *Tailor*
- *Personal shopper*
- *Office support staff*
- *Office equipment repairperson*
- *Office cleaning staff*
- *Child care provider*
- *Gardener*
- *Electrician and plumber*
- *Electronics repairperson*
- *Visiting nurse or nurse consultant*
- *Driver*
- *Temporary worker*

To stave off failure and help ensure that customer needs are identified and satisfied, owners and employees in such establishments must continually strive to gain new knowledge and skills while working hard to deliver a level of service equal to that offered by the bigger organizations. The public is generally unforgiving and, like elephants, they have long memories—especially when service breaks down.

If you work in this type of environment, look for opportunities to provide stellar service and really go out of your way to practice your people skills. Get back to the basics that you will learn more about in Chapters 3 to 5—listen, ask questions, provide feedback, communicate well—and do not miss an opportunity to let your customers know that they are special and that you are there to serve their needs.

Policies and Procedures

Although there are a lot of local, state, and federal regulations with which you and your organization must comply, many policies are flexible. If you go to your bank to deposit a fairly large check that exceeds the maximum amount that the bank will accept, the teller may inform you that there will be a seven-day hold put on the check until it clears the sender's bank. In this case, you might petition the branch manager and possibly get this period modified, since you are dealing with a "bank" policy.

Many customers meet organizational culture directly when a service person falls back on "company policy" to handle a problem. The goal should be to process customer requests and satisfy needs as quickly, efficiently, and cheerfully as possible. Anything less is an invitation for criticism, dissatisfaction, potential customer loss, and employee frustration.

Return policies are a case in point. Even though customers may not always be "right," they must be treated with respect and as if they are right to effectively provide service and generate future relationships.

An effective return process is part of the overall service process. In addition to service received, the return policy of an organization is another gauge customers use to determine where they will spend their time and money. The return statements shown in Figure 2-3 send specific messages concerning the organizational culture of both organizations. Notice the tone or service culture that radiates from each example. Think about your "gut" reaction as a customer when you read both policies.

FIGURE 2-3

Sample return policies.

POLICY 1

To err is human, to return is just fine...

Already read the book? Pages printed upside down? The package arrived bruised, battered, and otherwise weary from the trip? Actually, the only reason you need to return an item bought from us is this: You're not satisfied...

Having the chance to talk with our customer helps us learn and improve our service. It is also an opportunity to demonstrate the [organization's name] customer policy: YOU'RE RIGHT!

POLICY 2

Return Policy

Returns must meet the following criteria:

1. Books must be received within thirty (30) days of the invoice date. Please allow one week for shipping.

2. Books must be received in saleable condition. Damaged books will not be accepted for credit.

3. Refunds will not be made on videotapes and software unless they were defective at the time of purchase. Please notify [organization's name] of any such defects within ten (10) days of the invoice date.

Return Shipping Information

Returns must be shipped to [organization's name and full address].

Any returns not shipped to the above address will not be credited and FULL PAYMENT for shipping will be the responsibility of the shipper.

All charges incurred in returning materials, including customer's charges, if any, are the responsibility of the shipper.

Ensure that your returns are not lost or damaged.

Comments and Feedback

We value your opinion! If you need to return any of the enclosed material, please take a minute to let us know why. Your comments and suggestions will help us better meet your needs in the future.

Organizations often hang up fancy posters and banners touting such claims as, "The customer is always right," "The customer is No.1," or "We're here to serve YOU!" But at the moment of truth, when customers come into contact with employees, they frequently hear, "Please take a number so we can better serve you," "I can't do that," or (on the phone), "ABC Company, please hold—CLICK." Clearly, when these things occur, the culture is not customer-focused and a service has broken down. The important question for organizations is, "How do we fix our system?" The answer: make a commitment to the customer and establish an environment that will support that commitment. That's where you come in as a customer service professional. Through conscientious and concerned assistance to customers, the organization can form a solid relationship with the consumer through its employees.

WORKSHEET 2-1

Worksheet ▼
2-1

Return Policies

Review the two sample return policies shown in Figure 2-3, and then respond to the following questions.

1. *What do you expect in the way of service when you need to return or exchange an item?* _____

_____

_____

2. *How would you feel if you tried to return a product and were presented with policy No. 1? Why?* _____

_____

_____

_____

3. *How would you feel about policy No. 2? Why?* _____

_____

_____

_____

4. *What do you think the organization is trying to accomplish with policy No. 1? Why do you believe this?* _____

_____

_____

_____

5. *What do you believe the organization is trying to accomplish with policy No.2? Why do you believe this?* _____

_____

_____

_____

Products and Services

The type and quality of products and services also contribute to your organizational culture. If customers perceive that you offer reputable products and services in a professional manner and at a competitive price, your organization will likely reap the rewards of loyalty and positive "press." On the other hand, if products and services do not live up to expectations or promises, or if your ability to correct problems in products and services is deficient, you and the organization could suffer adversely.

Motivators and Rewards

In any employee environment, people work more effectively and productively when their performance is recognized and adequately rewarded. Whether the rewards are in the form of monetary or material items, or a simple verbal pat on the back by the manager, most employees expect and thrive on some form of recognition.

As a way of managing your own motivation level, it is important to remember that there will be many times when your only motivation and reward for accomplishing a goal or providing quality service will come from you. The reality is that every time you do something well or out of the ordinary, you may not receive a financial or any other kind of reward for it. On the other hand, many companies and supervisors go out of their way to recognize good performance. Many use public recognition, contests, games, employee activities (sporting or other events), financial rewards, incentives (gifts or trips), employee of the month or year awards, and a variety of other techniques to show appreciation for employee efforts. Whatever your organization does, there is always room for improvement and you should take time to make recommendations of your own.

Management Support

You cannot be expected to handle every customer-related situation that develops. In some instances, you will have to depend on the experience of your supervisor or manager and defer to his or authority.

A key role played by your manager, supervisor, and/or team leader is to provide effective, ongoing coaching, counseling, and training to you and your peers. By doing this, supervisors can pass on valuable information, guide, and aid your professional development. Also, it is their job to be alert to your performance and ensure that you receive appropriate rewards based on your ability to interact effectively with customers and fulfill the requirements of your job. Unfortunately, many supervisors have not had adequate training that would enable them to provide you with the support you need. They were probably good frontline service providers, with a high degree of motivation, initiative, and ability. As a result, their management promoted them, often without providing the necessary training, coaching, and guidance to develop their supervisory skills.

If you find that you are not receiving the support you need, there are some things you should consider doing in order to ensure that you have the information, skills, and support to provide quality service to your customers.

The key is to meet with your supervisor (or anyone else you feel could be helpful) to seek help as follows:

Ask Many Open-ended Questions

To get the information you need, you may have to take the initiative. Your customer does not want to hear you say, "Nobody showed me how," "I don't know," or "It's not my job." Remember what you read earlier about seamless service. Here are some questions you might ask your supervisor:

- *What are my exact duties? (Get a copy of your job description in writing if possible.)*
- *What are your expectations of me?*
- *How do I handle [name specific] situations?*
- *Who should I see about _____?*
- *Where are [materials, policies, equipment] located?*
- *Who is in charge when you are not available?*

Strive for Improvement

Customer service can be frustrating, and in some instances, monotonous. You may need to create self-motivation strategies and continue to seek fulfillment or satisfaction. By remaining optimistic and projecting a can-do image that makes customers enjoy dealing with you, you can influence yourself and others. Smile as an outward gesture of your "I care" philosophy. Many self-help publications and courses are available that can offer guidance in this area.

Look for ways to improve your skills and to raise the level of service you provide to your customer. Whether it is through formal training, mentoring, or simply observing positive service techniques used by others and mimicking them, work to improve your own skills. The more you know, the better you can assist customers and move your own career forward.

Look for a Strong Mentor in Your Organization

Mentors are people who are well acquainted with the organization, policies, politics, and processes well. They are well connected (inside and outside the organization), communicate well, have the ability and desire to assist you (the **mentee**), and are capable and experienced. Ask these people to provide support and help you grow personally and professionally. Many good books on the topic of mentoring are available. Figures 2-4 and 2-5 list some characteristics of a mentor and *mentee*.

Avoid Complacency

Anyone can go to work and just do what he or she is told. The people who excel are the ones who constantly strive for improvement and look for opportunities to grow professionally. Take the time to think about the systems, policies, and procedures in place in your organization. Can they be improved? How? Now take that information or awareness and make recommendations for improvements. Even though managers have a key

---

FIGURE 2-4

Characteristics of an effective mentor.

When searching for someone to mentor you, look for these characteristics:

- Willingness to be a mentor
- Experienced in the organization or industry and/or job you need help with
- Knowledgeable about the organization and industry
- Good communicator (verbal, nonverbal, and listening skills)
- Aware of the organizational culture
- Well connected inside and outside the organization
- Enthusiastic
- Good coaching skills and a good motivator
- Charismatic
- Trustworthy
- Patient
- Creative thinker
- Self-confident
- Good problem solver

FIGURE 2-5

Characteristics of a successful mentee.

Since mentoring is a two-way process, you should make sure that you are ready to have a mentor. You should have the following characteristics:

- Willingness to participate, listen, and learn
- Desire to improve and grow
- Commitment to working with mentor
- Self-confidence
- Effective communication skills
- Enthusiasm
- Openness to feedback
- Adaptability
- Willingness to ask questions

---

role, the implementation and success of cultural initiatives (practices or actions taken by the organization) rest with you, the frontline employee. You are the one who interacts directly with a customer and often determines the outcome of the contact.

Some people might throw up their hands and say, "It wasn't my fault," "Nobody else cares, why should I," or "I give up." A special person looks for ways around roadblocks in order to provide quality service for customers. The fact that others are not doing their job does not excuse you from doing yours. You are being paid a salary to accomplish specific job tasks. Do them with gusto and with pride. Your customers expect no less. You and your customers will reap the rewards of your efforts and initiative.

▶ Take a few minutes to respond to the following questions. Then your instructor will group you with others to discuss responses.

1. Have you ever witnessed or experienced a customer service situation in which a supervisor or manager became involved in an employee-customer encounter? If so, what occurred? _____

_____

_____

_____

_____

2. How do you feel the supervisor handled the situation? _____

_____

_____

_____

_____

3. Could the supervisor's approach have been improved? If so, how? _____

_____

_____

_____

_____

Training

The importance of effective training cannot be overstated. To perform your job successfully and create a positive impression in the minds of customers, you and other frontline employees must be given the necessary tools. Depending on your position and your organization's focus, this training might address interpersonal skills, technical skills, organizational awareness, or job skills, again depending on your position. Most important, your training should help you know what is expected of you and how to fulfill those expectations. Training is a vehicle for accomplishing this and is an essential component of any organizational culture that supports customer service.

Take advantage of training programs. Check with your supervisor and/or training department, if there is one. If you work in a small company, have a limited budget for training, or do not have access to training through your organization, look for other resources. Many communities have lists of public seminars available through the public library, college business programs, high schools, chambers of commerce, professional organizations, and a variety of other organizations. Tap into these to gain the knowledge and skills you will need to move ahead. Also, your training and skill level will often determine whether you keep your job if your organization is forced to downsize and reduce staff.

▶ Take a few minutes to think about and respond to these questions.

1. What type of skills training do you believe would be valuable for a customer service professional? Why? _____

_____

_____

_____

_____

2. What types of training have you had or do you need to qualify for a service position?

_____

_____

_____

_____

_____

2 | ESTABLISHING A SERVICE STRATEGY

▶ **CONCEPT:** A service provider helps determine approaches for service success.

The first step a company can take in creating or redefining its service environment is to do an inspection of its systems and practices to decide where the company is now and where it needs to be in order to be competitive in a global service economy. The manner in which internal and external customer needs are addressed should also be reviewed.

As a service provider, you should do your part in determining needed approaches for service success. From the prospective of a customer service professional, ask yourself the following questions to help clarify your role.

- *Who is my customer?*
- *What am I currently doing, or what can I do, to help achieve organizational excellence?*
- *Do I focus all my efforts on total customer satisfaction?*
- *Am I empowered to make the decisions necessary to serve my customer? If not, what levels of authority should I discuss with my supervisor?*
- *Are there policies and procedures that inhibit my ability to serve the customer? If so, what recommendations about changing policies and procedures can I make?*
- *When was the last time I told my customers that I sincerely appreciated their business?*
- *In what areas of organizational skills and product and service knowledge do I need additional information?*

The best way to create a service culture is to get everyone in the organization involved in planning and brainstorming. Everyone should be encouraged to share ideas about how and where internal changes need to be made to be more responsive to customer needs. How do you think these ideas can be shared most effectively?

3 CUSTOMER FRIENDLY SYSTEMS

> **CONCEPT:** System components are advertising, compaint resolution, and delivery systems.

A service culture starts at the top of an organization and filters down to the frontline employee. By demonstrating their commitment to quality service efforts, managers lead by example. It's not enough to authorize glitzy service promotional campaigns and send out directives informing employees of management's support for customer initiatives; managers must get involved. Further, employees must take initiative to solve problems and better serve the customer. They must be alert for opportunities and make recommendations for improvement whenever appropriate. Only in these situations can changes and improvements in the culture occur.

Typical System Components

Part of the effectiveness in serving customers can be accomplished through policies and practices that say, "We care" or "You're important to us." Some systems that can send positive messages are:

Advertising

Advertising campaigns should send a message that products and services are competitive in price and that the quality and quantity are at least comparable to those of competitors. Otherwise, customers will likely go elsewhere. An advertisement that appears to be deceptive can cost the organization customers and its reputation. For example if an advertisement states that something is "free," (a cup of coffee, a buy-one, get-one-free item, tire rotation, or a consultation) but somewhere in the advertisement (in small print), there are restrictions ("with a purchase of $20 or more," "while supplies last," "if you buy new two tires," or "if you sign a one-year contract," then it is deceptive. To prevent misunderstandings as a service provider, make sure that you point out such restrictions to customers when they call or ask questions. If you notice that an advertisement sounds a bit "tricky," inform your supervisor immediately. Possibly the ad was not proofread carefully enough before it was printed and/or aired. Remember, you have a vested interest in your organization's success. Take ownership.

Complaint Resolution

The manner in which complaints or problems are handled can signal the organization's concern for customer satisfaction. If an employee has to get approvals for the smallest decisions, the customer may have to wait for a supervisor to arrive (a supermarket cashier has to call for a manager to approve a check for $10, and when the supervisor arrives, he or she doesn't even look at the check before signing and walking away). This can lead to customer and employee frustration and irritation and makes the organization look inept.

As a service professional, you should make recommendations for improvement whenever you spot a roadblock or system that impedes provision of service excellence.

Service Delivery Systems

Your organization must determine the best way to deliver quality products and service and to provide effective follow-up support. Everything you do in customer service is crucial. This includes the way information is made available to customers, initial contacts and handling of customer issues, sales techniques (hard sell versus relationship selling), order collection and processing, price quotations, product and service delivery, invoicing, and follow-up. Customers should not have to deal with internal policies, practices, or politics. They should be able to contact you, get the information they need, make a buying decision, and have the product or service selected flawlessly delivered in a timely, professional manner. Anything less is poor service.

Customers also expect value for their money. Part of this is professional, easy-to-access service. For example, if your organization does not have an 800, 877, or 888 number with online customer support, extended hours of operation, top-quality merchandise, and effective resolution of problems, your customers may rebel. They can do this by complaining, speaking negative word-of-mouth publicity, writing letters to consumer advocacy groups (television or radio stations, Better Business Bureaus, local, state, and federal government agencies), and/or going elsewhere for their needs.

Many ways are available for delivering service to customers. Two key factors involved in delivery are transportation modes (how products and services are physically delivered—by truck, train, plane, U.S. Postal Service, courier, and electronically) and location (facilities located centrally and easily accessible by customers). You will explore the use of technology in service delivery in detail when you read Chapter 7.

Direct Versus Indirect Systems

The type of delivery system used (direct or indirect contact) is important because it affects staffing numbers, costs, technology, scheduling, and many other factors. The major difference between the two types of systems is that in a direct contact environment, customers interact directly with people, whereas in an indirect system their needs are primarily through technology (possibly integrated with the human factor).

Figure 2-6 shows some ways by which organizations are providing service to customers and prospective customers.

FIGURE 2-6

Service delivery systems.

Many industries are using technology to provide service that has traditionally been obtained by a customer going to a supplier and meeting face-to-face with an organization's representative. The following lists compare the traditional (direct) and technological (indirect) approaches.

Direct Contact	Indirect Contact
Face-to-face	800, 877, 888 number
Bank tellers	Automated teller machines or online banking
Reservationists (airlines, hotels)	Online computer reservations
Front desk staff (hotels)	On-screen, in-room television checkout and bill viewing
Ticket takers (theme parks)	Ticket scanners
Customer service representatives	Online viewing to provide balance or billing information (credit card companies)
Lawyers	Telephone tip lines or E-mail
Photo developers	Self-service film kiosk or Internet transmission of digital images
Supermarket clerks	Online ordering and delivery
Towing dispatchers	In-car navigation and notification systems

---

Third–Party Delivery

In recent years, as companies strive to reduce costs, increase profit, and stay ahead of the competition, an interesting trend has occurred. Many companies are eliminating internal positions and hiring outside (third-party) organizations and individuals to assume eliminated and newly created roles (call center customer support functions, human resource benefits administration, accounting functions, and marketing). This practice of outsourcing provides multiple benefits while bringing with it some down sides. On the positive side, companies can save money by:

- *Eliminating large ongoing salaries*
- *Reducing health benefits, retirement, and 401(k) payments*

- *Avoiding the need to purchase and update computers and equipment and a myriad of other equipment*
- *Bringing in new, fresh expertise and perspectives from outside the organization*

And, on the negative side:

- *Long-term employee expertise is lost*
- *Employee loyalty to the organization suffers*
- *The morale of the "survivors" (employees whose jobs were not eliminated) is adversely affected*
- *Managing becomes more complex*
- *Customers must deal with "strangers" with whom they cannot build a long-term relationship because their provider may be gone the next time they call or stop by*

Many organizations have adopted the practice of redesignating job positions as either part-time or shared (by two employees who are both part-time and therefore do not qualify for all benefits because of the number of hours they work). Another common strategy is to fill positions with "temporary" employees contracted through a temporary staffing agency. All of this is done in an effort to reduce rising employee costs (especially benefits) while providing the necessary customer support.

Worksheet 2-2

WORKSHEET 2-2

Delivery Systems

Think about organizations you have either worked for or patronized as you respond to the following questions.

1. What were some of the strategies and systems used for delivery of products and/or customer service? _____

_____

_____

_____

2. Were the strategies and systems effective or ineffective? Why do you believe this? _____

_____

_____

_____

3. What are some things that organizations could do to improve their delivery systems? _____

_____

_____

_____

Tools for Service Measurement

In a customer-oriented environment, it is important to constantly gauge service effectiveness. Organizations can use many ways to find out how well you and your peers are doing in servicing customers. Once the results of organizational self-assessments are obtained, they will likely be shared with you and other employees in an effort to determine ways to reduce shortcomings and enhance strengths. If your supervisor fails to share such results, simply ask. Again, you have a vested interest in improvement and if he or she forgets to include you in the improvement loop—or intentionally omits you, you should take initiative to demonstrate that you do care and are concerned with customer service delivery.

Here are some of the typical techniques or tools available for gathering customer service data:

Employee focus groups. In such groups, you and others might be asked to comment or develop ideas on various topics related to customer service or employee and organizational issues. Although you will be providing interesting and valuable insights from your own perspective, remember that your views may differ significantly from those of your customers. For this reason, if your ideas are not implemented, do not be discouraged. Overriding organizational and customer issues to which you are not privy may be the reason.

Customer focus groups. Similar to the employee groups, these forums provide an opportunity to gather a group of customers (selected geographically, demographically by factors such as age, sex, race, income, or interests, or randomly from lists). Customer focus groups are brought together to answer specific questions related to some aspect of product or service.

Mystery shoppers. These people may be internal employees or external consultants who pose as customers in on-site visits or over the telephone to determine how well customers are being served.

Customer satisfaction surveys. This type of survey can be written or orally administered. It could be something as simple as an employee or manager chatting with customers at a restaurant and gathering their feedback, or it could be something more formal. Customers are sometimes asked to complete a brief questionnaire at the end of their service transaction. Some organizations do follow-up telephone satisfaction surveys; others put their surveys on their Website and encourage feedback. Customers are often enticed to participate in a survey through the use of gifts, prizes, and discounts.

Profit and loss statements or management reports. These reports are invaluable in spotting trends or dramatic changes in profits or losses that might indicate or lead to a service breakdown.

Employee exit interviews. These interviews are typically administered by the human resources or personnel department, or in smaller organizations, an officer or owner might informally ask questions of a departing employee. Such information can identify

trends or concerns. Departing employees often feel that they have nothing to lose and will candidly provide valuable feedback about management practices, policies and procedures, and a multitude of other organizational issues.

On-site management visits. These visits provide firsthand observation of service practice and allow interaction between managers, employees, and customers. They are especially helpful when there are off-site workers (at construction sites or branch offices), or operations consulting projects, or in-home services, such as plumbing). A side benefit of these types of visits is that they show that the organization is committed to fulfilling the customers' needs.

4 TWELVE STRATEGIES FOR PROMOTING A POSITIVE SERVICE CULTURE

▶ **CONCEPT:** To perform effectively as a customer service professional, you will need a plan.

Here are 12 strategies for service success.

1. **Explore your organization's vision** by working to better understand the focus of the organization and asking yourself, "What's the Added Value And Results For Me? (AVARFM)," you can develop your own commitment to helping make the organization successful. An example of AVARFM might occur when a new policy is implemented that requires you to answer a phone by the third ring.

   A "mystery caller" system is in place as a means of monitoring compliance. Also, to each employee who meets the three-ring standard rewards are given. You now have a reason or added value associated with compliance.

2. **Help communicate the culture and vision to customers—daily.** Customers have specific expectations. It does no good for the organization to have a vision if you do not help communicate and demonstrate it to the customer. Many companies place slogans and posters throughout the workplace or service area to communicate the vision. Although these approaches reinforce the message, a more effective means is for you to deliver quality customer service regularly. Through your attitude, language, appearance, knowledge of products and services, body language, and the way you communicate with your customers, they will feel your commitment to serve them. You will read more about techniques for presenting yourself professionally in later chapters.

3. **Demonstrate ethical behavior.** Ethical behavior is based on values—those of the society, organization, and employees. These values are a combination of beliefs, ideologies, perceptions, experiences, and a sense of what is right (appropriate) and wrong (inappropriate). Successful demonstration of ethical behavior is often determined by the values of the customer and how they perceive your behavior, and the customer often holds you and your organization to high standards. Thus, it is crucial for you to be aware of your words and actions so that you do not inadvertently send a negative ethical message to your customers.

   How do you know which values your organization holds as important? Many times, they are communicated in an employee manual distributed during new hire orientation. Sometimes they are emblazoned on a plaque on the wall, possibly as part of the mission or philosophy statement or next to it. However, the reality test or "where the rubber meets the road" related to your organization's values comes in the day-to-day operational actions of you and your organization.

   From an ethical standpoint, it is often up to you and your frontline peers to assess the situation, listen to your customers' requests, scrutinize your organizational policies and procedures, consider all options, and then make the "right" decision. This decision is fair—to your customer and your organization—and it is morally and legally right. A 1999 movie (*The Insider* with Al Pacino and Russell Crowe) epitomized the issues of ethical behavior. The movie is based on a true story of a tobacco industry insider who blew the whistle on his company, which publicly denied the harmful side effects of smoking. Even though the man stood to lose everything, possibly even his life, he acted out of conscience in an effort to help others.

   The key to ongoing customer relations is trust. Without it, you have no relationship.

4. **Identify and improve your service skills.** Take an inventory of your interpersonal and customer service skills; use the strengths, and improve the weaker areas. By continually upgrading your knowledge and skills related to people, customer service, and products

As a frontline contact with customers, you will be asked a variety of questions about the company and its products. You may also be asked to conduct a tour. What skills will you need and what information should you give customers in this situation?

and services offered, you position yourself as a resource to the customer and an asset to the organization.

5. **Become an expert on your organization.** As the frontline contact person with customers, you are likely to receive a variety of questions related to the organization. Typical questions involve organizational history, structure, policies and procedures systems, products, or services. By being well versed in the many facets of the organization and its operation, related industry topics, and your competition, you can project a more knowledgeable, helpful, and confident image that contributes to total customer satisfaction.

6. **Demonstrate commitment.** As an employee with customer contact opportunities and responsibilities, you are the organization's representative. One mistake that many frontline employees (and many supervisors) make in communications with customers is to intentionally or unintentionally demonstrate a lack of commitment or support for their company and a sense of powerlessness. A common way in which this occurs is with the use of "they" language when dealing with customers. This can be in reference to management or policies or procedures, for example, "Mrs. Howard, I'd like to help but our policy says..." or "Mrs. Howard, I've checked on your request, but my manager (they) said we can't..."

An alternative to using "they" language is to take ownership or responsibility for a situation by telling the customer what you can do, not what you cannot do. Customers are not interested in internal strife or procedures; they want to have their needs satisfied. To try to involve customers in situations that are out of their control and that do not concern them is unfair and unwise. Positive language and effort on your part can reduce or eliminate unnecessarily dragging the customer in. Here's one approach: "Mrs. Howard, I'm terribly sorry that you were inconvenienced by our mistake (policy or omission). What I can do to help resolve this situation is . . . "

7. **Partner with customers.** Customers are the reason you have a job and the reason your organization continues to exist. With that in mind, you should do whatever you can to promote a positive, healthy customer-provider relationship. This can be done in a number of ways, many of which will be addressed in detail in later chapters. Here are some simple techniques:

   • *Communicate openly and effectively.*
   • *Smile—project a positive image.*
   • *Listen intently, and then respond appropriately.*
   • *Facilitate situations in which customer needs are met and you succeed in win-win situations helping accomplish organizational goals.*
   • *Focus on developing an ongoing relationship with customers instead of taking a one-time service or sales opportunity approach.*

8. **Work with your customer's interest in mind.** Think to yourself, "If I were my customer, what type of service would I expect?" Then, set out to provide that service.

9. **Treat vendors and suppliers as customers.** Some customer service employees view vendors and suppliers as salespeople whose only purpose is to serve them. In fact, each contact with a vendor or a supplier offers a golden opportunity to tap into a pre-established network and potentially expand your own customer service base while providing better service to existing customers. People remember how they are treated and often act in kind.

   (Here's a hint: Even if your organization does not have a formal policy regarding returning calls, business etiquette dictates that you return all calls and do so within 24 hours or by the next business day. Even better, do so by the close of the business day if possible. Telephone skills will be discussed in more detail in Chapter 7.)

10. **Share resources.** By building strong interpersonal relationships with coworkers and peers throughout the industry, you can develop a support system of resources. Sometimes customers will request information, products, or services that are not available through your organization. By being able to refer customers to such sources, you will have provided a service, and they are likely to remember that you helped them indirectly.

11. **Work with, not against, your customers.** Customers are in the enviable position of being in control. At no time in recent history has the cliché "it's a buyers market" been more true, and many consumers know it. To capitalize on this situation, many organizations have become

very creative and proactive in their efforts to grab and hold customers. One large Colorado-based national supermarket, Albertson's, developed a series of commercials touting, "Albertson's—it's your store" and stressing that corporate efforts were focused on customer satisfaction. Your efforts should similarly convey the idea that you are working with customers to better serve them.

12. **Provide service follow-up.** Providing follow-up is probably one of the most important service components. Service does not end when the service encounter or sale concludes. There are numerous follow-up opportunities to ensure that customer satisfaction was attained. This can be through a formal customer satisfaction survey or telephone call-back system or through an informal process of sending thank-you cards, birthday cards, special sale mailings, and similar initiatives that are inexpensive and take little effort. Think of creative ways to follow up, and then speak to your supervisor about implementing them. These types of efforts reinforce service commitment to customers and let them know that you want to keep them as your customers.

5 | SEPARATING AVERAGE COMPANIES FROM EXCELLENT COMPANIES

CONCEPT: Ask questions to determine the service environment in a company in which you need employment.

Whether you are currently a service provider in an organization or seeking employment as a service provider, it is important to recognize what makes organizations successful in serving customers. If you are seeking employment, these factors can be used as a basis for questions you might ask interviewers in order to determine what type of service environment exists:

- *Executives spend time with the customers.*
- *Executives spend time talking to frontline service providers.*
- *Customer feedback is regularly asked for and acted upon.*
- *Innovation and creativity are encouraged and rewarded.*
- *Benchmarking (identifying successful practices of others) is done with similar organizations.*
- *Technology is widespread, frequently updated, and used effectively.*
- *Training is provided to keep employees current of industry trends, organizational issues, skills, and technology.*
- *Open communication exists between frontline employees and all levels of management.*
- *Employees are provided with guidelines and empowered (in certain instances, authorized to act without management intervention) to do whatever is necessary to satisfy the customer.*
- *Partnerships with customers and suppliers are common.*
- *The status quo is not acceptable.*

6 WHAT CUSTOMERS WANT

▶ **CONCEPT:** Customers expect effective, efficient service and value for their money. Customers also expect certain common things that service providers can furnish.

Most customers are like to you. They want value for their money and effective, efficient service. They also expect certain intangible things during a service encounter. Here are seven common things that customers want and expect if they are to keep doing business with you and your organization:

1. **Personal recognition.** This can be demonstrated in a number of ways (sending thank-you cards or notes, or birthday cards, returning calls in a timely fashion, taking the time to look up information that might be helpful even if the customer did not ask for it). A simple way to show recognition to a customer who enters your work area, even if you cannot immediately stop what you are doing to serve them, is to smile and acknowledge their presence. If possible, you might also offer them the option of waiting, having a seat, and so on.

2. **Courtesy.** Basic courtesy involves pleasantries such as "please" and "thank you" as there is no place or excuse for rude behavior in a customer service environment. Even though customers may not always be right, you must treat them with respect. If a situation becomes too intense and you find yourself "losing it," call upon someone else to serve that customer.

3. **Timely service.** Most people don't mind waiting briefly for service if there is a legitimate reason (as when you are waiting on another customer or obviously serving another customer on the phone), but they do not like to spend what they believe is undue amounts of time waiting to be served. Your challenge as a customer service professional is to provide prompt yet effective service.

4. **Professionalism.** Customers expect and should receive knowledgeable answers to their questions, service that satisfies their needs and lessens effort on their part, and service personnel who take pride in their work. You can demonstrate these characteristics by exemplifying the ethics talked about earlier, and the communication behaviors outlined in later chapters of this book.

5. **Enthusiastic service.** Customers come to your organization for one purpose—to satisfy a need. This need may be nothing more than to "look around." Even so, they should find a dedicated team of service professionals standing by to assist them in whatever way possible. By delivering service with a smile, offering additional services and information, and taking the time to give extra effort in every service encounter, you can help guarantee a positive service experience for your customer.

6. **Empathy.** Customers also want to be understood. Your job as a service provider is to make every effort to be understanding, and to

provide appropriate service. To succeed, you must be able to put yourself in the customer's position or look at the need from the customer's perspective as much as possible. This is especially true when customers do not speak English well or have some type of disability that reduces their communication effectiveness. When a customer has a complaint or believes that he or she did not receive appropriate service, it is your job to calm or appease in a non-threatening, helpful manner and show understanding.

7. **Patience.** Customers should not have to deal with your frustrations or pressures. Your efficiency and effectiveness should seem effortless. If you are angry because of a policy, procedure, management, or the customer, you must strive to mask that feeling. This may be difficult to do when you believe that the customer is being unfair or unrealistic, however. By suppressing your desire to speak out or react emotionally, you can remain in control, serve the customer professionally, and end the contact sooner. Some tips on managing difficult customers and your own stress levels will be addressed in Chapters 9 and 11.

Work It Out 2-4

Work It Out 2-4. Your Customer Expectations

▶ Now that you know what goes into making a customer environment "customer-friendly," think about your own expectations when you patronize a company.

Based on your own experiences, list four or five expectations that you feel are typical of most customers. _____

_____

_____

_____

_____

_____

_____

_____

_____

_____

_____

_____

_____

_____

_____

_____

_____

_____

_____

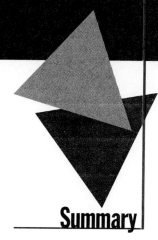

Chapter 2 Summary and Review

Professional customer service helps highlight and define service culture. Everything customers experience from the time they contact an organization in person, on the phone, or through other means, affects their perception of the organization and its employees. To positively influence their opinion, you must constantly be alert for opportunities to provide excellent service. Taking the time to provide a little extra effort can often mean the difference between total customer satisfaction and service breakdown.

CHAPTER REVIEW QUESTIONS

1. What are some of the key elements that make up a service culture?

_____

_____

_____

_____

_____

_____

2. How does management's service philosophy affect the culture of an organization?

_____

_____

_____

_____

_____

3. How does RUMBA help clearly define employee roles and expectations? Why is each component important?

_____

_____

_____

_____

_____

_____

4. How can policies and procedures affect the customer's impression of customer service?

_____

_____

_____

_____

_____

5. What questions should you ask yourself about your role as a service provider?

_____

_____

_____

_____

_____

6. What are some indicators that a company has customer-friendly systems in place?

_____

_____

_____

_____

_____

7. What are some of the tools used by organizations to measure their service culture?

_____

_____

_____

_____

_____

8. What are some strategies for helping promote a positive customer culture?

_____

_____

_____

_____

_____

9. What separates average organizations from excellent ones?

_____

_____

_____

_____

_____

10. What are some typical things that customers want?

_____

_____

_____

_____

_____

▼ SEARCH IT OUT

Customer Service and Corporate Culture

Log on to the Internet and gather research on any of the topics covered in this chapter. Make a list of the Websites you locate. Be prepared to share your findings at the next scheduled meeting. You can locate information by going to available search engines (Yahoo.com, Infoseek.com, AltaVista.com, Excite.com, or AskJeves.com) and typing in a topic header such as those listed below:

> *Corporate culture*
>
> *Ethical behavior in the workplace*
>
> *Service philosophy*
>
> *Corporate mission*
>
> *Customer needs and expectations*
>
> *Customer satisfaction surveys (assessment)*

COLLABORATIVE *Learning Activity*

Service Culture

Along with assigned group members, go on a field trip to several local organizations. Use Figure 2-1, Elements of a Service Culture, as a guideline to determine the level and quality of the service culture of each organization visited. Take notes and be prepared to share your observations with other groups when you return to class. As part of your note-taking, answer the following questions about each organization:

1. *Did you notice any overt signs that indicated the organizations cultural philosophy* (mission or philosophy statements on walls)? *If yes, what were they?*

2. *In what way was service delivered and how did the delivery indicate the organization's philosophy related to customer service?*

3. *What did the organization's products and services say about its approach to service* (quality and quantity, availability, and service support)?

4. *What evidence did you see of management support for the service initiatives being used by employees?*

5. *What indicators of motivators and rewards did you notice* (employee of the month or year plaques, parking space for employee of the month, visible indicators of rewards on employees' clothes or uniforms, for example items such as pins or buttons)?

6. *Were there any indications that training of employees is occurring* (employees have a consistent greeting or closing "Thanks for shopping at ____")?

FACE TO FACE

You and Your New Job in Customer Service

In the following case study, you are a new employee and are excited and happy to begin your position in customer service with United Booksellers. Read about the company and your role in customer service; then answer the questions at the end of the case study.

Background

United Booksellers is the fifth-largest retailer of publications on the West Coast of the United States. It started 15 years ago as a family-owned bookstore in Seattle, Washington, and has grown to over 125 stores in seven states. The organization currently employs 3,000 employees, each of whom receives extensive customer service training prior to being allowed to interact with customers.

Recent issues of *Booksellers Journal* and *Publishers Select* magazine have heralded the quality service and friendly atmosphere of the organization. United Booksellers has been praised for the appearance of the facilities, helpfulness and efficiency of employees, wide selection of publications, and intimate coffee shops where patrons can relax and read their purchases over a hot cup of fresh cappuccino.

Your Role

As a new customer service professional with United Booksellers, you are excited about starting your job, which will require continual customer contact. As a child, you watched your siblings perform customer service functions at the local Burger Mania Restaurant and always thought you'd like to follow their lead. Since you like people, enjoy a challenge, don't get stressed out easily, and have hopes of moving into management, you anticipate that this job should be just right for you. In this position, you'll be expected to receive new publications from publishers, log in receipts, stock shelves, assist customers, and occasionally work as backup cashier.

Critical Thinking Questions

1. Are there indicators of United Booksellers' service culture? If so, what are they? _____

   _____

   _____

   _____

2. If you were an employee, in what ways would you feel that you could contribute to the organizational culture? _____

   _____

   _____

3. If you were a customer, what kind of service would you expect to receive at United Booksellers? Why? _____

   _____

FROM THE FRONTLINE *Interview*

Ms. Pamela Howard
Owner
AudioBook Magic
Winter Springs, Florida

1. In one or two paragraphs, describe your customer service experience (please provide specific examples of how you have worked face-to-face with customers in any environment).

Customer service is the easiest part of any business, but it is the one aspect that people overcomplicate. At AudioBook Magic we listen to the customer, note his or her needs, and go about fulfilling them. For example, busy people often call and ask us to choose a book for them and have it ready when they stop by. Other customers ask to be notified immediately when their favorite author comes out with a new title. Once a customer whose leg was broken asked us to deliver some books. We take care of such requests.

2. What are your general impressions of service in the United States? Why do you feel that way?

I have a very negative impression of service in the United States today. When you make a telephone call, you are put on hold for an interminable length of time and then insulted when a recording tells you how important your business is to the company you have called. Then, when you go to a store, you usually have to search for an employee to help you—only to find out that the employee is uninformed.

3. In a corporate culture, what are some factors that you feel are crucial for helping ensure customer satisfaction?

As the owner of a small business, I give service that I would hope to receive as a customer. As a customer, I want and need to deal with individuals who smile, listen, care, and are sincere. I will always walk away satisfied regardless of whether I get what I wanted if these four things are present.

4. **What type of "system" (people or technology) does your organization use to identify and satisfy customer needs and to ensure delivery of quality service?**

   a. An associate answers the phone within two or three rings.

   b. Each customer is greeted when entering the store.

   c. The interests and identifying characteristics of each customer are entered in the computer, along with their rental and sales history (for example, age of children, profession, travel plans). This information can be a reference point in future conversations by any associate and can be valuable in mailings.

   d. Most important ... listen ... because the customer always tells you what he or she wants, whether directly or indirectly.

5. **In what ways do you think policies and procedures have an impact on customer service?**

   Policies and procedures are necessary to define boundaries for both the customer and the employee; however, in most organizations the rigidity with which they are enforced has had a very negative impact on customer service. Flexibility is a necessity in successful customer service.

6. **What advice——related to an employee's role in helping develop and maintain a customer-oriented environment—can you give someone entering the customer service profession?**

   a. Remember that you are there to meet the customers' needs; they are not there to meet yours.

   b. Listen and, where possible, make adjustments to fit for the customer's needs.

   c. Use the customer's name often.

   d. Smile.

CRITICAL THINKING

How do you think customer service operates in this organization? Would you handle it the same? Do you agree with the advice given?

PART

II

Skills for Success

Customer Service Skills Assessment

RATE YOUR COMMUNICATION BEHAVIOR:
We all have an image of how well we relate to others in various areas of our life—with family, in the workplace, or at social functions. To be successful in dealing with customers, you must know your skill levels for communicating and interacting with others. To help you get a better idea of how well you are currently performing in these areas, take a few minutes before beginning Part II, "Skills for Success," to rate the following statements using the key. This information is for your personal benefit and will help you focus on specific information as you read this book. The statements describe behavior commonly exhibited by people who are successful in customer relationships. Rate yourself honestly, as you feel others would.

NOTE: Since your self-image often differs from the image others have of you, make copies of this survey before you rate yourself. Once you have completed the survey, distribute the copies to people familiar with your behavior in dealing with others. Ask them to rate your general ability to relate. Even if you have not had customer service experience, their feedback will be helpful, for your interpersonal habits often carry over to customer encounters. Compare all the results and develop an action plan to improve your skills after you have read this book.

DIRECTIONS: Select the number that best describes your behavior when you work with internal customers (peers, coworkers, bosses, subordinates, external customers.

KEY: 1 = Rarely   2 = Sometimes   3 = Frequently   4 = Usually   5 = Always

_____   **1.** I smile when interacting with others.

_____   **2.** I attempt to set up relationship situations from which I and the other party gain.

_____   **3.** I strive to meet the needs and expectations of others.

_____   **4.** I provide prompt, specific feedback to inquiries I receive.

_____   **5.** I try to imagine how I would feel when dealing with irate people and then work actively toward calming them.

_____   **6.** I actively solicit, listen to, and follow up on questions, suggestions, and complaints.

_____   **7.** I offer alternatives when someone's original request of me cannot be fulfilled.

_____   **8.** I encourage continued association by demonstrating the benefits of future interactions.

_____   **9.** I answer the telephone promptly and in a professional manner.

_____   **10.** I am proactive (actively look for opportunities to improve) in finding ways to better deal with people.

SCORING:

45–50	Excellent people-oriented skills/attitude.
40–44	Good job; Keep it up.
30–39	Fair effort; Stay focused on improving relationships and work toward improvement.
20–29	Room for improvement; Get some personal coaching from experts (counselors/professors/supervisors) to help you improve.
Below 20	Evaluate your approach to dealing with people; Focus on Chapters 3–13.

Chapter 3

Positive Verbal Communication

OBJECTIVES

After completing this chapter, you will be able to:

- *Help ensure positive customer interactions in your workplace.*

- *Recognize the elements of effective two-way interpersonal communication.*

- *Project a professional customer service image.*

- *Avoid language that could send a negative message and harm the customer relationship.*

- *Provide feedback effectively.*

- *Deal assertively with others.*

"But words once spoke can never be recalled."

Horace, 65-8 B.C.
Roman poet

Before reviewing the chapter content, respond to the following questions by placing a "T" for true or an "F" for False on the rules. Use any questions you miss as a checklist of material to which you will pay particular attention as you read through the chapter. For those you get right, congratulate yourself, but review the sections they address in order to learn additional details about the topic.

_____ 1. Feedback is not an important element in the two-way communication model.

_____ 2. Customers appreciate your integrity, and they trust you more when you use language such as "I'm sorry" or "I was wrong" when you make a mistake.

_____ 3. Phrases such as "I'll try" or "I'm not sure" send a reassuring message that you're going to help solve a customer's problem.

_____ 4. When you use agreement or acknowledgment statements, customers can vent without their emotions escalating.

_____ 5. You should attempt to make a positive impression by focusing on the customer and his or her needs during your initial and subsequent contacts.

_____ 6. Having one prepared greeting and closing statement to use with all customers is a good practice.

_____ 7. When you are not certain of an answer, it is a good idea to express an opinion or speculate when something will occur if a customer asks.

_____ 8. An acceptable response to a customer's question about why something cannot be done is "Our policy does not allow . . ."

_____ 9. You should delay feedback whenever possible unless you're communicating in writing.

_____ 10. The appearance of your workplace has little impact on customer satisfaction as long as you are professional and help solve problems.

_____ 11. Assertive communication means expressing your opinions positively and in a manner that helps the customers recognize that you are confident and have the authority to assist them.

_____ 12. Assertiveness is another word for "aggressiveness."

3. F   6. F   9. F   12. F
2. T   5. T   8. F   11. T
1. F   4. T   7. F   10. F

1 THE IMPORTANCE OF EFFECTIVE COMMUNICATION

> **CONCEPT:** You represent your organization, and customers will respond according to you and your actions.

As a customer service professional, you have the power to make or break the organization. You are the front line in delivering quality service to your customers. Your appearance, actions or inactions, and ability to communicate say volumes about the organization and its focus on customer satisfaction. For all these reasons, you should continually strive to project a polished, professional image and go out of your way to make a customer's visit or conversation with you a pleasant and successful one.

A key element in making your interactions with customers successful is to recognize how you tend to communicate. The easiest way to find out how you communicate is to ask those who know you best. Unfortunately, many people are leery about requesting feedback because of what they might hear. Conversely, most people have difficulty giving useful feedback because they either never learned how to do it or are uncomfortable doing it. In any event, try it. Ask a variety of people for their feedback because each person will likely have a different perspective. In addition to any specifics you would like to learn for yourself, ask the following questions of those with whom you interact regularly:

Two-way communication is the foundation of effective customer service. How can you be sure that you are listening to the customer?

> *Do I tend to smile when I speak?*
>
> *What other body cues (nonverbal signals) do I use regularly when I speak?*
>
> *What mannerisms do I typically use when speaking?*
>
> *How would you categorize my overall presence when I speak (confident, uncertain, timid, relaxed)? Why do you perceive that?*
>
> *What "pet" words or phrases do I use regularly?*
>
> *When I speak, how does my tone sound (assertive, attacking, calming, friendly, persuasive)? What examples of this can you provide?*

2 ENSURING TWO-WAY COMMUNICATION

> **CONCEPT:** Two-way communication involves the sender and the receiver who each contribute to the communication process. Part of the process is deciding which is the best channel to ensure clear message delivery.

As a customer service professional, you are responsible for ensuring that a meaningful exchange of information takes place. By accepting this responsibility, you can perform your job more efficiently, generate goodwill and customer loyalty for the organization, and provide service excellence. To facilitate this, you should be aware of all the elements of **two-way communication** and the importance of each. Figure 3-1 shows a communication model that clarifies the process.

Interpersonal Communication Model

Environment. The environment (office, store, and group or individual setting) in which you send or receive messages affects the effectiveness of your message.

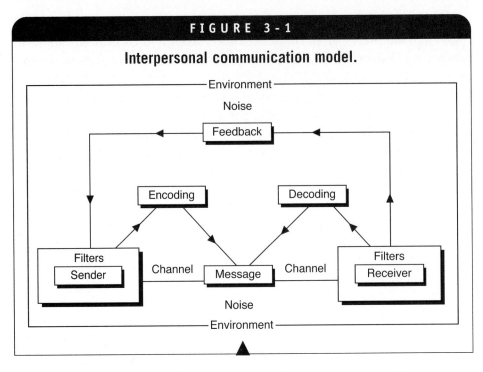

FIGURE 3-1

Interpersonal communication model.

Sender. You take on this role as you initiate a message with your customer. Conversely, when customers respond, they assume that role.

Receiver. Initially, you may be the recipient of your customer's message; however, once you offer feedback, you switch to the sender role.

Message. The message is the idea or concept that you or your customer wish to convey.

Channel. The method you choose to transmit your message (over the phone, in person, by fax, by modem, or by other means).

Encoding. Encoding occurs as you evaluate what must be done to effectively put your message into a format that your customer will understand (language, symbols, and gestures are a few options). Failing to correctly determine your customer's ability to decode your message could lead to confusion and misunderstanding.

Decoding. Decoding occurs as you or your customer converts messages received into familiar ideas by interpreting or assigning meaning. Depending on how well the message was encoded or whether filters interfere, the received message may not be the one originally sent.

Feedback. Unless a response is given to messages received, there is no way to determine whether the intended message was received. Feedback is one of the most crucial elements of the two-way communication process. Without it, you have a monologue.

Filters. Filters are factors that distort or affect the messages you receive. They include, among other things, your attitude, interests, biases, expectations, education, beliefs, and values.

Noise. Noises are physiological or psychological factors (your physical characteristics, level of attention, message clarity, loudness of message, or environmental factors) that interfere with the accurate reception of information.

AVOIDING NEGATIVE COMMUNICATION

> **CONCEPT:** Use positive words or phrases, rather than emphasize the negative.

You can squelch customer loyalty and raise customer frustration in a number of ways when communicating. Your choice of words or phrasing can often lead to either satisfaction or confrontation or it can destroy a customer-provider relationship. Customers do not want to hear what you can't do; they want to hear how you're going to help satisfy their needs or expectations. Focus your message on how you can work with the customer to accomplish needs satisfaction. Don't use vague or weak terminology. Instead of "I'm not sure . . ." or "I'll try . . ." say, "Let me get that answer for you . . ." or "I can do . . ."

Another pitfall to watch out for is the use of **global terms** (inclusive expressions such as *always, never, everyone, all*). If your customer can give just one example for which your statement is not true, your credibility comes into question and you might go on the defensive. Suppose you say, "We always return calls in four hours," yet the customer has personally experienced a situation when that did not happen. Your statement is now false. Instead, phrase statements to indicate possible variances such as, "We attempt to return all calls within four hours" or "Our objective is to return calls within four hours." Be careful, too, about "verbal finger pointing," especially if your customer is already upset. This tactic involves the use of the word *"you."* (as in "You were supposed to have called back to remind me" or "You didn't follow the directions I gave you."). This is

---

FIGURE 3-2

Words and phrases that damage relationships.

Here are some words and phrases that can lead to trouble with your customers. Avoid or limit their use.

You don't understand.	You're wrong or mistaken.
You'll have to . . .	You aren't listening to me.
You don't see my point.	Listen to me.
Hold on (or hang on) a second.	I never said . . .
I (we, you) can't . . .	In my opinion . . .
Our policy says (or prohibits) . . .	What's your problem?
That's not my job (or responsibility).	The word *problem*.
You're not being reasonable.	Do you understand?
You must . . .	Are you aware . . .
You should . . .	The word *but*.
What you need to do is . . .	Global terms (always, never, nobody).
You'll have to . . .	The word *no*.
Why don't you . . .	Endearment terms (honey, sweetie, sugar, baby).

like pointing your finger at someone or using a patronizing tone to belittle them. People are likely to react powerfully and negatively to this type of treatment. See Figure 3-2.

To practice identifying positive speech patterns, complete Worksheet 3-1.

Worksheet ▼
3-1

Correcting Negative Communication

Using the concepts given in Figure 3-2, list alternative positive phrases for each of the negative ones.

NEGATIVE	POSITIVE
You don't understand.	_____
You'll have to . . .	_____
You don't see my point.	_____
Hold on (or hang on) a second.	_____
	_____
I (we, you) can't . . .	_____
	_____
	_____
Our policy says (or prohibits) . . .	_____
	_____
You'll have to . . .	_____
	_____
That's not my job (or responsibility).	_____
	_____
You're not being reasonable.	_____
You must . . .	_____
You should . . .	_____
What you need to do is . . .	_____
Why don't you . . .?	_____
You're wrong (or mistaken).	_____
You aren't listening to me.	_____
	_____

Listen to me.

_____

_____

I never said . . .

_____

_____

In my opinion . . .

_____

_____

What's your problem?

_____

The word *problem*.

_____

_____

Do you understand?

_____

_____

_____

_____

Are you aware . . .

_____

The word *but*.

_____

The word *no*.

_____

_____

_____

_____

Global terms *(always, never, nobody)*.

_____

_____

Endearment terms (honey, sweetie, sugar, baby).

_____

Work It Out 3-1 Analyzing Your Verbal Communication Skills

Work It Out

3-1

▶ To help you determine how you sound to others, try a bit of objective self-analysis. To do this, place a cassette recorder nearby, either at home or in the office, and leave it on for about 45 minutes to an hour while you interact with other people. Then play the cassette to hear what your voice sounds like when you communicate verbally with others. Be especially alert for verbal cues that send a negative message or seem to be misinterpreted by the other people involved. Also, listen carefully to the manner in which others respond to you. Do their words or voice tone seem different from what you expected? Did they seem to respond to your comments in a way that shows confusion, frustration, or irritation because of what you said or how you said it? If you answer yes to

these questions, and this occurs several times on the tape, go back to the people involved in the conversation and ask them to help you interpret what's on the tape. You may find that your communication style is doing more to hurt than help in gathering information and building relationships with others.

4 COMMUNICATING POSITIVELY

▶ **CONCEPT:** A positive approach can produce positive results.

Just as you can turn customers off with your word choice, you can also win them over.

Figure 3-3 contains some tips.

FIGURE 3-3

Words and phrases that build relationships.

Some phrases can assist you in strengthening relationships with your customers. Such language reinforces your integrity and encourages customers to trust you. How do you or could you use these words? Which ones do you use most?

Please.	You're right.
Thank you.	May I . . . ?
I can or will . . .	Have you considered . . .
How may I help?	I'm sorry (I apologize) for . . . *However, and, or yet* (instead of *but*).
I was wrong.	It's my (our) fault.
I understand (appreciate) how you feel.	Would you mind . . . .
Situation, issue, concern (instead of *problem*).	What do you think?
Often, many times, some (instead of *global terms*).	

Positive Language

Take a few minutes to review the words and phrases in Figure 3-3. What additions can you make to that list? _____

_____

_____

_____

_____

Plan Your Messages

You should think out everything from your greeting to your closing statements before you come into contact with a customer. Know what you want and need to say, avoid unnecessary details or discussion, and be prepared to answer questions about the organization, its products and services, and the customer's order.

Greet Customers Warmly and Sincerely

If appropriate, shake hands, smile often, and offer a sincere welcome, not the canned "Welcome to . . ." Instead, use whatever your organizational policy dictates, such as, "Good morning/afternoon, welcome to . . . , my name is . . . , how may I assist or help you?"

Even on the telephone you should smile and verbally shake your customer's hand, because your smile can definitely be heard in your voice. You will learn more about customer service and telephone etiquette in Chapter 7.

Use Eye Contact Effectively

In addition to greeting the customer, make regular eye contact (no longer than 3 to 5 seconds at a time) and assume a positive approachable posture throughout your interaction with a customer. More discussion on the topics of eye contact and nonverbal communication appears in Chapter 4.

Listen Carefully and Respond Appropriately

Listening is the key element of two-way verbal communication. The manner in which you listen and respond often determines the direction of the conversation. When customers feel that they are not being listened to, their attitude and emotions can quickly change from amiable to confrontational. If necessary, review Chapter 5 for specific suggestions on effective listening.

Be Specific

Whenever you have to answer questions, especially details relating to costs, delivery dates, warranties, and other important areas of customer interest, give complete and accurate details. If you leave something out, possibly because you believe that it isn't important, you can bet that the customer will feel it was important, and will be upset.

Examples:

If deliveries are free, but only within a 50-mile radius, make sure that you tell the customer about the mileage policy. (The customer may live 51 miles away!) If a customer calls to ask for the price of an item and your quote does not include tax, shipping and handling, say so. Give the total cost, so that there are no surprises when they drive to the store to make the purchase.

Look for opportunities to communicate in a friendly atmosphere.
Do you think a friendly conversation can facilitate working through a conflict or problem?

Use Positive "I" or "We" Messages

In addition to avoiding the "you" statements mentioned earlier, focus on what "I" or "we" can do for or with the customer. In addressing the customer, state the specific service approaches you will take, for example, "I'll handle this personally," as opposed to "I'll do my best" or "I'll try." Expressions like "I'll handle this personally" sound proactive and positive. They go a long way in subtly letting the customer know that you have the knowledge, confidence, and authority to help out.

Use "Small Talk"

Look for opportunities to communicate on a personal level or to compliment your customer. If you establish quickly a relationship with your customers, they are less likely to attack you verbally or complain. Listen to what they say. Look for things specific that you have in common. For example, suppose your customer mentions that she has just returned from Altoona, Pennsylvania, where she visited relatives. If you grew up in or near Altoona, comment about this and ask questions. By bonding with the customer, you show that you recognize the customer as more than a nameless face.

Use Simple Language

Many interpersonal impartation decompositions can be ascribed to one singular customer service professional fallacy—that all customers can discern the significance of the employee's vernacular. Simply stated: *Many customer service professionals fail to use language their customers can understand.*

When dealing with customers, especially if you are selling or servicing in a technical field, use terms and explanations that are easily understood. Watch the customer nonverbal body language for signs of confusion or frustration as you speak, and frequently ask for feedback and questions.

If you are on the telephone, listen for sounds of confusion or pauses that may indicate that the customer either did not understand something you said or has a question.

Paraphrase

To ensure that you get the message that the customer intended to communicate, take the time to ask for feedback. Do this by repeating to the customer the message you heard, but do so in your own words. An example would be, "If I understand the problem, Mrs. Hawthorne, you bought this item on June 28 as a present for your son. When he tried to assemble it, two parts were missing. Is that correct?"

Ask Positively Phrased Questions

Sometimes the simplest things can cause problems, especially if someone is already irritated. To avoid creating a negative situation or escalating customer emotions, choose the wording of your questions carefully. Consider these two specific techniques. The first is to find a way to rephrase any question that you would normally start with "Why?" The reason is that this word cannot be inflected in a way that doesn't come across as potentially abrasive, intrusive, or meddlesome. As with many experiences you have, the origin of negative feelings toward the word likely stem from childhood. Remember when you used to want to do something as a child and were told no? The word that probably came out of your mouth (in a whiney voice) was "Why?" This was a verbal challenge to the person who was telling you that you couldn't do something. And the response you probably heard was "Because I said so" or "Because I'm the mommy (or daddy), that's why." Most likely, you didn't like that type of response then, and neither did your customers when they were children. The result of this early experience is that when we hear the word *why*, it can sound like a challenge and can prompt a negative emotional reaction. To prevent this from occurring, try rewording your "Why" questions.

Examples:

Instead of	Try
Why do you feel that way?	What makes you feel that way?
Why don't you like . . . ?	What is it that you don't like about . . . ?
Why do you need that feature?	How is that feature going to be beneficial to you?
Why do you want that color?	What other colors have you considered?

The second technique to consider regarding question phrasing is to ask questions that do not create or add to a negative impression. This is especially important if you have a customer who is already saying negative things about you, your product or service, or the company. By asking questions that start with a negative word and trying to lead customers to an answer, you can be subtly adding fuel to a fire. For example, suppose your customer is upset because he ordered window blinds through the mail and did not get the color he wanted. He has called you to complain. You have asked a few questions to determine the color scheme of the room in which the blinds will be installed. You say, "Based on what you have told me, don't you think the color you received would work just as well?" Your customer now launches into a tirade. He probably thinks that you were not listening to him, were not concerned about his needs, and presumed you could lead him to another decision.

Here are some more examples of questions that could cause communication breakdowns, along with some suggested alternatives.

Example:

Instead of	Try
Don't you think . . . ?	What do you think . . . ?
Wouldn't this work as well?	How do you think this would work?
Couldn't we do . . . instead?	Could we try . . . instead?
Aren't you going to make a deposit?	What amount would you like to deposit?
Don't you have two pennies?	Do you have two pennies?
Shouldn't you try this for a week before we replace the part again?	How do you feel about trying it for a week to see how it works before we replace the part again?

Communicate to Your Customer's Learning Style

People process information in one of three ways—visually (seeing), aurally (hearing), or kinesthetically (touching). (Figure 3-4 gives examples of people's styles and how they express their preferences.) To increase the likelihood that the messages you send are received in the most positive and successful manner, you should strive to encode them based on your customers' preferred style of learning. By being aware of their verbal and physical reactions and mannerisms, you can often determine the best way to send messages.

Ask Permission

Get customer approval before taking action that was not previously approved or discussed, such as putting a telephone caller on hold or interrupting. By doing so, you can raise the customers to a position of authority, boost their self-esteem, and empower them (to say yes or no). They'll likely appreciate all three. You'll learn more about telephone etiquette and effective usage in Chapter 7.

Agree With Customers

Like most other people, customers like to hear that they are right. This is especially true when a mistake has been made or something goes wrong. When a customer has a complaint or is upset because a product and/or service does not live up to expectations, acknowledge the emotion he or she is feeling and then move on and help resolve the issue. Defusing by acknowledgment is a powerful tool. However, listen carefully for the level of emotion. If the customer is very angry, you may want to choose your words carefully. For example, suppose you have a customer who has called or returned to your store on four occasions to address a single problem with a product. She has been inconvenienced, has not gotten satisfaction in the previous encounters and has spent extra time in an effort to correct

FIGURE 3-4

Personal learning orientations.

Message Preference	Orientation	Environmental Influences	Verbal Clues
Visual (Seeing)	Images or pictures	Amount of stimulus Lighting Colors Design patterns	• I see what you mean. • I think I get the picture. • Some people can't see the forest for the trees. • Look at it this way. • Help me visualize what you're saying. • That gives me the big picture. • The way I see it . . . • It appears to me.
Aural (Hearing)	Words or language	Noise levels Sound pitch (high or low) Speed of message Diversity of sounds	• That sounds okay. • That's music to my ears. • Let me hear more about that. • If I'm hearing you correctly. • It sounds like you're saying . . . • As I hear it. • We'd better keep our ear to the ground. • In one ear and out the other. • Sounds a little strange to me. • I hear exactly what you're saying. • Talk is cheap. • Something doesn't sound right.
Kinesthetic (Hands-on)	Experience or practical application	Proxemics (space) Touch Room temperature Room arrangement	• I think I've got a grip on what you're saying. • It feels to me . . . • That's a little too close for comfort. • How do you feel about this? • I'm not sure I'm comfortable with . . . • Things are really heating up. • Let's roll up our sleeves and get started. • I'm not sure I can go for that. • How do you feel about . . . ? • Let's analyze this. • I can't quite grasp your meaning. • If the shoe fits.

the problem. When she calls or arrives, her voice tone and volume are elevated and she is demanding that you get a supervisor. In this situation, your best approach probably is to let her vent and describe the problem without interrupting, apologize as often as appropriate, and do everything you can to resolve the issue fairly (assuming that she has a legitimate complaint). You would not want to use a statement that could further enflame her. Phrases such as, "You sound upset Ms. O'Malley," or "I can understand how you feel" can come across as patronizing and insincere when someone is really angry. Instead of using such terminology, try looking for something she is saying that you can agree with. Also, remember that when customers get angry, raise their voices and say certain things, they are not typically angry with the customer representative—they are frustrated and angry with the organization and/or system. For example, suppose Ms. O'Malley says something like, "You people are a bunch of idiots. I've been coming in here for years and I always have problems. Why don't you hire someone with brains to serve your customers?" The normal human response would be to retaliate. However, think back on what happened when you were a child at the playground. When someone pushed you or called you a name and you responded with name-calling or pushed back, emotions escalated until someone either struck out or ran away crying. No one won. The relationship was damaged, possibly irreparably. In the case of Ms. O'Malley, if you strike back with similar comments, neither of you will win. Moreover, you will likely lose a valued customer who will tell her story to many friends—and you will have to explain to your boss why you acted the way you did. Instead, try a defusing technique in which you seek something to agree upon. For example, you might reply, "I know this is frustrating, especially when it seems we haven't done a good job solving your problem." After this, assuming she doesn't launch back in with another tirade, you might then offer, "Let me help you take care of this right now." If she does verbally attack again, let her vent and then try another calm agreement response, followed by a second offer to assist. The value in this approach is that in letting Ms. O'Malley vent, you are discovering her emotions and possibly the history of the problem by listening actively. If you need more information, you can ask questions once you have defused her emotions and she calms down a bit. Typically, if you remain calm and objective and look for minor things with which you can agree, the customer will back off. Also, the customer will likely start to see that she is the one out of control and that you are being professional while trying to help her. If the customer truly wants the problem to be solved, she soon realizes that cooperation with you is necessary.

In many cases, if you resolve the customer's problem professionally, the customer will often apologize for his or her actions and words.

Solicit Customer Feedback and Participation

Make customers feel as if they are a part of the conversation by asking questions. Ask opinions, find out how they feel about what you're doing or saying, and get them involved by building **rapport** through ongoing dialogue. Acknowledge their ideas, suggestions, or information with statements such as, "That's a good idea (or suggestion or decision)." This will foster a feeling that the two of you are working together to solve a problem. The beauty of such an approach is that if the customers come up with an idea and you follow through on it, they feel a sense of ownership and are less likely to complain later or feel bad if things don't work out as planned.

Close the Transaction Professionally

Instead of some parroted response used for each customer like, "Have a nice day," offer a sincere "thank-you" and encourage the customer to return in the future. Remember that part of a service culture is building customer loyalty. You will have an opportunity to examine that subject in depth in Chapter 13.

WORKSHEET 3-3

Looking For Positive Experiences

It is often easy to spot exceptional or substandard service, but we sometimes overlook solid, positive service delivery. To raise your awareness of what positive service consists of and how it is delivered, take a day during a weekend or holiday and go on a service "scavenger hunt." First review the techniques covered in the section "Communicating Positively." Visit as many stores or businesses as possible in your area (maybe a local mall). Search for instances in which service providers used these or other techniques to deliver quality service. Afterward, answer the following questions.

1. What types of positive communication did you find? (Give examples.) _____

_____

_____

_____

2. How did you (or whoever you witnessed) react to the techniques experienced? (Be specific.) _____

_____

_____

_____

3. What techniques (other than the ones from the text) did you witness or experience? _____

_____

_____

_____

---

5 | PROJECTING A POSITIVE IMAGE

▶ **CONCEPT:** Make the customer feel special and important. Take responsibility for what you say and do.

Knowing what to say and when to say it in a customer service environment can often determine the outcome of a customer encounter. As mentioned before, it is not only what you say but how you say it that makes an impression on your customers. As a customer service professional, you should always attempt to make a positive impression by focusing on the customer and his or her needs during your initial contact and all subsequent ones. This effort benefits you and the customer immediately and the organization in the long term. Here are some tips for projecting a positive image and communicating professionally.

Make Customers Feel Welcome

Most people like to feel as if they belong, to be recognized as special, and to be seen as individuals. Know the customer's name, use it in greeting him or her, several times throughout the conversation, and when closing the encounter. Try to avoid using negative-sounding "you" messages as a primary means of addressing your customer. For example, instead of "You'll need to fill out this form before I can process your refund," try "Mr. Renaldi, if you could please provide some information on this form while I start processing your refund, we'll have you out of here in a minute." The latter approach makes it sound as if you recognize customers as being important, respect their time, and are not dictating to them. This can often mean the difference between a smile from your customer and a confrontation and demand to speak to a supervisor.

Many companies go out of their way to send the message of "family." For example, the Saturn automobile company advertisements tout that customers become part of the "Saturn family" once they buy a car from the company. Similarly, CarMax and several other national automobile chains go to great lengths to make the customer feel welcome and special. For example, they drape a huge ribbon over a newly purchased vehicle in a well-lighted garage, available sales representatives gather round with the customer to congratulate him or her on being part of the "family," and photographs are taken of this "special moment."

Focus on the Customer as a Person

Strive to let customers know that you recognize them as persons and appreciate their time, effort, patience, trust, and business. This is important. To deliver quality service effectively, you must deal with the human being before you deal with his or her needs or business concerns. For example, if someone has waited in a line or on hold for service, as soon as this person steps up or you come back on the line; smile warmly (yes, even on the phone, since a smile can be heard in your voice), thank him or her for being patient, apologize for the wait, and ask what you can do to assist him or her. Often in such situations the service provider says something like, "Next," (sounds canned and not customer-focused) or "Can I help the next person?" (better, but still goes straight to business without an apology or without recognizing the customer's inconvenience or wait). On the phone the service provider goes straight to, "This is Jean, how may I help you?" (with no recognition of the customer's inconvenience).

Another opportunity to focus on the customer occurs at the end of a transaction or call. If your organization does not have a standard parting comment to use with customers, simply smile and say something like, "Mr. Rinaldi, thank you for coming to (or calling) ABC Corporation. Please come back (or call) again." The key is that you must sound sincere. You may even want to modify your parting statement for subsequent customers so that it sounds more personal—and so the next person in line doesn't hear you parrot the same words with each customer.

Work It Out 3-2 Feeling Special

▶ Think of times when you have been put on hold or stood in a line.

*1. How did the service provider address you when it was your turn for service?*_____

_____

_____

2. Did you feel special or did you feel like the next in a long line of bodies being processed? Why? _____

_____

*3. When the service provider simply picked up the phone and offered to assist you or shouted "Next" while you waited in line, what thoughts went through your mind about the provider and the organization?*_____

_____

4. What could service providers do or say to eliminate negative customer feelings in such situations? _____

_____

Offer assistance. Even if a problem or question is not in your area of responsibility, offer to help get answers, information, or assistance. Your customer will likely appreciate the fact that you went out of your way to help.

Be prepared. Know as much as possible about the organization, its products and services, your job, and as appropriate, the customer. Also, make sure that you have all the tools necessary to serve the customer, take notes, and do your job in a professional manner. This allows you to deliver quality information and service while better satisfying customer needs and expectations.

Provide factual information. Don't express opinions or speculate why something did or didn't, or will or will not occur. State only what you are sure of or can substantiate. For example, if you are not sure when a delivery will take place or when a coworker who handles certain functions will return, say so, but offer to find the answer or handle the situation yourself. Don't raise customer expectations by saying, "This should be delivered by 7:30 tomorrow morning," or "Sue should be back from lunch in 10 minutes." If neither event occurs, the customer is likely to be irritated.

Be helpful. If you cannot do something or don't have a product or service, admit it but be prepared to offer an alternative. Do not try to "dance around" an issue in an effort to respond in a manner that you feel the customer expects. Most people will spot this tentative behavior, and your credibility will suffer as a result. Do not insult your customer's intelligence by taking this approach. You and the organization will lose in the long run.

Accept responsibility. Take responsibility for what you do or say and, if necessary, for actions taken by someone else that failed to satisfy the customer. Don't blame others or hide behind "they said" or "policy says" excuses. When something goes wrong, take responsibility and work to resolve the problem positively and quickly. If you don't have the authority needed, get someone who does, rather than referring the customer to someone else.

Take appropriate action. You should take whatever action is necessary to satisfy the customer. Sometimes this may mean bending the rules a bit. In such cases, it may be easier to ask forgiveness from your supervisor than to explain why you lost the organization a good customer. If a request really cannot be honored because it is too extreme (a customer demands a free $100 item because he or she had to return one that did not work properly), explain why and then negotiate and offer alternatives. In Chapter 14 you will find some suggestions for appropriate service recovery strategies.

6 | PROVIDING FEEDBACK

> **CONCEPT:** Your feedback could affect the relationship you have or are building with your customers. The effect may be positive or negative, depending on the content and delivery.

Feedback is a response to messages a listener receives. This response may be transmitted verbally (with words) or nonverbally (through actions or inaction). Depending on the content and delivery, your feedback could positively or negatively influence your relationships with your customers. Figure 3-5 offers some tips on providing feedback effectively, and the two types of feedback are discussed in the following sections.

Verbal Feedback

The words you choose in providing feedback to your customers are crucial to interpretation and understanding. Before providing feedback, you should take into consideration the knowledge and skill level of your customer(s). This is part of the "encoding" discussed earlier in the section "Interpersonal Communication Model" earlier in this chapter. Failure to consider the customer could result in breakdowns in understanding. For example, if you choose words that are not likely to be part of your

---

FIGURE 3-5

Guidelines for providing positive feedback.

Here are 10 tips for effectively providing feedback:

1. When appropriate, give feedback immediately when communicating face to-face or over the telephone.

2. Communicate in a clear, concise manner.

3. Remain objective and unemotional when providing feedback.

4. Make sure that your feedback is accurate before you provide it.

5. Use verbal and nonverbal messages that are in congruence (agree with each other).

6. Verify the customer's meaning before providing feedback.

7. Make sure that your feedback is appropriate to the customer's original message (active listening helps in getting the original message).

8. Strive to clarify feedback when the customer seems unclear of your intention.

9. Avoid overly critical feedback or negative language (as described in this chapter).

10. Do not provide feedback if it could damage the customer-provider relationship.

▲

---

customer's vocabulary, because of the customer's education and/or experience, your message may be confusing. Also, if you use acronyms or technical terms (jargon or unfamiliar to the customer), the meaning of the message could get lost. When providing feedback, you should also be conscious of how your customer is receiving your information. If the customer's body language or nonverbal cues (gestures, facial expressions) or words indicate misunderstanding, you should pause, and take any corrective action necessary to clear up the misunderstanding.

To check your perception of nonverbal cues, use the following process:

1. Identify the behavior observed
   Example: "Mr. Warlinkowski, when I said that it would be seven to ten days before we could get your new sofa delivered to your home, your facial expression changed to what appeared to be one of concern."

2. Offer one or two interpretations.
   Example: "I wasn't sure whether you were indicating that the time frame doesn't work for you, or whether something else went through your mind."

3. Ask for clarification.
   Example: "Which was it?"

By asking for clarification, you reduce the chance of having a dissatisfied customer. You also send a message that you are paying attention to the customer.

Nonverbal Feedback

Nonverbal feedback will be explored in depth in Chapter 4. Here are a few ways in which feedback can be given nonverbally.

Body Language

The ways in which you sit, stand, gesture, position your body (face to face or at an angle), or use facial expressions can all send positive or negative messages.

Actions

By responding to the request of a coworker or external customer in a timely, correct manner, you can send a message of "I care" or "You're important." On the negative side, failure to act or a delay could be perceived as a lack of concern. Moreover, it is important to recognize that the amount of time you allocate to individuals can send a powerful message. For example, suppose a coworker comes into your work area and says that she needs to speak with you about information that you have which is needed for a project deadline she has. You invite her to have a seat and then tell her you have only a few minutes to talk because you're expecting an important call. Two minutes later, the phone rings and you ask to be excused while you take the call. She leaves, and from her cubicle, which is next to yours, she can overhear your conversation. From your laughter, comments, and tone of voice, she concludes that you are on a personal call. She waits patiently for almost 20 minutes and then has to go to another meeting.

The messages that you have sent nonverbally are that you are not a team player, for you do not appear to be supporting her in the project, and that you value personal calls over important business issues with an internal customer. Such actions could haunt you when your coworker relates the incident to others or possibly to a supervisor. Also, if you need her support in the future, you may find that she is reluctant to help you out.

A workplace that is unkempt and untidy may give the impression that the person is also untidy and disorganized. What do you think of a person who has a messy workplace? Do you think the company is responsible for getting an employee to clean up?

Appearances

The way you look physically (hygiene and grooming), dress, and how you maintain your work area sends a message of either professionalism or indifference. Even though you provide attentive, quality service, the customer will typically form an opinion of you and your organization within 30 seconds based on your appearance and that of your work space. This opinion may make the difference in whether the customer will continue to patronize your organization or go to a competitor. For example, a disorganized desk with piles of papers scattered over it

may seem functional to you, but many people think of a person with such a work space as disorganized, unmotivated, and unprofessional. Likewise, your clothing, grooming, and choice of jewelry or other accessories could send a negative message to some people. It is crucial to be able to distinguish between what is appropriate for the workplace and what is appropriate for a night out. We'll cover nonverbal cues more thoroughly in Chapter 4.

Work It Out 3-3 Perceptions Are Reality

▶ To emphasize that different people often have different perceptions of what they see, and the importance of appearance, look at the photographs of the people below. Describe your reactions to and perceptions of each in the spaces provided.

Photo 1

1. Your perceptions: _____

_____

2. Explain why you have these perceptions: _____

_____

3. Is your perception of the organization affected by your reaction to this person? If so, how? _____

Photo 2

1. Your perceptions: _____

_____

2. Explain why you have these perceptions:_____

_____

3. Is your perception of the organization affected by your reaction to this person? If so, how? _____

Photo 3

1.Your perceptions:_____

_____

2. Explain why you have these perceptions:_____

_____

Work It Out
3-3

Work It Out 3-3 Perceptions Are Reality (continued)

3. Is your perception of the organization affected by your reaction to this person? If so, how? _____

Photo 4

1. Your perceptions: _____

_____

2. Explain why you have these perceptions: _____

3. Is your perception of the organization affected by your reaction to this person? If so, how? _____

Work it Out
3-4

Work It Out 3-4 Improving Feedback Skills

▶ To strengthen your ability to provide feedback, work with two other people (one partner and one observer) to practice your skill in delivering feedback.

Select a topic for discussion.

Spend 10 minutes talking about your selected topic with your partner.

During the conversation, you and your partner should use verbal and nonverbal feedback.

At the end of the 10 minutes, ask your partner, and then the observer, the following questions.

1. How did I do in providing appropriate verbal feedback? Give examples.

_____

_____

2. How did I do in providing appropriate nonverbal feedback? Give examples.

_____

_____

3. How well did I interpret verbal and nonverbal messages? Give examples.

_____

_____

4. What questions did I ask to clarify comments or feedback provided? Give examples.

_____

5. What could I have done to improve my feedback?

_____

_____

7 | DEALING ASSERTIVELY WITH CUSTOMERS

CONCEPT: Express ideas simply without weakening your position.

Your level of assertiveness is directly tied to your style of behavior. Some people are direct and to the point; others are calm and laid back. Neither style is better or worse than the other. What is important is to be able to recognize which style to call upon in various situations. You will explore behavioral styles in detail in Chapter 6.

Generally, assertive communication deals with expressing ideas positively and with confidence. An example would be to stand or sit erect, make direct eye contact, smile, listen empathetically, and then calmly and firmly nod and explain what you can do to assist the customer.

Figure 3-6 lists several examples of nonassertive and assertive language and behaviors. Additional resources are listed in the Bibliography.

FIGURE 3-6

Nonassertive and assertive behaviors.

The following list contains examples of nonassertive and assertive language and behaviors, along with tips for increasing your assertiveness.

Nonassertive	Assertive
Poor eye contact while speaking.	Look customer in the eye as you speak.
Weak ("limp fish") handshake.	Grasp firmly without crushing (web of your hand against web of the other person's hand).
Rambling speech, not really stating.	Think, Plan, Speak a specific question or information.
Use of verbal paralanguage (ah, um, you know).	Stop, gather thoughts, speak.
Apologetic in words and tone.	Apologize if you make a mistake; (I'm sorry, please forgive me) then take control and move on with the conversation.
Soft, subdued tone.	Increase volume, sound firm and convincing.
Finger pointing; blaming others.	Take responsibility; resolve the problem.
Nervous gestures, fidgeting.	Hold something; grasp a table or chair; fold your hands as you talk.

---

8 ASSERTIVE VERSUS AGGRESSIVE SERVICE

> **CONCEPT:** Assertive service is good for solving problems; aggressive service may escalate them.

Do not confuse assertive with aggressive service. Why is the distinction so important in customer service? What's the difference? The answer: **Assertiveness** can assist in solving problems, aggression can escalate and cause relationship breakdowns. Asserting yourself means that you project an image of confidence, are self-assured, and state what you believe to be true in a self-confident manner. Aggression involves hostile or offensive behavior, often in the form of a verbal or even physical attack. An assertive person states (verbally and nonverbally) "Here's my position. What's your reaction to that?" An aggressive person sends the message, "Here is my position. Take it or leave it." Obviously, the two modes of dealing with customers create very different service experiences. The manner in which you nonverbally or verbally approach, address, and interact with customers may label you as either assertive or aggressive. Consider the following interactions between a customer and a service provider:

Aggressive behavior can lead to relationship failure. When someone verbally attacks another, the chances of emotions escalating and relationships failing increase significantly. How can you avoid aggressive behavior in a relationship?

Assertive Behavior Example

Customer: (returning an item of merchandise): Excuse me, I received this sweater as a present and I'd like to return it.

Service Provider (smiling): Is there something wrong with it?

Customer (still smiling): Oh no. I just don't need another sweater.

Service Provider (still smiling): Do you have a receipt?

Customer (not smiling): No. As I said, it was a gift.

Service Provider (handing over a form): That's all right. But I will need you to fill out the top portion of this form with your name, phone number, and reason for return. And please sign at the bottom.

Customer (not smiling): Does this mean I have to get out of line and then wait again? I've already been in line for ten minutes.

Service Provider (smiling): Well, rather than delay the line, if you could step over to that table to fill out the form, and then bring it back to me, I'll take care of you.

Customer (smiling): Okay, thanks.

In this example, the service provider is trying to assure the customer, through words and body language, that he or she is there to assist the customer.

Aggressive Service Example

Customer (returning an item of merchandise): Excuse me, I received this sweater as a present and I'd like to return it.

Service Provider (not smiling): What's wrong with it?

Customer (smiling): Oh nothing, I just don't need another sweater.

Service Provider (still not smiling): Do you have a receipt?

Customer (not smiling): No. As I said, it was a gift.

Service Provider (handing over a form): Well, our policy requires that you'll have to fill out this form since you don't have a receipt.

Customer (not smiling): Does that mean I have to get out of line and then wait again? I've already been in line ten minutes.

Service Provider (not smiling): The line's getting shorter. It shouldn't take long. Next . . .

In this example, the service provider is not doing well on service delivery, nor is he or she projecting a positive image. The nonverbal and verbal messages convey an almost hostile attitude. This type of behavior can easily escalate into an unnecessary confrontation.

Providing Assertive Service

You will find that it is important to recognize your own level of knowledge, ability, and authority in any situation. If you do not send a message of confidence and competence through your personal demeanor, the customer-provider relationship can quickly be spoiled. To project an assertive image as opposed to aggressive one try focusing in the following areas:

Facial expressions. Smile and demonstrate warmth and a willingness to help.

Voice. Remain calm, steady, and self-assured. Use inflection without raising volume to emphasize your speech. State your issues, ideas, or concerns in a manner that does not project an assumptive or threatening tone. Remember to smile and maintain a delivery pace that shows you are not rushed or stressed.

Posture. Stand or sit erect, but not rigid. Occasionally lean forward to emphasize key points.

Gestures. Use open gestures with arms and hands. Gesture with open palms as opposed to pointing.

Eye contact. Maintain intermittent eye contact as you smile. Avoid squinting or glaring.

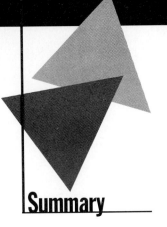

Chapter Summary

Providing service that makes a customer feel special can lead to customer satisfaction and loyalty to you and your organization. By responding appropriately and in a positive manner (verbally and nonverbally), you will increase your likelihood of success. When additional information is needed, it is up to you to ask questions that will elicit useful customer feedback. You must then interpret and respond in kind with feedback that lets the customer know you received the intended message. You must also let your customers know that you'll take action on their needs or requests.

Summary

CHAPTER REVIEW QUESTIONS

1. What are some things you can do as a customer service professional to project a positive image to the customer?

   _____

   _____

   _____

2. What element(s) of the Interpersonal Communication Model do you believe are the most important in a customer service environment? Explain.

   _____

   _____

   _____

3. What are some strategies to use in order to avoid words or phrases that will negatively affect your relationship with your customer?

   _____

   _____

4. What are some of the tips outlined in this chapter for ensuring effective customer interactions?

   _____

   _____

5. What is feedback?

   _____

   _____

   _____

6. How can verbal feedback affect customer encounters?

   _____

   _____

   _____

7. Give some examples of nonverbal feedback and explain how they can affect customer interactions.

_____

_____

_____

8. List at least five tips for providing positive feedback.

_____

_____

_____

▼ SEARCH IT OUT

Search the Web for Information on Verbal Communication

Log on to the Internet to research topics related to verbal communication, such as those presented in this chapter. Use various search engines (Yahoo.com, AltaVista.com, and Excite.com); your results will be different with each. Look for one or more of the following, print out pages you feel are helpful, and be prepared to share your findings with your peers in class. Some possible topics are:

Interpersonal communication

Two-way communication

Questioning

Learning styles

Positive image

Verbal feedback

Nonverbal feedback

Assertiveness

COLLABORATIVE *Learning Activity*

Role-Playing to Improve Verbal Communication

Find a partner and use the following role-plays to improve your verbal communication skills. After reading the scenarios, pick the two for which you want the most feedback. Next, take a moment to think about how each of you will play your part and then have a 2- or 3-minute dialogue centering on the situation.

For the four scenarios, alternate roles with your partner: each of you should role-play twice, and each of you will be the debriefer twice. If possible, videotape or audiotape the conversation. This will allow each of you to see or hear how you seem when you interact with others. After the role-play, discuss how each of you felt about the way the other person handled the situation. Each of you should ask the other these questions about your own performance:

What did I do well?

What did I not do so well?

What can I do to improve in the future?

Scenario 1

You are a customer service professional in a dry cleaner's shop. A customer who has been coming in for years stops by with a silk shirt that has a stain that, according to him, was not there before the most recent dry cleaning. He is upset because the garment is expensive and was to have been worn to a class reunion yesterday.

Scenario 2

You are a member services representative in an automobile club that provides maps, trip information, towing and travel services, and a variety of travel-related products. A member has stopped by to find out whether she can get a replacement membership card and assistance in planning an upcoming vacation.

Scenario 3

You are a counter clerk in a fast-food restaurant. It is lunchtime, and the restaurant is full of patrons. As you are taking an order from a customer, a second customer steps to the front of the line, interrupts the first customer, and demands a replacement sandwich because the one she received is not what she ordered.

Scenario 4

As a clerk in a local video rental store, you see many of the same patrons regularly and have a fairly good relationship with many of them. One of the regular customers has just come in to rent a video but is not sure what he wants. You must determine his needs and properly assist him. Be sure to ask probing, open-ended questions, phrased positively, to help you get the information you need.

FACE TO FACE

Seeking Information from a Client

Background

LKM Graphics has been in business in Norfolk, Virginia, for almost five years. The company employs 17 full-time graphic employees, a part-time administrative assistant, and 3 interns from Old Dominion University's graphic arts program. During a typical week, LKM prints 300,000 to

CHAPTER 3 REVIEW

400,000 documents for businesses in the surrounding Tidewater metropolitan area. Most clients have 15 or fewer employees, although there are two active and ongoing government contracts with the Naval Operations Base, which is nearby. The owner of LKM, Linda McLaroy, hired you three years ago when you graduated from the graphic arts program. You are now one of the senior graphics account managers with the company and supervise four other team members.

Your Role

As a quality control measure, each month you are required to visit the clients assigned to your region. During those visits, you are to answer questions, deliver completed orders, verify customer satisfaction, collect feedback data, and look for new orders. On a recent visit to Brickman Bakery, you met the new office manager, Sylvia Greco. You had been told by a friend who works at Brickman's that Sylvia is considering closing her account with LKM Graphics and moving it to a competitor. Prior to joining Brickman's last month, she had been employed by another organization in the area and had developed a strong relationship with your competitor. Since she is comfortable with the competitor's operation and has friends there, she wants to maintain the relationship. You've also heard through the grapevine that Sylvia prefers to work with your competitor's account representative.

Critical Thinking Questions

1. Since you don't have a relationship with Sylvia, what will you do to get off to a solid start during your visit? _____

_____

_____

_____

2. How should you approach Sylvia verbally and nonverbally? _____

_____

_____

_____

3. What strategies among the ones discussed in this chapter can you use to find out where you and LKM stand in Sylvia's mind? _____

_____

_____

_____

FROM THE FRONTLINE
Interview

Michael O'Hora
Internal Communica-
tions Specialist
United Parcel Service
Orlando, Florida

1. In one or more paragraphs, describe your customer service experience.

I have worked in the Human Resources Department at United Parcel Service for over three years now. I work with both internal and external customers on a regular basis as the internal communications specialist for central Florida. My most recent exposure to a large number of external customers came when I donned our traditional brown uniform to help our drivers deliver some packages. Because of the backup of packages caused by Hurricane Floyd, I visited over 200 different customers in one day.

I also work with local business customers to promote charity events throughout central Florida. We have a myriad of activities and events for which we need sponsors, and I recruit many of our customers to join in for the good of our community.

On a daily basis, I meet with internal customers to promote effective communication skills at UPS. Part of my job is to show our employees the value of interpersonal communication in the corporate environment and give them the skills necessary to improve customer service and relations.

2. What are your general impressions of customer service in the United States? Why do you feel this way?

My general impressions of customer service in the United States vary from business to business. Some companies such as UPS, Disney, and McDonald's excel at customer service because they train their employees very well. They instill in them the reasons for genuine smiles, sincerity, and quality service. However, many companies just throw their employees into the "fire" without the proper customer service training. Employees who aren't trained properly, at least from my perspective, make you feel as if you should be happy just because you are being waited on. Their form of thank-you, if you are lucky enough to get any response, is "No problem." There doesn't seem to be any middle ground when it comes to good customer service. My experience has been that employees are either noticeably customer-friendly or are severely lacking in both customer relations and communication skills.

3. **In your experience in working with customers, what are some of the most effective verbal communication techniques you have used or seen used?**

Many techniques are crucial when one is engaged in conversation with a customer. In my experience, I have found that maintaining eye contact while speaking is extremely important for both the sender and the receiver of the message. Speaking clearly and in a friendly tone is another key quality. Make the customers feel relaxed and show that you are glad to answer their questions, instead of giving the impression that you are being inconvenienced. Don't act rushed when talking with customers and show genuine concern for their needs. Be empathetic. Never be rude or offensive, or use slang, and avoid any terminology that could be misconstrued as a racial or ethnic slur.

4. **What are some of the communication techniques you have witnessed which have resulted in poor customer service?**

Poor customer service usually results when employees use inappropriate communication skills, for example, not maintaining eye contact with a customer. If an employee makes customers feel as if they are a distraction or are unimportant, their conversation and relationship will suffer immediately. The way you say things has a greater impact on customer service than what you say. Answering questions and concerns in an abrupt, negative tone will turn a customer off. Customer service also suffers if the focus is not solely on the customer. Laughing or joking with another employee is a no-no if you want to win a customer's confidence and respect.

5. How does the way you and other employees communicate affect UPS?

I am a direct representative of my company, and the way I act and communicate has a direct impact on UPS. Treating customers inappropriately by using poor communicating techniques has a negative impact on our business. Therefore, my job as an employee of UPS is to treat every customer the same way. Respect, courtesy, and friendliness are the hallmark communication traits that I use to show them that I care about them and their business. Communicating effectively with customers is the key to opening the door to true customer satisfaction.

6. What advice related to verbal communication would you give people entering the customer service profession?

I would recommend taking as many verbal communication courses, seminars, and training classes as possible to upgrade and add to their communication arsenal. Verbal communication is difficult enough without training, so one must always be open to learning more about how to do it effectively and efficiently. I would also recommend that employees learn about people by observing them in a customer-employee environment where they can sit back and see what is good communication and what is bad. This can help in understanding the dynamics that occur when two people are engaged in face-to-face communication.

CRITICAL THINKING
What verbal communication skills would you use while dealing with Internal Communications Specialist customers? Do you agree with the United Parcel Service advice given?

Chapter 4

Nonverbal Communication in Customer Service

OBJECTIVES

After completing this chapter, you will be able to:

• *Define nonverbal communication.*

• *Recognize the potential impact on customers of nonverbal communication.*

• *Effectively use nonverbal cues to achieve and improve customer satisfaction.*

• *Explain the effect that gender and culture have on communication.*

• *Describe the advantages of customer-focused behavior.*

• *Project a customer-focused image through the effective use of nonverbal cues.*

"Silence can be a speech."

Unknown

Before reviewing the chapter content, respond to the following questions by placing a "T" for true or an "F" for false on the rules. Use any questions you miss as a checklist of material to which you will pay particular attention as you read through the chapter. For those you get right, congratulate yourself, but review the sections they address in order to learn additional details about the topic.

_____ 1. It is possible for you to not send nonverbal messages.

_____ 2. By becoming knowledgeable about body language, you can use the cues you observe to accurately predict the meaning of someone's message.

_____ 3. By leaning toward or away from people as they speak, you can communicate your level of interest in what they are saying.

_____ 4. Smiling may mean that someone agrees with what you say. Smiling may also mean that the person is listening.

_____ 5. The use of open, flowing gestures could encourage listening and help illustrate key points.

_____ 6. Taking the time to polish your shoes and clean and press your clothing can help in presenting a positive personal image.

_____ 7. Vocal qualities have little impact on the way others perceive you.

_____ 8. Pauses in your oral message delivery can nonverbally say, "Think about what I just said" or "It's your turn to speak."

_____ 9. The words you use can distort message meaning.

_____ 10. Spatial preferences are the same throughout the world.

_____ 11. People often draw inferences about you based on the appearance of your office.

_____ 12. The amount of time you allocate for meetings with people could nonverbally communicate your feelings about the importance of those people.

3. T   6. T   9. T   12. T
2. F   5. T   8. T   11. T
1. F   4. T   7. F   10. F

1 WHAT IS NONVERBAL COMMUNICATION?

CONCEPT: Nonverbal messages can contradict or override verbal messages. When in doubt, people tend to believe nonverbal messages.

The phenomenon of messages sent via nonverbal means has fascinated people for decades. The general public became aware of this subject when the book *Body Language*[1] and several others were published three decades ago. In *Body Language,* Julius Fast defined various postures, movements, and gestures by ascribing to them the unspoken messages that they might send to someone observing them (for example, defensiveness or accessibility). Since then, hundreds of articles, books, and research studies have explored the topic and expanded the knowledge on the subject.

---

[1] Julius Fast, *Body Language*, Pocket Books, New York, NY 1960.

By being aware that you constantly send **nonverbal messages** to others and that it is impossible for you to *not* communicate, you can increase your effectiveness in customer encounters or anywhere you come into contact with another person. A significant fact to remember is that, according to a classic research study on how feelings are transmitted between two people during communication, nonverbal signals can contradict or override verbal messages.[2] This is especially true when emotions are high. In Mehrabian's study, it was found that in communication between two people, 55 percent of message meaning (feelings) is extracted from facial and other body cues, 38 percent is taken from vocal cues, and 7 percent is received from the actual words used. (The various cues will be discussed in more detail later in this chapter.) This should not be construed to mean that your words are not important; they are just typically overridden by facial and vocal cues. When in doubt about your message meaning, people tend to believe the nonverbal (facial and vocal) parts. Figure 4-1 illustrates the importance of the different types of cues.

Although nonverbal cues carry powerful messages, it is important to understand that there is considerable room for misinterpretation of the cues used by different people. The skill of recognizing, assigning meaning, and responding appropriately to nonverbal messages is not exact. Human behavior is too unpredictable and the interpretation of nonverbal cues is too subjective for accuracy of interpretation to occur with consistency. This is because different cues have different meanings depending on where they were learned, who is interpreting them, and so on.

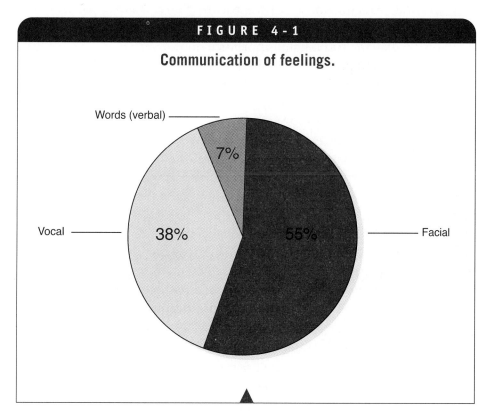

FIGURE 4-1

Communication of feelings.

Words (verbal) — 7%

Vocal — 38%

55% — Facial

---

[2] Albert Mehrabian, *Silent Messages: Implicit Communication of Emotions and Attitudes,* 2nd Ed., Wadsworth Publishing Co., Blemont, CA 1981, pgs 75–80.

2 | THE SCOPE OF NONVERBAL BEHAVIOR

▶ **CONCEPT:** Background, culture, physical conditions, communication ability, and many other factors influence whether and how well people use body cues.

In addition to verbal and written messages, you continually provide nonverbal cues that tell a lot about your personality, attitude, and your willingness and ability to assist customers. Customers receive and interpret the messages you send, just as you receive and interpret their messages. The following categories of nonverbal cues are discussed in this chapter.

Body language

Vocal cues

Appearance or grooming

Spatial cues (proxemics)

Environmental cues

Miscellaneous cues (habits, time usage, follow-through)

Body Language

Recognizing, understanding, and reacting appropriately to the body language of others, as well as using positive body language yourself, allow you to communicate with your customers more effectively. The key to "reading" body language is to realize that your interpretations should be used only as an indicator of the customer's true message meaning. This is because background, culture, physical condition, communication ability, and many other factors influence whether and how well people use body cues. Remember that not everyone uses nonverbal cues in the same manner that you do. Placing too much importance on nonverbal cues could lead to miscommunication and possibly a service breakdown. Some typical forms of body language are discussed in the following sections.

Eye Contact

It has been said that the eyes are "the windows to the soul." Eye contact is very powerful. Criminal investigators are often taught to observe eye movement in order to determine whether a suspect is being truthful or not. In most Western cultures, the typical period of time that is comfortable for holding eye contact is 5 to 10 seconds; then an occasional glance away is normal. Looking away more often can send a message of disinterest or dishonesty. If either the length or the frequency of eye contact differs from the "norm," many people might think that you are being rude or offensive. They might also interpret your behavior as an attempt to exert power or as flirting. In any case, your customer might become uncomfortable and may react in an undesirable manner (for example, become upset or end the contact). Also, looking down before answering questions, glancing away continually as your customer talks, blinking excessively, and other such eye movements can create a negative impression. The customer's eye contact can also send meaningful messages to you. A customer's lack of direct eye contact with you could send a variety of messages, such as lack of interest, confidence or trust, or honesty. For example, if you are watching a customer shop and notice a quick loss of eye contact, the customer might be nervous because he or she is shoplifting, or the customer simply might not want your attention and assistance. Eye contact accomplishes a number of purposes; for example, it can

- *Indicate degrees of attentiveness or interest.*
- *Help indicate and sustain intimate relationships.*
- *Influence attitude change and persuasion.*
- *Regulate interaction.*
- *Communicate emotions.*
- *Define power and status relationships.*
- *Assume a central role in the management of impressions.*[2]

Another aspect of nonverbal communication has to do with the size of the pupils. Much research has been done on the correlation between a person's interest in an item or object being viewed and the size of the person's pupils. Typically, when a customer is interested in an item, his or her pupils will *dilate* (grow larger). This fact can be parlayed into increased sales and customer satisfaction because an astute and experienced salesperson can watch for dilation as a customer looks over merchandise. For example, even if a customer displays only mild interest in an item after asking the price, and then moves on to another, the salesperson who has observed the customer's interest as revealed by dilation of the pupils might be able to influence the customer's buying decision. But, as with all nonverbal communication, if you are using this technique, remember that there is room for misinterpreting a cue. To avoid this kind of mistake, listen carefully to voice tone and observe other signals so that you do not appear to be pushy.

Posture

Basically, *posture* (or stance) involves the way you position your body. Various terms describe posture (for example, formal, rigid, relaxed, slouched, awkward, sensual, defensive). By sitting or standing in an erect manner, or leaning forward or away as you speak with customers, you can send a variety of messages. By standing or sitting with an erect posture, walking confidently, or assuming a relaxed, open posture, you might appear to be attentive, confident, assertive, and ready to assist your customer. On the other hand, slouching in your seat, standing with slumped shoulders, keeping your arms crossed while speaking to someone, shuffling or not picking up your feet when walking, or averting eye contact can say that you are unsure of yourself, are being deceitful, or just have a poor customer service attitude.

In addition, your behavior when listening to a customer speak can affect his or her feedback and reaction to you. For example, if you lean forward and smile as the customer speaks, you signal that you are interested in what is being said and that you are listening intently. Leaning away could send the opposite message.

---

[2] Leathers p. 54.

Facial Expressions

The face is capable of making many expressions. Your face can signal excitement, happiness, sadness, boredom, concern, dismay, and dozens of other emotions. By being aware of the power of your expressions and using positive ones, such as smiling, you can initiate and sustain relationships with others. In fact, smiling seems to be one of the few nonverbal cues that has a universal meaning of friendship or acceptance. Smiling typically expresses a mood of friendship, cheerfulness, pleasure, relaxation, and comfort with a situation. On the other hand, some people smile to mask nervousness, embarrassment, or deceit. In some situations, smiling (yours and a customer's) may even lead to problems. For example, suppose that you are a male service representative working at a customer service desk in an electronics store. A male customer from the Middle East and his wife step up to your counter. You smile and greet the husband, and then turn your attention to the wife and do likewise, possibly adding, "How are you today?" She smiles and giggles as she looks away in an embarrassed effort to avoid eye contact. At this point, you notice that the husband looks displeased. A cultural factor may be involved. Although your intention was to express friendliness and openness, because of his cultural attitudes the husband may interpret your words and smiling as flirtatious and insulting.

Don't think that you should ignore the wives of your customers. Rather, be cognizant of cultural and personal differences that people may have, and take your cue from the customer. As the world grows smaller, it is more crucial than ever that you expand your knowledge of different cultural attitudes and recognize that your ways are not the ways of everyone.

Work It Out
4-1

Work It Out 4-1. Facial Expressions

▶ Take a few minutes to look at each of the faces shown below. Write the emotion that you believe each image portrays on the rules.

Nodding of the Head

Nodding of the head is often used (and overused) by many people to signal agreement or to indicate that they are listening to a speaker during a conversation.

You must be careful when you are using this technique, and when you are watching others who are doing so, to occasionally pause to ask a question for clarification. Stop and ask for or provide feedback through a paraphrased message. A question such as, "So what do you think of what I just said?" will quickly tell you whether the other person is listening and understands your meaning. The answer will also make it clear if the other person is simply politely smiling and nodding—but not understanding.

If you are a woman, be careful not to overuse the nodding technique. Research has shown that women often nod and smile more than men do during a conversation. Doing so excessively might damage your credibility or effectiveness, especially when you are speaking to a man. The interpretation may be that you agree or that you have no opinion, whether you do or not.

Although nodding your head generally signals agreement, if you nod without a verbal acknowledgment or **paralanguage** (a vocal effect such as tone of voice) a missed or misinterpreted cue could result. For example, suppose that you want to signal to a customer that you are listening to and understand her request. You may nod slowly, vocalize an occasional "I see" or "Uh-huh," and smile as she speaks. She might interpret this to mean that you are following her meaning and are nonverbally signaling acceptance of it. But if she is stating something contrary to your organization's policy or outside your level of authority, she might misinterpret your signals thinking that you *agree* with her, not that you are merely signaling *understanding*. Later, she might be upset, saying something like, "Well, earlier you nodded agreement when I said I wanted a replacement."

Gestures

The use of the head, hands, arms, and shoulders to accentuate verbal messages adds color, excitement, and enthusiasm to your communication. Using physical movements naturally during a conversation with a customer may help make a point or result in added credibility.

Typically, such movements are designed to gain and hold attention (for example, waving a hand to attract the attention of someone), clarify or describe further (for example, holding up one finger to indicate the number 1), or emphasize a point (for example, pointing a finger while angrily making a point verbally).

Open, flowing gestures encourage listening and help explain messages to customers (gesturing with arms, palms open and upward, out and away from the body). On the other hand, closed, restrained movements could send a message of coolness, insecurity, or disinterest (tightly crossed arms, clinched fists, hands in pockets, hands or fingers intertwined and held below waist level or behind the back).

The key is to make gestures seem natural. If you do not normally use gestures when communicating, you may want to practice in front of a mirror until you feel relaxed and the gestures complement your verbal messages without distracting.

Figure 4-2 summarizes positive and negative communication behaviors discussed in this chapter.

FIGURE 4-2

Positive and negative communication behaviors.

Positive	Negative
Brief eye contact (3 to 5 seconds)	Yawning
Eyes wide open	Frowning or Sneering
Smiling	Attending to matters other than the customer
Facing the customer	Manipulating items impatiently
Nodding affirmatively	Leaning away from customer as he or she speaks
Expressive hand gestures	Subdued or minimal hand gestures
Open body stance	Crossed arms
Listening actively	Staring blankly or coolly at customer
Remaining silent as customer speaks	Interrupting
Gesturing with open hand	Pointing finger or object at customer
Maintaining professional appearance	Casual unkempt appearance
Clean, organized work area	Disorganized, cluttered work space

---

Simple nonverbal cues like smiling at a customer send powerful messages that a service provider is customer-focused. How do you feel when a service provider smiles at you?

Work It Out 4-2. Gesture Practice

▶ To see what you look like when you gesture and communicate nonverbally, stand in front of a mirror or videotape yourself as you practice expressing nonverbal cues that demonstrate the following emotions:

1. Sadness
2. Frustration
3. Disgust
4. Happiness
5. Love
6. Fear
7. Anger

8. Excitement
9. Concern
10. Boredom
11. Skepticism
12. Complacency
13. Frustration
14. Optimism

Vocal Cues

Vocal qualities, that is, pitch, volume (loudness), rate, quality, and articulation and other attributes of verbal communication can send nonverbal messages to customers.

Pitch

Changes in voice tone (either higher or lower) add vocal variety to messages and can dramatically affect interpretation of meaning. These changes are referred to as **inflection** or **pitch** of the voice or tone. Inflection is the "vocal punctuation" in oral message delivery. For example, a raised inflection occurs at the end of a question and indicates a vocal "question mark." Some people have a bad habit of raising inflection inappropriately at the end of a statement. This practice can confuse listeners for they hear the vocal question mark, but they realize that the words were actually a statement. To rectify this communication error, be sure that your inflection normally falls at the end of sentence statements. Another technique is to use a vocal "comma" in the form of a brief pause as you speak.

Volume

The range in which vocal messages are delivered is referred to as the degree of loudness or **volume**. Depending on surrounding noise or your customers' ability to hear properly, you may have to raise or lower your volume as you speak. Be careful to listen to customer comments, especially on the telephone. If the customer keeps asking you to speak up, check the position of the mouthpiece in relation to your mouth, adjust outgoing volume (if your equipment allows this), try to eliminate background noise, or simply speak up. On the other hand, if he or she is saying, "You don't have to shout, " adjust your voice volume or the positioning of the mouthpiece accordingly.

Also, be aware of the volume of your voice, for changes in volume can indicate emotion and may send a negative message to your customer. For example, if a communication exchange with a customer becomes emotionally charged, your voice might rise, indicating that you are angry or upset. This may escalate emotions and possibly lead to a relationship breakdown.

Rate of Speech

Rate of speech varies for many people. This is often a result of the person's communication abilities, the region of the United States in which he or she was reared, or his or her country of origin. An average rate of speech for most adults in Western cultures is 125 to 150 words per minute (wpm). You should recognize this because, as we discussed in Chapter 3, speed of delivery can affect whether your message is received and interpreted correctly. Speech that is either too fast or too slow can be distracting and cause loss of message effectiveness.

Voice Quality

Message interpretation is often affected by the sound or quality of your voice.

The variations in your **voice quality** can help encourage customers to listen (for example, if your voice sounds pleasant and is accompanied by a smile) or discourage them (for example, if it is harsh-sounding), based on their perception of how your voice sounds. Some terms that describe unpleasant voice quality are *raspy, nasal, hoarse,* and *gravelly.* Such qualities can be a problem because others are less likely to listen to want to listen to or interact with you if your voice quality is irritating. If you have been told, or you recognize, that your voice exhibits one or more of these characteristics, you may want to meet with a speech coach who specializes in helping improve vocal presentation of messages. Most local colleges and universities can supply the name of an expert, possibly someone on their staff. By taking the initiative to improve your voice quality, you can enhance your customer service image.

Work It Out
4-3

Work It Out 4-3. Adding Emphasis to Words

▶ To practice how changes in your vocal quality affect the meaning of your message, try this activity. Pair up with someone. Take turns verbally delivering the following sentences. Each time, place the vocal emphasis on the word in boldface type.

I said I'd do it.   I said I'd **do** it.

I **said** I'd do it.   I said I'd do **it**.

I said **I'd** do it.

Articulation

Also known as *enunciation* or *pronunciation* of words, **articulation** refers to the clarity of your word usage. If you tend to slur words ("Whadju say?" "I hafta go whitja") or cut off endings (goin', doin', gettin', bein'), you can distort meaning or frustrate listeners. This is especially true when communicating with customers who do not speak English well and with customers who view speech ability as indicative of educational achievement or your ability to assist them effectively. If you have a problem articulating well, practice by gripping a pencil horizontally between your teeth, reading sentences aloud, and forcing yourself to enunciate each word clearly. Over time, you will find that you slow down and form words more precisely.

Pauses

Pauses in communication can be either positive or negative depending on how you use them. From a positive standpoint, they can be used to allow a customer to reflect on what you just said, to verbally punctuate a point made or a sentence (through intonation and inflection in the voice), or to indicate that you are waiting for a response. On the negative side, you can irritate someone through the use of too many vocal pauses or interferences. These can be audible sounds ("uh," "er," "um," "uh-huh") and are often used when you have doubts or are unsure of what you are saying, not being truthful, or nervous.

Silence

Silence is a form of tacit communication that can be used in a number of ways, some more productive than others. Many people have trouble dealing with silence in a conversation. This is unfortunate, because silence is a good way to show respect or show that you are listening to the customer while he or she speaks. It is also a simple way to indicate that the other person should say something or contribute some information after you have asked a question. You can also indicate agreement or comprehension by using body language and paralanguage, as discussed earlier. On the negative side, you can indicate defiance or indifference by coupling your silence with some of the nonverbal behaviors listed in Figure 4-2. Obviously, this can damage the customer-provider relationship.

Semantics

Semantics has to do with choice of words. Although not nonverbal in nature, **semantics** is a crucial element of message delivery and interpretation. You can aid or detract from effective communication depending on the words you use and how you use them. Keep in mind what you read earlier about the Mehrabian study and the fact that 7 percent of message meaning comes from the words you choose to use.

If you use a lot of jargon (technical or industry-related terms) or complex words that customers may not understand because of their background, education, culture, or experience, you run the risk of irritating, frustrating, or dissatisfying them and thus damaging the customer-provider relationship.

Appearance and Grooming

Through your appearance and grooming habits, you project an image of yourself and the organization. Good personal hygiene and attention to your appearance are crucial in a customer environment. Remember, customers do not have to return if they find you or your peers offensive in any manner. And, without customers, you do not have a job.

Hygiene

Effective **hygiene** (regular washing and combing of hair, bathing, brushing teeth, use of mouthwash and deodorant, and washing hands and cleaning fingernails) is basic to successful customer service. This is true, even when you work with tools and equipment, or in other skilled trades in which you get dirty easily. Most customers accept that some jobs are going to result in more dirt and grime than others. However, they often have a negative feeling about someone who does not take pride in his or her personal appearance and/or hygiene. Such people are often perceived as inconsiderate, lazy, or simply dirty. For example, if you failed to wash prior to reporting to work, you could be offensive in appearance to customers and coworkers (you might even have an unpleasant odor). This could result in people avoiding you or complaining about you. Naturally, this would reduce your effectiveness on the job and lower customer satisfaction.

Although good hygiene and grooming are important, going to an extreme through excessive use of makeup, cologne, or perfume can create a negative impression and may even cause people to avoid you. This is especially true of people who have allergies or respiratory problems, or people with whom you work in confined spaces.

Clothing and Accessories

Cleaned and pressed clothing, as well as polished shoes, helps project a positive, professional image. Certain types of clothing and accessories are acceptable in the work environment, but others are inappropriate. If your organization does not have a policy outlining dress standards, always check with your supervisor before wearing something that might deviate from the standards observed by other employees or might create an unfavorable image to the public. For example, spike heels and miniskirts, or jeans, bare midriffs, T-shirts, and tennis shoes, might be appropriate for a date or social outing, but they may not be appropriate on the job. They could actually cause customer disapproval and/or complaints and lost business to your organization.

If you are in doubt about appropriate attire, many publications and videos are available on the subject of selecting the right clothing, jewelry, eyeglasses, and accessories. Check with your corporate and/or local public library or the Internet.

Spatial Cues

Each culture has its own **proxemics** (zones in which interpersonal interactions take place) or **spatial cues** for various situations. When you violate this distance, the comfort level of other people is likely to decrease, and they may become visibly anxious, move away, and/or become defensive or offended. For example, suppose that you have an intimate or friendly spatial relationship with a coworker or with someone who regularly comes into your place of business. Outside the workplace, you and this person typically engage in interactions from 0 to 4 feet (joking around, touching, kissing, and holding hands). But if you exhibited similar behavior in the workplace, you could create a feeling of discomfort in others, especially customers or other people who do not know you. Even if they are aware of your relationship with this person, the workplace is not the appropriate place for such behavior. Any touching should be restricted to standard business practices (for example, shaking hands palm to palm). In fact, touching other than this can lead to claims of a hostile work environment and could lead to a lawsuit according to numerous federal and state laws.

In the United States and many Western cultures, studies have resulted in definitions of approximate comfort zones. These may vary, for example, when someone has immigrated to a Western environment and still retains some of his or her own culture's practices related to space.

Intimate distance (0 to 18 inches). Typically this distance is reserved for your family and intimate relationships. Most people will feel uncomfortable when a service provider intrudes into this space uninvited.

Personal distance (18 inches to 4 feet). This distance is used when close friends or business colleagues, with whom you have established a level of comfort and trust, are together. It might also occur if you have established a long-term customer relationship that has blossomed into a semifriendship. In such a situation, you and the customer may sometimes exchange personal information (vacation plans, children, and so forth) and feel comfortable standing or sitting closer to one another than would normally be the case.

Social and work distance (4 to 12 feet). This is usually the distance range in the customer service setting. It is typically maintained at casual business events and during business transactions.

Public distance (12 or more feet). This distance range is likely to be maintained at large gatherings, activities, or presentations where most people do not know one another, or where the interactions are formal in nature.

Being aware of how people may react to violations of their space is necessary for those in customer service. How do you feel when someone gets too close to you during a conversation? What is "too close" for you?

Work It Out 4-4. Spatial Perceptions

▶ Pair up with someone and stand facing him or her from across the room. Start a conversation about any topic (for example, how you feel about the concepts addressed in this chapter or how you feel about the activity in which you are participating) and slowly begin to move toward one another. As you do so, think about your feelings related to the distance at which you are communicating. Keep moving until you are approximately 1 inch from your partner. At that point, start slowly backing away, again thinking about your feelings.

When you get back to your side of the room, have a seat and answer these questions:

1. How did you feel when you were communicating from the opposite side of the room (what were your thoughts)? _____

_____

_____

_____

2. At what distance (moving forward or back) did you feel most comfortable? Why?

_____

_____

_____

3. Did you feel uncomfortable at any point? Why or why not?

_____

_____

_____

4. How can you use the information learned from this activity in the customer service environment? _____

_____

_____

_____

Environmental Cues

The *environment* (surroundings) in which you work or service customers also sends messages. For example, if your work area looks dirty or disorganized, with pencils, files, and papers scattered about, or if there are stacks of boxes, papers stapled or taped to walls, and trash or clutter visible, customers may perceive that you and the organization have a lackadaisical attitude or approach to business. This perception may cause customers to question your ability and commitment to serve.

Granted, in some professions keeping a work area clean all the time is difficult (service station, construction site office, manufacturing environment). However, that is no excuse for giving up on cleanliness and organization of your area. If each employee takes responsibility for cleaning his or her area, cleaning becomes a routine event during a work shift and no one has to get stuck with the job of doing cleaning tasks at a specific time. Also, the chance that a customer may react negatively to the work area is reduced or eliminated.

To help reduce negative perceptions, organize and clean your area regularly, put things away and out of sight once you have used them (calculators, extra pencils, order forms, extra paper for the printer or copier, tools and equipment, supplies). Also, clean your equipment and desk area regularly (telephone mouthpiece, computer monitor and keyboard, cash register and/or calculator key surface, tools).

It is also important to remove any potentially offensive items (photos of or calendars displaying scantily clad men or women; cartoons that have ethnic, racial, sexual, or otherwise offensive messages or that target a particular group; literature, posters, or objects that support specific political or religious views; or any item that could be unpleasant or offensive to view). Failure to remove such material might result in legal liability for you and your organization and create a hostile work environment.

Miscellaneous Cues

Other factors, such as the ones discussed in the following sections, can affect customer perception or feelings about you or your organization.

Personal Habits

If you have annoying or distracting habits, you could send negative messages to your customer. For example, eating, smoking, drinking, or chewing food or gum while servicing customers can lead to negative impressions about you and your organization. Any of the following nonverbal and verbal habits can lead to relationship breakdowns:

Touching the customer.

Scratching or touching parts of your body.

Using pet phrases or speech patterns excessively ("Cool," "You know," "Groovy," "Am I right?" "Awesome," "Solid").

Talking endlessly without letting the customer speak.

Talking about personal problems.

Complaining about your job, employer, coworkers, or other customers.

Time Allocation and Attention

Some organizations have standards for servicing customers within a specific time frame (for example, returning phone calls within 4 hours), but these standards are ranges because customer transactions cannot all be resolved in a specified period of time. The key is to be efficient and also effective in your efforts. Continually reevaluate your work habits and patterns to see whether you can accomplish tasks in a more timely fashion. The amount of time you spend with customers often sends subliminal messages of how you perceive their importance. For example, suppose that you are a salesperson in an exclusive clothing store. A teenage male customer (cutoff jeans, sandals, and T-shirt) enters and encounters one of your coworkers who says courteously "May I help you?" without smiling. As she meanders near the customer, she gives a disapproving look as she searches for other customers to serve. At some point, a well-dressed older woman wearing a suit arrives. The salesperson greets her warmly with a smile and proceeds to follow her around, assisting attentively, for the next 10 minutes, while the original customer waits to have a question answered. This certainly could tell the first customer that he is not welcome or respected.

Follow-Through

Follow-through, or lack of it, sends a very powerful nonverbal message to customers. If you tell a customer you will do something, it is critical to your relationship that you do so. If you can't meet agreed-upon terms or time frames, get back to the customer and renegotiate. Otherwise, you may lose the customer's trust. For example, suppose you assure a customer that an item that is out of stock will arrive by Wednesday. On Tuesday, you find out that the shipment is delayed. If you fail to inform the customer, you may lose that sale and the customer.

Proper Etiquette and Manners

People appreciate receiving appropriate respect and like to deal with others who have good manners and practice **etiquette**. Many books and seminars address the dos and don'ts of servicing and working with customers. From a nonverbal message standpoint, the polite things you do (saying "please," "thank you," asking permission, or acknowledging contributions) go far in establishing and building relationships. Such language says, "I care" or "I respect you." In addition, behavior that affects your customer's perception of you can also affect your interaction and ability to provide service (interrupting others as they speak, talking with food in your mouth, pointing with your finger or other items such as a fork while eating). Many good books are available on manners and dining etiquette if you are unsure of yourself.

Color

Although color is not as important as some other factors related to non-verbal communication in the customer service environment, the way in which you use various colors in decorating a work space and in your clothing can have an emotional impact. Much research has been done by marketing and communication experts to determine which colors evoke the most positive reactions from customers. In various studies involving the reaction people had to colors, some clear patterns evolved. Figure 4-3 lists various colors and the emotional reactions they can induce.

FIGURE 4-3

The emotional messages of color.

Color	Emotion or Message
Red	Stimulates and evokes excitement, passion, power, energy, anger, intensity. Can also indicate "stop," negativity, financial trouble, or shortage.
Yellow	Indicates caution, warmth, mellowness, positive meaning, optimism, and cheerfulness. Yellow can also stimulate thinking and visualizing.
Dark blue	Depending on shade, can relax, soothe, indicate maturity, and evoke trust and tranquillity or peace.
Light blue	Projects a cool, youthful, or masculine image.
Purple	Projects assertiveness or boldness and youthfulness. Has a contemporary "feel." Often used as a sign of royalty, richness, spirituality, or power.
Orange	Can indicate high energy or enthusiasm. Is an emotional color and sometimes stimulates positive thinking.
Brown	An earth tone that creates a feeling of security, wholesomeness, strength, support, and lack of pretentiousness.
Green	Can bring to mind nature, productivity, positive image, moving forward or "go," comforting, growth, or financial success or prosperity. Also, can give a feeling of balance.
Gold and silver	Signals prestige, status, wealth, elegance, or conservatism.
Pink	Projects a youthful, feminine, or warm image.
White	Not really a color (actually, an absence of it). Typically used to indicate purity, cleanliness, honesty, and wholesomeness. Is visually relaxing.
Black	Lack of color. Creates sense of independence, completeness, and solidarity. Often used to indicate financial success, death, or seriousness of situation.

Using Nonverbal Cues

Think about the nonverbal cues you use when you communicate with others. Do you cross your arms? Interrupt the other person? Lean away from or toward the speaker? Avoid eye contact when you talk? Chew gum loudly? Pay attention to these cues as you communicate with several people during the day.

1. At the end of the day, list common cues that you use often.

_____

_____

_____

2. Are any of these cues potentially distracting? If so, use your list as an action plan to reduce these cues in the future.

_____

_____

_____

3 THE ROLE OF GENDER IN NONVERBAL COMMUNICATION

▶ **CONCEPT:** Research indicates that boys and girls and men and women behave differently. Young children are sometimes treated differently by their parents because of their gender preference (either female or male child may be preferred).

Much has been discovered and written about how females and males communicate and interact with others differently. For example, some researchers have found that females are more comfortable being in close physical proximity with other females than males are being close to other males.[3] Although similarities exist between the ways in which males and females relate to one another, there are distinct differences in behavior, beginning in childhood and carrying through into adulthood.

In the book *The Difference*, Judy Mann hypothesizes that boys and girls are different in many ways, are acculturated to act and behave differently, and have some real biological differences that account for their actions (and inactions) which are examined from a number of perspectives. The book discusses various studies that have found that boys and girls typically learn to interact with each other, and with members of their own gender, in different ways. Girls tend to learn more nurturing and relationship skills early, whereas boys approach life from a more aggressive, competitive stance. Girls often search for more "relationship" messages during an interaction and strive to develop a collaborative approach; boys typically focus on competitiveness or "bottom-line" responses in which

---

[3] Howard, p. 52.

there is a distinct winner. Obviously, these differences in approaches to relationship building can have an impact in the customer service environment, where people of all walks of life come together.

The lessons learned early in life usually carry over into the workplace and affect customer interactions. If you fail to recognize the differences between the sexes and do not develop the skills necessary to interact with both men and women, you could experience some breakdowns in communication and ultimately in the customer-provider relationship.

The basis for gender differences is the fact that the brains of males and females develop at different rates and focus on different priorities throughout life. For example, women often tend to be more bilateral in the use of their brain (they can switch readily between the left and right brain hemispheres in various situations). Men, on the other hand, tend to be more lateral in their thinking. This means that they favor either the left hemisphere (analytical, logical, factual, facts-and-figures-oriented) or the right hemisphere (emotional, creative, artistic, romantic, expressive of feelings). This results in a difference in the way each gender communicates, relates to others, and deals with various situations. Figure 4-4 lists some basic behavioral differences between females and males.

FIGURE 4-4

Men and women differ in their approach to relationships. Here are some general behavioral differences that are seen in many men and women.

	Females	**Males**
BODY	Claim small areas of personal space (e.g., cross legs at knees or ankles).	Claim large areas of personal space (e.g., use figure-four leg cross, or armrests on airplanes).
	Cross arms and legs frequently.	Use relaxed arm and leg posture (e.g., over arm of a chair).
	Sit or stand close to same sex.	Sit or stand away from same sex but closer to females.
	Use subdued gestures.	Use dramatic gestures.
	Touch more (both sexes).	Touch males less, females more.
	Nod frequently to indicate receptiveness.	Nod occasionally to indicate agreement.
	Lean forward toward speaker.	Lean away from speaker.
	Glance casually at watch.	Glance dramatically at watch (e.g., with arm fully extended and retracted to raise sleeve).
	Hug and possibly kiss. both sexes upon greeting.	Hug and possibly kiss females upon greeting.

VOCAL	Use high inflection at end of statements inflection (sounds like a question)	Use subdued vocal inflection
	Use high pitch.	Use low pitch.
	Speak at faster rate.	Speak at slower rate.
	Use paralanguage frequently.	Use paralanguage occasionally.
	Express more emotion.	Express less emotion.
	Use more polite "requesting" language (e.g., "Would you please?	Use more "command" language (e.g., "Get me the . . .)
	Focus on relationship messages.	Focus on business messages.
	Use vocal variety.	Often use monotone.
	Interrupt less, more tolerant of interruptions.	Interrupt more, but tolerate interruptions less.
	Use more precise articulation.	Use less precision in word endings and enunciation (e.g., drop the "g" in –ing endings).
FACIAL	Maintain eye contact.	Glance away frequently.
	Smile frequently.	Smile infrequently (with strangers).
	Use expressive facial movements.	Show little variation in facial expression.
BEHAVIOR	Focus more on details.	Focus less on details.
	Are more emotional in problem solving	Are analytical in problem solving. (e.g., try to find cause and fix problem).
	View verbal rejection as personal.	Do not dwell on verbal rejection.
	Apologize after disagreements.	Apologize less after disagreements.
	Hold grudges longer.	Do not hold grudges.
ENVIRONMENTAL	Commonly display personal objects in the workplace.	Commonly display items symbolizing achievement in the workplace
	Use bright colors in clothing and decorations.	Use more subdued colors in clothing and decorations
	Use patterns in clothing and decoration.	Use few patterns in clothing.

Work It Out 4-5. Gender Communications

▶ To get a better idea of how males and females communicate and interact differently, go to a library or to the Internet and gather information on the topic. Look specifically for information on the following topics:

Brain differences between men and women and the impact of these differences on communication and relationships.

Differences in nonverbal cues used by men and women.

Base for the communication differences in the workplace or business world between men and women.

WORKSHEET 4-2

Watching Others

To emphasize how people interpret nonverbal signals based on their own experiences and beliefs, try the following activity:

Pair up with someone and go to a local mall or airport. Take along a pen and paper as well as a copy of this chapter. Decide how many people you will observe. Assign a number to each person you observe. Select a site from which you will both have a clear line of vision in a busy area (food court or entrance area). Choose individuals to watch at random and together observe them discreetly for an agreed-upon amount of time. At the end of the time, jot down your observations of nonverbal cues and what you thought the cues conveyed in terms of general messages. Finally, compare notes and discuss any differences between your observations. Then answer these questions:

1. Were there differences in perception between you and your partner? If so, why might they have occurred? _____

_____

_____

2. What trends or typical body signals were noted? What do these mean to each of you? _____

_____

_____

3. Did men and women differ in their nonverbal behaviors? If they differed, describe how they differed. _____

_____

_____

_____

4. *Did behaviors differ between people under and over the age of twenty years? If they differed, describe how they differed.* _____

_____

_____

_____

5. *Did you notice any trends in dress and grooming between men and women and among people of similar age groups? What were they?* _____

_____

_____

_____

6. *How can you use what you learned in your own customer service environment?*

_____

_____

_____

_____

---

4 THE IMPACT OF CULTURE ON NONVERBAL COMMUNICATION

▶ **CONCEPT:** To be successful in a global economy, you need to be familiar with the many cultures, habits, values, and beliefs of a wide variety of people.

As you read in Chapter 1, and will again in Chapter 10, cultural diversity is having a significant impact on the customer service environment. The number of service providers and customers with varied backgrounds is growing at a rapid pace. This trend provides a tremendous opportunity for personal knowledge growth and interaction with people from cultures you might not otherwise encounter. However, with this opportunity comes challenge. If you are to understand and serve people who might be different from you, you must first become aware that they are also very similar to you. In addition, if you are to be successful in interacting with a wide variety of people, you will need to learn about many cultures, habits, values, and beliefs from around the world. The Internet is a fertile source for such information. Take advantage of it, or visit your local library to check out books on different countries and their people. Join the National Geographic Society, and you will receive its monthly magazine, which highlights different cultures and people from around the globe.[4]

To become more skilled at dealing with people from other cultures, develop an action plan of things to learn and explore. At a minimum, familiarize yourself with common nonverbal cues that differ dramatically from one culture to another. Specifically, look for cues that might be perceived as negative in some cultures so that you can avoid them. Learn to

---

[4] National Geographic Society, http://www.nationalgeographic.com

recognize the different views and approaches to matters such as time, distance, touching, eye contact, and use of colors so that you will not inadvertently violate someone's personal space or cause offense.

5 UNPRODUCTIVE BEHAVIORS

▶ **CONCEPT:** You should be aware of habits or mannerisms that can send annoying or negative messages to customers.

Many people develop unproductive nonverbal behaviors without even realizing it. These may be nervous habits or some mannerism carried to excess (scratching, pulling an ear, or playing with hair). In a customer environment, you should try to minimize such actions because they might send a negative or annoying message to your customers. An easy way to discover whether you have such behaviors is to ask people who know you well to observe you for a period of time and tell you about anything they observe that could be a problem. Here are some more common behaviors that can annoy people and cause relationship breakdowns or comments about you and your organization.

Unprofessional Handshake

Hundreds of years ago, a handshake was used to determine whether a person was holding a weapon. Later, a firm handshake became a show of commitment, of one's word, or of "manhood." Today, in Western cultures and many others in which the Western way of doing business has been adopted, both men and women in the workplace are expected to convey greeting and/or commitment with a firm handshake. Failure to shake hands appropriately (palm to palm), with a couple of firm pumps up and down, can lead to an impression that you are weak or lack confidence. The grip should not be overly loose or overly firm.

Fidgeting

Using nervous mannerisms can indicate to a customer that you are anxious, annoyed, or distracted, and should therefore be avoided, if possible. Such signals can also indicate that you are nervous or lack confidence. Cues such as playing with or putting hair in your mouth, tugging at clothing, hand-wringing, throat-clearing, playing with items as you speak (pencil, pen, or other object), biting or licking your lips, or drumming your fingers or tapping on a surface with a pencil or other object can all send a potentially annoying and/or negative message.

Pointing a Finger or Other Object

This is a very accusatory mannerism and can lead to anger or violence on the part of your customer. If you must gesture toward a customer, do so with an open flat hand (palm up) in a casual manner. The result is a less threatening gesture that almost invites comment or feedback, because it looks as if you are offering the customer an opportunity to speak.

Raising Eyebrow

This mannerism is sometimes called the *editorial eyebrow* because some television broadcasters raise their eyebrow. With the editorial eyebrow, only one eyebrow is arched, usually in response to something that the person has heard. This mannerism signals skepticism or doubt about what you have heard. It can be viewed as questioning the customer's honesty.

Peering Over Glasses

This gesture might be associated with a professor or someone who is in a position of authority looking down on a student or subordinate. For that reason, a customer may not react positively if you peer over your glasses. Typical nonverbal messages that this cue might send are displeasure, condescension, or disbelief.

Crossing Arms

Typically viewed as a closed or defiant posture, crossing your arms may send a negative message to your customer and cause a confrontation. People often view this gesture as demonstrating a closed mind, resistance, or opposition.

Holding Hands Near Mouth

By holding your hands near your mouth, you will muffle your voice or distort your message. If someone is hearing impaired or speaks English as a second language and relies partly on reading your lips, this person will be unable to understand your message. Also, placing your hands over or in front of your mouth can send messages of doubt or uncertainty, or can suggest that you are hiding something.

---

6 STRATEGIES FOR IMPROVING NONVERBAL COMMUNICATION

CONCEPT: Nonverbal cues are all around us. Vocal and visual cues related to customers' feelings or needs are important and may mean the difference between a successful or unsuccessful customer service experience.

The four strategies discussed in this section will help you improve your nonverbal communication skills if you practice them and try to understand the behavior of others.

Seek Out Nonverbal Cues

Too often, service providers miss important vocal and visual clues related to customer feelings or needs because they are distracted doing other things or not being attentive. These missed opportunities can often mean the difference between a successful and an unsuccessful customer experience. Train yourself to look for nonverbal cues by becoming a "student of human nature." Nonverbal cues are all around you, if you simply open your eyes and mind to them. Start spending time watching people in public places (at supermarkets, malls, airports, bus stops, school, or wherever you have the chance). Watch the behavior of others you see, and the behavior of the people with whom they are interacting. Try to interpret the results of each behavior. However, keep in mind that human nature is not exact and that many factors affect the nonverbal cues used by yourself and others (culture, gender, environment, and many more). Be aware that you may be viewing through your own filters or biases, so evaluate carefully. Also, look at **clusters,** or groups of nonverbal behaviors, and the language accompanying them instead of interpreting individual signals. These clusters might be positive (smiling, open body posture, friendly touching) or negative (crossed arms, looking away as someone talks, or angry facial expressions or gestures). Evaluating clusters can help you gain an accurate view of what is going on in a communication exchange.

From your observations, objectively evaluate what works and what doesn't, and then modify your behavior accordingly to mimic the positive things you learn.

Confirm Your Perceptions

Let others know that you have received and interpreted their nonverbal cues. Ask for clarification by **perception checking,** if necessary. This involves stating the behavior observed, giving one or two possible interpretations, and then asking for clarification of message meaning. For example, suppose that you are explaining the features of a piece of office equipment to a customer and he reacts with a quizzical look. You might respond with a statement such as, "You seem surprised by what I just said. I'm not sure whether you were surprised by something I said or whether I was unclear in my explanation. What questions do you have?" By doing this, you focus on his behavior and also provide an opportunity for him to gain additional necessary information.

Seek Clarifying Feedback

In many instances you need feedback in order to adjust your behavior. You may be sending cues you do not mean to send or to which others may react negatively. For example, assume that you are on a cross-functional work team with members of various departments in your organization and have been in a meeting to discuss ideas for creating a new work process. During a heated discussion of ideas, you excuse yourself briefly to get a drink of water in order to take a pill. Later, a teammate mentions that others commented about your frustration level and the fact that you bolted out of the room. To determine what behaviors led to the team's reaction, you might ask something like, "What did I do that made people perceive that I was upset?" If you find out why people viewed your behavior the way they did, you offer an explanation in your next team meeting and avoid exhibiting similar behaviors in the future.

Another example might be to ask a coworker whether the clothing you have on seems too formal for a presentation you will give later in the day. Keep in mind, though, that some people will not give you honest, open feedback. Instead, they tell you what they think you want to hear or what they think will not hurt your feelings. It is usually best to elicit information from a variety of sources before making any behavioral changes, or deciding not to make them.

Analyze Your Interpretations of Nonverbal Cues

One way to ensure that you are accurately evaluating nonverbal cues given by variety of people is to analyze your own perceptions, stereotypes, and biases. The way you view certain situations or groups of people might negatively affect your ability to provide professional and effective customer service to all your customers. This is especially true of customers in the groups toward which you feel a bias. Without realizing it you may send negative nonverbal cues that could cause a relationship breakdown and lead to a dissatisfied customer.

You will explore interactions with various groups and relationship-building strategies in more detail in Chapter 10.

Work It Out 4-6. Practicing Nonverbal Communication

To help you understand the importance that nonverbal cues play in effective interpersonal communication, select any section from this chapter and review the information in it. Once you are familiar with the section you have chosen, meet with a partner (preferably someone you know well) and have a 5- to 10-minute conversation about any topic of your choice. Do not inform your partner of what you're doing, but as you talk, intentionally send negative signals. For example, you might use any of the following nonverbal cues as you talk: stare blankly, do not smile, do not nod or use paralanguage when he or she speaks, look distracted, cross your arms, lean away, look at your watch frequently, play with a pencil or pen, or fidget.

As the conversation progresses, mentally note your partner's reaction to your cues. After 5 to 10 minutes, stop and explain what you've been doing. Ask what he or she noted about your behavior as you were talking. Chances are that he or she will be able to list several of your behaviors. Next, ask how your behaviors made him or her feel. Finally, ask what you might have done to seem more positive during the conversation.

7 CUSTOMER-FOCUSED BEHAVIOR

CONCEPT: Being customer-focused in your behavior may help you solve a customer's problem or eliminate the opportunity for a problem to develop. The nonverbal cues discussed in this section can help you stay customer-focused.

The nonverbal behavior you exhibit in the presence of a customer can send powerful messages. You should constantly remind yourself of advice you may have heard often: "Be nice to people." One way you can indicate that you intend to be nice is to send customer-focused messages regularly and enthusiastically through your nonverbal cues. Here are some simple ways to accomplish this when you are dealing with internal and external customers:

Stand up, if appropriate. If you are seated when a customer arrives or approaches you, stand up and greet him or her. This shows that you respect the person as an equal and are eager to assist her or him.

Act promptly. The speed with which you assist customers, gather information, or respond to customers tells them what you think of their importance. If your service to the customer will take longer than planned or will be delayed, notify the customer, tell him or her the reason, and offer service alternatives if they are appropriate and available.

Guide rather than direct. If customers must go to another person or area of the organization, or if they ask directions, personally guide them or have someone else do so, if possible. Do not simply point or direct. If you are on the telephone and you need to transfer a customer, give the extension of the person you're connecting to (in case of disconnection), transfer the call, and stay on the line to introduce the customer to the other service provider. Once the connection is made, excuse yourself and thank the customer for calling; then disconnect quietly.

Don't rush customers. Provide whatever assistance is necessary without appearing to push customers away. Take the time to determine whether a customer has additional needs, and don't be impatient in the process. It is fine to ask questions such as, "Will there be anything else I can assist you with?" to signal the end of your interaction with a customer. Just be sure that you do it with a smile and pleasant tone so that the customer does not feel "dumped" or abandoned.

Offer assistance. Offer to assist with packages, especially if a customer is elderly, has a disability, has numerous packages, or appears to need help. Similarly, if someone needs assistance with a door or in getting from one place to another, offer to help. If the person says, "No, thank you," smile and go on your way. Do not assume that someone needs help, grab an arm to guide him or her, or push open a door. Such actions could surprise a person and throw him or her off balance. This is especially true of someone with a mobility or sight impairment who has learned to navigate using canes or other assistance. Upsetting a person's momentum or "system" could cause a fall or injury, which in turn could result in embarrassment and/or a liability situation for you or your organization.

Don't keep customers waiting. Nobody likes waiting, so keep waits to a minimum. If long delays are anticipated, inform the customer, offer alternatives, and work to reduce wait time.

Allow customers to go first. As a show of respect, encourage and allow customers to precede you through cafeteria lines, through doors, onto escalators or elevators, into vehicles, and so on. This projects an air of respect and courtesy. If he or she declines, do not make a scene and insist; simply go first yourself.

Offer refreshments, if appropriate. Take care of your "guests" the same way you would at home. Offer to get them something to drink if they come to your office or if they are attending lengthy meetings. You may also want to offer reading materials if they are in a waiting area. Be sure that reading materials are current and professional-looking. Discard old or worn materials.

Avoid unprofessional actions. Avoid smirking, making faces, or commenting to other customers after a customer leaves or turns his or her back. Such activity is unprofessional and will probably make the second customer wonder what you'll do when he or she leaves.

Worksheet ▼

4-3

Customer-Focused Behavior in Action

Consider the points in the preceding section on sending positive customer-focused messages. Now, think about a situation in which you were an internal customer in an organization (a business, an office, or an educational institution). Select one occasion when you went to someone's office in that organization. List the things the person you visited did that made you feel either welcome or important or like an intruder.

Positive	Negative
_____	_____
_____	_____
_____	_____
_____	_____
_____	_____
_____	_____
_____	_____

Use this reflection to help guide you in selecting positive steps in the future when someone visits your work area.

8 ADVANTAGES OF CUSTOMER-FOCUSED BEHAVIOR

CONCEPT: As you have learned in this chapter, many different factors affect behavior and influence how a customer perceives your ability to provide good customer service. By treating customers with respect, communication improves. This applies to both internal and external customers.

Because of the competitive nature of business, organizations and customer service professionals should strive to pull ahead of the competition in any positive way possible. Simple courteous nonverbal behavior can be one way to beat the service quality levels of other companies. Why should you be courteous?

Image is enhanced. First impressions are often lasting impressions. A more professional impression is created when you and the organizational culture are customer-focused. When your customers feel comfortable about you and the image projected, they are more likely to develop a higher level of trust and willingness to be more tolerant when things do go wrong occasionally.

Customer loyalty increases. People often return to organizations where they feel welcome, serviced properly, and respected. In Chapter 13, you will explore specific strategies for increasing customer loyalty.

Word-of-mouth advertising increases. Sending regular positive nonverbal messages can help create a feeling of satisfaction and rapport. When customers are satisfied, and feel comfortable with you and your organization, they typically tell three to five other people. This increases your customer base while holding down formal advertising costs (newspapers and other publications, television, and radio).

Complaints are reduced. When people are treated fairly and courteously, they are less likely to complain. If they do complain, their complaints are generally directed to a lower level (below supervisory level) and are generally expressed with low levels of anger. Simple things like smiling or attentive actions can help customers relax and feel appreciated.

Employee morale and esteem increase. If employees feel that they are doing a good job and get positive customer and management feedback, they will probably feel better about themselves. This increased level of self-esteem affects the quality of service delivered.

Keep in mind your role in helping peers feel appreciated. They are often your internal customers and expect the same consideration and treatment as your external customers expect.

Financial losses decrease. When customers are satisfied, they are less likely to file lawsuits, steal, be abusive toward employees (who might ultimately resign), and spread negative stories about employees and the organization. Building good rapport through communication can help in this area.

Employee-customer communication improves. By treating customers in a professional, courteous manner, you encourage them to freely approach and talk to you. Needs, expectations, and satisfaction levels can then be more easily determined.

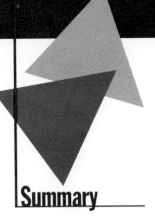

Chapter Summary

Once you become aware of the potential and scope of nonverbal communication, it can be one of the most important ways you have of sharing information and messages with customers. Limitless messages can be conveyed through a look, a gesture, a posture, or a vocal intonation. To be sure that the messages received are the ones you intended to send, be vigilant about what you say and do and how you communicate. Also, watch carefully the responses of your customers. Keep in mind that gender, culture, and a host of other factors affect the way you and your customers interpret received nonverbal cues.

To avoid distorting customer messages, or sending inappropriate messages yourself, keep these two points in mind: (1) Do not use a nonverbal cue you receive from others as an absolute message. Analyze the cue in conjunction with the verbal message to more accurately assess the meaning of the message. (2) Continually seek to improve your understanding of nonverbal signals.

One final point: Do not forget that you are constantly sending nonverbal messages. Be certain that they complement your verbal communication and say to the customer, "I'm here to serve you."

CHAPTER REVIEW QUESTIONS

1. What are six categories of nonverbal cues?

_____

_____

_____

_____

2. What are some of the voice qualities that can affect message meaning?

_____

_____

_____

_____

3. What are some examples of inappropriate workplace attire?

_____

_____

_____

_____

4. How can grooming affect your relationship with customers?

_____

_____

_____

5. What are the four spatial distances observed in Western cultures, and for what people or situations are each typically reserved?

_____

_____

_____

_____

6. What are some of the miscellaneous nonverbal cues that can affect your effectiveness in a customer environment?

_____

_____

_____

_____

7. What are some ways in which men and women differ in their nonverbal communication?

_____

_____

_____

_____

8. What are some examples of unproductive communication?

_____

_____

_____

_____

9. List four strategies for improving nonverbal communication.

_____

_____

_____

_____

10. What are five examples of customer-focused behavior?

_____

_____

_____

_____

SEARCH IT OUT

Use the Internet to Further Your Knowledge of Nonverbal Communication
Now that you have learned some of the basics of nonverbal communication and the impact it can have on your customer relationships, use the Internet to explore the topic further.

Select two topics from the following list, check out as many sites as you can find, and prepare a report of at least two pages in length to present to your peers.

Body language

Nonverbal cues

Albert Mehrabian

The impact of gender differences on nonverbal communication

Spatial distances

The role of vocal cues in nonverbal communication

Professional appearance and grooming for the workplace

The impact of culture on nonverbal cues

COLLABORATIVE *Learning Activity*

Focus on Your Speech Patterns
Set up an audiocassette player. Then pair up with someone to discuss what you believe are the benefits of understanding and using nonverbal cues for building customer relations (spend at least 5 minutes presenting your ideas). Your partner should then present his or her views to you. Once both of you have presented your ideas, listen to the audiocassette with your partner and focus on your speech patterns.

1. Are you using appropriate verbal cues in your relationships with others? In what ways?_____

_____

2. Do you use silence effectively? If so, how? _____

_____

_____

3. How did you sound in regard to the following?

   Rate _____

   Pitch _____

   Volume _____

   Articulation _____

4. Once you've identified positive and negative areas in your communication, set up an action plan for improvement by targeting the following:

Area(s) for improvement _____

_____

Target improvement date _____

Resources needed to improve (assistance of others, training, training materials) _____

_____

Support person(s)—who will coach or encourage you toward improvement? _____

_____

FACE TO FACE

Handling Customer Complaints at Central Petroleum National Bank

Background

Central Petroleum National Bank is one of the largest financial institutions in the Dallas–Fort Worth, Texas, area. With revenues of more than $200 million and investment holdings all over the world, the bank does business with many individuals and organizations in the region and other parts of Texas. The bank has 17 branch offices in addition to the home office in downtown Dallas.

Your Role

As one of the 125 employees of Central Petroleum's Western Branch Office, you provide customer service and establish new checking and savings accounts.

On Tuesday, a new customer, Mr. Gomez, came in to open an account. He stated that he was moving his money, over $200,000, from an account at a competing bank because of poor service. As you spoke with Mr. Gomez, one of your established patrons, Mrs. Wyatt, came into the office. As she signed in, you looked over, smiled, nodded, and held up one finger to indicate that you'd be with her momentarily. She smiled in return as she went to sit in the waiting area. As you were finishing the paperwork with Mr. Gomez, his teenage son came in and joined him. The son had been working at a summer job and had saved several hundred dollars. He also wished to establish a checking account. He placed his money on your desk and asked what he needed to do. He stated that he was on his lunch break and had only 20 more minutes to fill out the necessary forms. By then, you noticed that Mrs. Wyatt was looking at her watch and glancing frequently in your direction. Shortly thereafter, she left abruptly.

When you arrived at work the next day, the branch vice president called you into her office to tell you that she had received a complaint letter from Mrs. Wyatt concerning your lack of customer service and uncaring attitude.

Critical Thinking Questions

1. What did you do right in this situation? _____
   _____
   _____

2. What could you have done differently? _____
   _____
   _____

3. Do you believe that Mrs. Wyatt was justified in her perception of the situation? Explain. _____
   _____
   _____

4. Could Mrs. Wyatt have misinterpreted your nonverbal messages? Explain. _____
   _____
   _____

FROM THE FRONTLINE
Interview

Ms. Ruth Marchwinski
Account Representative
Paragon Computer
Professionals
Maitland, Florida

1. In one or two paragraphs describe your experience in dealing with external and internal customers.

I have been an account representative for a little over three years. I spend most of my time with external customers who are mainly in the telecommunications industry. Most of the people I interact with are technical, so their manner is usually very analytical and straightforward.

2. What are your general impressions of customer service in the United States? Why do you feel this way?

I think that the introduction of automated systems and on-line shopping has added a new twist to the world of customer service. Nowadays speaking with a human being in a customer service situation is becoming the exception rather than the rule. However, once you do have the opportunity to speak with someone, it usually turns out to be a pleasant experience—not all the time, but most of the time. I think that automated systems have helped customer service by reducing the number of general calls service reps have to answer. This means that the reps have more time to deal with customers' problems and complaints.

3. In your experience in working with customers, what are some of the most effective nonverbal communication techniques you have used or seen used? Please explain.

One of the most effective forms of nonverbal communication is eye contact. Eye contact is a way of showing interest and indicating that you are an active participant in a conversation. Customers like to feel that they are being heard and, that what they're saying is important. By maintaining eye contact and acknowledging what they are saying with head nods and such, you start to build the foundation of trust in a business relationship.

4. How does the way you and other employees communicate affect your organization and your customers?

If a customer is upset about something, the way in which that customer is handled can make or break a situation. Telling a person that he or she is wrong or has nothing to be upset about will not solve the problem. A customer cannot be treated with indifference, either. For example, once I called to question a late charge that was put on a bill. Actually, I had never received the bill. The customer service rep's response was, "So. Just because you didn't receive it, doesn't mean you don't have to pay it!" This is poor customer service. I believe that, as an account representative, I not only represent myself but also the company. If I do not communicate in a professional and respectful manner, it affects more than just me—it affects the name and reputation of my company.

5. What advice, related to nonverbal communication, would you give to someone entering the customer service profession?

Whether the customer service is via telephone or in person, the representative needs to sound concerned and focused on the person he or she is dealing with. The representative needs to let the customer know that he or she is listening to what is being said and will do everything possible to help solve the problem. Being pleasant is also a very important factor. When I am a customer, I know that I have a tendency to be pleasant when the person helping me is being pleasant and helpful.

CRITICAL THINKING
What role does eye contact play in nonverbal communication, according to Ms. Marchwinski? Do you agree?

Chapter 5

Listening to the Customer

OBJECTIVES

After completing this chapter, you will be able to:

• *Describe the four steps in the listening process.*

• *Actively gather and provide information in customer contact situations.*

• *Recognize internal and external obstacles to effective listening.*

• *Develop strategies to improve your listening ability.*

• *Create relationships with customers through effective listening.*

"You just listen to the customers, then act on what they tell you."

Charles Lazarus
Founder, Toys "R" Us, Inc.

Before reviewing the chapter content, respond to the following questions by placing a "T" for true or an "F" for false on the rules. Use any questions you miss as a checklist of material to which you will pay particular attention as you read through the chapter. For those you get right, congratulate yourself, but review the sections they address in order to learn additional details about the topic.

_____ **1.** Listening is a passive process similar to hearing.

_____ **2.** Listening is a learned process.

_____ **3.** During the comprehending stage of the listening process, messages received are compared and matched to memorized data in order to attach meaning to the messages.

_____ **4.** The two categories of obstacles that contribute to listening breakdowns are personal and professional.

_____ **5.** Biases sometimes get in the way of effective customer service.

_____ **6.** A customer's inability to communicate ideas effectively can be an obstacle to effective listening.

_____ **7.** A faulty assumption arises when you react to or make a decision about a customer's message based on your past experiences or encounters.

_____ **8.** A customer's refusal to deal with you, coupled with a request to be served by someone else, could indicate that you are viewed as a poor listener.

_____ **9.** Many people can listen effectively to several people at one time.

_____ **10.** By showing a willingness to listen and eliminate distractions, you can encourage meaningful customer dialogue.

_____ **11.** Two types of questions that are effective for gathering information are reflective and direct.

_____ **12.** Open-ended questions elicit more information than closed-ended questions do because they allow customers to provide what they feel is necessary to answer your question.

1. F   4. F   7. T   10. T
2. T   5. T   8. T   11. F
3. T   6. T   9. F   12. T

1 | WHY IS LISTENING SO IMPORTANT?

▶ **CONCEPT:** To be a better customer service professional, it is necessary to improve your listening skills.

Listening effectively is the primary means customer service professionals use to determine the needs of their customers. Needs are whatever the customer wants or expects you to provide. Many times, these needs are not communicated to you directly but through inferences, indirect comments, or nonverbal signals. A skilled listener will pick up on these cues and conduct follow-up questioning or probe deeper to determine the real need.

Most people take the listening skill for granted. They incorrectly assume that anyone can listen effectively. Unfortunately, this is untrue. Many people are complacent about listening and only go through the motions of listening. According to Andrew Wolvin and Carolyn Coakley in their book *Listening*, one survey found that three-fourths (74.3 percent) of 129 managers surveyed perceived themselves to be passive or detached listeners.

In a classic study on listening conducted in 1957 by Dr. **Ralph G. Nichols,** who is sometimes called the **father of listening,** data revealed that the average white-collar worker in the United States typically has only about a 25 percent efficiency rate when listening. This means that 75 percent of the message is lost. Think about what such a loss in message reception could mean in an organization if the poor listening skills of customer service professionals led to a loss of 75 percent of customer opportunities. Figure 5-1 gives you some idea of the impact of this loss.

FIGURE 5-1

Missed opportunities.

Opportunities	Action Taken	Impact
100 customers a day, each with a $10 order	25 orders were filled successfully	Loss of $750 per day ($273,750 per year)
1000 customers went to a store in one day	250 were serviced properly	750 were dissatisfied
1,000,000 members were eligible for membership renewal in an association	250,000 returned their application	750,000 members were lost

---

Work It Out 5-1. Personal Listening Experience

Work It Out
5-1

▶ Think about experiences you have had as a customer in which the provider did not do a good job listening to you.

Describe some of these experiences. _____

_____

_____

_____

How did the behavior of the provider make you feel? _____

_____

_____

_____

Work It Out 5-1. Personal Listening Experience (continued)

How did you react to the behavior of the provider? _____

_____

_____

_____

Did you take your business elsewhere? _____

_____

_____

_____

What did you tell others about your experience? _____

_____

_____

_____

_____

Worksheet ▼

5-1

WORKSHEET 5-1

Listening Awareness Self-Assessment

How well do you really listen? Before going further in this chapter, take a moment to respond objectively to the following statements by placing a check mark in the appropriate column. Key: A; Always O: Often N: Never

A   O   N

___ ___ ___ **1.** *I focus all my attention on the speaker when conversing.*

___ ___ ___ **2.** *I consciously look for issues or action items during conversations.*

___ ___ ___ **3.** *I avoid planning my next remarks until after I have heard the entire message.*

___ ___ ___ **4.** *I approach conversations with interest and a desire to truly listen.*

___ ___ ___ **5.** *I avoid letting my emotions get in the way of my listening.*

___ ___ ___ **6.** *I avoid daydreaming as I listen.*

___ ___ ___ **7.** *I try to put myself in the speaker's place and empathize with what he or she is saying.*

___ ___ ___ **8.** *To avoid jumping ahead in the conversation, I avoid assumptions about what someone will say.*

A O N

__ __ __   **9.** *I feed back, in my own words, what I heard the speaker say in order to verify my understanding of the message.*

__ __ __   **10.** *I check my understanding of a speaker's meaning by asking for clarification of words or comments I do not understand.*

__ __ __   **11.** *I use a variety of techniques to stay focused while someone speaks.*

__ __ __   **12.** *I make eye contact or look at the person as he or she speaks.*

__ __ __   **13.** *I consciously think about how someone might respond to what I say.*

__ __ __   **14.** *I allow the speaker to present his or her ideas even when I am emotional about the topic.*

__ __ __   **15.** *I do not let other sounds or activities distract me as I listen.*

__ __ __   **16.** *I listen objectively and don't judge the speaker.*

__ __ __   **17.** *When appropriate, I take notes as I listen.*

__ __ __   **18.** *I listen for ideas and concepts, and not just details or facts.*

__ __ __   **19.** *I select a location that provides the best environment for effective listening and limits distractions.*

__ __ __   **20.** *I observe and evaluate the speaker's physical posture and gestures as he or she speaks.*

If you did not rate yourself with an "A" for always in each instance, reflect on your weak areas and focus on strategies for improvement in those areas as you go through this chapter.

2 WHAT IS LISTENING?

▶ **CONCEPT:** Listening is a learned process, not a physical one.

Listening is your primary means of gathering information from a customer or any other person. True listening is an active learned process, as opposed to hearing, which is the physical action of gathering sound waves through the ear canal. When you listen actively, you go through a process consisting of various phases—hearing or receiving the message, attending, comprehending or assigning meaning, and responding. Figure 5-2 illustrates the process.

FIGURE 5-2

The listening process.

Attending (2)

Comprehending (3)

Hearing (1)

Responding (4)

Hearing and Receiving the Message

Hearing is a passive physiological process of receiving sound waves and transmitting them to the brain, where they are analyzed. This is usually a simple process. Because of external noises and internal distracters (psychological and physical), however, a customer's message(s) may be lost or distorted. Using some of the strategies for improvement given in this chapter can help change your ability to listen more effectively.

Attending

Once your ears pick up sound waves, your brain goes to work focusing on, or attending to, what was heard. In the process, it sorts out everything being heard. The effort involves deciding what's important so that you can focus attention on the proper sound. This becomes extremely difficult when you are receiving multiple messages or sounds. That is why it's important to eliminate as many distractions as possible. For example, during a meeting you could forward phone calls, or turn off your computer, or shut your door—or you could find a quiet place to meet.

Comprehending or Assigning Meaning

Once you've decided which message or customer you will listen to, your brain begins a process of **comprehending**, or **assigning meaning** to, what you heard. Just like a computer, your brain has files of information—sounds, sights, shapes, images, experiences, knowledge on various topics—it sorts through. As it compares what was heard to what is stored, it tries to match the pieces. For example, when you hear a voice on the phone that sounds familiar, the brain goes to work trying to match the voice to a name or person you've dealt with before. This is called *memory* and *recognition*.

Responding

The last phase of the listening process is **responding**. Selecting an appropriate response is crucial to the success of your customer interactions. The words you select, the way you deliver them, the timing and location, and the nonverbal signals you send all have meaning, and all affect the way others perceive and interpret your message. This is why you should be careful to consciously select the appropriate response and method of delivery when dealing with customers. A wrong choice could mean lost business or worse (the customer could get angry or violent).

Figure 5-3 gives some suggested questions you might ask yourself to check on your listening skills.

FIGURE 5-3

Questions for the listener.

In analyzing your customer's message(s), ask yourself the following questions:

- Am I practicing active listening skills?
- What message is the customer trying to get across?
- What does the customer want or need me to do in response to his or her message?
- Should I take notes or remember key points being made?
- Am I forming premature conclusions, or do I need to listen further?
- Are there biases or distractions I need to avoid?
- Is the customer failing to provide information needed to make a sound decision?
- What other feedback clues are being provided in addition to words? Are they important to message meaning?
- What questions do I need to ask as a follow-up to the customer's message?

WORKSHEET 5-2

Evaluating Good Listeners

Take a few minutes to think about all the people you have known whom you consider to be good listeners. List the names of five of these people below, along with the characteristics or skills (they focused on their speaker, didn't interrupt, made eye contact, faced their listener) that you feel made their listening effective.

Name	Characteristics
_____	_____
	_____
	_____
	_____
	_____

Worksheet ▼
5-2

WORKSHEET 5-2 (CONTINUED)

Name	Characteristics
_____	_____
	_____
	_____
	_____
	_____
_____	_____
	_____
	_____
	_____
	_____
_____	_____
	_____
	_____
	_____
	_____
_____	_____
	_____
	_____
	_____

Now that you have identified the characteristics of a good listener, ask yourself which of the characteristics you display. Use your answers as a basis for working toward enhancing your own listening skills.

3 CHARACTERISTICS OF A GOOD LISTENER

▶ **CONCEPT:** Listening will improve as you "learn" in the customer's shoes.

To help in your efforts in improving your listening skills, use information you entered in Worksheet 5-2 as a checklist as you read through this chapter.

Successful listening is essential to service excellence. Like any other skill, listening is a learned behavior that some people learn better than others. Some common characteristics possessed by most effective listeners are discussed in the following sections. The characteristics of effective and ineffective listeners are summarized in Figure 5-4.

Empathy. By putting yourself in the customer's place and trying to relate to the customer's needs, wants, and concerns, you can often reduce the risk of poor service. Some customer service professionals neglect the customer's need for compassion, especially when the customer is dissatisfied. Such negligence tends to magnify or compound the effect of the initial poor service the customer received.

Understanding. The ability to listen as customers verbalize their needs, and to ensure that you understand them, is essential in properly servicing the customer. Too often, you hear people say, "I understand what you mean," when it is obvious that they have no clue as to the level of emotion being felt. When this happens while a customer is upset or angry, the results could be flared tempers, loss of business, bad publicity, and at the far end of the continuum, acts of violence. Some techniques for demonstrating understanding will be covered later in this chapter.

Patience. Many people spend time thinking about what they will say next rather than listening to what is being said. Taking time to slow down and actively listen to customers makes them feel important and allows you to better meet their needs. Patience is especially important when a language barrier or speech disability is part of the situation. Your job is to take extra care to determine the customer's needs and then respond appropriately. In some cases, you may have to resort to the use of an interpreter or written communication in order to determine the customer's needs.

Attentiveness. By focusing your attention on the customer, you can better interpret his or her message and satisfy his or her needs. Attentiveness is often displayed through nonverbal cues (nodding or cocking of the head to one side or the other, smiling, or using paralanguage), which were discussed in detail in Chapter 4. When you are reading, talking on the phone to someone while servicing your customer, or doing some other task while "listening" to your customer, you are not really focusing. In fact your absorption rate will fall into the 25 percent category discussed earlier.

Objectivity. In dealings with customers, avoid subjective opinions or judgments. If you have a preconceived idea about customers, their concerns or questions, the environment, or anything related to the customers, you could mishandle the situation. Listen openly and avoid making assumptions. Allow customers to describe their needs, wants, or concerns, and then analyze them fairly before taking appropriate action.

FIGURE 5-4

Characteristics of effective and ineffective listeners.

Many factors can indicate an effective or ineffective listener. Over the years, researchers have assigned the following characteristics to effective and ineffective listeners:

Effective Listeners	Ineffective Listeners
Focused	Inattentive

▼

FIGURE 5-4 (CONTINUED)

Effective Listeners	Ineffective Listeners
Responsive	Uncaring
Alert	Distracted
Understanding	Unconcerned
Caring	Insensitive
Empathetic	Complacent
Unemotional	Emotionally involved
Interested	Self-centered
Patient	Judgmental
Cautious	Haphazard
Open	Defensive

Worksheet ▼ 5-3

WORKSHEET 5-3

Identifying Personal Listening Characteristics

List the characteristics that you believe you typically exhibit as a listener. If they are in the ineffective category, list strategies for improvement.

Effective	Ineffective	Strategies
_____	_____	_____
_____	_____	_____
_____	_____	_____
_____	_____	_____
_____	_____	_____
_____	_____	_____
_____	_____	_____
_____	_____	_____

Attention in Listening. Active listening involves complete attention, a readiness and willingness to take action, and an open mind to evaluate customers and determine their needs. What should customer service professionals do to achieve these goals of active listening?

> Concept: Poor customer service may result from a breakdown of the listening process.

Many factors contribute to ineffective listening. Some are internal, but others are external and you cannot control them. The key is to recognize actual and potential factors that can cause ineffective listening and strive to eliminate them. The factors discussed in the following sections are some of the most common.

Personal Obstacles

As a listener, you may have individual characteristics or qualities that get in the way of listening effectively to the customer. Some of these are discussed in the following sections.

Biases

Your opinions or beliefs about a specific person, group, situation, or issue can sometimes cloud your ability to listen objectively to what is being said. These biases may result in preconceived and sometimes incorrect assumptions. They can also lead to service breakdown, complaints, and angry or lost customers.

Psychological Distracters

Your psychological state can impede effective listening. If you are angry, upset, or simply don't want to deal with a particular person or situation, your listening may be negatively affected. Think about a time when you had a negative call or encounter with a customer or someone else and you became frustrated or angry. Did your mood, and possibly your voice tone, change as a result? Did that emotion then carry over and affect another person later?

When a customer service professional gets angry, his or her tone and mood may likely carry over to a customer. How do you feel when a customer service professional is angry and raises his or her voice?

Often when people become upset, time is needed to cool off before they deal with someone else. If you do not cool off, the chance that you will raise your voice or become frustrated with the next person you encounter is increased greatly. And, if this second encounter escalates because of the person's reaction to a negative tone or attitude, you might respond inappropriately. Thus, a vicious cycle is started. You get angry at a person, your tone carries over to a second, who in turn gets upset with your tone, your emotions escalate, and you carry that mood to a third person, and so on. All of this lessens your ability to listen and serve customers effectively.

Physical Condition

Another internal factor that can contribute to or detract from effective listening is your state of wellness and fitness. When you are ill, fatigued, in poor physical condition, or just not feeling well, listening can suffer. We often hear that a good diet and exercise are essential to good health. They are also crucial for effective listening. Try not to skip meals when you are working, stay away from foods high in sugar content, and get some form of regular exercise. These all affect physical condition. Try something as simple as using the stairs rather than the elevator or escalator. Another option is a brisk walk at lunchtime. All of these can help you maintain your "edge" so that you will be better prepared for a variety of customer encounters.

Work It Out
5-2

Work It Out 5-2. Personal Habits

▶ Take a few minutes to think about your personal nutritional and exercise habits; then create a list of the ones that are positive and negative:

Name   **Characteristics**

_____   _____
_____   _____
_____   _____
_____   _____
_____   _____
_____   _____
_____   _____
_____   _____
_____   _____

Circadian Rhythm

All people have a natural 24-hour biological pattern (**circadian rhythm**) by which they function. This "clock" often establishes the body's peak performance periods. Some people are said to be morning people; their best performance typically occurs early in the day. They often wake early, "hit the ground running," and continue until after lunch, when the natural rhythm or energy level in their body begins to slow down. For such people afternoons are often a struggle. They may not do their best thinking or perform physically at peak during that point in the day.

Evening people often have just the opposite pattern of energy. They struggle to get up or perform in the morning; however, during the afternoon and in the evening they are just hitting their stride. They often stay awake and work or engage in other activities until the early hours of the next day, when the morning people have been sound asleep for hours. From a listening standpoint, you should recognize your own natural body pattern so that you can deal with the most important listening and other activities during your peak period if possible. For example, if you are a morning person, you may want to ask your boss to assign you to customer contact or to handling problem situations early in the day. At that time, you are likely to be most alert and productive, less stressed, and less apt to become frustrated or irritated by abusive or offensive behavior by others.

Preoccupation

When you have personal or other matters on your mind (related to financial matters, school, marriage, family, or personal or work projects), it sometimes becomes difficult to focus on the needs and expectations of the customer. This can frustrate both you and the customer. It is difficult to turn off personal problems, but you should try to resolve them before going to work, even if you must take time off to deal with them. Many companies offer programs to assist employees in dealing with their personal and performance issues. Through employee assistance programs (EAPs), many organizations are offering counseling in such areas as finance, mental hygiene (health), substance abuse, marital and family issues, and workplace performance problems. Check with your supervisor to identify such resources in your organization, or ask about these services during the interview process when you apply for a position.

Hearing Loss

Many people suffer from hearing loss caused by physiological (physical) problems or extended exposure to loud noises. Sometimes they are not aware that their hearing is impaired. Often, out of vanity or embarrassment, people take no action to remedy the loss. If you find yourself regularly straining to hear someone, having to turn one ear or the other toward the speaker, or having to ask people to repeat what they said because you didn't get the entire message, you may have a hearing loss. If you suspect that you have hearing loss, go to your physician or an audiologist (hearing specialist) quickly to avoid complications or further loss of hearing.

Listening Skill Level

People communicate on different levels depending on their knowledge and experiences in the area of communication. Adults are influenced by the experiences they had as children; that is, they are likely to repeat behavior they learned during childhood. For example, if you grew up in an environment where the people around you practiced positive skills related to listening, providing feedback and using nonverbal communication (covered in Chapter 4), and effective interpersonal skills for dealing with others, you will likely use similar techniques as an adult. On the other hand, if your childhood experiences were negative and you did not have good communication role models, the chances are that you struggle in dealing with others effectively.

Listening is the primary skill most people have for gathering information. Unfortunately, in the United States, listening as a skill is not taught in most public school systems. People learn the proper techniques involved in the skill only if they read, listen to audiotapes, watch videos, and attend seminars or college courses on listening. Too often, even though an adult's intentions might be well meant, techniques used to teach listening to children are often ineffective.

Think about your own experiences or times when you have observed an adult "teaching" a child to listen. You might have seen the adult grasp the child, look directly at the child, and say something like, "Look at me when I'm talking to you." Or the adult might have used a harsh tone to say the same kind of thing without touching the child. Now think of this from an adult standpoint. If someone treated you like that today, would you want to focus your attention and say, "Yes, what is it?" Or would a barrier go up and listening stop as your emotions escalated? Remember, if you learned the negative behavior as a child, you will likely repeat it as an adult unless new behavior replaces the old.

Thought Speed

Your brain is capable of comprehending messages delivered at rates of as much as four to six times faster than the speed at which the average adult in the United States speaks (approximately 125 to 150 words per minute, or wpm). The difference between the two rates can be referred to as a **lag time** or **listening gap** during which the mind is actually idle. The result is that your brain does other things to occupy itself (for example, daydreaming). To prevent or reduce such distraction, you must consciously focus on your customer's message, look for key points, ask pertinent questions, and respond appropriately. If the customer has a complaint or suggestion, you may even want to take notes. This not only helps you focus on and recall information but also can demonstrate to the customer that you are truly interested in the ideas or subject of the conversation.

Faulty Assumptions

Because of past experiences or encounters with others, you may be tempted to make **faulty assumptions** about your customer's message(s). Don't. Each customer and each situation is different and should be regarded as such. Because you had a certain experience with one customer does not mean that you will have a similar experience with another. Suppose, for example, that your are college registrar. You see lots of students and hear lots of stories when they try to change from one class to another or drop a course. One day a student comes into your office and asks to cancel her registration in one class in order to register for another even though the designated time for such a change has passed. Your immediate inclination might be to quote policy since you've "heard this one before." Your response might sound like, "I'm sorry, Ms. Molina, the period for adds or drops has passed." Don't respond so quickly; instead, hear the customer out. She may provide information (verbally or nonverbally) that will change your view. For example, Ms. Molina (crying) might say, "I've got to get out of that class. I need one more course to graduate, but I can't stay in this class."

If you are proactive in this situation and practicing active listening, you will pick up on the emotions and ask some questions in order to find out her real need or issue. For example, you might say, "Ms. Molina, you seem very upset, is anything wrong?" She might respond, "Yes. I need to graduate this semester and return to my country to help support my family. But I can't stay in Mr. Broward's class. He's . . . he's always leering at me and making lewd remarks." Obviously, the rules don't apply in this case. If you didn't listen, you'd never know, and there would be a dissatisfied and distraught customer as a result. Also, you might be setting up the institution for a harassment lawsuit by forcing Ms. Molina to stay in the class or to seek other solutions (lawsuit, violence, or going to the media to expose the teacher).

External Obstacles

You cannot remove all barriers to effective listening, but you should still try to reduce them when dealing with customers. Some typical examples might include the following.

Information Overload

Each day you are bombarded with information from many sources. You get information in meetings, from the radio and television, from customers, and in a variety of public places. In many instances, you spend as much as 5 to 6 hours a day listening to customers, coworkers, family members, friends, and strangers. Such overloads can result in stress, inadequate time to deal with individual situations, and reduced levels of customer service.

Other People Talking

It is not possible for you to give your full attention to two speakers simultaneously. In order to serve customers effectively, deal with only one person at a time. If someone else approaches, smile, acknowledge him or her, and say, "I'll be with you in just a moment" or at least signal that message by holding up your index finger to indicate "1 minute" while you smile.

Work It Out 5-3. Dealing With Interruptions

▶ Think about a situation in which you were talking to a customer or someone else and another person arrived, interrupted, and started asking questions or talking to you.

What was the reaction of the first person to whom you were talking? _____

_____

_____

What was your reaction? _____

_____

_____

How did you handle the situation? _____

_____

_____

Ringing Phones

Ringing telephones can be annoying, but you shouldn't stop helping one customer to get into a discussion with or try to serve another customer over the phone. This creates a dilemma, for you cannot ignore customers or others who depend on you to serve their needs over the telephone.

Several options are available. You might arrange with your supervisor or coworkers to have someone else take the calls. Those people can either provide service or take messages (as we'll explore in Chapter 7), depending on the business your organization conducts. Another option is the use of a voice mail system, answering service, or pager for message collection. Still another possibility would be to ask the person to whom you are speaking face-to-face to excuse you, professionally answer the phone, and either ask the caller to remain on hold or take a number for a callback.

No one solution is best. You can only try to provide the best service possible, depending on your situation. Before such situations develop, it is a good idea to speak with your supervisor or team leader and peers to determine the policy and procedures for handling customers in these instances.

Speakerphones

These devices allow for hands-free telephone conversations. They are great because you can continue your conversation while searching for something the customer has requested. Unfortunately, many people put callers on the loudspeaker while continuing to do work not related to the caller. This not only is rude but it results in ineffective communication. Because the speakerphone picks up background noise, it is often difficult to hear the caller, especially if you are moving around the room and are not next to the phone. Many people dislike speakerphones. Be aware that improper use of the speakerphone could cause customers to stop calling. An additional issue with the speakerphone is confidentiality. Since others can hear the caller's conversation, the caller may be reluctant to provide certain information (credit card and social security numbers, medical information, or personal data). Whenever you use a speakerphone, to inform the caller that someone else is in the room with you and/or close your office door, if possible.

Office and Maintenance Equipment

Noisy printers, computers, photocopying machines, electric staplers, vacuum cleaners, and other devices can also be distractions. When servicing customers, eliminate or minimize the use of these types of items. If others are using noisy equipment, try to position yourself or them as far away from the customer service area as possible.

Physical Barriers

Desks, counters, furniture, or other items separating you from your customer can stifle communication. Depending on your job function, you might be able to eliminate barriers. If possible, do so. These obstacles can distance you physically from your customer or depersonalize your service. Be conscious of how you arrange your office or work space. Side-by-side (facing the customer at an angle) seating next to a table is preferable to sitting across from a customer in most situations. An exception to this approach would be appropriate if you provide service to customers who might become agitated or violent. Some examples: city or state clerks who deal with people who have been charged with traffic or other violations of the law; public utility employees who deal with people who are complaining about service problems; employees in motor vehicle offices where people may have frustrating problems with drivers' licenses or vehicle registration.

An Additional Obstacle

In addition to the issues already addressed, customers themselves can negatively affect communication—through their inability to convey a message.

Although it is not specifically a listening issue, if customers are unable to deliver their message effectively, you will be unable to receive and properly analyze their meaning. No amount of dedication and effort on your part will make up for a language barrier, a disability (speech, physical) that limits speech and nonverbal body language, or poor communication skills. In these situations, it is often necessary to seek out others to help (translators, signers) or to use alternative means of communication (gestures, written, symbols, or a text telephone, or **TTY/TDD**) to discover the customers' meaning and satisfy their needs.

By recognizing these limiting factors, you can improve your chances of communicating more effectively. Use Worksheet 5-4 to evaluate listening distractions in your environment.

WORKSHEET 5-4

Worksheet ▼
5-4

Eliminating Distractions

Take a moment to think of obstacles you've seen, experienced, or had to deal with in a customer service setting (as a provider or customer). List them along with two or three strategies to eliminate them.

Obstacles　　　　　　　　　**Strategies**

Personal

_____　　_____

_____　　_____

_____　　_____

External

_____　　_____

_____　　_____

_____　　_____

Additional

_____　　_____

_____　　_____

_____　　_____

Work It Out 5-4. Inattentive Listening Behavior

▶ To help you improve your listening skills and offer better service to your customers, complete the following activity. Think of a time when you were trying to verbally communicate ideas to someone but you realized (based on verbal and nonverbal responses) that this person was not listening to you.

1. What led you to believe that this person was not paying attention to your message(s)? How was your ability to get your message across affected? How did you feel?

_____

_____

_____

Next, think of times when you were involved in conversations but were not really focused and listening to the other person.

2. What was going on that prevented you from listening effectively? What reaction did your listener have to your distraction or lack of focus?

_____

_____

_____

Use your responses to these questions to improve your listening skills.

---

5   INDICATORS OF POOR LISTENING

▶ **CONCEPT:** Improve your listening skills through self-analysis.

You cannot afford the luxury of failing to listen to your customer. Periodically, you should do a self-check on your listening style to see whether you need to improve. If any of the following events occur, you may need to refocus.

Customers specifically ask to speak to or be served by someone else.

You find yourself missing key details of conversations.

You regularly have to ask people to repeat information.

You end phone calls or personal encounters not knowing for sure what action is required of you.

Customers often make statements such as, "Did you hear what I said?" "Are you listening to me?" or "You're not listening."

You find yourself daydreaming or distracted as a customer is speaking.

You miss nonverbal cues sent by the customer as the two of you communicate.

You answer a question incorrectly because you didn't actually hear it.

▶ Here are some common listening problems. Try to think of one or two means for reducing or eliminating them in your customer service.

Problem	Strategy for Improvement
Listening to words, not concepts, ideas, or emotions.	_____ _____
Pretending interest in a customer's problem, question, suggestion, or concern.	_____ _____ _____
Planning your next remarks while the customer is talking.	_____ _____
Being distracted by external factors.	_____ _____
Listening only for what you perceive is the real issue or point.	_____ _____
Reacting emotionally to what the customer is saying.	_____ _____

6 STRATEGIES FOR IMPROVED LISTENING

▶ **CONCEPT:** You can improve your listening skills in several different ways. One important way is to listen more than you talk.

Numerous techniques can be used to become a more effective listener. The following tips can be used as a basis for improvement.

Stop Talking!

You cannot talk and actively listen at the same time. When the customer starts talking, stop talking and listen carefully. One common mistake that many people make is to ask a question, hesitate, and if no answer is immediately offered, ask a second question or "clarify" the meaning by providing additional information. A habit like this is not only confusing to the listener, but rude.

Some people like to reflect on what they have heard and then formulate just the right answer before responding. People who speak another language, or who have a disability, may either be translating the information received into their own language or trying to assimilate your message before making an appropriate response. If you interrupt with additional information or questions, you may interfere with their thought patterns and cause them to become frustrated. The end result is that the listener may not speak or respond at all because he or she believes that you aren't really listening or interested in the response anyhow, or because he or she is embarrassed or confused. To avoid such a scenario, plan what you want to say, ask the question, and then stop speaking. You might ask, "Mr. Swanson, how do you think we might resolve this issue?" Once you have asked the question, stop talking and wait for a response. If a response does not come in a minute or so, try asking the question another way (paraphrase), possibly offering some guidance to a response and concluding with an open-ended question (one that encourages the listener to give opinions or longer responses). You might say, "Mr. Swanson, I'd really like to help resolve this issue. Perhaps we could try _____ or _____. How do you think that would work?"

Prepare Yourself

Before you can listen effectively to someone, you must be ready to receive what this person has to say. Stop reading, writing, talking to others, thinking about other things, working on your computer, answering phones, and dealing with other matters that distract you. For example, if a customer approaches while you're using a calculator to add up a row of figures, smile and say, "I'll be with you in just a moment" or smile and hold up your index finger to indicate "1 minute." As quickly as possible, complete your task, apologize for the delay, and then ask, "How may I assist you?"

Work It Out 5-6. Active Listening Strategies

▶ Think about strategies used by people whom you believe are listening to you. List some of the behaviors and techniques they use.

_____

_____

_____

_____

_____

_____

_____

_____

Listen Actively

Use the basics of sound communication when a customer is speaking. The following strategies are typically helpful in sending an "I care" message when done naturally and with sincerity:

SMILE!

Do not interrupt to interject your ideas or make comments unless they are designed to clarify a point made by the customer.

Sit or stand up straight and make eye contact with the customer.

Lean forward or turn an ear toward the customer, if appropriate and necessary.

Paraphrase their statements occasionally.

Nod and offer affirmative paralanguage statements ("I see," "Uh-huh," "Really," "Yes") to show that you're following the conversation.

Do not finish a customer's sentence. Let the customer talk.

In addition, focus on complete messages. A complete message consists of the words, nonverbal messages, and emotions of the customer. If a customer says that she's satisfied with a product but is sending nonverbal signals that contradict her statement, you should investigate further. Suppose that the supply of blue bowls being given away as gifts to people who stop by your trade show exhibit is gone. The customer might say, "Oh, that's okay. I guess a green one will do." Her tone and facial expression may, however, indicate disappointment. You could counter with, "I'm sorry we're out of the blue bowls, Mrs. Zagowski. If you'd like one, I can give you a certificate that will allow you to pick one up when you visit our store, or I can take your address and ship one to you when I get back to the store. Would you prefer one of those options?" By being "tuned in" to your customer and taking this extra initiative, you have gone beyond the ordinary and moved into the realm of exceptional customer service. Mrs. Zagowski will probably appreciate your gesture and tell others about the wonderful, customer-focused person she met at the trade show exhibit.

Show a Willingness to Listen

By eliminating distractions, sending positive verbal and nonverbal responses, and actively focusing on what is being said, you can help the customer relax and have a more meaningful dialogue. For example, when dealing with customers, you should make sure that you take some of the positive approaches to listening outlined earlier (turning off noisy equipment, facing the person, making eye contact, and smiling while responding in a positive manner). These small efforts can pay big dividends in the form of higher satisfaction, lowered frustration, and a sense of being cared for on the customer's part.

Show Empathy

Put yourself in the customer's place by empathizing, especially when the customer is complaining about what he or she perceives to be poor service or inferior products. This is sometimes referred to as "walking a mile in your customer's shoes." For example, if a customer complains that she was expecting a specific service by a certain date but didn't get it, you might respond as follows: "Mrs. Ellis, I apologize that we were unable to complete _____ on the tenth as promised. We dispatched a truck, but the driver was involved in an accident. Can we make it up to you by _____? (Offer a gift, suggest an alternative such as hand delivery and so on.) This technique, known as **service recovery**, is a crucial step in delivering quality service and remaining competitive into the twenty-first century.

Service recovery is discussed in detail in Chapter 14.

Listen for Concepts

Instead of focusing on one or two details, listen to the entire message before analyzing it and responding. For example, instead of trying to respond to one portion of a message, wait for the customer to provide all the details. Then ask any questions necessary to get the information you need to respond appropriately. For example, "Mr. Chi, if I understand you correctly, you'd like us to build a new prototype part to replace the one currently being used in the assembly. You're looking for a total cost for development and manufacture not to exceed $10,000. Is that correct?"

Be Patient

Not everyone communicates in the same manner. Keep in mind that it is your job to serve the customer. Do your best to listen well so that you can get at the customer's meaning or need. Don't rush a customer who seems to be processing information and forming opinions or making a decision. This is especially important after you have presented product information and have asked for a buying decision. Answer questions, provide additional information requested, but don't push. Doing so could frustrate, anger, and ultimately alienate the customer. You could end up with a complaint or lost customer.

Listen Openly

Avoid the biases discussed earlier. Remember that you don't have to like everyone you encounter, but you do have to respect and treat customers fairly and impartially if you want to maintain a business relationship. For example, whenever you encounter a person who is rude or is the type of person for whom you have a personal dislike, try to maintain your professionalism. Remember that you represent your organization and that you are paid by your employer to serve the customer (whoever he or she is). If a situation arises that you feel you cannot or prefer not to handle, call in a coworker or supervisor. However, be careful in taking this action because you will likely reveal a personal preference or bias that could later be held against you when you apply for other positions in your organization or positions in other companies. Try to work through your differences or biases rather than letting them hinder your ability to deal with others. Your ability to serve each customer fairly and competently is important to your job success.

Send Positive Nonverbal Cues

Be conscious of the nonverbal messages you are sending. Even when you are verbally agreeing or saying yes, you may be unconsciously sending negative nonverbal messages. When sending a message, you should make sure that your verbal cues (words) and nonverbal cues (gestures, facial expressions) are in **congruence**. For example, if you say, "Good morning. How may I help you?" in a gruff tone, with no smile, and while looking away from the customer, that customer is not going to feel welcome or believe that you are sincere in your offer to assist. (Nonverbal cues were covered in detail in Chapter 4.)

Don't Argue

Remember the "Did not," "Did too" quarrels you had when you were a child? Such verbal exchanges got heated, voices rose and tempers escalated, and someone might have started hitting or pushing. Who won? No one. You should avoid similar childish behaviors in dealing with others—especially your customers or potential customers.

When you argue, you become part of the problem and cannot be part of the solution. Learn to phrase responses or questions positively (as discussed in Chapter 3). Even when you go out of your way to properly serve customers, some of them will respond negatively. Some people seem to enjoy conflict. In such situations, maintain your composure (count to ten silently before responding), listen, and attempt to satisfy their needs. If necessary, refer such customers to your supervisor or a peer for service.

Take Notes, if Necessary

If information is complicated, or if names, dates, numbers, or numerous details are involved in a customer encounter, you may want to take notes for future reference. Notes can help prevent your forgetting or confusing information. Once you have made your notes, verify your understanding of the facts with your customer before proceeding. For example, in an important client or customer meeting, you may want to jot down key issues, points, follow-up actions, or questions. Doing so shows that you are committed to getting it right or taking action.

Ask Questions

Use questions to determine customer needs and to verify and clarify information received. This will ensure that you thoroughly understand the customer's message prior to taking action or responding. For example, when you first encounter a customer, you must discover his or her needs or what is wanted. Through a series of open-ended questions (typically they start with words such as *when*, *what*, *how*, or *why*, and seek substantial amounts of information) and closed-ended questions (they often start with words such as *do*, *did*, *are*, and *will*, and elicit one-syllable or single-word responses), you can gain useful information.

WORKSHEET 5-5

Benchmarking Customer Service

You can often improve your own listening behavior by observing that of others and benchmarking (identifying the best practices). During the next five to seven days, make note of contacts (in person and on the phone) that you have with a variety of service providers (gas station attendants, telephone operators, vendors, bank tellers, drive-through service attendants, taxi or bus drivers, and coworkers). As you interact with each of these people, pick one who provided excellent service and one whose service was less than satisfactory. Note how well each listened in your encounter and respond to these questions.

1. What did the successful listener do that you considered effective? _____

_____

_____

2. What did the unsuccessful listener do that you considered ineffective? _____

_____

_____

3. How did the behavior of both listeners affect your reaction as a customer?

_____

_____

4. What could each listener have done differently to improve effectiveness?

_____

_____

7 INFORMATION-GATHERING TECHNIQUES

▶ **CONCEPT:** Use questions to sort out facts from fiction.

Your purpose in listening to your customers is to gather information about their needs on which you can base decisions on how to best satisfy them. Sometimes, you will need to prompt your customers to provide additional or different types of information. To generate and gather information, you can use a variety of questions. Most questions are either open-ended or closed-ended.

Open-ended Questions

This type of questioning follows the time-tested approach of the 5 Ws and 1H used by journalists who ask questions that help determine who, what, when, where, why, and how. Basically, **open-ended questions** establish a number of facts. They:

Identify Customer Needs

By asking questions, you can help determine **customer needs**, what he or she wants or expects. This is a crucial task because some customers are either unsure of what they need or want or do not adequately express their needs or wants.

Examples:

"Ms. Deloach, what type of car are you looking for?"
"Mr. Petell, why is an extended warranty important to you?"

Gather a Lot of Information

Open-ended questions are helpful when you're just beginning a customer relationship and aren't sure what the customer has in mind or what's important. By uncovering more details, you can better serve your customer.

Example:

"Mr. and Mrs. Milton, to help me better serve you, could you please describe what your ideal house would look like if you could build it?"

Uncover Background Data

When a customer calls to complain about a problem, often he or she has already taken unsuccessful steps to solve it. In such cases, it is important to find out the background information about the customer or situation. By asking open-ended questions, you allow customers to tell you as much information as they feel is necessary to answer your question. This is why open-ended questions are generally more effective for gathering data than are closed-end questions. If you feel you need more information after your customer responds to an open-ended question, you can always ask further questions.

Example:

"Mrs. Chan, will you please tell me the history behind this problem, including all of your previous contacts with this office?"

Uncover Objections During a Sale

If you are in sales or cross-selling or upselling products or services (getting a customer to buy a higher quality or different brand of product or extend or enhance existing service agreements) to current customers as a service representative, you will likely encounter **objections**. The reasons for a customer not wanting or needing your product and/or service can be identified through the use of open-ended questions. Such questions can be used to determine whether your customer has questions or objections. Many times, people are not rejecting what you are offering outright; they simply do not see an immediate need for the product or cannot think of appropriate questions to ask. In these cases, you can help them focus their thinking or guide their decision through the use of open-ended questions. Be careful to listen to your customer's words and tone when he or she offers objections. If the customer seems adamant, such as, "I really don't think I want it," don't go any further with your questions. The customer will probably become angry because he or she will feel that you are not listening. A fine line exists between helping and pushing, and if you cross it, you could end up with a confrontation on your hands. Often active listening and experience will help you determine what course of action to take.

Example:

"Ms. Williams, from what you told me, all the features of the new RD10 model that we talked about will definitely ease some of your workload, so let me get the paperwork started so you can take it home with you. What do you think?"

Give the Customer an Opportunity to Speak

Although it is important to control the conversation in order to save time and thus allow you to serve more customers, sometimes you may want to give the customer an opportunity to talk. This is crucial if the customer is upset or dissatisfied about something. By allowing a customer to "vent" as you listen actively, you can sometimes reduce the level of tension and help solve the problem.

Examples of open-ended questions:

"What suggestions for improving our complaint-handling process should I present to my boss?"

"Why is this feature so important to you?"

"How has the printer been malfunctioning, Jim?"

"What is the main use of this product?"

"When would you most likely need to have us come out each month?"

"Where have you seen our product or similar ones being used?"

"Why do you feel that this product is better than others you've tried?"

"How do you normally use the product?"

"Mr. O'Connell, I can see you're unhappy. What can I do to help solve this problem?"

Closed-ended Questions

Open-ended questions are designed to draw out a lot of information. Traditionally, **closed-ended questions** elicit short, one-syllable responses and gain little new information. Many closed-ended questions can be answered yes or no or with a specific answer, such as a number or a date. Closed-ended questions can be used for:

Verifying Information

Closed-ended questions are a quick way to check what was already said or agreed on. Using them reinforces that you're listening and also helps prevent you from making mistakes because you misinterpreted or misunderstood information.

Example:

"Mr. Christopherson, earlier I believe you said you've used our service before. Is that correct?"

Closing an Order

Once you've discovered needs and presented the benefits and features of your product and service, you need to ask for a buying decision. This brings closure to your discussion. Asking for a decision also signals the customer that it is his or her turn to speak. If the customer offers an objection, you can use the open-ended questioning format discussed earlier.

Example:

"Mr. Jones, this tie will go nicely with your new suit. May I wrap it for you?"

Gaining Agreement

When there has been ongoing dialogue and closure or commitment is needed, closed-ended questions can often bring about that result.

Example:

"Veronica, with everything we've accomplished today, I'd really like to be able to conclude this project before we leave. Can we work for one more hour?"

Clarifying Information

Closed-ended questions can also help ensure that you have the details correct and thus help prevent future misunderstandings or mistakes. Closed-ended questions also help save time and reduce the number of complaints and/or product returns you or someone else will have to deal with.

Example:

"Ms. Jovanovich, if I heard you correctly, you said that the problem occurs when you increase power to the engine. Is that as soon as you turn the ignition key or after you've been driving the car for a while?"

Examples of closed-ended questions:

"Do you agree that we should begin right away?" (obtaining agreement)

"Mrs. Leonard, did you say this was your first visit to our restaurant?" (verifying understanding)

"Mr. Morris, did you say you normally travel three or four times a month and have been doing so for the past ten years?" (verifying facts)

"How many employees do you have, Mr. Carroll?" (obtaining information)

8 ADDITIONAL QUESTION GUIDELINES

> **CONCEPT:** Use questions to further your feedback.

In order to generate meaningful responses from customers, keep the following points in mind.

Avoid Criticism

Be careful not to seem to be critical in the way you ask questions. For example, a question like, "You really aren't going to need two of the same item, are you?" sounds as if you are challenging the customer's decision making. And the bottom line is that what customers choose should not be your concern. Your job is to help them by providing excellent service. Also, as you read in Chapter 4, nonverbal messages delivered via tone or body language can suggest criticism, even if your spoken words do not.

Ask Only Positively Phrased Questions

You can ask for the same information in different ways, some more positive than others. As you interact with your customers, it is crucial to send messages in an open, pleasant manner. This is done by tone of voice and proper word selection. In the examples, you can see how a negative or positive word choice affects meaning.

> ***Examples:***
>
> "You really don't want that color do you, Mrs. Handly?" (potentially negative or directive)
>
> "We offer a wide selection of colors. Would you consider another color as an alternative, Mrs. Handly?" (positive or suggestive)

Ask Direct Questions

You generally get what you ask for. Therefore, being very specific with your questions can often result in your receiving useful information. Being specific can also save time and effort. This should not be construed to mean that you should be abrupt or curt in your communication with customers or anyone else.

Effective questioning is important. Asking open-ended questions is one way to get information and better meet your customers' needs. Do you like it when a listener asks you open-ended questions?

Example:

If you want to know what style of furniture the customer prefers, but you know that only three styles are available, don't ask a general open-ended question, such as, "Mrs. Harris, what style of furniture were you looking for?" Instead, try a more structured closed-ended question such as, "Mrs. Harris, we stock Colonial, French provincial, and Victorian styles. Do any of those meet your needs?"

This approach prevents you from having to respond, "I'm sorry, we don't stock that style," when Mrs. Harris answers your open-ended question by telling you that she's looking for Art Deco style furniture.

Ask Customers How You Can Better Serve

You will find no better or easier way to determine what customers want and expect than to ask them. They'll appreciate it, and you'll do a better job serving them. *Note:* If appropriate, a good follow-up question to gain additional information after a customer has responded to a question is, "That's interesting, will you please explain to me why you feel that way or believe that's true?"

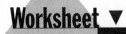

Worksheet 5-6

Asking Questions

To give you practice in formulating open-ended questions, take a few minutes to review the following closed-ended questions. Then convert them to open-ended questions without changing the goal of each.

Example:

Closed-ended: "Have you had experience with negative customers?"

Open-ended: "What experience have you had with negative customers?"
_____

Now, you try . . .

Closed-ended: "Will you use this primarily in an office?"

Open-ended:_____

_____

_____

Closed-ended: "Do you think that this product will fit your needs?"

Open-ended:_____

_____

_____

Closed-ended: "Have you often done business with us?"

Open-ended:_____

_____

_____

Closed-ended: "What word would you use to describe the best feature of this stereo system?"

Open-ended:_____

_____

_____

Closed-ended: "You look unhappy about the lease. Is everything all right?"

Open-ended:_____

_____

_____

Chapter Summary

No matter what your current level of listening skill is, there is usually room for improvement. Customers expect and should receive your undivided attention in any encounter they have with you. You should continually reevaluate your own listening style, decide which areas need development, and strive for improvement. In addition, you should keep in mind that active listening involves more than just focusing on spoken words. Remember that there are many obstacles that can impede listening. To overcome them, you need to develop the characteristics of an effective listener and strive to minimize negative habits. Through the use of the active listening process and positive questioning, you can better determine and satisfy customer needs.

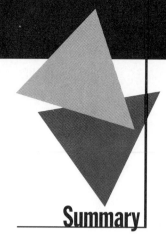

Summary

CHAPTER REVIEW QUESTIONS

1. What phases make up the active listening process? _____

_____

_____

_____

_____

_____

2. How does hearing differ from listening? _____

_____

_____

_____

_____

_____

3. According to studies, what is the average rate of listening efficiency for most adults in the United States? Why is this significant in a customer service environment? _____

_____

_____

_____

_____

_____

4. List 14 characteristics of effective listeners. _____

_____

_____

_____

_____

_____

Summary

5. What is an important reason for practicing good listening skills in a customer service environment? _____

_____

_____

_____

_____

6. Of the characteristics common to good listeners, which do you consider the most important in a customer service organization? Explain. _____

_____

_____

_____

_____

7. What obstacles to effective listening have you experienced, either as a customer service professional or as a customer? _____

_____

_____

_____

_____

8. How can you determine when someone is not listening to what you say? _____

_____

_____

_____

_____

9. What techniques or strategies can be used to improve your listening skills? _____

_____

_____

_____

_____

10. How is the outcome of customer service encounters improved by using a variety of questions? _____

_____

_____

Search the Internet for Items on Listening Skills

To find out more about the listening process and how you can improve your listening skills, log on to the Internet and type in Listening or any of the other topic headings or subheadings in this chapter. Search for the following items:

Listening activities

Quotations about listening

Books and articles on listening (create a bibliographic list) or interpersonal communication

Research data on listening

Any other topic covered in this chapter (open-ended or closed-ended questions, handling sales objections)

COLLABORATIVE *Learning Activity*

Bring your findings to class and be prepared to discuss them with your group.

Developing Team Listening Skills

To give you some practical experience in using the techniques described in this chapter, you will now have an opportunity to interact with others in your group. The activity will be done in groups of three or four members. One person will be the listener, one the speaker, and one or two observers. Each person will have an opportunity to play the different roles. For example, if there are four people in the group, there will be four rounds of activity. In the first round one member of the group will be the listener, one will be the speaker, and the other two will be observers. The roles will change in each of the next three rounds so that everyone will have had a turn at each role.

The speaker will spend about 5 to 7 minutes sharing a customer service experience he or she has had in the past few weeks (it can be positive or negative). The experience should have been one that lasted for several minutes so that there will be enough detail to share with the other members of the group. The speaker should describe the type of organization, why he or she was there, how he or she was greeted, the behavior of the customer service provider, how the provider dealt with concerns and questions, and any other important point the speaker can recall.

As the speaker talks, the listener should pay attention and use as many of the positive listening skills discussed in this chapter as possible. The observers should watch and take notes on what they see. Specifically, they should look for use of the positive listening skills and any other behaviors exhibited (positive or negative). After each speaker has finished his or her story, the listener, then the speaker, and finally the observers (in that order) should answer the following questions about the listener's behavior:

What was done well from a listening standpoint?

What needed improvement?

What comments or suggestions came to mind?

FACE TO FACE

Handling an Irate Customer at Regal Florists

Background

Regal Florists is a small, third-generation family-owned flower shop in Willow Grove, Pennsylvania. Most customers are local residents, but Regal has a Website and an FTD delivery arrangement so that it serves customers throughout the United States. Mr. and Mrs. Raymond Boyle have been doing business with Regal for more than 20 years and know the owners well. Quite often they order centerpiece arrangements for holidays and dinner parties, which they host frequently because of Mr. Boyle's position with a public relations firm. They also occasionally send flowers to their six children and four grandchildren living in various parts of the United States and overseas. Regal's owners and employees are usually especially cheerful, helpful, and efficient. That's one of the reasons the Boyles are loyal customers even though Regal's prices have risen above the industry average in recent years.

Your Role

During the past four years you have worked part-time at Regal's, at first delivering arrangements and for the past year creating arrangements and managing the shop.

Mr. Boyle stopped by first thing this morning, just as you were opening the store. He was irate, demanding to know what happened with the arrangement delivered yesterday to his assistant for Secretary's Day, and swearing he'd never patronize Regal's again. Apparently, he had phoned in the order last week. The order was taken by a 16-year-old part-time employee who has since resigned. According to Mr. Boyle, he'd ordered a small arrangement with carnations and various other bright spring flowers for his assistant. Instead, his assistant received a dozen red roses along with a card, on the outside of which was a border of little hearts and the statement "Thinking of you." Inside the card was a message intended for his wife: "I don't know what I'd do without you." Unfortunately, Mrs. Boyle had dropped by Mr. Boyle's office and was near the assistant's desk when the flowers arrived, saw the card and flowers, and was quite upset. Rumor has it that Mr. and Mrs. Boyle are having marital problems. You were the only person in the shop when Mr. Boyle came in. Answer these questions.

Critical Thinking Questions

1. Do you think that Mr. Boyle should take Regal's past performance record into consideration? Why or why not? _____

   _____

   _____

   _____

   _____

   _____

2. What listening skills addressed in this chapter should you use in this situation? Why? _____

   _____

   _____

   _____

   _____

   _____

3. What can you possibly do or say that might resolve this situation positively? _____

   _____

   _____

   _____

   _____

   _____

4. Based on information provided, how would you have reacted in this situation if you were Mr. Boyle? Why? _____

   _____

   _____

   _____

   _____

   _____

5. If you were Mr. Boyle, what could be done or said to convince you to continue to do business with Regal? _____

   _____

   _____

   _____

   _____

   _____

FROM THE FRONTLINE
Interview

Ms. Andrea Burns
Assistant Call Center
Manager
Boston Communica-
tion Group, Inc.,
Deland, Florida

1. Please provide one or two paragraphs describing your experience in dealing with external and internal customers (number of years, type of customers, organizations).

I have been involved in the customer service industry since the summer of 1987 as an entertainment coordinator and later as front desk attendant and foreign exchange teller for a resort in Jamaica. My work involved greeting guests and ensuring that they had a memorable vacation at the resort. In 1990 I worked briefly as a receptionist for a sales and promotion company in London. In this position I met clients on a daily basis and represented the company while I completed a work and travel program. In 1992 I joined a retail sales company where I remained for six years, five of them in management. In this capacity I assisted customers in planning for major events in their lives—engagement and weddings, which can be a difficult and stressful time for people. Now I am the assistant call center manager for a company that handles billing questions for the customers of our clients. I deal mostly with the clients, ensuring that their calls are answered promptly and successfully while following all company and FCC policies. Sometimes I handle difficult issues with customers.

2. What are your general impressions of customer service in the United States? Why do you feel this way?

Consumers have so many choices because of competition that companies are spending resources on providing quality service in order to create customer loyalty. Any American company that I can think of provides customer service to customers. Customers have become very educated, particularly since computers have become so widely used, and companies must train their employees to represent their interest, to provide quality service, and to efficiently resolve customers' concerns in order to gain customer loyalty. Customer service is indeed a growing industry that can never be replaced by technology. People will always be needed to address customers' concerns, listen to their opinions and suggestions, and quickly solve their problems.

3. What is the biggest challenge related to listening to customers (internal and external) that you have observed in your environment? Please explain.

One of the biggest challenges related to listening to customers has to do with time. Customer Service Representatives (CSRs) are given goals regarding calls per hour (CPHs) and average handling time (AHT). CSRs tend to rush their calls in order so that they will achieve a high CPH and a low AHT. This means that they often do not listen effectively to customers and therefore do not completely satisfy their needs or concerns. CSRs need to understand that quality and quantity go together. If both are not achieved, the company and the customers suffer. There are no shortcuts.

4. In your experience, when listening breaks down, what is the result? Please explain.

When listening breaks down, the communication flow is interrupted and customers' problems cannot be solved. If the CSR does not closely listen to customers' needs, customers may, for example, receive inaccurate billing information. They become irate. They may call the customer service department two or three more times, and the situation may escalate. This customer may have experienced a similar situation before and described this negative experience to 20 friends. Not only has the company's reputation been damaged, the customer—and the 20 friends—are lost because of poor listening skills.

5. What are some pitfalls service providers should remember to avoid when listening to customers? Please explain.

Service providers should avoid a number of pitfalls. First, they should not interrupt customers. This can be frustrating to customers and create unnecessary problems. By not interrupting the caller, a CSR will have an opportunity to get a complete understanding of the situation at hand. Second, it is important to customers not to have to repeat information. A CSR should make a note of information given by a customer (name, account numbers) to avoid having to ask the customer to repeat. Third, be sure to acknowledge a customer's statement. CSRs should use some statement or sound to indicate that they are listening ("Absolutely," "Hmmm," "Yes, I understand," "All right"). This helps to develop rapport and lets the customer know that you are listening, responding, and understanding to eliminate asking unnecessary questions. Finally, give the customer your undivided attention.

6. From your perspective, what is the most important thing to remember when dealing with a customer?

The most important thing to remember is to consistently represent the company's interest by providing the quality of service that you would expect as a customer. Summarizing a customer's concerns is very important because it shows the customer that you understand and are assuring the customer that you will help. Empathy is one of the most important qualities you can exhibit to make a customer feel appreciated ("I'm sorry to hear you were misinformed, Mr. Smith"). Try to use the customer's name throughout a call; it makes customers feel special if you can remember their names. Promptly resolve customers' concerns and ensure that follow-ups are done when promised.

7. What advice related to listening would you give someone entering the customer service profession?

Listening is an acquired skill that is basic in providing quality service. Give customers the opportunity to vent or explain concerns without interrupting. When service representatives listen attentively, they can summarize to show the customer that they understand and can effectively solve the problem.

CRITICAL THINKING

How do you think customer service operates in this organization? Would you handle it the same? Do you agree with the advice given?

Chapter 6

Customer Service and Behavior

OBJECTIVES

After completing this chapter, you will be able to:

- *Recognize four key behavioral styles and the roles they play in customer service.*

- *Use techniques outlined to interact with various customer behavioral styles.*

- *Develop strategies for communicating effectively with customers.*

- *Interpret customer nonverbal cues effectively on the basis of behavioral styles.*

- *Respond to customer problems effectively.*

"The basic cause of most inharmonious human relationships is the tendency to impose our values on other people."

Robert Anthony
Assistant Secretary of
Defense 1965–68

Before reviewing the chapter content, respond to the following questions by placing a "T" for true or an "F" for false on the rules. Use any questions you miss as a checklist of material to which you will pay particular attention as you read through the chapter. For those you get right, congratulate yourself, but review the sections they address in order to learn additional details about the topic.

_____ **1.** Understanding behavioral styles can aid in establishing and maintaining positive customer relationships.

_____ **2.** You should treat others as individuals, not as members of a category.

_____ **3.** People whose primary behavioral style category is "E" focus their energy on working with people.

_____ **4.** People whose primary behavioral style category is "D" focus their energy on tasks or getting the job done.

_____ **5.** Some behavioral styles are better than others.

_____ **6.** People who exhibit the "D" style often tend to move slowly and speak in a low-key manner.

_____ **7.** People who exhibit the "E" style often tend to be highly animated in using gestures and speaking.

_____ **8.** People who exhibit the "R" style often tend to be very impatient.

_____ **9.** People who exhibit the "I" style often tend to express their emotions easily.

_____ **10.** You should attempt to determine a customer's behavioral style and then tailor your communication accordingly.

_____ **11.** To deliver total customer satisfaction, you need to make your customers feel special.

_____ **12.** When you say no to a customer, it is important to let him or her know what you cannot do and why.

_____ **13.** Service to your customers should be seamless; customers should not have to see or deal with problems or process breakdowns.

_____ **14.** Perceptions are based on education, experiences, events, and interpersonal contacts, as well as a person's intelligence level.

_____ **15.** Once you've made a perception, you should evaluate its accuracy.

1. T 5. F 9. F 13. T
2. T 6. F 10. T 14. F
3. T 7. T 11. T 15. T
4. T 8. F 12. F

1 | WHY BE CONCERNED WITH BEHAVIORAL STYLES?

CONCEPT: Behavioral styles are observable tendencies. An awareness of your own style can lead you to understand customers and improve your relationships with customers.

As a customer service professional, you need to understand human behavioral style characteristics. The more proficient you become at identifying your own behavioral characteristics and those of others, the better you will be at establishing and maintaining positive relationships with customers. Self-knowledge is the starting point. To help in this effort, we will examine some common behavior that you exhibit and that you may observe in various other people.

A key to successfully dealing with others is recognizing your own style. Too often we try to impose our *beliefs, values, attitudes,* and *needs* on others. This can lead to frustration for them and us. When dealing with your customers, you should recognize that just because someone else does something differently, or acts differently, from the way you do doesn't mean that they are wrong. Relationships are built on accepting the characteristics of others. In customer service, adaptability is crucial, for many people do not always act the way you want them to. As you will read later in this chapter, there are many strategies that can be used to help modify and adapt your behavior so that it does not clash with that of your customers. This does not mean that you must make all the concessions when behaviors do not mesh. It simply means that, although you do not have control over the behavior of others, you do have control over your own behavior. Use this control to deal more effectively with your customers.

2   WHAT ARE BEHAVIORAL STYLES?

> **CONCEPT:** Behavioral styles are actions exhibited when you and others deal with tasks or people. As a customer service professional, you need to be aware that everyone is not the same.

Behavioral styles are observable tendencies (actions that you can see or experience) that you and other people exhibit when dealing with tasks or people. As you grow from infancy, your personality forms, based on your experiences and your environment. For example, if you had a lot of interaction with others as a child and were exposed to "people-based" activities, you likely will relate well to others in the workplace as an adult. On the other hand, if your childhood was a lonely one, as an adult you may have difficulties interacting with people.

For thousands of years, people have devised systems in an attempt to better understand why people do what they do and how they accomplish what they do—and to categorize behavioral styles. Many of these systems are still in use today. For example, early astrologers grouped the 12 signs into the four categories Earth, Air, Fire, and Water. Hippocrates, and other ancient physicians and philosophers, observed and categorized people as sanguine, phlegmatic, melancholy, and choleric. Modern researchers have examined behavior from a variety of perspectives.

Have you ever come into contact with someone with whom you simply did not feel comfortable or someone with whom you felt an immediate bond? If so, you were possibly experiencing and reacting to the impact of behavioral style. As a customer service professional, you need to be aware that everyone is not the same, or just like you. For this reason, you should strive to provide service in a manner that addresses others' needs and desires, not the ones you prefer.

Because you have certain behavioral preferences, you may want to impose your preferences on others. This type of behavior from a service provider may cause a customer to become angry, withdrawn, or even disruptive. You will be better informed about yourself if you learn your own behavior preferences. The next section addresses how to do that.

3 IDENTIFYING BEHAVIORAL STYLES

> **CONCEPT:** Each contact in a customer service environment has the potential for contributing to your success. Each person should be valued for his or her strengths and not belittled for what you perceive as shortcomings.

Through an assessment questionnaire you can discover your own behavioral tendencies in a variety of situations. An awareness of your own style preferences can then lead you to a better understanding of customers, since they also possess style preferences. By understanding these characteristics, you can improve communication, build stronger relationships, and offer better service to the customer.

Many self-assessment questionnaires and research related to behavioral styles are based on the work begun by psychiatrist Carl Jung and others in the earlier part of the twentieth century. Jung explored human personality and behavior. He divided behavior into two "attitudes" (introvert and extrovert) and four "functions" (thinking, feeling, sensing, and intuitive). These attitudes and functions can intermingle to form eight psychological types, a knowledge of which is useful in defining and describing human behavioral characteristics.

From Jung's complex research have come many variations, additional studies, and a variety of behavioral style self-assessment questionnaires and models for explaining personal behavior. Examples of these questionnaires are the Myers-Briggs Type Indicator (MBTI), the Personal Profile System (DiSC), and the Social Styles Profile (SSP).

Although everyone typically has a *primary behavioral pattern* (the way a person acts or reacts under certain circumstances) to which they revert in stressful situations, people also have other characteristics in common and regularly demonstrate some of the other behavioral patterns. Identifying your own style preferences helps *you* identify similar ones in others.

To informally identify some of your own behavioral style preferences, use Worksheet 6-1.

Describing Your Behavior

STEP 1: Read the following list of words and phrases and rate yourself by placing a number (from 1 to 5) to the left of each item. A 5 means that the word is an accurate description of yourself in most situations, a 3 indicates a balanced agreement about the word's application, and a 1 means that you do not feel that the word describes your behavior well. Before you begin, refer to the sample assessment in Figure 6-1.

__ Decisive

__ Logical

__ Relaxed

__ Talkative

__ Calculating

__ Nonaggressive (avoids conflict)

__ Consistent

__ Fun-loving

__ Competitive

__ Quality-focused

__ Loyal

__ Enthusiastic

__ Pragmatic (practical)

__ Accurate

__ Sincere

__ Popular

__ Objective

__ Detail-oriented

__ Patient

__ Optimistic

__ **TOTAL D=   I=   R=   E=**

STEP 2: Once you have rated each word or phrase, start with the first word, *Decisive,* and put the letter "D" to the right of it. Place an "I" to the right of the second word, an "R" to the right of the third word, and an "E" to the right of the fourth word. Then start over with the fifth word and repeat the "DIRE pattern until all words have a letter at their right.

STEP 3: Next, go through the list and count point values for all words that have a "D" beside them. Put the total at the bottom of the grid next to "D=." Do the same for the other letters.

Once you have finished, one letter will probably have the highest total score. This is your natural style tendency. For example, if "D" has the highest score, your primary style is Decisive. If "I" has the highest score, you exhibit more Inquisitive behavior. "R" indicates Rational, and "E" is an Expressive style preference.

If two or more of your scores have the same high totals, you probably generally put forth similar amounts of effort in both these style areas.

Note: Keep in mind that this is only a quick indicator. A more thorough assessment, using a formal instrument (questionnaire), will be better at predicting your style preferences. For more information or to obtain written or computer-based surveys and reports, write the author at the address shown in the author information section of this book.

FIGURE 6-1

Sample completed self-assessment.

5	Decisive	D
3	Logical	I
1	Relaxed	R
4	Talkative	E
5	Calculating	D
3	Nonaggressive (avoids conflict)	I
5	Consistent	R
3	Fun-loving	E
5	Competitive	D
1	Quality-focused	I
3	Loyal	R
2	Enthusiastic	E
5	Pragmatic (practical)	D
1	Accurate	I
3	Sincere	R
1	Popular	E
5	Objective	D
2	Detail-oriented	I
1	Patient	R
1	Optimistic	E

TOTAL	D = 25	I = 10	R = 13	E = 11

You should be aware that you should not try to use behavioral characteristics and cues as absolute indicators of the type of person you are dealing with. (This is similar to the situation with nonverbal cues.) Human behavior is complex and often unpredictable. You have some of the characteristics listed for all four style ca7tegories; you simply have learned through years of experience which behavior you are most comfortable with and when adaptation is helpful or necessary. Generally, most people are adaptable and can shift style categories or exhibit different characteristics based on the situation. For example, a person who is normally very personable and amiable can revert to more directive behavior, if necessary, to manage an activity or process for which he or she will be held accountable. Similarly, a person who normally exhibits controlling or task-oriented behavior can socialize and react positively in "people" situations. People are adaptable.

An important point to remember is that there is no "right" or "wrong" style. Each person should be valued for his or her strengths and not belittled because of what you perceive as shortcomings. In a customer environment, each contact has the potential for contributing to your success and that of your organization. By appreciating the behavioral characteristics of people with whom you interact, you can avoid bias or prejudice and better serve your customer.

4 | STYLE TENDENCIES

CONCEPT: A person may demonstrate strong tendencies toward one style preference or another. By being familiar with these styles and their general characteristics, you can adapt to various behaviors your customers may exhibit.

How can a person who demonstrates one of the four styles be described? How might this person act, react, or interact? Some generalizations about behavior are listed in this section. Keep in mind that even though people have a primary style, they demonstrate other style behaviors too. By becoming familiar with these style characteristics, and observing how others display them, you can begin to learn how to better adapt to various behaviors.

D: Decisive

People who have a strong tendency toward this style preference may tend to:

- *Move quickly.*
- *Seek immediate gratification of needs or results.*
- *Work proactively toward a solution to a problem.*
- *Be forceful and assertive in their approach (sometimes overly so).*
- *Project a competitive nature.*
- *Display a confident, possibly arrogant demeanor.*
- *Ask specific, direct questions and give short, straight answers.*
- *Discuss rather than write about something (e.g., call or come in rather than write about a complaint).*
- *Talk and interrupt more than listen.*
- *Display symbols of power to demonstrate their own importance (e.g., expensive jewelry, clothes, cars, power colors in business attire such as navy blue or charcoal gray).*
- *Be solemn and use closed, nonverbal body cues.*
- *Have firm handshakes and strong, direct eye contact.*
- *Have functionally decorated offices (all items have a purpose and are not there to make the environment more attractive).*
- *Prefer active, competitive leisure activities.*

I: Inquisitive

People who have a strong tendency toward this style preference may tend to:

- *Rarely volunteer feelings freely.*
- *Ask specific, pertinent questions rather than making statements of their feelings.*
- *Rely heavily on facts, times, dates, and practical information to make their point.*
- *Prefer to interact in writing rather than in person or on the phone.*
- *Prefer formality and distance in interactions. They often lean back when talking, even when emphasizing key points.*
- *Use formal titles and last names as opposed to first names. They may also stress the use of full names, not nicknames (e.g., Cynthia instead of Cindy or Charles instead of Chuck).*
- *Use cool, brief handshakes, often without a smile. If they do smile, it may appear forced.*
- *Wear conservative clothing although their accessories are matched well.*
- *Be impeccable in their grooming but may differ in their choice of styles from those around them (e.g., hair and makeup).*
- *Be very punctual and time-conscious.*
- *Carry on lengthy conversations, especially when trying to get answers to questions.*
- *Be diplomatic with others.*
- *Prefer solitary leisure activities (e.g., reading or listening to relaxing music).*
- *Keep their personal life separate from business.*

R: Rational

People who have a strong tendency toward this style preference may tend to:

- *Be very patient.*
- *Wait or stand in one place for periods of time without complaining, although they may be irritated about a breakdown in the system or lack of organization.*
- *Exhibit congenial eye contact and facial expressions.*
- *Prefer one-on-one or small-group interactions over solitary or large-group ones.*
- *Seek specific or complete explanations to questions (e.g., "That's our policy" does not work well with an "R" customer).*
- *Dislike calling attention to themselves or a situation.*
- *Avoid conflict and anger.*
- *Often wear subdued colors and informal, conservative, or conventional clothing styles.*
- *Ask questions rather than state their opinion.*

- *Listen and observe more than they talk (especially in groups).*
- *Communicate more in writing and like the use of notes, birthday, or thank-you cards just to stay in touch.*
- *Like to be on a first-name basis with others.*
- *Have intermittent eye contact with brief, businesslike handshake.*
- *Have informal, comfortable office spaces, possibly with pictures of family in view.*
- *Like leisure activities that involve people (often family).*

E: Expressive

People who have a strong tendency toward this style preference may tend to:

- *Look for opportunities to socialize or talk with others (e.g., checkout lines at stores, bus stops, waiting areas).*
- *Project a friendly, positive attitude.*
- *Be enthusiastic, even animated when talking, using wide, free-flowing gestures.*
- *Use direct eye contact and enthusiastic, warm (often two-handed) handshake.*
- *Smile and use open body language.*
- *Get close or touch when speaking to someone.*
- *Talk rather than write about something (e.g., call or come in with a complaint rather than writing to complain).*
- *Initiate projects.*
- *Wear bright, modern, or unusual clothes and jewelry because it gets them noticed or fits their mood.*
- *Dislike routine.*
- *Share feelings and express opinions or ideas easily and readily.*
- *Get distracted in conversations and start discussing other issues.*
- *Prefer informal use of names and like first-name communication.*
- *Not be time conscious and may often be late for appointments.*
- *Speak loudly and expressively with a wide range of inflection.*
- *Like action-oriented, people-centered leisure activities.*

5 | COMMUNICATING WITH EACH STYLE

CONCEPT: Each behavior style features various indicators of this style in practice. Remember, these cues are indicators, not absolutes, as you begin to use them to interact appropriately with others.

Once you recognize peoples' style tendencies, you can improve your relationships and chances of success by tailoring your communication strategies. As you examine Figure 6-2, think about how you can use these strategies with people you know in each style category. Keep in mind that these and other characteristics outlined in this chapter are only general in nature. Everyone is a mixture of all four styles and can change to a different style to address a variety of situations. Use these examples as indicators of style and not as absolutes.

FIGURE 6-2

Communicating with different personality styles.

Style	Behaviors	Strategy
DECISIVE	*Nonverbal Cues*	
	Steady, direct eye contact.	Return eye contact (3 to 5 seconds) and smile.
	Writing tends to be short and specific.	Respond in similar fashion; Minimize small talk and details.
	Gestures tend to be autocratic (e.g. pointing fingers or hands on hips).	Stand your ground without antagonizing. Maintain a professional demeanor.
	Verbal Cues	
	Forceful tone.	Don't react defensively or in a retaliatory manner.
	Speaks in statements.	Use facts and logic and avoid unnecessary details.
	Direct and challenging (short, abrupt).	Listen rather than defend.
	Fast rate of speech.	Match rate somewhat.
	Additional Cues	
	Short attention span when listening.	Keep sentences and communication brief.
	Very direct and decisive.	Support opinions, ideas, and vision.
INQUISITIVE	*Nonverbal Cues*	
	Deliberate body movements.	Use careful, restrained body cues.
	Uses little physical contact.	Avoid touching.
	Correspondence is formal and includes many details.	Respond similarly.
	Verbal Cues	
	Quiet, slow-paced speech (especially in groups).	Mirror rate and pattern.
	Minimal vocal variety.	Use subdued tone and volume.
	Additional Cues	
	Values concise communication.	Use brief, accurate statements.
	Uses details to make points.	Provide background information and data.

▼

Prefers confirmation and backup in writing.	Respond in writing and provide adequate background information.
Uses formal names instead of nicknames.	Address them by title and last name unless told otherwise.
Additional Cues	
Sharing of personal information is minimal.	Communicate on business level unless they initiate personal conversation.
Focuses on task at hand.	Organize thoughts before responding.

RATIONAL *Nonverbal Cues*

Gentle handshake, flowing, nondramatic gestures.	Return firm, brief handshake; avoid aggressive gestures.
Fleeting eye contact.	Make intermittent (3 to 5 seconds) eye contact.

Verbal Cues

Steady, even delivery.	Mirror their style somewhat.
Subdued volume.	Relax your message delivery.
Slower rate of speech.	Slow your rate if necessary; be patient.
Keeps communication brief.	Ask open-ended questions to draw out information.
Communication follows a logical pattern (e.g., Step 1, Step 2).	Use structured approach in communications.
Additional Cues	
Avoids confrontation.	Attempt to solve problems without creating a situation in which they feel challenged or obliged to defend themselves.

EXPRESSIVE *Nonverbal Cues*

Enthusiasm and inflection in voice.	Listen and respond enthusiastically.
Active body language.	Use open, positive body language and smile easily.
Enthusiastic, possibly two-handed handshake.	Return firm, professional one-handed shake.
Uses touch to emphasize points.	Acknowledge but use caution in returning touch (this action could be misinterpreted by them or others).

▼

Very intense, dramatic.	Show interest and ask pertinent questions.
Writing tends to be flowery and includes many details.	When writing, use a friendly reader-focused style.

Verbal Cues

Excessive details when describing something.	Ask specific open-ended questions to help them refocus.
Fast rate of speech.	Mirror or match their rate and excitement where appropriate.
Emphasizes storytelling and fun.	Relax, listen, and respond appropriately.

Additional Cues

Inattentive to details in tasks.	Ask questions to involve them.
Shares personal information and virtually anything else freely.	Reciprocate if you are comfortable doing so; however, stay focused on task at hand.

Work It Out 6-1. Monitoring Behavior

▶ To practice matching behavior with styles, try this activity. Make four or five copies of Worksheet 6-2. Select four or five friends or coworkers whom you see and interact with regularly. Write one of their names at the top of each worksheet copy. Covertly (without their knowledge) observe these people for a week or so and make notes about their behavior under each category listed on the worksheet. Focus specifically on the following areas:

Writing pattern or style

Interpersonal communication style (e.g., direct, indirect, specific or nonspecific questions, good or poor listener)

Body movements and other nonverbal gestures

Dress style (e.g., flashy, conservative, formal, informal)

Surroundings (e.g., office decorations or organization, car, home)

Personality (e.g., activities and interactions preferred—solitary, group, active, passive)

At the end of the week, decide which primary and/or secondary style of behavior each person exhibits most often. Then ask these people to assist you in an experiment that will involve them completing the quick style assessment that you did earlier (Worksheet 6-1).

After they have rated themselves, explain that you have been observing them for the past week.

Compare their ratings to the characteristics described in this chapter, and to your own assessment. Were you able to predict their primary or, at least, their secondary style?

Observing Others

Person Observed _____

Writing style: _____

_____

_____

_____

_____

_____

_____

Body movements and gestures: _____

_____

_____

_____

_____

_____

_____

_____

_____

_____

Interpersonal style: _____

_____

_____

_____

_____

_____

_____

Dress style: _____

_____

_____

_____

_____

_____

_____

Surroundings: _____

_____

_____

_____

_____

_____

WORKSHEET 6-2 (CONTINUED)

Personality: _____

_____

_____

_____

_____

Primary Style _____   Secondary Style _____

---

6 BUILDING STRONGER RELATIONSHIPS BY SOLVING PROBLEMS

▶ **CONCEPT:** Sometimes building stronger customer relationships means that you discover customer needs, seek opportunities for service, and respond appropriately to customers' behavioral styles. Occasionally you will need to de-emphasize a no and say it as positively as you can.

Recognizing and relating to customers' behavioral styles is just the first step in providing better service. To deliver total customer satisfaction, you will need to make the customer feel special. Whether a situation involves simply answering a question, guiding someone to a desired product or location, or performing a service, customers should leave the interaction feeling good about what they experienced. Providing this feeling is not only good business sense on your part but also helps guarantee the customers' return or favorable word-of-mouth advertising. Many ways of partnering with customers produce a *win-win situation* (one in which the customer and you and your organization succeed). Whatever you do to achieve this result, your customers should realize that you are their advocate and are acting in their best interests to solve their problems. Some suggestions for building stronger customer relationships are given in the following paragraphs.

Discover Customer Needs

Using the communication skills addressed in earlier chapters, engage customers in a dialogue that allows them to identify what they really want or need. If you can determine a customer's behavioral style, you can tailor your communication strategy to that style. Keep in mind that some customer needs may not be expressed aloud. In these instances, you should attempt to validate your impressions or suspicions by asking questions or requesting feedback. Gather information about a customer from observing vocal qualities, phrasing, nonverbal expressions and movements, and emotional state. For example, while providing service to Mr. Delgado, you told him that the product he was ordering would not arrive for three weeks. You noticed that he grimaced and made a concerned sound of "Um." At this point, a perception check would have been appropriate. You could have said, "Mr. Delgado, you looked concerned or disappointed when I mentioned the delivery date. Is that a problem for you?" You might have discovered that he needed the item sooner but resigned himself to the delay and didn't ask about other options. In effect, he was exhibiting "I" or possibly "R" behavior (silence and low-key reaction). Rather than have a confrontation, he accepted the situation without voicing disappointment or concern. He might then have gone to a competitor. By reacting positively to his nonverbal signals, you could identify and address a concern and thus prevent a dissatisfied and/or lost customer.

Avoid Saying No

If you must decline a request or cannot provide a product or service, do so in a positive manner. De-emphasizing what you cannot do and providing an alternative puts the customer in a power position. That is, even though she may not get her first request, she is once again in control because she can say yes or no to the alternative you have offered, or she can decide on the next step. For example, when a customer requests a brand or product not stocked by your organization, you could offer alternatives. You might counter with, "Mrs. Hanslik, although we don't stock that brand, we do have a comparable product which has been rated higher by *Consumer's Report* than the one you requested. Let me show you." This approach not only serves the customer but also (sometimes) results in a sale.

Seek Opportunities for Service

View complaints as a chance to create a favorable impression by solving a problem. Watch the behavioral characteristics being exhibited by your customer. Based on what you see and hear, take appropriate action to adapt to the customer's personality needs and solve the problem professionally. For example, Mrs. Minga complained loudly to you that the service woman who installed her new washing machine tracked oil onto the dining room carpet. As she is speaking, Mrs. Minga is pointing her finger and threatening to go to the manager if you do not handle this situation immediately. You can take the opportunity to solve the problem and strengthen the relationship at the same time. You might try the following. Make direct eye contact (no staring), smile, and say, "Mrs. Minga, I'm terribly sorry about your carpet. I know that it must be very upsetting. If you'll allow me to, I'll arrange to have your dining room carpet cleaned, and for your inconvenience, while they're at it we'll have them clean all the carpets in your house at no cost to you. How does that sound?" In reacting this way, you have professionally and assertively taken control of the situation. This is important because Mrs. Minga is exhibiting high "D" behavior. Responding in a less decisive manner might result in an escalation of her emotions and a demand to see someone in authority.

The process just described, which involves an attempt at righting a wrong and compensating for inconvenience, is called *service recovery*. The concept will be addressed in detail in Chapter 14.

FIGURE 6-3

Strategies for responding to customer problems.

Figure 6-3 provides some strategies to use when responding to customer complaints and solving problems involving people who demonstrate the four behavioral styles you have learned about. By tailoring customer service strategies to individual style preferences, you address the customer's specific needs. As you read in Chapter 5, active listening is a key skill in any service situation. As you review these strategies, think of other things you might do to better serve each behavioral type.

Style	Behaviors	Strategies
DECISIVE	Loud voice.	Be patient; listen empathetically.
	Finger pointing or aggressive body gestures.	Don't internalize; they are angry with the product or service, not necessarily you.
	Firm, active handshake.	Return a firm businesslike handshake.
	Directly places blame on service provider.	Be brief; tell them what you can do; offer solutions.
	Direct eye contact.	Be formal, businesslike.
	Sarcasm.	Don't take a happy-go-lucky or flippant approach.
	Impatient.	Be time-conscious; time is money to a "D."
	Demanding verbiage (e.g., "You'd better fix this";, "I want to see the manager now!").	Project competence; find the best person to solve problem.
	Irrational assertions (e.g., "You people *never* or *always...*")	Ask questions that focus on what they need or want (e.g., "What do you think is a reasonable solution?").
	Threats (e.g., "If you can't help, I'll go to a company that can.").	Reassure; say what you can do.
INQUISITIVE	Demands specifics.	Have details and facts available.
	Mild demeanor.	Approach in nonthreatening manner.
	Intermittent eye contact	Listen actively, make eye contact and focus on the situation.
	Gives list of issues, in chronological order.	Be specific in outlining actions to be taken by everyone.

	Exhibits patience.	Follow through on commitments.	
		Seeks reassurance.	Offer guarantees of resolution if possible.
		Focuses on facts.	Give facts and pros and cons of suggestions.
		Seeks to avoid conflict; just wants resolution.	Use low-pitched, unemotional speech; be patient; listen.
RATIONAL	Seeks systematic resolution to the situation.	Stress resolution and security of the issue.
	Avoids conflict or disagreement.	Smile, when appropriate.
	Strives for acceptance of ideas.	Provide references or resources.
	Intermittent eye contact.	Listen actively; make eye contact.
	Uses hand and subdued body movements and speech to emphasize key points.	Focus on personal movements to convey your feelings about the incident (e.g., How do you feel we can best resolve this problem?").
	Listens to explanations.	Focus on the problem, not the person.
EXPRESSIVE	Intermittent smiling along with verbalizing dissatisfaction.	Be supportive; tell them what you *can* do for them.
	Uses nonaggressive language (e.g., "I'd like to talk with someone about...").	Allow them to vent frustrations or verbalize thoughts.
	Steady eye contact.	Smile, if appropriate; return eye contact while conversing.
	Elicits your assistance and follow-up (e.g., "I really don't want to run all over town searching. Will you please call...").	Take the time to offer assistance and comply with their requests, if possible.
	Shows sincere interest.	Focus on feelings through empathy (e.g.,"I feel that...")
	Enthusiastic active handshake.	Return a firm businesslike handshake.
	Enthusiastically explains a situation.	Patiently provide active listening; offer ideas and suggestions for resolution.

Focus on Process Improvement

Customers do not like being kept waiting when your system is not functioning properly. They rightfully view their time as valuable. To expect them to patiently wait while a new cashier tries to figure out the register codes, someone gets a price check because the product was coded incorrectly, you have to call the office for information or approvals, and so on, is unfair and unreasonable. Defects or delays should be handled when the customer is not present. Service should be seamless to customers. This means that they should get great service and never have to worry about your problems or breakdowns. When breakdowns do occur, they should be fixed quickly, and the customer relationship smoothed over. In addition, it is important to recognize that customers with different behavioral styles will react differently to such breakdowns. Someone who exhibits "D" behavior may get loud, aggressive, and vocal and demand a supervisor after only a brief delay. Those with "I" styles may seem to be patient and not say anything or cause a confrontation but will possibly request directions to the supervisor's office and/or later send a detailed letter of complaint. The "R" style customers are likely to complain in an inoffensive manner and may even smile but may also seek out a supervisor. The "E" types may get upset but will often make the best of their time complaining to other customers and comparing notes on similar past experiences. No matter what style the customer exhibits, you should strive to reduce or eliminate customer inconvenience.

In all cases, after a delay you may want to compensate the customer for the inconvenience. At the least, such a situation warrants a sincere apology. Such an occurrence might be handled in the following manner. "Mr. Westgate, I am sorry for the delay. We've been experiencing computer problems all day. I'd like to make up for your inconvenience by giving you a 10 percent discount off your meal check. Would that be acceptable?" Although this is not a significant offering, your intention is to show remorse and to placate the customer so that he or she will continue to use your products and/or services.

After you have dealt with the situation, your next concern should be to personally fix the process that caused the breakdown or make a recommendation to your supervisor or other appropriate person. Quality and improvement are the responsibility of all employees.

Make Customers Feel Special

No matter which style tendencies a customer has, everyone likes to feel appreciated. By taking the time to recognize customers' value and by communicating effectively, you can bolster their self-esteem. When customers feel good about themselves as a result of something you did or said, they are likely to better appreciate what you and your organization can offer them. For example, as appreciation for long-term patronage, you may want to recognize a customer as follows: "Mr. and Mrs. Hoffmeister, we really appreciate your loyalty. Our records indicate that you've been a customer for over 20 years. In recognition, on behalf of _____ I'd like to present you with a complimentary weekend stay at _____ and two tickets to see the opening night of _____, along with a coupon for $50 toward dinner for two at _____. Please accept these with our compliments." This type of strategy goes a long way in guaranteeing customer loyalty.

Be Culturally Aware

The reality of a multicultural customer service environment further challenges your ability to deal with behaviors. This is because in today's multicultural business environment, it is likely that you will come into contact with someone of a different background, belief system, or culture. Many problems that develop in these encounters are a result of diversity ignorance. Even after you master the concepts of behavioral styles, you must remember that because values and beliefs vary from one culture to another, behavior is also likely to vary. For example, in many countries or cultures, the nonverbal gestures that Americans use have completely different meanings. Also, the reactions to such gestures will differ based on the recipient's personality style. Variations of symbols such as joining the thumb and index finger to form an O, signaling "Okay," have sexual connotations in several countries (e.g., Germany, Sardinia, Malta, Greece, Turkey, Russia, the Middle East, and parts of South America). Likewise, variations of the V symbolizing "victory" or "peace" to many people in Western cultures, have negative connotations in some parts of the world (e.g., British Isles and parts of Malta).[1] Symbols and gestures, therefore, might anger or offend some customers. Also, seemingly innocent behaviors such as crossing your legs so that the sole of your shoe points toward someone or patting a small child on the top of his or her head may cause offense. The sole of the foot is the lowest part of the body and touches the ground. In some parts of the world, pointing the sole of the foot toward a person implies that the person is lowly. Males from a Western culture, and specifically males who have "D," "I," and "R" styles and tend to adopt a formal posture when seated, should be aware of the effect of crossing their legs might have on certain customers. ("E" style people tend to be more relaxed and sprawling in their posture.) As for the head, many countries (e.g., in the Far East, especially Thailand)[2] view it as a sacred part of the body. Patting a child on the head is sometimes considered to invite evil spirits or bad omens. This action might easily be taken by people who have high "E" behavioral tendencies, for they tend to be touchy-feely.

Some books listed in the Bibliography address these kinds of issues. Also, we will explore other culturally related subjects in Chapter 10.

To help send a positive message to customers from other cultures, you can do simple things that might have major impacts. For example, if you work in a restaurant and want to show appreciation for the large numbers of customers from another country who patronize the restaurant, you might recommend to your boss that a special dish from that area of the world be added to the menu. This offering could be promoted through flyers or advertisements. Such a strategy shows appreciation of the customers and their culture while encouraging them to eat at your

---

[1] Morris, pp. 118–119; 130–131.

[2] Morris, p. 142.

establishment. However, be sure that the special dish is correctly prepared and uses the correct ingredients. Otherwise, you might offend rather than please the customer.

All these strategies, combined with a heightened knowledge of behavioral styles, can better prepare you to serve a wide variety of customers.

Know Your Products and Services

Customers expect that you will be able to identify and describe the products and services offered by your company. Depending on the behavioral style of the customer, the type of questions will vary. For example, a person with a strong "D" behavioral tendency may want to know the "bottom line" of using your service or product, an "I" may ask many questions related to options, testing, rebates, and similar detailed technical information, an "R" may want to know who uses your services and products and ask to see the instructions, and an "E" may want to talk about uses, colors, and sizes. If you cannot answer their questions, frustration, complaints, and/or loss of a customer may result.

Service providers need to know the products they are offering so that they can provide the best customer service possible. For example, when a new product line is introduced, orientation classes for employees can be arranged. In the classes, the features, benefits, and operation of the new items can be explained and demonstrated. Taking this approach increases knowledge of products and helps ensure better customer service.

Continue to Learn About People

To better prepare yourself for serving others, read whatever you can get your hands on related to customer service and take classes on how to interact and communicate with a variety of different types of people. Courses in psychology, sociology, and interpersonal communication are invaluable for providing a basis of understanding why people act as they do. Focus on issues of differences and similarities between men and women, cultural diversity, behavioral styles, and any other topic that will expand and round out your knowledge of people.

Of course, each person is unique, but the more you know about human behavior in general, the more successful you will be in dealing with the individuals you serve.

Prepare Yourself

Before you come into contact with customers, take a minute to review your appearance. Ask yourself, "What image do I project?" Think about how well your appearance is in tune with that of your typical customer. Evaluate your knowledge of your job and of the products and services offered by your organization. Are you ready and able to describe them to people regardless of their style preference? If not, start getting ready by learning as much as you can and practicing your message delivery by reviewing and implementing some of the strategies related to each style preference discussed earlier in this chapter.

▶ Read the following descriptions and then determine which behavioral style you are dealing with. Keep in mind that each person can switch behavioral styles depending on the situation. To help you determine styles, refer to the style tendencies described in previous sections of this chapter. Suggested answers are given in the margin.

Situation 1

You are a salesperson at a jewelry counter and observe a professionally dressed female customer waiting in line for several minutes. She is checking her watch frequently, anxiously looking around, and sighing often. When she arrives at the counter, she makes direct eye contact with you and without smiling states, "I want to buy a 16-inch 14-karat gold twisted-link necklace like the one advertised in today's paper. I also want a small gold heart pendant and would like these to cost no more than $125. Can you help me? Oh yes, I almost forgot. Wrap that in birthday paper. This gift is for my daughter's birthday."

STYLE	INDICATORS
_____	_____
	_____
	_____
	_____
	_____

ANSWERS
The behavioral styles and telltale indicators are described for each situation.

Situation 1 = D
Impatience, directive "D" language, direct eye contact, and no indication of smiling.

Situation 2

You stop by the office of a director of a department that provides data you use to prepare your end-of-month reports. As you look around, you see a photograph of his family. Your coworker smiles weakly and asks you to have a seat. As you begin to state your purpose by saying, "Thanks for taking the time to see me Mr. Cohen," he interrupts and says, "Call me Lenny, please."

STYLE	INDICATORS
_____	_____
	_____
	_____
	_____
	_____

Situation 2 = R
Low-key, friendly approach to communicating, smiling, offering a seat, suggesting that the less formal name _Lenny_ be used, family photos present.

Situation 3

As a customer service representative for an automobile dealer, you return a phone message from Cynthia McGregor. When the phone is answered, you say, "Good morning, may I speak with Cindy McGregor?" The curt response is, "This is *Cynthia* McGregor. How may I help you?" During the conversation, Ms. McGregor asks a variety of very specific questions about an automotive recall. Even though it seems obvious that the recall does not apply to her car, she asks very detailed follow-up questions such as why the recall was necessary, who was affected, and what was being done. Throughout the conversation, she is very focused on facts, times, dates, and technical aspects of the recall.

STYLE	INDICATORS
_____	_____
	_____
	_____
	_____
	_____

Situation 3 = I

Insistence on formal name *Cynthia* as opposed to more informal *Cindy*, direct, to the point, specific questions, detail-focused approach to gathering information

Situation 4

You are a teller in a bank. Mrs. Vittelli, one of the customers, comes into your branch several times a week. You know that she has just become a grandmother because she has brought along photos of her grandson. She has shared them, and all the details of her daughter's pregnancy, in a loud, exuberant manner with several of your coworkers. As she speaks, you have noticed that she has a beautiful smile, and that throughout conversations she is very animated, using gestures and often reaching over to lightly touch others as they speak.

STYLE	INDICATORS
_____	_____
	_____
	_____
	_____
	_____

Situation 4 = E

Freely sharing personal information about her family with strangers, outgoing demeanor, smiling, gesturing, and communicating in a loud, animated voice

7 | DEALING WITH PERCEPTIONS

CONCEPT: Often there are many different perceptions of an event. Our perceptions are often influenced by many factors such as physical qualities, social roles and behaviors, psychological qualities, and group affiliations.

Everyone has *perceptions* about the people and events he or she encounters. A person's background, based on education, experiences, events, and interpersonal contacts, influences how he or she views the world. In effect, there are sometimes as many different perceptions of an event as there are people involved.

WORKSHEET 6-3

Perception Evaluation

Many people are different from you or have different beliefs. Based on your perceptions, honestly rate the importance you think that each of the following factors should have in your relationships with others. Rate each from 1 (least important) to 5 (most important).

Rating   *Characteristic*

_____   *Physical characteristics*

_____   *Clothing, grooming, accessories*

_____   *Gender*

_____   *Education level*

_____   *Interpersonal communication ability (verbal, nonverbal, listening skills)*

_____   *Ability to speak English well*

_____   *Sexual orientation*

_____   *Height and weight*

_____   *Race and color of skin*

_____   *Job title*

_____   *Age*

_____   *Economic status (rich, middle income, poor)*

_____   *Behavioral style*

_____   *Self-confidence level*

_____   *Ability to deal with stress*

_____   *Active participation with religious groups*

_____   *Active participation with ethnic groups*

_____   *Active participation with political groups*

Worksheet ▼

6-3

Factors Affecting Perceptions

How are our perceptions shaped within a customer service framework? In essence, there are five categories that form the basis of many perceptions. We tend to base our perceptions of others and categorize people by thinking about the following:

- *Physical qualities. What does a person look like? What gender? What body shape? Color of skin? Physical characteristics (hair color or type, facial features, height or weight)?*
- *Social roles. What is a person's position in society? Job title? Honors received? Involvement in social or volunteer organizations?*
- *Social behaviors. How does this person act, based on the behavioral style characteristics? What social skills does he or she exhibit in social and business settings? How well does he or she interact with people (peers, customers, seniors, subordinates, and people of other races, gender, or backgrounds)?*
- *Psychological qualities. How does he or she process information mentally? Is this person confident? Stressed out? Insecure? Curious? Paranoid?*
- *Group affiliations. Does this person belong to a recognizable religious, ethnic, or political group? What kinds of qualities are associated with each group? Does he or she assume leadership roles and demonstrate competence in such roles?*

Perceptions and Stereotypes

People's perceptions of events vary greatly, as do their perceptions of each other. As a customer service provider, you should be aware of how you perceive your customers and, in turn, how they perceive you.

In some cases, you may **stereotype** people and, in doing so, adversely affect delivery of services. For example, your perception of older customers may be that they are all slow, hard of hearing, cranky, and politically conservative. This perception may be based on past experiences or from what you've heard or seen on television. This view might cause you to treat most older people in the same way, rather than treating each person as unique. However, you are basing your behavior on a stereotype, not on reality. Think about it—aren't there many older people who don't have these characteristics? Thus, you need to be very careful that your perceptions are not influenced by stereotypes, because this clearly works against treating each customer as an individual.

Stereotyping people affects our relationships with customers. For this reason, you should consciously guard against stereotyping when you interact with others. If you pigeonhole people right away because of preconceptions, you may negatively affect future interactions. For example, suppose you use your new knowledge about behavioral styles to walk up to a coworker and say something like, "I figured out what your problem is when dealing with people. You're a 'D.'" Could this create a confrontational situation? Might this person react negatively? What impact might your behavior have on your relationship with your coworker (and possibly others)? Based on what you have read regarding communication in earlier chapters, several things are wrong with such an approach. First of all, no one is always a "D." Although a person might exhibit this behavior a lot, he or she draws from all four styles, just as you do. Second, exhibiting any particular style is not a "problem." As you have seen in this chapter, "D" behavior can provide some valuable input to any situation. And finally, although a behavioral style may contribute to a person's actions, many other factors come into play (communication ability, timing, location, situation, etc.).

To avoid categorizing people, spend time observing them, listen to them objectively, and respond based on each situation and person. Doing this can lead to better relationships and improved customer service.

WORKSHEET 6-4

Worksheet ▼
6-4

Stereotype Evaluation

When we think of certain individuals or categories of people, we often conjure up mental images. Based on your life experiences, when you hear the following groups mentioned, what is the first word or picture that comes to mind? List several adjectives to describe each category listed? (Answers will vary.)

Category	Descriptors
Older people (over 65)	_____
Younger people (under 18)	_____
Gay or lesbian	_____
Male	_____
Female	_____
Wealthy	_____
Poor	_____
College students	_____
Military personnel	_____
Blacks	_____
Whites	_____
Hispanics	_____
Disabled people	_____
American Indians	_____
Middle Easterners	_____

▼

WORKSHEET 6-4 (CONTINUED)

Vietnamese _____

Asians _____

Tourists _____

8 STRATEGIES FOR SUCCESS

CONCEPT: Being aware of the possible behavioral styles of others can help you determine which strategies for success will be most useful to you.

Now that you have a better understanding about behavioral style(s), you can improve your chances of building successful relationships with others. In order to successfully deal with customers, try focusing on the following strategies:

Decisive

People whose style is "D" often want to save time and money. To help them accomplish this:

- *Focus on their need for control by finding out what they wish to do, what they want or need, or what motivates them.*
- *Provide direct, concise, and factual answers to their questions.*
- *Keep explanations brief and provide solutions, not excuses.*
- *Avoid trying to "get to know them." They often perceive this as a waste of time, and they may distrust your motives.*
- *Be conscious of time, by making your point and then concluding the interaction appropriately.*
- *Provide opportunities for the customer to talk by alternately providing small bits of information and asking specific questions aimed at solving the problem and serving the customer.*
- *Be prepared with information, necessary forms, details, warranties, and so on, before they arrive.*
- *When appropriate, provide options supported by evidence and focus on how the solution will affect their time, effort, and money.*
- *Focus on new, innovative products or services, emphasizing especially those that are environmentally sensitive or responsive.*

Inquisitive

People whose style is "I" often desire quality, efficiency, and precision. To help them attain these things:

- *Focus on their need for accuracy and efficiency by methodically outlining steps, processes, or details related to a product or service.*

- *Tie communication into facts, not feelings.*
- *Prepare information in advance and be thoroughly familiar with it.*
- *Approach encounters in a direct, businesslike, low-key manner.*
- *Avoid small talk and speaking about yourself.*
- *Ask specific open-ended questions about their background or experiences related to the product or service.*
- *Present solutions in a sequential fashion, stressing advantages, value, quality, reliability, and price. Also, be prepared to point out and discuss disadvantages.*
- *Have documentation available to substantiate your claims.*
- *Don't pressure their decisions.*
- *Follow through on promises.*

Rational

People who demonstrate the "R" behavioral style often want to maintain peace and group stability. To help them accomplish this:

- *Focus on their need for security and amiable relationships.*
- *Show a sincere interest in them and their views.*
- *Organize your information in a logical sequence and provide background data, if necessary.*
- *Take a slow, low-key approach in recommending products or services.*
- *Use open-ended questions to obtain information.*
- *Explain how your product or service can help simplify and support their relationships and systems.*
- *Stress low risk and benefits to them.*
- *Encourage them to verify facts, and so on, with others whose opinions they value.*
- *When change occurs, explain the need for the change and allow time for them to adjust.*
- *Provide information on available warranties, guarantees, and support systems.*

Expressive

People exhibiting the "E" style are typically people-oriented and want to be around people. To help them succeed in this goal:

- *Focus on their need to be liked and accepted by appealing to their emotions.*
- *Give positive feedback, acknowledging their ideas.*
- *Listen to their stories and share humorous ones about yourself.*
- *Use an open-ended, friendly approach.*
- *Ask questions such as "What attracted you to this product or service?"*

- *Keep product details to a minimum unless they ask for them.*
- *Describe how your product or service can help them get closer to their goals or to fulfilling their needs.*
- *Explain solutions or suggestions in terms of the impact on them and their relationships with others.*
- *If appropriate, provide incentives to encourage a decision.*

Work It Out 6-3. Discovering Common Characteristics

Use the copies of Worksheet 6-1 ("Describing Your Behavior") you received earlier in the chapter. Select four to eight friends or coworkers and ask them to rate themselves using the worksheet. Next, ask each person to complete the following statements on a separate sheet of paper:

When I shop I look for _____

My main reason for shopping is _____

When I need to buy or replace something, _____ I

The most important thing to me when I'm looking to replace something is _____

_____

Once everyone has finished, gather in a group to compare and discuss answers. Focus on the fact that each person and each style is unique but that we all have common characteristics and needs. Discuss how this knowledge of common needs or drives can be used to provide customer service more effectively.

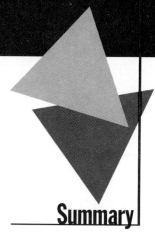

Summary

Chapter Summary

Everything a customer experiences from the time he or she makes contact with an organization, in person, on the phone, or through other means, affects that customer's perception of the organization and its employees. To positively influence the customer's opinion, customer service professionals must be constantly alert for opportunities to provide excellent service. Making a little extra effort can often mean the difference between total customer satisfaction and service breakdown.

As you have seen in this chapter, people are varied and have different behavioral styles. Recognizing the differences and dealing with customers on a case-by-case basis is the foundation of solid customer service. By examining individual behavioral tendencies, actions, communication styles, and needs, you can better determine a course of action for each customer. The test of your effectiveness is whether your customers return and what they tell their friends about you and your organization.

CHAPTER REVIEW QUESTIONS

1. What are behavioral styles?

_____

_____

2. What are the four behavioral style categories discussed in this chapter?

_____

_____

3. What are some of the characteristics that can help you identify a person who has the following style preferences?

D _____

_____

I _____

_____

R _____

_____

E _____

_____

4. When communicating with someone who has a "D" preference, what can you do to improve your effectiveness? _____

_____

5. When communicating with someone who has an "I" preference, what can you do to improve your effectiveness? _____

_____

6. When communicating with someone who has an "R" preference, what can you do to improve your effectiveness? _____

_____

7. When communicating with someone who has an "E" preference, what can you do to improve your effectiveness? _____

_____

8. What are some strategies for eliminating service barriers by using your knowledge of behavioral styles? _____

_____

_____

9. What are perceptions? _____

_____

10. How can perceptions affect customer relations? _____

_____

▼ SEARCH IT OUT

Search for Behavioral Styles on the Internet

Log onto the Internet and look for information and research data on behavioral styles. Specifically look for the various theories and surveys that describe and categorize behavior. Also try to find information about some of the people who have done research on behavior:

> *Sigmund Freud*
>
> *Carl Jung*
>
> *Alfred Adler*
>
> *Abraham Maslow*
>
> *William Moulton Marston*
>
> *Ivan Pavlov*
>
> *B. F. Skinner*

Be prepared to present some of your findings at the next scheduled class.

COLLABORATIVE *Learning Activity*

Observing and Analyzing Behavioral Styles

With a partner or team, go to a public place (park, mall, airport, train or bus station, or restaurant) to observe three different people. Using the copies of Worksheet 6-5 given to you by your instructor, note the specific behaviors each person exhibits. After you have finished this part of the activity, take a guess at each person's behavioral style preference based on behaviors you saw. Compare notes with your teammates and discuss similarities and differences among findings. Also, discuss how this information can be helpful in your workplace to deliver better customer service.

Observing Behaviors in Others

As part of the Collaborative Learning activity, complete this form for a person you observe in a public place.

Person (general description) _____

Appearance and dress _____

Posture (erect, slouched, slumped shoulders, eyes down) _____

_____

Vocal quality (assertive, meek, hesitant) _____

_____

Facial expressions _____

_____

_____

Gestures _____

_____

_____

Perceived behavioral style preference _____

Perceived secondary style preference (if any) _____

FACE TO FACE

Working Through Technology and People Problems at Child's Play Toy Company

Background

Since opening its newest store in Princeton, New Jersey, Child's Play Toy Company of Minneapolis, Minnesota, has been getting mixed customer reviews. Designed to be state-of-the-art, open, and customer-friendly, the store includes an attended activity area where small children can play while parents shop. In addition, an innovative system makes it possible for local customers to order products from catalogs or from the company's Website and then go to a drive-up window to pick up their purchases without leaving their cars. Another creative feature involves interactive television monitors in the store—where customers can see a customer service representative at the same time the representative sees them. To reduce staffing costs, the customer service representatives are at a Philadelphia, Pennsylvania, location and are remotely connected via satellite and computer to all new stores. This system is used for special ordering, billing questions, and complaint resolution. Customers can use a computer keyboard to enter data.

In recent months, the number of customer complaints has been rising. Many people complain about not getting the product that they ordered over the system, they are uncomfortable using the computer keyboard, they dislike the lack of personal touch and the fact that they have to answer a series of standard questions asked by a "talking head" on the screen, they have encountered system or computer breakdowns, and they cannot get timely service or resolution of problems.

Your Role

As a customer service representative and cashier at the store, you are responsible for operating a cash register when all lines are operational and more than two customers are in each line. You are also responsible for supervising other cashiers on your shift and dealing with customer questions, complaints, or problems. You report directly to the assistant store manager, Meg Finochio. Prior to coming to this store, you worked in two other New Jersey branches during the five preceding years.

This afternoon, Mrs. Sakuro, a regular customer, came to you. She was obviously frustrated and pointed her finger at you as she shouted, "You people are stupid!" She also demanded to speak with the manager and threatened that, "If you people do not want my business, I will go to another store!" Apparently, a doll that Mrs. Sakuro had ordered two weeks ago over the in-store system had not arrived. The doll was to be for her daughter's birthday, which is in two days. Although Mrs. Sakuro has a heavy accent, you understood that she had been directed by a cashier to check with a customer service representative via the monitor to determine the status of the orders. When she did this, she was informed that there was a problem with the order. The representative who took the order wrote the credit card number incorrectly, and the order was not processed. When Mrs. Sakuro asked the customer service representative why someone hadn't called her, the representative said that the customer service department was in another state and that long-distance calls were not allowed. She was told that the local store is responsible for verifying order status and handling problems.

Mrs. Sakuro's behavior and attitude are upsetting to you.

Critical Thinking Questions

1. Based on the behavioral style information in this chapter and other subjects discussed in this book, what do you think is causing the complaints being made?

_____

_____

_____

_____

_____

_____

2. What system changes would you suggest for Child's Play? Why?

_____

_____

_____

_____

_____

_____

_____

_____

_____

_____

_____

3. What can you do at this point to solve the problem?

_____

_____

_____

_____

_____

_____

_____

_____

_____

_____

_____

4. What primary behavioral style is Mrs. Sakuro exhibiting? What specific strategies should you use to address her behavior?

_____

_____

_____

_____

_____

_____

_____

_____

_____

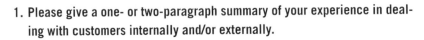

Boni Sivi
Managing Partner
Thomas Baker
Associates(.com)
Sorrento, Florida

1. **Please give a one- or two-paragraph summary of your experience in dealing with customers internally and/or externally.**

We develop customized training for customer service employees in high-technology companies—engineers, field service people, technicians, and so on. Technical people often don't view themselves as suppliers to customers, so providing the training is more challenging than when we deal with people who naturally view themselves as customer service representatives.

2. **Why is it helpful to have a solid knowledge of behavioral styles in the customer environment?**

Employees nearly always gain new insights into customer interactions when they have considered the notion of behavioral styles. They then make comments such as "Aha! Now I know why I don't see eye-to-eye with Edna!"

Learning the key points in dealing with people who have a variety of behavioral styles is very helpful in keeping interactions smooth and effective: in fact, it avoids having to start over again. So, do it right the first time!

3. **How have you seen a knowledge of behavioral styles help frontline customer service providers in dealings with customers?**

Employees can customize their responses to people instead of responding in the way they would want to be responded to or in a way that is dictated by their anger and irritation at the situation.

One engineer who routinely gave long, detailed answers to even the simplest questions said, "No wonder my kids tell me it takes a half hour to answer a yes-no question!"

4. **What advice related to behavioral styles would you give to someone new to customer service?**

First, observe yourself as you respond to people. If possible, record your conversations and listen to them to get ideas on how you can be more effective. I did this once accidentally. I was recording conversations that involved interviewing engineers about a product. I realized, when I listened to the tapes, that I was asking questions but cutting off answers.

You may find that you are spending too much time socializing. You may find that your answers to customers' questions are too brief, and that customers have to ask you the same question many times to get the information they need. Maybe they need information in a step-by-step format, and you are giving the information out of order.

CRITICAL THINKING

How can a knowledge of behavioral styles help you in customer service? Do you agree with the advice that Boni Sivi would give a new customer service representative?

Chapter 7

Customer Service via Technology

OBJECTIVES

After completing this chapter, you will be able to:

- *Understand the extent to which customer service is facilitated by the effective use of technology.*

- *Use technology to enhance service delivery capabilities.*

- *Communicate effectively via e-mail, the Internet, and facsimile.*

- *Deliver quality service through effective telephone techniques.*

- *Recognize the impact of verbal cues during telephone conversations.*

- *Send and receive messages via voice mail.*

"The newest innovations, which we label information technologies, have begun to alter the manner in which we do business and create value, often in ways not readily foreseeable even five years ago."

Alan Greenspan
Chairman
U.S. Federal Reserve Board

Before reviewing the chapter content, respond to the following questions by placing a "T" for true or an "F" for false on the rules. Use any questions you miss as a checklist of material to which you will pay particular attention as you read through the chapter. For those you get right, congratulate yourself, but review the sections they address in order to learn additional details about the topic.

_____ **1.** According to the U.S. Department of Commerce, over 94 percent of U.S. homes have telephones.

_____ **2.** *E-commerce* is a term that means that the commerce of the United States is in excellent condition.

_____ **3.** A customer service representative might also have one of the following job titles: associate, sales representative, consumer affairs counselor, consultant, technical service representative, operator, account executive, attendant, or engineer.

_____ **4.** The acronym *TTY* is used by call center staff members to indicate that something is *to* be *do*ne *to*day.

_____ **5.** Many organizations think of technology as a way to reduce staff and save money.

_____ **6.** One way to improve your image over the telephone is to continually evaluate your speech.

_____ **7.** Jargon, slang, and colloquialisms can distort message meaning.

_____ **8.** Adjusting your rate of speech to mirror a customer's rate can aid comprehension.

_____ **9.** Quoting policy is one way to ensure that customers understand why you can't give them what they want.

_____ **10.** To ensure that accurate communication has taken place, you should summarize key points at the end of a telephone conversation.

_____ **11.** Blind transfers are effective if you don't take too much time explaining who is calling.

_____ **12.** Chewing food and gum, drinking, or talking to others while on the telephone can be distracting and should be avoided.

_____ **13.** Using voice mail to answer calls is an effective way to avoid interruptions while you are speaking to a customer.

_____ **14.** Planning calls and the information you will leave is an effective way to avoid telephone tag.

1. T   8. T
2. F   9. F
3. T   10. T
4. F   11. F
5. T   12. T
6. T   13. T
7. T   14. T

THE INCREASING ROLE OF TECHNOLOGY IN CUSTOMER SERVICE

> **CONCEPT:** Customer service is a 24/7 responsibility, and technology can assist in making it effective.

To say that technology has permeated almost every aspect of life in most developed countries would be an understatement. Computers are continually becoming smaller, more complex, and powerful; we have only started to see the impact that technology will have on shaping the future. Most businesses in the United States are technologically dependent in some form. Calculators, cash registers, maintenance equipment, telephones, radios, cellular phones, pagers, computer systems, and handheld personal planners are typical examples of technology that we rely upon. We have become a 24/7 society (we access technology 24 hours a day, 7 days a week) and can communicate at any time and any place. Roughly 28 percent (76 million) of the American population own a cellular phone as shown in Figure 7-1.[1] By the year 2010, it is projected that 70 percent of the population will be using wireless devices. This is in addition to the more than 94 percent of U.S. households that have telephones.[2] A result is that more people are accessing telephone-related customer service. There are about 100,000 call centers in the United States, with over 3 million agents to answer those calls and serve the people who have access to technology.

This means that companies that are not prepared to meet the future will lose business as customers migrate to providers that are better prepared. With access to products and services at almost any time through telephones, e-mail, facsimile machines, and the Internet, customers are in a power position as never before. They will likely use alternative resources considering the fact that the United States has enjoyed the lowest unemployment rate in almost two decades. Thus, fewer service providers are available to fill jobs. That translates to longer wait times and increased frustration that many customers will simply not accept.

THE CALL CENTER OR HELP DESK

> **CONCEPT:** Electronic commerce is a new and powerful way to employ technology to conduct business.

The growing trend to reduce staff and costs, while maintaining or increasing service effectiveness, necessitates employing technology in addition to people. In the past, operations that used technology were seen as labor-intensive (because of the need to maintain and operate equipment) and behind-the-scenes or "back-office" functions. They typically supplemented the frontline service providers and were not viewed as a strategic initiative

---

[1] Cellular Telecommunications Industry Association.

[2] U.S. Department of Commerce, National Telecommunications and Information Administration.

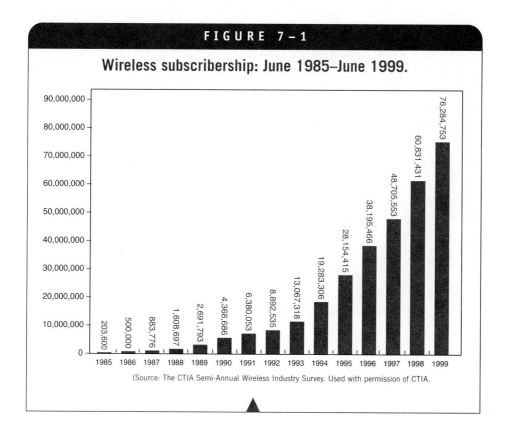

FIGURE 7-1

Wireless subscribership: June 1985–June 1999.

- 1985: 203,600
- 1986: 500,000
- 1987: 883,776
- 1988: 1,608,697
- 1989: 2,691,793
- 1990: 4,368,686
- 1991: 6,380,053
- 1992: 8,892,535
- 1993: 13,067,318
- 1994: 19,283,306
- 1995: 28,154,415
- 1996: 38,195,466
- 1997: 48,705,553
- 1998: 60,831,431
- 1999: 76,284,753

(Source: The CTIA Semi-Annual Wireless Industry Survey. Used with permission of CTIA.

related to the overall operation of the organization. With the availability of technically literate and trained employees, and a shift in expectations of customers who are capable of accessing products and services through technology, customer support through call centers is now an integral part of business. Corporate and organizational officers now recognize the potential of such operations and are pumping billions of dollars into the development, maintenance, and improvement of call center operations. Call centers are more powerful and complicated than ever before. They also provide more functions than their rather ineffectual predecessors.

The influence is so significant in terms of dollars that the way that organizations do business using technology has been labeled *electronic commerce (e-commerce)*.

Even with all the technological advances, one thing remains clear: customers still appreciate old-fashioned personalized customer service. Whether service is delivered face-to-face or via technology, there is no substitute for a dedicated, knowledgeable, and well-trained employee. You and your peers are the lifeline of your organization.

Types of Technology

Technology is advancing at such a rapid rate that the typical organization and its employees are unable to cope with the changes. Previously when a customer had a question or needed assistance, he or she would call an 800 number. When the call arrived at the call center, a customer service representative would answer, and after obtaining various information, might be able to handle the customer's situation.

Today, the representatives have a vast amount of technology at their disposal. Some of the typical systems found in call centers nowadays are described in the following sections.

Automatic Call Distribution (ACD) System

This system routes incoming calls to the next available agent when lines are busy. This is the most typical system. You may get a recording cueing you to select a series of numbers on the phone to get to certain people or information.

Today's customers want access to service and products 24 hours a day, 7 days a week. Can you name some technology advances that can make this possible?

Automatic Number Identification (ANI)

The ANI (pronounced "Annie") is a form of caller ID similar to home telephones. The system allows customers to be identified and their call directed appropriately before an agent talks to them. For example, a customer could be routed to special agents (an agent who is multilingual or who has specialized product or service knowledge). This saves time for the agent, for the customer's telephone number does not have to be keyed in and the agent can identify the customer's geographic location before speaking with him or her. Based on the information about the customer that the agent sees on a computer screen, he or she might also access information about the customer's history with the organization. Also, calls can be routed to the same agent who most recently handled a specific caller. Finally, with ANI, calls can be routed to the service center closest to the customer's home.

Electronic Mail (E-Mail)

This form of technology provides an inexpensive, rapid way of communicating with customers in writing worldwide. E-mail allows customers to access information via telephone and then, through prompting (using the telephone keypad), have the information delivered to them via e-mail. A big advantage of e-mail is that you can write a single message and have it delivered to hundreds of people worldwide in a matter of minutes at little or no cost.

Facsimile (Fax) Machine

This device allows graphics and text messages to be transported as electronic signals via telephone lines or from a personal computer equipped with a modem. Information can be sent anywhere in the world in minutes, or a customer can make a call, key in a code number, and have information delivered to his or her fax machine or computer without ever speaking to a person ("fax-on-demand" system).

Internet Call Back

Internet call-back system allows someone browsing the Internet to click on words or phrases (e.g., *Call me*), enter his or her phone number, and continue browsing. This triggers the predictive dialing system (discussed later in this chapter) and assigns an agent to handle the call when it rings at the customer's end.

Internet Telephony

Internet telephony allows users to have voice communications over the Internet. Although widely discussed in the industry, call center Internet telephony is in its infancy, lacks standards, and is not currently embraced by consumers.

Interactive Voice Response (IVR) or Voice Response Unit (VRU)

This type of system allows customers to call in 24 hours a day, 7 days a week, even when customer service representatives are not available. By keying in a series of numbers on the phone, customers can get information or answers to questions. Such systems also ensure consistency of information. Banks and credit card companies use such systems to allow customers to access account information.

Media Blending

Media blending allows agents to communicate with a customer over a telephone line at the same time information is displayed over the Internet to the customer. As with Internet telephony, this technology has not yet been taken to its fullest potential.

On-Line Information Fulfillment System

This technology allows customers to go the World Wide Web, access an organization's Web page, and click on desired information. This is one of the fastest-growing customer service technologies. Every competitive business will eventually use this system so that customers can get information and place orders.

Predictive Dialing System

A predictive dialing system automatically places outgoing calls and delivers incoming calls to the next available agent. This system is often used in outbound (telemarketing) operations. Because of numerous abuses, the government is continually restricting its use.

Screen Pop-Ups

Screen pop-ups are used in conjunction with ANI and IVR systems to identify callers. As a call is received and dispatched to an agent, the system provides information about the caller that "pops" onto the agent's screen before he or she answers the telephone (e.g., order information, membership data, service history, contact history).

Teletype Systems (TTY)

Partly because of the passage of the 1990 Americans With Disabilities Act, which required that telecommunication services be available to people with disabilities, organizations now have the technology to assist customers who have hearing and speech impairments. By using a TTY (a typewriter-type device for sending messages back and forth over telephone lines), a person who has a hearing or speech impairment can contact someone who is using a standard telephone. The sender and the receiver type their messages using the TTY. To do this, the sender or receiver can go through an operator-assisted relay service provided by local and long-distance telephone companies for example, 1-800-855-1155 (AT&T) and 1-800-855-4000 (Sprint), to reach companies and individuals who do not have TTY receiving technology, or the user can get in touch directly with companies that have TTYs. The service is free of charge. Operators can help first-time hearing users understand the rules in using TTY. Also, local speech and hearing centers can often provide training on the use of TTY in a call center environment.

The federal government has a similar service (Federal Information Relay Service, or FIRS) for individuals who wish to conduct business with any branch of the federal government nationwide.

Video

For customers and call centers equipped with video camera-computer hookups, this evolving technology allows customers and agents to interact via the computer. Like the interactive video kiosks discussed earlier in this book, this technology allows customers and agents to see one another during their interactions. Because of privacy concerns or preference, some software allows customers to block their image, yet they still see the agent to whom they are speaking.

Voice Recognition

This relative newcomer to the market is advancing rapidly. The technology is incorporated into a call center's voice response system. It is typically used by individuals to dictate data directly into a computer, which then converts the spoken words into text. There are potential applications of voice-recognition systems for all call centers. Some companies are recording customers' voices (passwords and phrases) as a means of identification so that customers can gain access to their accounts. With other applications agents speak into a computer, rather than typing data, and people who have disabilities can obtain data from their accounts by speaking into the computer.

Advantages and Disadvantages of Technology

Like anything else related to customer service, technology offers advantages and disadvantages. The following sections briefly review some of the issues resulting from the use of technology.

Organizational Issues

Distinct advantages accrue to organizations that use technology. Through the use of computers, software, and various telecommunication devices, a company can extend its presence without physically establishing a business site and without adding staff. Simply by setting up a Website, organizations can become known and develop a worldwide customer base. Information and services can be provided on demand to customers. Often, many customers can be served simultaneously through the telephone, fax, and so on.

The challenge for organizations is to have well-maintained state-of-the-art equipment and qualified, competent people to operate it. In a low unemployment era, this can be a challenge and can result in disgruntled customers who have to wait on hold for service until an agent is available to help them.

Staying on top of competition with technology is an expensive venture. New and upgraded software and hardware appear almost every day. If a company is using systems that are six months old, these systems are on their way to becoming obsolete. Also, new technology typically brings with it a need to train or retrain staff. The end result is that employees have to be taken away from their jobs for training.

Employee Issues

Technology brings many benefits to employees. The greatest benefit is that it frees them from mundane tasks such as taking information and mailing out forms, information, or other materials. These tasks can be done by using fax-on-demand, IVR, or on-line fulfillment systems. Technology also allows employees to serve more people in a shorter period of time—and to do it better.

The downside for employees is that many organizations see technology as a way to reduce staff costs and overhead related to employees, and they therefore eliminate positions. Moreover, as mentioned before, new technology requires new training and skills. Some people have difficulty using technology and are not able to master it. This in turn can lead to reassignment or dismissal. To avoid such negative outcomes, you and your peers should continually work to stay abreast of technology trends by checking the Internet or taking refresher courses through your organization's training department or local community resources.

Another problem created is an increase in stress levels of both employee and customer. This arises from the increased pace of business and daily life, from the need for employees to keep up to date with technology, and so on. Stress accounts for some of the high turnover rate in call center staff and for customer defection. But, it doesn't necessarily have to be that way. Read Chapter 11 carefully for tips on controlling and reducing stress.

Customer Issues

From a customer standpoint, technology can be a blessing. From the comfort and convenience of a home, office, car, or anywhere a customer may have a telephone and laptop computer, he or she can access products and services. More people than ever have access to the Internet (Figure 7-2) and computers (Figure 7-3). Technologies allow a customer to get information, order products, have questions about billing or other matters answered, and access virtually anything she or he wants on the World Wide Web.

However, this convenience comes with a cost to customers, just as it does for organizations. To have the latest gadgets is costly in terms of time and money. For example, when a customer calls an 800 or 888 support number, or must pay for a call to a support center, it is not unusual for the customer to wait on hold for the next available agent. Also, technology does not always work as it is designed to. For example, a Website might not provide clear instructions about how to enter an account number or how to get a password. Even if a customer follows the instructions exactly, he or she might repeatedly get a frustrating error message instructing him or her to reenter the data. At some point, the customer will simply give up and go to another Website. Another example would be to get caught in "voice mail jail." In this situation the customer follows the

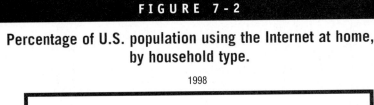

Percentage of U.S. population using the Internet at home, by household type.

1998

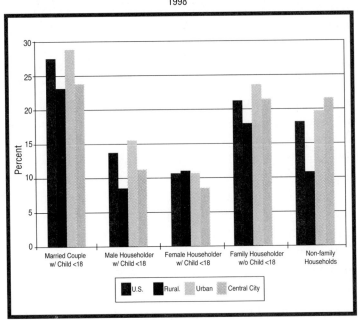

	U.S.	Rural	Urban	Central City
Married Couple w/ Child <18	27.7	23.9	29.3	23.8
Male Householder w/ Child <18	13.5	8.7	15.2	11.1
Female Householder w/ Child <18	10.6	11.0	10.5	8.4
Family Householder w/o Child <18	21.5	17.4	23.1	21.5
Non-family Households	18.2	10.7	19.9	21.7

(Source: U.S. Department of Commerce, National Telecommunications and Information Administration.)

instructions, pressing the appropriate phone keys to get to a representative, only to find that the representative has forwarded his or her calls to another voice mail box. Eventually the instructions lead the customer back to the first message.

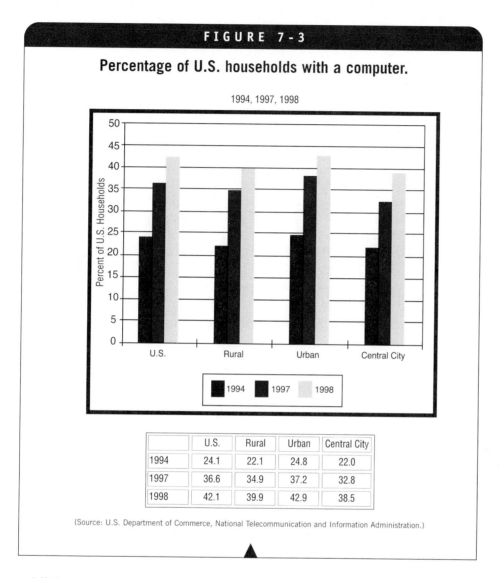

FIGURE 7-3

Percentage of U.S. households with a computer.

1994, 1997, 1998

	U.S.	Rural	Urban	Central City
1994	24.1	22.1	24.8	22.0
1997	36.6	34.9	37.2	32.8
1998	42.1	39.9	42.9	38.5

(Source: U.S. Department of Commerce, National Telecommunication and Information Administration.)

Additional Issues

Just as with any system, there are people who will take advantage of it. Technology, especially the Internet, has spawned a new era of fraud and manipulation. This is a major concern for consumers and can create many challenges for you and your peers when you work in a call center. One of the biggest problems you must deal with is customers' fear of fraud and violation of privacy. According to the National Fraud Information Center, a division of the National Consumers League in Washington, D.C., the number of Internet fraud complaints has risen over 600 percent since 1997.

Informed customers go to great lengths to protect credit card, merchant account, and social security numbers, addresses, and personal data (e.g., arrest records, medical history, and family data). Many news stories have warned of criminal activity associated with technology. The result is that customers, especially those who are technically naive, have a level of distrust and paranoia related to giving information via the Internet. This is why many Websites involved in e-commerce offer the option of calling an 800 number instead of entering credit card and other personal information into an Internet order form. If you, as a customer service provider, encounter a lot of this type of reluctance, notify your supervisor. Some systemic issues may be adding to your customers' fears. Helping identify these issues and dealing with them can make life easier for you and your customers while helping the organization improve the quality of service delivered.

One thing to remember is that a customer's reluctance to provide you with information is not necessarily a reflection on you or your service-providing peers; it is based more on a distrust in the system. Figure 7-4 lists some strategies you can use to help reduce customer fears related to communicating via technology.

---

3 | TECHNOLOGY ETIQUETTE AND STRATEGIES

▶ **CONCEPT:** Using technology ethically and with correct etiquette is important.

As with any other interaction with people, you should be aware of some basic dos and don'ts related to using technology to interact with and serve your customers. Failure to observe some commonsense rules can cause loss of a customer.

E-Mail

The e-mail system was designed as an inexpensive, quick way of communicating via the World Wide Net. E-mail was not designed to replace formal written correspondence. E-mail has its own set of guidelines for effective usage to ensure that you do not offend or otherwise create problems when dealing with customers via e-mail. Here are some e-mail tips to remember, as well as some etiquette for effective usage.

- *Use abbreviations and initials.* Since e-mail is an informal means of communicating, using acronyms and other short forms or abbreviations (e.g., USA versus United States of America) works fine in some cases. Just be sure that your receiver knows what the letters stand for; otherwise miscommunication could occur. Figure 7-5 lists some common abbreviations employed by e-mail users who typically know one another and e-mail one another frequently (e.g., internal customers). When communicating with external customers, you may want to use abbreviations sparingly or avoid them altogether in order to prevent confusion, communication breakdown, and the perception that you are unprofessional.

- *Proofread and spell-check before sending a message.* Checking your message before sending an e-mail may help prevent damage to your professional image. This is especially true when writing customers, for you represent your organization. Poor grammar, syntax, spelling, and usage can paint a poor picture of your professionalism.

FIGURE 7-4

Reducing customer fears about technology.

Avoiding customer concerns is often as simple as communicating effectively. Try some of the following approaches to help reassure your customers about the security of technology:

- Emphasize the organization's policy on security and service (e.g., if customers voice concerns about providing a credit card number over the phone, you might respond with "This is not a problem. You can either fax or mail the information to us.").

- Stress participation in consumer watchdog or community organizations (e.g., Better Business Bureau or Chamber of Commerce).

- Ask for only pertinent information.

- Answer questions quickly and openly (e.g., if a customer asks why you need certain information, respond in terms of customer service (e.g., "We need that information to ensure that we credit the right account.").

- Explain why you need information (e.g., "To verify your account information, could I please have the last four digits of your social security number or your account password?")

- Inform customers of security devices that are in place to protect information.

- Avoid asking for personal and account information when possible.

- Offer other options for data submission, if they are available.

- When using the telephone, smile and sound approachable in order to establish rapport (customers can "hear" a smile over the telephone).

- Listen carefully for voice tones that indicate hesitancy or uncertainty and respond appropriately (e.g., "You sound a bit hesitant about giving that information, Mr. Hopkins. Let me assure you that nothing will be processed until we have actually shipped your order.").

- Communicate in short, clear, and concise terms and sentences. Also, avoid technical or "legal" language that might confuse or frustrate the customer.

- *Think before writing.* This is especially important if you are answering an e-mail when you are upset or emotional. Take time to cool off before responding to a negative message (An insulting or provocative e-mail message is called a *flame.*) or when you are angry. Remember that once you send an e-mail, you cannot take back your words. Your relationship with your receiver is at stake.

- *Use short, concise sentences.* The average person will not read lengthy messages sent by e-mail. Scrolling up and down pages of text is time-consuming and frustrating. Therefore, put your question or key idea in the first sentence or paragraph. Keep your sentences short and use new paragraphs often, for easier reading. A good rule of thumb is that if the entire message does not fit on a single viewing screen, consider whether another means of communication is more appropriate. An option would be to use the attachment feature so that lengthy documents can be printed out.

FIGURE 7-5

Common abbreviations.

LOL	Lots of luck	ROTFL	Rolling on the floor laughing
BCNU	Be seeing you	TTFN	Ta ta for now
FYI	For your information	TTYL	Talk to you later
IMHO	In my humble opinion	BTW	By the way
FWIW	For what it's worth	ASAP	As soon as possible

- *Avoid using all-capital letters.* With e-mail, writing a sentence or message in all-capital letters is like shouting at a person and could offend or cause relationship problems.

- *Be careful with punctuation.* As with all-capital letters, you should use caution with punctuation marks, especially exclamation points, which can cause offense because, like all-capital letters, they indicate strong emotion.

- *Use e-mail only for informal correspondence.* Do not use e-mail when a more formal format is appropriate. For example, it would be inappropriate to send a cancellation notice via e-mail. The receiver might think that the matter is not significant enough to warrant your organization's buying a stamp to mail a letter. However, this caution does not mean that you should not attach letters or other documents to an e-mail. Just consider the impact on the recipient.

  Another important thing to remember about e-mail is that it is sometimes unreliable. Many people do not check their e-mail regularly, computer systems fail, and individuals often change service providers without notifying you. If your message is critical and delivery is time-sensitive, choose another method (e.g., a telephone call or express mail). In some cases, e-mail that is not delivered is not returned to the sender, so you may not know why the recipient did not respond.

- *Do not use organization e-mail for personal reasons.* Many companies have policies prohibiting sending personal e-mail via their system. Some companies have started to monitor outgoing messages. Do not violate your company's policy on this. Remember, too, that while you are sending personal messages, you are wasting productive time and your customers may be waiting.

- *Use care in the type of information you send.* Avoid sending personal information (e.g., account numbers, personal data) or proprietary information via e-mail. Unless you have security software that will decode and mask the information, hackers or others who do not have a right or need to know such information can gain access to it. A good rule of thumb is to never send anything by e-mail that you would not want to see in tomorrow's newspaper.

- *Use blind courtesy copies (BCCs) sparingly.* Most e-mail systems allow you to send a copy to someone without the original addressee knowing it (a blind courtesy copy, or bcc). If the recipient becomes aware of the bcc, your actions might be viewed as suspicious, and your motives brought into question. Thus, a relationship break-down could occur if the original recipient discovers the existence of the bcc or if the recipient of the bcc misuses the information.

- *Do not "reply to all."* Nowadays, most people are overloaded with work and do not have the time to read every e-mail. If someone does not need to see a message, do not send them a copy.

- *Avoid sending unsolicited advertisements or promotional materials.* As mentioned earlier, people have little time or patience to read lengthy e-mail messages, especially from someone trying to promote or sell them something. This is viewed the same way you probably think of unsolicited junk mail or telemarketing calls at home.

- *Be cautious in using emoticons.* Emoticons (for *emotional icons*) are the faces created though the use of computer keyboard characters. Many people believe that their use in business correspondence is inappropriate and too informal. Also, since humor is a matter of personal point of view, these symbols might be misinterpreted and confusing. This is especially true when you are corresponding with someone from a different culture. Figure 7-6 shows examples of emoticons.

- *Fill in your address line last.* This is a safety mechanism to ensure that you take the time to read and think about your message before you send the e-mail. The message cannot be transmitted until you address it. You will have one last chance to think about the impact of the message on the recipient.

FIGURE 7–6

Some emoticons.

:-)	Happy		:-}	Embarrassment or sarcasm
:-(	Sad		:-D	Big grin or laugh
;-)	Flirting or wink		<:-)	Stupid question (dunce cap)
O < > / \	Defiant or determined		0:-)	Angel or saint
:-O	Yelling or surprise		>:-)	Devil
:-x	Lips are sealed		:~/	Really confused

Facsimile

As with any other form of communication, there are certain dos and don'ts to abide by when using the facsimile (fax) to transmit messages. Failing to adhere to these simple guidelines can cause frustration, anger, and a breakdown in the relationships between you and your customers or others to whom you send messages.

- *Be considerate of your receiver.* If you plan to send a multipage document to your customer, telephone in advance to make sure that it is okay to send it. This is especially true if you will be using a business number during the workday or if there is only one line for the telephone and fax machine. It is frustrating and irritating to customers when a fax is tied up because large documents are being transmitted. If you must send a large document, try to do so before or after working hours (i.e., before or after 9 A.M. to 5 P.M.). Also, keep in mind geographic time differences. Following these tips can also help maintain good relationships with coworkers who may depend on the fax machine to conduct business with their customers.

- *Limit graphics.* Graphic images that are not needed to clarify written text waste the receiver's printer cartridge ink, tie up the machine unduly, and can irritate your receiver. Therefore, delete any unnecessary graphics, including your corporate logo on a cover sheet if it is heavily colored and requires a lot of ink to print (if appropriate, create a special outline image of your logo for your fax cover sheets).

- *Limit correspondence recipients.* As with e-mail and memorandums, limit the recipients of your messages. If they do not have a need to know, do not send them messages. Check your broadcast mailing list (a list of people who will receive all messages, often programmed into a computer) to ensure that it is limited to people who "have a need to know." This is also important from the standpoint of confidentiality. If the information you are sending is proprietary or sensitive in any way, think about who will receive it. Do not forget that unless the document is going directly to someone's computer fax modem, it may be lying in a stack of other incoming messages and accessible by people other than your intended recipient.

4 | THE TELEPHONE IN CUSTOMER SERVICE

▶ **CONCEPT:** The telephone is the second most important link in customer service.

Not all service via technology, and specifically the telephone, is delivered from a call center. Although many small- and medium-sized organizations have dedicated customer service professionals to staff their telephones, others do not. In the latter cases, the responsibility for answering the telephone and providing service falls on anyone who is available and hears the telephone ring (e.g., administrative assistant, salesperson, driver, partner, owner, CEO). Remember that in order to provide quality customer service, everyone in the organization has to take ownership for customer satisfaction.

Modern businesses rely heavily on the use of telephones to conduct day-to-day operations and communicate with internal as well as external customers. Effective use of the telephone saves employee time and effort. Employees no longer have to take time to physically travel to another location to interact with customers and vendors. By simply lifting the telephone receiver and dialing a number, you are almost instantaneously transported anywhere in the world. And with the use of the fax and computer modem, documents and information can also be sent in minutes to someone thousands of miles away—even during nonbusiness hours.

With these tools, more businesses are setting up inbound (e.g., order taking, customer service, information sources) and outbound (e.g., telemarketing sales, customer service, customer surveys) telephone staffs. Through these groups of trained specialists, companies can expand their customer contact and be more likely to accomplish total customer satisfaction.

Advantages of Telephone Customer Service

Even though there are some disadvantages to telephone communication (e.g., lack of face-to-face contact with the customer), there are many advantages. Some of the advantages are discussed in the following sections.

- *Convenience.* Sales, information exchange, money collection, customer satisfaction surveys, and complaint handling are only a few of the many tasks that can be effectively handled using the telephone and related equipment. If a quick answer is needed, the telephone can provide it without the need to travel and meet with someone face-to-face or to endure the delays caused by the mail.

- *Ease of communication.* Although some countries have more advanced telephone systems and capabilities than others, you can call someone in nearly any country in the world. And, with advances in cellular phone technology, even mobile phones have international communication capability.

- *Economy.* Face-to-face visits or sales calls are expensive and can be reduced or eliminated by making contacts over the telephone as opposed to traveling to a customer's location. With competitive rates offered by many telephone companies since the deregulation of the telecommunication industry years ago, companies and customers have many options for calling plans. For example, customers can purchase a calling card and use it from any telephone. All of this makes accessing customer services a simple and relatively inexpensive task, especially when combined with the other technology discussed in this chapter.

- *Efficiency.* You and your customer can interact without being delayed by writing and responding. Telephone usage is so simple that it is taught to kindergarten and grade school children.

Communication Skills for Success

In Chapters 3 to 5, you read about the skills you need in face-to-face customer service. The same skills apply to providing effective customer service over the telephone, especially the use of vocal quality and listening skills. Your customer cannot communicate with or understand you if she or he doesn't accurately receive your message. To reduce the chances of message failure, think about the communication techniques discussed below.

- *Speak clearly.* By pronouncing words clearly and correctly, you increase the chances that your customer will accurately receive your intended message. Failure to use good diction could decrease a customer's comprehension of your message and be interpreted as a sign that you are lazy, unprofessional, or lack intelligence and/or education. If you are unsure how to improve your diction, review Chapter 3.

- *Avoid jargon, slang, and colloquialisms.* Technical jargon (terms related to technology, an industry, a specific organization, or a job), slang (informal words used to make a message more colorful (e.g., *whoopee, blooper, groovy*), and colloquialisms (regional phrases or words such as, "fair to middling," "if the good Lord's willing and the creek don't rise," or "faster than a New York minute") can distort your message and detract from your ability to communicate effectively. This is especially true when your recipient speaks English as a second language (see Chapter 10 for more information on this topic). By using words or phrases unfamiliar to the customer, you draw the customer's attention away from listening to your message. This is because, when people encounter a word or phrase that is unfamiliar, they tend to stop and reflect on that word or phrase. When this occurs, the next part of the message is missed while the mind tries to focus on and decipher the unfamiliar element it encountered. You must then repeat the missed portion or end up with a miscommunication.

- *Adjust your volume.* As your conversation progresses, it may become apparent that you need to speak more loudly or more softly to your customer. Obvious cues are statements from the customer, such as, "You don't have to yell" or "Could you speak up?" Or if your customer is speaking really loudly, he or she may have a hearing impairment. To find out if this is the case, you could say, "I'm sorry, Mrs. _____, are you able to hear me clearly? I'm having trouble with loud volume on my end."

- *Speak at a rate that allows comprehension.* Depending on the person to whom you are speaking, you may find yourself having to adjust your rate of speech (covered in Chapter 3) by either speeding up or slowing down. A good rule of thumb is to mirror or match the other person's rate of speech to some extent, since he or she is probably comfortable with it. Otherwise you risk boring the customer by speaking too slowly, or losing the customer by speaking too rapidly. Be careful not to be too obvious or unnatural when doing this; otherwise, some customers may think that you're making fun of them.

- *Use voice inflection.* By using inflection and avoiding a tendency to speak in a monotone, you can help communicate your message in an interesting manner that will hold your customer's attention. The result might be saved time since your message may be received correctly the first time and you will not have to repeat it.

- *Use correct grammar.* Just as important as enunciation, good grammar helps project a positive, competent image. When you fail to use good grammar in your communication, you may be perceived as lazy or uneducated. Keep in mind that your customer forms an image of you and the company you represent simply by listening to you and the way you speak. Chapter 8 explores grammar in more detail.

- *Pause occasionally.* This simple yet dramatic technique can sometimes affect the course of a conversation. By pausing after you make a statement or ask a question, you give yourself time to breathe and think. You also give your customer an opportunity to reflect on what you have said or to ask questions. This practice can greatly aid in reducing tension when you are speaking with an upset customer or one who does not speak your language fluently.

- *Smile as you speak.* By smiling, you project an upbeat, warm, and sincere attitude through the phone. This can often cheer the customer, diffuse irritation, and help build rapport. A technique some telephone professionals use to remind themselves to smile when placing or answering a call is to put a small mirror or a picture of a "smiling face" in front of them or next to their telephone. This reminds them to smile as they talk.

- *Project a positive image and attitude.* All the tips related to using your voice that were presented in earlier chapters contribute to how people envision you. Customers generally do not want to hear what you cannot do for them or about the bad day you're having. They want a timely, affirmative answer to their questions or solution of their problems. Giving anything less is likely to discourage or annoy them and result in a service breakdown.

- *Don't interrupt.* Many people tend to interrupt a customer to add information or ask a question. As you read in Chapter 5, this is not only rude but can cause a breakdown in communication and possibly anger the customer. If you ask a question or if the customer is speaking, allow him or her to respond or to finish speaking before interjecting your thoughts or comments.

- *Listen actively.* Just as with face-to-face communication, effective listening is a crucial telephone skill for the customer service provider. The need to focus is even more important when you are speaking on the phone since you do not have nonverbal cues or visual contact to help in message delivery or interpretation. Information on active listening was covered in Chapter 5.

To help prevent breakdowns in communication, avoid distractions while you are on the phone. It is difficult to listen effectively when you are reading something, writing notes to yourself, using a cash register, typing, polishing your fingernails, and so on.

Tips for Creating a Positive Telephone Image

People form an opinion of you and your organization quickly. The message they receive often determines how they interact with you during the conversation and in your future relationship. Keep in mind that when you answer your organization's telephone, or call someone else as part of your job, you represent yourself *and* the organization. And, since many telephone calls are short, you have limited opportunity to make a positive impression.

When you feel good about yourself, you normally project a naturally confident and pleasant image. On days when things aren't going so well for you, your self-image may tend to suffer. Here are some suggestions to help serve your customers effectively and leave them thinking well of you and your organization.

- *Continually evaluate yourself.* You are your own best critic. From time to time, think about your conversation—what went well, what could have been improved. If possible, occasionally tape-record your conversations and evaluate your voice qualities and message delivery. Have someone else listen to the tape and provide objective feedback. To help in your self-assessment, you may want to make copies of Worksheet 7-1 and evaluate all your calls for a specific period of time (for example, a couple of hours or a day).

- *Use proper body posture.* The following can negatively affect the sound and quality of your voice:

  Slouching in your chair.

  Sitting with your feet on a desk with your arms behind your head as you rock back and forth in your chair.

  Looking down, with your chin on your chest, to read or search through drawers.

  Resting the telephone handset between your cheek and shoulder as you do other work (e.g., type data into a computer, look for something, writing, or doodling).

  Strive to sit or stand upright and speak clearly into the mouthpiece whether you are using a headset or handheld receiver. If you are using a handheld receiver, make sure that the earpiece is placed firmly against your ear and the mouthpiece is directly in front of your mouth.

- *Be prepared.* Answer a ringing phone promptly and use a standard greeting as outlined later in this chapter.

Personal Telephone Effectiveness Survey

To determine your level of service quality over the telephone, make copies of this worksheet and use it to monitor your phone conversations for one week. Several times a day, following calls, do a quick, honest self-analysis of your service delivery. After you receive a call and hang up, fill out one of the copies. Do this for at least seven days. At the end of that time, review your responses and look for patterns (positive and negative).

Number of rings before I answered _____

What greeting did I use (good morning, good afternoon, etc.)? _____

_____

_____

	Yes	No
Did I give my:		
Name?	_____	_____
Organization's name?	_____	_____
Department's name?	_____	_____
Did I offer to assist?	_____	_____

   If yes, how did I phrase the offer? _____

_____

	Yes	No
Did I listen actively? (using strategies from Chapter 5)	_____	_____
Did I use the caller's name frequently?	_____	_____
Did I use good communication techniques by:		
Speaking clearly?	_____	_____
Adjusting my rate of speech?	_____	_____
Adjusting my volume?	_____	_____
Using correct grammar?	_____	_____
Employing vocal variety?	_____	_____
Speaking in a conversational tone?	_____	_____
Smiling?	_____	_____
Pausing frequently?	_____	_____
Eliminating distractions?	_____	_____
Was I prepared?	_____	_____
Did I use the telephone effectively by:		
Using the receiver or headset properly?	_____	_____
Transferring the call correctly?	_____	_____
Avoiding unnecessary holds?	_____	_____
Taking effective messages?	_____	_____
Did I handle the customer's need, complaint, or question effectively?	_____	_____
Did I allow the customer to disconnect first?	_____	_____

- *Speak naturally.* Whether you are calling someone or providing information to a caller, speak in a conversational voice. Don't use a "canned" or mechanical presentation, and don't read from a prepared script, unless you are required to do so by your company. If you must read from a script, *practice, practice, practice.* Before you connect with a customer, become very comfortable with your presentation so that you can deliver it in a fluid, warm, and sincere manner. Nothing sends a more negative message than a service provider who mispronounces a customer's name, stumbles through opening comments, and seems disorganized.

- *Be time-conscious.* Customers appreciate prompt, courteous service. Be aware that time is money—yours, your organization's, and the customer's. Have your thoughts organized when you call a customer. It is a good idea to use a list of questions or key points (see Worksheet 7-2 as an example). If a customer calls you and you don't have an answer or information readily available, offer to do some research and call back instead of putting the customer on hold. Respect your customer's time. Chances are that customers will prefer to hold if they will be waiting only a short time, but give them the option. In addition to helping better organize your calls, a written call-planning sheet will provide a good record of the call.

- *Do not quote policy.* If you must say no to a customer, do so in a positive manner without quoting policy. Tell the customer what you can do. For example, if your policy prohibits refunds on one-of-a-kind or closeout items, you might make an offer such as this (depending on your level of authority or empowerment):

    "Mr. _____, I see that the computer you ordered from our Website was a closeout item. I understand that you have decided that you need more RAM. Although I cannot give refunds on a closeout item, I can give you a voucher good at any of our retail locations for a $50 discount on a memory chip upgrade or free installation, whichever you prefer."

    Doing more than the customer expects following a breakdown (this is called *service recovery* and is discussed in Chapter 14) is important, especially if you or your company made an error. When you or your company is not responsible for the error, but you want to maintain a positive customer-provider relationship, going out of your way to help make it better is just good business practice.

- *Conclude calls professionally.* Ending a call on an upbeat note, using the caller's name and summarizing key actions to be taken by both parties are all recommended practices. For example, you might say, "All right, Ms. _____, let me confirm what we've discussed. I'll get _____ by the 23d, and call you to confirm _____. You'll take care of _____. Is that correct?" Once agreement has been reached, thank the customer for calling, ask what other questions he or she has or what else you can assist with, and then let the customer hang up first. By following this type of format, you can

Call Planning Sheet

Before placing a call, complete this form and have it handy to use as a guide.

Time _____   Date _____

Person called _____

Organization _____

Topic 1 _____

Questions _____

_____

_____

Topic 2 _____

Questions _____

_____

_____

Topic 3 _____

Questions _____

_____

_____

Topic 4 _____

Questions _____

_____

_____

Worksheet ▼

7.2

reduce misunderstandings and elicit any last-minute questions or comments the customer might have. If you fail to bring the conversation to a formal close and hand up abruptly, the customer may feel you are in a hurry to service him or her (regardless of the fact that you have just spent 15 minutes talking with him or her!). Think of this final step as wrapping a gift: it looks fine, but adding a nice ribbon and bow makes it look even better. The thank-you and polite sign-off are your ribbon and bow.

Effective Telephone Usage

One basic strategy for successfully providing effective customer service over the telephone is to thoroughly understand all phone features and use them effectively. This may seem to be a logical and simple concept, but think about times when you called a company and someone attempted to transfer you, or put you on hold, or did not communicate clearly. If the transfer was successful, you were lucky. If not, you probably couldn't understand what happened, got disconnected, were connected to the wrong party, or heard the original person come back on the telephone to apologize and say something like, "The call didn't go through. Let me try again." Sound familiar? If so, use the following strategies to ensure that you never deliver similar poor service.

- *Eliminate distractions.* Don't eat food, chew gum, drink, talk to others, read (unless for the purpose of providing the customer with information), or handle other office tasks (filing, stapling, stamping, sealing envelopes, etc.) while on the phone. Your voice quality will alert the customer to the fact that you are otherwise occupied.

- *Answer promptly.* A lot is communicated by the way a phone call is handled. One tip for success is to always answer by the second or third ring. This sends a nonverbal message to your customers of your availability to serve them. It also reduces the irritating ringing that you, coworkers, or customers have to hear.

- *Use titles with names.* It has been said that there is nothing sweeter than hearing one's own name. However, until you are told otherwise, use a person's title (e.g., Mr., Mrs., Ms., or Dr.) and last name. Do not assume that it is all right to use first names. Some people regard the use of their first name as insolent or rude. This may especially be true of older customers and people from other cultures where respect and use of titles are valued. When you are speaking with customers, it is also a good idea to use their name frequently (don't overdo it, though, or you'll sound mechanical). Repeat the name directly after the greeting (e.g., "Yes, _____, how may I help you?"), during the conversation (e.g., "One idea I have, _____, is to . . ."), and at the end of the call (e.g., "Thanks for calling, _____. I'll get that information right out to you.")

- *Ask questions.* You read about the use of questions earlier in the book. Use them on the telephone to get information or clarify points made by the customer. Ask open-ended questions; then listen to the response carefully. To clarify or verify information, use closed-ended questions.

- *Use equipment properly.* Your success or failure in receiving and delivering messages often hinges on simply holding the receiver or wearing a headset properly. Ensure that the earpiece and mouthpiece rest squarely against your ear and in front of your mouth, respectively. This allows you to accurately hear what is said and accurately transmit your words to the customer clearly.

- *Use speakerphones with caution.* Speakerphones make sense for people who have certain disabilities and in some environments (where you need free hands or are doing something else while you are on hold or are waiting for a phone to be answered). From a customer service standpoint, they can send a cold or impersonal message, and their use should be minimal. Many callers do not like them and even think that speakerphone users are rude. Also, depending on the equipment used and how far you are from the telephone, the message received by your customer could be distorted, or it might seem as though you are in an echo chamber. Before using a speakerphone, ask yourself whether there is a valid reason for not using a headset or handheld phone. When you are using a speakerphone, make sure that your conversation will not be overheard if you are discussing personal, proprietary, or confidential information. Also, if someone is listening in on the customer's conversation, make sure that you inform the customer of that fact and explain who the listener is and why he or she is listening. As you read earlier, some people are very protective of their privacy and their feelings should be respected.

- *Transfer calls properly.* Be sure you understand how the telephone transfer (sometimes called the *link*) and hold functions work. Nothing is more frustrating or irritating for callers than to be shuffled from one person to the next or to be placed on what seems to be an endless hold. Here are some suggestions that can help to increase your effectiveness in these areas.

  Always request permission before transferring a caller. This shows respect for the caller and psychologically gives the caller a feeling of control over the conversation. You can also offer options (you can ask the caller to allow a transfer or let you take a message). This is especially helpful when the customer is already irritated or has a problem. Before transferring the call, explain why you need to do so. You might say, "The person who handles billing questions is Shashandra Philips at extension 4739. May I transfer you, or would you rather I take a message and pass it along to her?" This saves you and the caller time and effort, and you have provided professional, courteous service. If the caller says, "Yes, please transfer me," follow by saying something like, "I'd be happy to connect you. Again, if you are accidentally disconnected, I'll be calling Shashandra Philips at extension 4739."

  Once you have successfully reached the intended person, announce the call by saying, "Shashandra, this is (your name), from (your department). I have (customer's name) on the phone. She has a (question, problem). Are you the right person to handle that?" If Shashandra answers yes, connect the caller and announce, "(Customer's name), I have Shashandra Philips on the line. She will be happy to assist you. Thanks for calling (or some similar positive disconnect phrase)." You can then hang up, knowing that you did your part in delivering quality customer service.

  If the call taker is not available or is not the appropriate person, reconnect with the customer and explain the situation. Then offer to take a message rather then trying to transfer to different people while keeping the customer on hold. You would make an exception if the call taker informed you of the appropriate person to whom you should transfer, or if the customer insisted on staying on the line while you tried to transfer to the right person.

You should avoid making a *blind transfer*. This practice is ineffective, rude, and not customer-focused. A blind transfer happens when a service provider asks a caller, "May I transfer you to _____?" or may even say, without permission, "Let me transfer you to _____." Once the intended transfer party answers, the person transferring the call hangs up. Always announce your caller by waiting for the phone to be picked up and saying, "This is (your name) in (your department). I have (customer's name) on the line. Can you take the call?" Failure to do this could result in a confrontation between the two people. If the calling customer is already upset, you have just set up a situation that could lead to a lost customer and/or angry coworker.

If you place someone on hold, it is a good idea to go back on the line every 20 to 30 seconds to let the person know that you have not forgotten the call. This action becomes more important if the phone system you are using does not offer information that the customer hears during the holding time.

One final word about holds: once you return to the phone to take the call, thank the caller for waiting.

- *Use call waiting*. A useful feature offered by many phone systems is call waiting. While you are on the phone, a signal (usually a beep) indicates that there is an incoming call. When you hear the signal, you have a couple of options: Excuse yourself from your current call, by getting permission to place the person on hold, or ignore the second caller. If you have a voice mail system, the system makes the choice for you by transferring incoming calls to your message system. Both options have advantages and disadvantages.

  By taking the second call, you may irritate your current caller, who might hang up. This results in lost business. (On the other hand, by not taking the second call, you might miss an important message and/or irritate that caller.)

  By ignoring the signal, you might offend the second caller. Research indicates that many customers forget to or decide against placing later calls to busy number, especially if they have already made several attempts. Customers may feel that you're too busy to properly serve them.

  So, how do you handle the dilemma? Make a judgment about how the customer to whom you are speaking might react and then act accordingly. In some instances, company policies tell you what to do, so you don't have to decide.

Voice Mail and Answering Machines or Services

Although voice mail is hailed by many people as a time-saver and vehicle for delivering messages when an intended recipient is unavailable, many other people have difficulty dealing with voice mail (including answering machines). Let's take a look at some ways to use voice mail.

- *Managing incoming calls.* To effectively use voice mail, you must first understand how your system works. Check the manuals delivered with your system or speak with your supervisor and/or the technical expert responsible for its maintenance.

  A key to using voice mail effectively is to keep your outgoing message current, indicating your availability, the type of information the caller should leave, and when the caller can expect a return call. If your system allows the caller the option of accessing an operator or another person, you should indicate this early in your outgoing message to save the caller from having to listen to unnecessary information. Figure 7-7 provides a sample outgoing message. Also, Work It Out 7-1 can be used to evaluate the voice mail messages of others when you call them. Another key to effective voice mail usage is to retrieve your calls and return them as soon as possible. Usually 24 hours, or by the next working day, is a good guideline for returning calls. Doing so sends a positive customer service message.

FIGURE 7-7

Sample outgoing message.

"Hello. This is the voice mail of (your name) of (company and department). I'm unavailable to take your call at the moment, but if you will leave your name, number, and a brief message, I'll call you as soon as possible. Thanks for calling." If you know when you will be returning calls (e.g., at the end of the workday), tell the caller so. If your voice mail system offers callers the option to press a number to speak with someone else, let them know this right after you tell them whose voice mail they have reached. This avoids requiring them to listen to a lengthy message before they can select an option.

Work It Out 7-1. Evaluating Voice Mail

Work It Out
7-1

▶ To help increase your awareness of the impact of voice mail messages, place a copy of this form next to your phone during the coming week. As you call people or organizations, take note of the outgoing messages that they leave on their voice mail or answering machines. Evaluate the following:

	Yes	No
1. Was the call answered by the third ring?	_____	_____
2. Did the announcement contain the following:		
Greeting (Hello, Good morning or Good afternoon)?	_____	_____
Organization's name?	_____	_____
Departmental name?	_____	_____
A statement of when the person would return?	_____	_____

An early announcement of an option to
press a number for assistance? _____ _____

Instructions for leaving a message? _____ _____

When calls would be returned? _____ _____

- *Placing calls to voice mail.* Many normally articulate people cannot speak coherently when they encounter an answering machine or voice mail. One technique for success is to plan your call before picking up the phone. Have a 30-second or less "sales" presentation in mind that you can deliver whether you get a person or machine. For example, if you get a person, try, "This is (your first and last name) from (company) calling (or returning a call) for _____. Is he available?" Also, have available a written list of the key points you want to discuss so you don't forget them as you talk.

  If you get a machine, try, "This is (first and last name) from (company) calling (returning a call) for _____. My number is _____. I will be available from _____ to _____." If you are calling to get or give information, you may want to add, "The reason I am calling is to _____." This allows the return caller to leave information on your voice mail or with someone else and thus avoid the game of telephone tag.

- *Avoiding telephone tag.* You have probably played telephone tag. The game starts when the intended call receiver is not available and a message is left. The game continues when the call is returned, the original caller is not available, a return message is left, and so on.

WORKSHEET 7-3

Planning Return Calls

Date and time _____

Person called _____

Phone number (with area code and country code if necessary) _____

Reason for call _____

_____

Person who took call _____

Message left _____

_____

Follow-up required _____

_____

Telephone tag is frustrating and a waste of valuable time. It results in a loss of efficiency, money, and in some cases, customers. To avoid telephone tag, plan your calls and make your messages effective by giving your name, company name, phone number, time and date of your call, and a succinct message, and by indicating when you can be reached. If appropriate, emphasize that is all right to leave the information you have requested on your voice mail or with someone else. Also, you may suggest that your message recipient tell you a time when you can call or meet with him or her face-to-face. By doing this, you end the game and get what you need. Use Worksheet 7-3 to help plan your calls effectively.

Taking Messages Professionally

If you have ever received an incomplete or unreadable telephone message, you can appreciate the need for practice in this area. At a minimum, when you take a message you should get the following information from the caller:

Name (correctly spelled)

Company name

Phone number (with area code and country code, if appropriate)

Brief message

When call should be returned

Time and date of the call and your name (in case a question about the message arises)

If you are answering people's phones while they are away, let the caller know right away. This can be done by using a statement such as, "Hello, (person's name) line. This is (your name). How may I assist you?" In addition, be cautious of statements you make regarding the intended recipient's availability. Sometimes, well-meant comments can send a negative message to customers. See Figure 7–8 for typical problem messages and better alternatives.

General Advice

Don't communicate personal information (someone is at the doctor's, on sick leave, etc.), belittle yourself (i.e., "I don't know", "I'm only...") or the company (i.e., "Nobody knows"), or use weak or negative language (i.e., "I think," "I can't"). Instead, simply state "_____ is unavailable. "May I take a message?" or if appropriate, "I'd be happy to assist you." After you have taken the message, thank the caller before hanging up and then deliver the message to the intended receiver in a timely manner. If you discover that the receiver will not be available within a 24 hour period, you may want to call the customer and convey this information. If you do so, again offer to assist or suggest some other alternative, if one is available.

FIGURE 7-8

Communicating messages.

Message	Possible interpretation	Alternative
"I'm not sure where he is" or "He's out roaming around the building somewhere."	"Don't they have any control or structure at this company?"	"He's not available. May I take a message?"
"I'm sorry. She is *still* at lunch."	(Depending on the time of the call.) "Must be nice to have two-hour lunch breaks!"	Same as above or "I'm sorry, She is at lunch. May I assist you or take a message?"
"We *should* have that problem taken care of soon."	"Don't you know for sure?"	"I apologize for the inconvenience. We'll attempt to resolve this by ____."
"He isn't available right now. He's taking care of a crisis."	"Is there a problem there?"	"He isn't available right now. May I assist you or take a message?"
"She's not in today. I'm not sure when she'll be back."	Same as above.	She's not in today. May I assist you or take a message?"
"He left early today."	"Obviously, you people are not very customer-focused or she would be there during normal business hours to assist me."	He is out of the office. May I assist you or take a message?"
"I don't know where she is. I was just walking by and heard the phone ringing."	"Nice that you're so conscientious. Too bad others are not."	"She isn't available right now, but I'd be happy to take a message."
"I'll give him the message and try to get him to call you back."	"So there's a 50–50 chance I'll be served."	"I'll give him the message when he returns and ask him to call you back."
"Hang on a second while I find something to take a message with."	"Doesn't sound as if people at this company are very prepared to serve customers."	"Would you please hold while I get a pen and paper?"

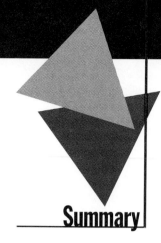

Summary

Chapter Summary

Delivering customer service via technology can be an effective and efficient approach to use to achieve total customer satisfaction. However, you must continually upgrade your personal technology knowledge and skills, practice their application, and consciously evaluate the approach and techniques you use to provide service.

In the quality-oriented cultures now developing in the United States and in many other countries, service will make the difference between survival or failure for individuals and organizations. You are the front line, and you are often the first and only contact a customer will have with your company. Strive to use technology to its fullest potential, but do not forget that you and your peers ultimately determine whether expectations are met in the eyes of your customer.

CHAPTER REVIEW QUESTIONS

1. In what ways can technology play a role in the delivery of effective customer service? Explain. _____

_____

_____

2. What are some advantages of using technology for service delivery?

_____

_____

3. What are some disadvantages of using technology for service delivery?

_____

_____

4. What are some of the communication skills for success? _____

_____

_____

5. How can you project a more positive image over the telephone?

_____

_____

6. What information should you always get when taking telephone messages? _____

_____

_____

_____

7. When transferring calls, what should you avoid and why?

_____

_____

8. When you leave a message on voice mail, what information should you give? _____

_____

_____

9. What is telephone tag, and how can it be avoided or reduced?

_____

_____

▼ SEARCH IT OUT

Search the Internet for Customer Service Technology

1. Log onto the Internet and search for sites that deal with the technology used to deliver quality customer service. Also, look for the Websites and organizations that focus on the technology and people involved in the delivery of customer service. Some starting points are the following:

   http://www.ccsmag.com   _http://www.csr.co.za_

   http://www.icsa.org   _http://www.the-resource-center.com_

   http://www.customercare.com   _http://www.fcc.gov_

   http://www.csm-us.com   _http://www.helpdeskinst.com_

   http://www.telemkt.com

2. Log onto the Internet to search for books and other publications that focus on customer service and technology. Develop a bibliographic listing of at least seven to ten publications, make copies of the list, and share it with your classmates.

COLLABORATIVE _Learning Activity_

Practice Customer Service with Your Team Members

Get together in teams of three members each. One person will take the role of a customer service provider, one will be a customer, and one will be the observer. Use the following scenarios to practice the skills you have learned in this chapter. Incorporate other communication skills covered in previous chapters as you deal with your "customer." Use three of the four scenarios so that each person in a group has a chance to play each of the three roles. Depending on the scenario, you might use copies of Worksheet 7-4 to plan your call.

Scenario 1: You are a customer service representative in a call center that provides service to customers who have purchased small appliances from your company. A customer is going to call complaining that she purchased a waffle iron from one of your outlet stores two weeks ago and it no longer works. She is upset because her in-laws and family are arriving in two days for an extended visit and they love her "special" waffles.

Scenario 2: You are a customer care specialist for a company that provides answers to travel-related questions for a national membership warehouse retail store. A customer will call to find out about the types of travel-related discounts for which he qualifies through his membership.

Scenario 3: You are a telemarketing sales representative for a company that sells water filtration systems. You are calling current customers who purchased a filtration system seven to ten years ago to inform them of your new Oasis line of filters, which is better than any other system on the market. You can offer them:

A 30-day money-back guarantee.

Billing by all major credit cards or invoice.

A one-year limited warranty on the system that replaces all defective parts but does not cover labor.

If they find a less expensive offer for the same product, a refund for the difference and an additional 50 percent of the difference.

Scenario 4: This scenario has two parts. In Part 1, you are a mechanic in an automotive repair shop. You answer a phone call from a customer calling to complain about what he perceives is an inflated billing charge for a recent air-conditioning repair. He is calling for your manager, who is at lunch and won't be back for 45 minutes. You take the incoming call, using the message-taking format covered in this chapter. In Part 2, you are the manager. You have just returned from lunch and find a message from the irate customer described in Part 1 and must call the customer. Use Worksheet 7-3 to plan your return call based on the message you received.

Telephone Techniques at Staff-Temps

Background

Staff-Temps International is a temporary employment agency based in Chicago, Illinois. It has six full-time and three part-time employment counselors. The office is part of a national chain owned by Yamaguchi Enterprises, Ltd., headquartered in Tokyo. The chain annually places over 100,000 temporary employees in a variety of businesses and offices.

Most of Staff-Temps' contacts are made by telephone; therefore, great emphasis is placed on selecting and training employees who have a good phone presence. Each employee is required to meet certain standards of quality in dealing with customers on the telephone. To ensure that these standards are applied uniformly, an outside quality control company (Morrison and Lewis) is used to make "phantom calls" to staff members. In these calls, Morrison and Lewis staff pretend to be potential clients seeking information. Employee-customer calls are also randomly taped. Through the calls and tapes, levels of customer service are measured.

Your Role

Your name is Chris Walker. As an employment counselor with Staff-Temps, you are aware of the customer service standards, which include the following:

Answer a ringing telephone within three rings.

Smile as you speak.

Use a standard salutation (Good morning, afternoon, or evening).

Give your name and the name of your department and company.

Offer to assist the customer ("How may I assist you?").

On the way back to the office after lunch, you were involved in a minor automobile accident. Even though it was not your fault, you are concerned that your insurance may be canceled since you had another accident and got a speeding ticket earlier this year. Because of the accident, you were an hour late in returning from lunch. Upon your arrival, the receptionist handed you six messages from vendors and customers. Two of the messages were from Aretha Washington, human resources director for an electronics manufacturing firm that has been a good client for over two years. The two of you had spoken earlier in the day.

As you walked into your office, the telephone started to ring. By the time you took your coat off and got to your desk, the phone had rung five or six times.

When you answered, you heard Aretha's voice on the line. Her tone told you that she was upset. This was the conversation:

You: "Staff-Temps. Chris speaking."

Aretha: "Chris, what's going on? You told me when I called first thing this morning that you would find out why my temp didn't show up today and would call me back. I've left messages all day and haven't heard a thing! We've got a major deadline to meet for a very important client, and I can't get the work done. My boss has been in here every half hour checking on this. What is going on?"

You: Aretha, I'm sorry. I just got in from lunch and haven't been able to get back to you."

Aretha: "Just got back from lunch! It's after 2:30! It must be nice to have the luxury of a long lunch break. I didn't even get to eat lunch today!"

You: "Listen, Aretha, I couldn't help..." Obviously anxious and raising your voice

Aretha: "Don't you listen me. I'm the customer, and if you can't handle my needs, I know someone else who can. If I don't hear from you within the next half hour, I don't ever want to hear from you again! Goodbye!" [Slamming receiver down.]

Questions

1. How well was this customer call handled? Explain. _____

_____

_____

_____

2. What should you have done differently? _____

_____

_____

_____

3. Do you believe that Aretha was justified in how she treated you? Explain._____

_____

_____

_____

4. How do personal problems or priorities sometimes affect customer service? _____

_____

_____

_____

_____

FROM THE FRONTLINE
Interview

Stephen A. Tanzer
President
Tanzer & Associates
Lake Mary, Florida

1. What is your background related to internal and external customer service?

I have worked with Fortune 1000 companies as a consultant as well as an employee. The industries include telecommunications, entertainment, manufacturing, high tech, service, and transportation. I have found a general understanding and acceptance among these firms of the concept of internal and external customers.

2. What are your general impressions of customer service in the United States?

Since the early 1990s, customers have noticed a significant change in the quality of customer service. The change seems to coincide with the use (or misuse) of technology to replace people in the customer service delivery process.

In preparing for this interview, I asked a number of professional contacts and friends to describe their experience with customer service. Interestingly, they all could immediately think of one or two bad experiences. However, one person described a very positive experience, and others related similar experiences with the same company. In addition, they all said that they would choose not to do business in the future with companies that had poor customer service programs.

3. In your experience working with customers in a technology-based environment, what are some of the issues with which they must deal?

On the positive side:

- There are more choices in levels of customer service (e.g., basic, preferred).
- The cost of receiving customer service (e.g., service levels, telephone costs) is borne by the provider.

On the negative side:

- There are long waits on hold and frequent busy signals (a 3- to 5-minute wait is fairly standard, but there are too many waits of 20 to 30 minutes).

- The menu choices are too complex (they cover all possibilities).

- Customer service is poor (incorrect information, inability to solve problems, poorly trained agents, etc.).

- Technology failures are common (disconnects, menu loops, etc.)

4. **What suggestions do you have for service providers?**

In embracing technology, companies (and frontline providers) must remember that the use of technology should enhance the customer service process. If reducing costs is the driving force behind using technology, the objective of the customer service program will be compromised. Several points to remember are:

- A customer service program should be part of the organization's strategy to win and keep customers.

- Customer feedback should be continually sought when a customer service program is set up.

- Specific program standards should be set and reviewed often.

- When introducing technology, use the service yourself so that you can experience what the customers are experiencing.

- Keep it simple (too many choices and menu levels lead to confusion).

- Most important: Just because customers go away doesn't mean that they have been served well. They may have simply become frustrated and have chosen to take their business to a company that can provide quality customer service.

CRITICAL THINKING
How should technology be used in customer service? Do you agree that a lot of the changes in customer service relate to technology?

Chapter 8

Customer Service Through Written Means

OBJECTIVES

After completing this chapter, you will be able to:

- *Recognize the importance of written messages in business.*

- *Correctly apply the basic rules of grammar when writing.*

- *Create professionally written documents.*

- *Apply a three-step approach to ensure effectiveness of written documents.*

- *Write in a way that enhances service.*

- *Set the right tone when you write.*

- *Deliver bad news and say no positively.*

- *Identify reference sources that will help improve your writing.*

"Learn to write well, or not at all."

John Dryden, 1631–1700
English poet
Essay on Satir

Before reviewing the chapter content, respond to the following questions by placing a "T" for true or an "F" for false on the rules. Use any questions you miss as a checklist of material to which you will pay particular attention as you read through the chapter. For those you get right, congratulate yourself, but review the sections they address in order to learn additional details about the topic.

_____ 1. Even if done professionally, written communication doesn't necessarily send a more formal message than verbal communication does.

_____ 2. It is important to show readers early in the written message why they should read on.

_____ 3. Nouns can be substituted for pronouns.

_____ 4. A pronoun names a person, place, or thing.

_____ 5. A verb aids others verbs, shows or indicates action, or states a condition.

_____ 6. Choosing the right words when writing can mean the difference between understanding and confusion.

_____ 7. When writing any correspondence, you should plan, write a draft, and edit and proofread before sending it.

_____ 8. Communicating in person or over the telephone is better than doing so through written means, if you want to help ensure correct understanding and allow for feedback.

_____ 9. The four parts of a typical letter are the heading, opening, body, and closing.

_____ 10. Memorandums are mainly for use within your organization (internal) and often act as a follow-up to verbal communications.

_____ 11. Most people do not respond well to letters that are written using pronouns such as *you, your, we,* or *I.*

_____ 12. When writing customers, you would be wise to follow the old saying, "If you can't say anything nice, don't say anything at all."

1. F   7. T
2. T   8. T
3. F   9. T
4. F 10. T
5. F 11. F
6. T 12. F

1 WHY WRITE TO CUSTOMERS?

CONCEPT: Writing to customers is an important activity in several instances that you will study about in this section. What you say and how you say it can affect business relationships positively or negatively.

You may wonder why you should bother writing when it is so easy to meet with customers face-to-face or to pick up the telephone and call them. Speaking with someone, face-to-face or over the phone, probably is the best and most expedient way to share information. However, writing allows you a further outlet for exchanging ideas and thoughts. If done professionally, written communication can send a more formal message while making your message visual. People gather information differently. Giving people something in writing allows them to read and reread the message at their leisure. If customers are unsure of something they read, having it in hand allows them to review it and then call you for clarification if necessary. In addition, you can use written documentation to summarize verbal discussions you have with a customer. This helps ensure that you both have the same interpretation of the discussion. Still another advantage is that you can plan your message and edit it before the customer receives it. You can also ask someone else to read it and provide input before you send it.

Of course, there is a downside to putting your thoughts in writing. Unless your customer acts or reacts to what you have written, you may never know how (or whether) the person received your message. You can deal with customers' reactions that are in the form of a telephone call or written response, a complaint, or an order. The ones you never know about are customers who do not respond at all. Did they get the letter, fax, or e-mail? Did they open it? Did they read part or all of it? Are they planning to respond later? These are all questions for which you have no answers. To help ensure your success of getting your message, and that of your organization, into the right person's hands, and having the person open, read, and respond to the message, you will need to communicate effectively.

2 | THE IMPORTANCE OF BUSINESS WRITING

▶ **CONCEPT:** Whether you are writing a letter, a memorandum, a report, or an e-mail, you must understand and apply the principles of good business writing.

The reality is that no matter what business you are in, you need to master the basics of business writing and effective written communication in order to deal effectively with others. There is much to consider. From a legal standpoint, the cliché "If it isn't in writing, it didn't happen" is very important to remember. If you get nothing else from this chapter, remember: document, document, document. By putting your thoughts and important details in writing, you create a "paper trail" that will help you in the future. Whether the format is a letter, memorandum, report, or e-mail, having on hand the key elements of a conversation or agreement along with background information can help successfully solve many problems in a customer service environment. Depending on the situation, you may send a brief reminder to someone or you may provide in-depth documentation. In either case, the way in which you express yourself can leave a lasting impression on how others view you and your organization. Remember the power of nonverbal communication. Writing is just another form of sending an image of yourself nonverbally.

An additional reason for taking time to express yourself effectively is that you are often competing with all the other people in your department for advancement, pay increases, and other employment opportunities. By communicating well, you set yourself above most of your peers, for many people cannot write effectively.

The importance of employee communication skills was highlighted in a 1994 study of employers conducted by the National Center on the Evaluation of Quality in the Workplace. The study asked employers to rate the job skills most critical to job performance. The results showed that employers list communication skills as the second most important job skill (attitude was No. 1)[1]

This chapter will address some basic issues related to effectively dealing with customers in writing; however, one chapter cannot adequately answer all questions related to communicating in writing. Some sources are listed at the end of the chapter, and others are given in the Bibliography. You are also encouraged to take a course or attend a seminar dealing with grammar, usage, editing, proofreading, and communicating effectively in writing.

Like any other worthwhile project in life, writing requires conscious effort and preparation. This is especially important when you are writing to prospective or current customers, for your reputation and that of your company is at stake. For customers to react, they must receive your message. You have to reach out through your writing and grab their attention. In most cases, you have only a few seconds to accomplish this before the customer makes the "use or lose" decision. Whatever the decision, you may not hear from the customer immediately, or you may never hear, if your material is tossed into the trash.

The easiest way to get your customer's attention when writing is to apply the **AVARFM principle** (**A**dded **V**alue **A**nd **R**esults **F**or **M**e) so that the customer can identify the rewards of reading your message. To do this, state your purpose for writing early in your correspondence. For example: "Thank you for your recent telephone call in which you shared your comments about our latest product line." "I am writing to ask your assistance in improving our service to you." "Please take a moment to read over the enclosed update to your product warranty for..."

Each of these examples is either an expression of appreciation or a reference to something that will help the customer or make his or her life better. Once you get the customer's attention, you need to prompt him or her to take action. You should do this in the body of your correspondence. This action might be one of the following:

To respond (e.g., answer a survey, call for additional information, or share an opinion).

To use your products or services.

To tell others about your organization and its products and/or services.

To contact you in the future (e.g., with questions or to order additional products or services).

---

[1] Lindsell-Roberts, p. 7.

3 BACK TO BASICS

▶ **CONCEPT:** Choosing the right words to communicate clearly is essential. To do that, you must know the basics of correct English usage.

Your image, and that of your organization, is at stake each time you pick up a pen or sit down at your computer to create some form of written communication. All the things you learned about grammar in high school English *are* important when you start to express your thoughts and ideas to customers and others. If your use of grammar is poor, it reflects negatively on your professionalism. In many cases, it can be the determining factor in whether you win, lose, retain, or regain a customer. People often form an opinion of your organization's ability to perform and meet their needs based on the information they receive from you and others who represent the organization. Many computer software packages have grammar and syntax checkers as well as spell checkers. However, remember that they are only tools to assist you; they do not replace you. Human beings, who make mistakes, designed them. You cannot afford to have your reputation rest solely on such technology. Improve your skills related to grammar, spelling, and composition and/or ask someone else who has strong skills in those areas to proofread what you write. The following sections provide a brief overview of the rules of effective grammar and should be just a beginning for you. If you think that you need help in strengthening your skills, find out about classes at some of the local colleges and professional training organizations in your area.

Over time, the "rules" for sentence and word usage change. However what you learned in high school is still relevant. Mastery of written English cannot only help you deal with customers but can often strongly influence your career opportunities. Remember the study on critical job skills mentioned earlier in this chapter? Refer to Figure 8-1 as you begin your review of the parts of speech.

Parts of Speech

Although you may be able to communicate well without knowing the roles of the various parts of speech, to communicate most effectively with your customers, you should be able to use all the tools available to you. In the case of written communication, your tools are the words in the English language. These words are divided into eight categories called **parts of speech:** nouns, pronouns, verbs, adverbs, adjectives, prepositions, conjunctions, and interjections (see Figure 8-1).

To help you better understand the way words are used, a brief description of each part of speech, along with some examples of how each is used, is given in the following sections. Keep in mind what you were taught in high school English classes, and remember that there are exceptions to most grammar rules. To help refresh your memory and prepare for writing professional-looking documents, you are encouraged to review the basic rules of grammar or attend a seminar on the topic. References are available at bookstores or libraries. Courses can be found on the Internet.

FIGURE 8-1

Parts of speech.

Part of Speech	Purpose	Example
Nouns	Name a person	Hamilton, Pat, Sui Ling
	Name a place	New Orleans, England
	Name a thing	Book, car, house
	Name an idea	Peace, love
	Name an ability	Walking, sitting
	Name a quality	Strength, intelligence
Pronouns	Take the place of nouns	She, it, them, his, her
Verbs	Aid or help other verbs,	Has been (helping)
	show or indicate action,	Has, receive, act, lift (action)
	state a condition	Is, was (condition)
Adverbs	Modify (describe or explain) a verb, adjective, or another adverb	Extremely, very, particularly
Adjectives	Modify, describe, or limit a noun or pronoun	Big, bigger, biggest, all, every
Prepositions	Link words, phrases, or clauses	In, to, for, from, by
Conjunctions	Links words, phrases, or clauses together	And, but, however, although
Interjections	Express emotion or excitement	Yikes!, Wow!, Oh!

Nouns

The easiest way to remember what nouns do is to think of their function. Nouns *name* a person, place, thing, idea, ability, or quality. Nouns also have subcategories. Nouns are either *proper* (specific and capitalized) or *common* (neither specific nor capitalized), for example:

Proper nouns: *Canterbury Avenue, Tallahassee, Howard University*

Common nouns: *street, capital, university, women, people, income, soccer*

Nouns are categorized by *gender* (masculine or male, feminine or female, or neuter), for example:

Masculine: *man, father, boy*

Feminine: *woman, mother, girl*

Neuter: *shirt, car, sofa*

Nouns can be collective or individual:

Collective: *family, tribe, class, team*

Individual: *person, employer, customer, student*

Pronouns

Pronouns are words that can be used in place of nouns. Using pronouns reduces the need to repeat nouns several times and creates a smoother flow to your writing. Here are some tips for using pronouns:

Make sure that the pronoun matches (agrees with) the noun (antecedent) that it replaces in terms of gender, number, and person.

> *All of my* customers *have paid* their *invoices (their refers to the plural noun* customers*)*.

> *The* woman *who ordered the new* draperies *said that* she *would pick* them *up this week (the pronoun* she *refers to the singular noun* woman; *the pronoun* them *refers to the plural noun* draperies*)*.

> *Everyone, except Sylvia and Marvin, called* her *or* his *supplier this morning (everyone is a singular noun, as are* her *and* his*)*.

Demonstrative pronouns (e.g., *these, those, that, this*) should be used only when referring to a specific noun (e.g., *those* items, *that* blouse, *this* form, *these* books), not to an entire thought or sentence. Using demonstrative pronouns to refer to a sentence can confuse your reader and cause your intended message to be lost.

> **Unclear:** *Ten customers ordered the special luncheon salads at approximately the same time.*
>
> *This is why we ran out of salads. (Did the shortage of salads result from ten customers ordering, or was it because they ordered at approximately the same time?)*

> **Clear:** *Ten customers ordered the special prepared luncheon salads at approximately the same time.*
>
> *Because of the large number of customers, we ran out of salads.*

Verbs

Verbs are the drivers behind sentences because they tell the condition, action, or state of being related to the subject of the sentence (see Figure 8-2). For example: A customer *called* to request a copy of our catalog (*customer* is the subject and *called* is the action).

Adverb

An adverb modifies (describes, explains, or limits) another adverb, an adjective, or a verb. An adverb answers the questions When? Where? Why? How? How much? And to what degree? One clue to identifying adverbs is that they often end in *ly*—but not always. Be sure to place an adverb as close as possible to the word it is modifying. Otherwise, you may inadvertently change the meaning of the sentence. For example, if you were writing a sentence in which you intended to say that your subject (John) explained a contract to someone and did nothing else, place the adverb appropriately.

> **Unclear:** *John explained the contract* only *to her. Only John explained the contract to her.*

> **Clear:** *John explained* only *the contract to her.*

FIGURE 8-2

Sample verbs.

be	have	read	tell
become	hold	rid	think
begin	keep	say	understand
break	know	see	wear
bring	lead	sell	win
build	leave	send	write
buy	lend	sit	
choose	let	speak	
come	lie	spend	
cost	make	split	
deal	mistake	strive	
do	pay	take	
feel	put	teach	

Adjectives

Adjectives enliven your sentences by modifying, limiting, or describing a noun or pronoun. Adjectives can be modified only by an adverb. Adjectives may be single words, phrases, or clauses, for example,

> The customer was *perfectly* happy.
>
> A *time of* great happiness.
>
> A *service provider* who is very stressed.

Prepositions

Prepositions connect a noun or pronoun with other words in a sentence. Prepositions also show direction or location. In the past, many educators taught students that a sentence should not end with a preposition. This rule has been relaxed in many cases. It is now permissible to use a preposition at the end of a sentence for emphasis or to avoid an awkward sentence construction, for example:

> The customer asked about *the sale merchandise shown* in the window *(the prepositional* about *makes a connection, and the prepositional phrase* in the window *gives a location).*
>
> We need the equipment to work with *(preposition* with *answer the question what.).*

Some common prepositions are listed in Figure 8-3.

Conjunctions

Conjunctions are words or phrases used to connect words, phrases, clauses, or sentences. Such words are also referred to as *transition words, transition phrases,* or *adverbial conjunctives* (see Figure 8-4), for example:

> I returned the customer's call, but *she was not in her office.*
>
> We do not have blue pillows; however, *we do have green ones.*

FIGURE 8-3

Common prepositions.

about	before	down	into	past	under
above	behind	during	like	pending	until
across	below	except	near	regarding	up
after	beneath	for	of	since	upon
among	between	from	off	through	with
around	beside	in	on	to	within
at	by	inside	onto	toward	without

Interjections

Interjections are words or phrases added to a sentence to express emotion or surprise, for example:

> Oh, my gosh, *I forgot to mail the information that a customer requested yesterday.*

> Wow, *I never expected to get a bonus for helping that customer.*

Word Choice

Use care in choosing the words to convey your meaning. Keep in mind that people outside your organization, industry, culture, or geographic area may not have heard the term(s) you are using. They may not have the same level of experience in the business world or the education that you have. Using **jargon**, buzzwords, or **slang** that people outside a particular group do not understand can cause a breakdown in communication and might signal your lack of interest in the reader's ability to comprehend your message (see Figure 8-5).

FIGURE 8-4

Common conjunctions or transitions.

in addition	either	meanwhile	therefore
also	eventually	nevertheless	toward
although	evidently	next	whenever
and	finally	on the other hand	whereas
at any rate	for	otherwise	wherever
as	for example	possibly	while
as a result	furthermore	rather	whoever
at the same time	however	since	yet
because	in comparison	similarly	
but	instead	so	
clearly	likewise	still	

Selecting the wrong word can change the meaning of your sentence entirely and make you look foolish, careless, or uneducated. To prevent this from occurring, have someone who has a good command of the English language look over documents that you have written before you

---

FIGURE 8-5

Common jargon, buzzwords, and slang.

Terms	Translation
annual premium	yearly payment
ballpark figure	estimate
brainstorm	generate ideas
carte blanche	unlimited power or freedom
ceiling	upper limit or highest level
CPU (central processing unit)	the brain of the computer
deep-six	discard
downsize	reduce workforce size
EEOC	Equal Employment Opportunity Commission
faked out	tricked or confused
gratis	free or no cost
hit a home run	succeed
iffy	doubtful
input	ideas, thoughts, or comments
jog your memory	prompt a thought or memory
kick around an idea	discuss something
laid back	casual or relaxed
mickey mouse	petty or trite
modus operandi	method of operating
nuts and bolts	basics or fundamentals
off the record	confidentially
out of whack	bad or defective
peripheral	equipment attached to a computer (e.g., printer or monitor)
power trip	arrogant display of personal power
quick fix	fast or hasty solution
run of the mill	common or ordinary
screwed up	made a mistake or confused
tab or check	bill or accounting of costs
ten-four	message was received
up the ante	raise or escalate a price or cost
uptight	anxious
vet	a veteran or to evaluate
whistle-blower	one who tells about or reveals wrongdoing
wild card	outside the rules or undefined
X-rated	obscene
zinger	a quick, caustic reply

send them. Doing this is one way of preventing the appearance of carelessness or of being unprofessional.

Keep It Simple

In addition to choosing the correct words, apply the **KISS principle** (<u>K</u>eep <u>I</u>t <u>S</u>hort and <u>S</u>weet) by using only the words you need to make your point. Using extra words usually does little to enhance the meaning of your message. In other words, be concise. Many people think that, by using more words, they appear to be better educated or more intelligent. Actually, they often confuse the reader and cloud the message by using unnecessary words (see Figure 8-6).

There is an additional problem created by using too many words—people do not have time to read them, especially managers and executives. If you cannot make your point in a few words, you will likely lose your reader.

Look at the following two examples. The first sentence in each example has the same meaning as the second; however, the first sentence has too many words.

Wordy: *As a point of fact, the customer who buys the advertised special will get the greatest value.*

Concise: *The advertised special offers the greatest customer value.*

Wordy: *A great many customers believe that we offer the best deals in the area a majority of the time.*

Concise: *Many customers believe that we typically offer the best deals in the area.*

FIGURE 8-6

Avoid wordiness.

Instead of This	Use This
a majority of	most
absolutely essential	essential
advance warning	warning
along the line of	like
as a result of	because
at a later date	later
at this time	now
based on the fact that	because
by means of	by
completely unanimous	unanimous
cooperate together	cooperate
depreciate in value	depreciate
due to the fact that	because
each and every	every
enclosed herewith is	enclosed

▼

FIGURE 8-6 (CONTINUED)

fell down	fell
final conclusion	conclusion or end
for the purpose of	for or to
for the reason that	because
had occasion to be	was
in regard to	about
in the course of	during
in the first place	first
large in number	many
large in size	large
month of March	March
mutual agreement	agreement
new innovation	new or innovation
on the grounds that	because
owing to the fact that	because
perform an analysis of	analyze
prior to	before
relative to	concerning or about
repeat again	repeat
small in numbers	few
subsequent to	after
take into consideration	consider
the only difference being that	except
until such time as	until
with reference to	about
within the realm of possibility	possible or possibly
with this in mind	clearly, according, or therefore

4 THE THREE-STEP PROCESS IN PREPARING WRITTEN MATERIAL

CONCEPT: When you start to create a communication of any kind, you must plan, write a draft, and edit and proofread the document carefully.

In most cases, the format and appearance of written materials sent to customers are dictated by tradition, organizational and industry precedence, and established procedure. Many companies have standard formats for written customer materials (e.g., rejection letters, collection letters, and solicitations). These formats are often stored in a computer database. When the letter is needed, a customer's name, address, and so on, are added, an envelope is addressed, and the letter is ready to be sent.

Whenever you are going to write anything that will go to a customer, it is a good idea to think first. Whether you are creating a letter, a memorandum, or an e-mail, you should follow three simple steps: (1) plan, (2) write a draft, and (3) edit or proofread. Only after you have completed

Work It Out 8–1. Reducing Wordiness

With your teammates, take about 5 minutes to determine a less wordy way to phrase the statements in the first column. Write your suggestions in the second column.

Instead of This	Use This
a great many	_____
a long period of time	_____
add the point that	_____
all of the	_____
another aspect of the situation to consider	_____
at a later date	_____
be of the opinion that	_____
during the course of	_____
except in a small number of cases	_____
exhibit a tendency to	_____
I want to take this opportunity to thank you	_____
in light of the fact that	_____
in the majority of instances	_____
on the order of	_____
some reason or another	_____
taking this factor into consideration	_____
it is apparent that	_____
the question as to whether	_____
to summarize the above	_____
with the exception of	_____

these phases are you ready to put your masterpiece into an envelope or click on "send."

Planning

The following are some specific points to consider in your planning phase.

Audience or Customer

Your format and tone typically depend on who will receive the correspondence. When deciding who will get the information, you need to consider a number of factors. To select your recipient(s), answer these questions before you start writing:

Who is the appropriate person to receive this information?

Is there anyone else who needs to receive this information? If so, why?

Purpose or Objective for Writing

In deciding your purpose, you should consider desired outcomes. Ask yourself some basic questions:

What do I want the recipient to think, know, or do differently?

What actions do I want the recipient to take?

What are the key points that I am trying to make?

What information does the recipient need?

Why does the recipient need this information?

What does the recipient already know about this topic?

What else does the recipient need to know about this topic?

How does he or she feel about this topic?

Format, Appearance, and Content

Numerous formats or styles can be used to create memorandums, business letters, proposals, reports, and all the other written documentation that you usually encounter in a customer service environment. In general, before you put ideas on paper, remember that you should write only what you would not mind seeing on the 6 o'clock news. If you keep this in mind when you are assembling information and selecting a style of writing, you are likely to end up with a professional-looking product. A key determinant in deciding on your style is your intended audience. For example, you would probably not use the same format and approach with your customers that you would with a coworker. With customers, you might use a formal letter, whereas with your coworkers, a memorandum may do.

Two approaches to writing your letters and memorandums—formal and informal—are available.

Formal formatting involves using a salutation that includes titles and last names of recipients. When writing an individual, use *Dear Mr., Mrs., or Ms.* _____ if you know the person's last name. Other appropriate salutations use a title such as *Dear Dr.* _____, *Dear General* _____, *Dear Mayor* _____, or *Dear Professor* _____.

Address your correspondence to a specific individual when possible. However, if you do not know the name, it is appropriate to use *Dear Sir or Madam* or *Ladies and Gentlemen*. Do not use *Gentlemen*, for it is a gender-biased term, except when you are writing to a group composed of all men. Or, in the case of a group composed of all women, use *Ladies* as your salutation.

An alternative is to address an individual by his or her position title or to address a department. For example, *Dear Human Resources Director* or *Dear Accounting Department*.

Many larger dictionaries typically list the correct salutations for various public officials. Reference manuals such as *The Gregg Reference Manual* by William H. Sabin provide comprehensive guidelines on writing business correspondence.

You can use *informal formatting* when you know the recipient personally, or have spoken to the person on the telephone, or when the person has corresponded with you or left a voice mail message using his or her first name. In such cases, you may use a salutation such as, *Dear Pat*.

As you will read in Chapter 10, many people with whom you will interact in the workplace are from different cultures. These people may have differing views on what is acceptable in the business environment. If you are writing to someone from another culture or country, it is typically better to err on the side of conservatism when addressing correspondence. Use the person's title and last name until you are given permission to do otherwise. Being careful in this regard can reduce the possibility of offense and avoid the perception that you are rude or arrogant.

Timing

The timing of correspondence can often have a major impact on how it is received. For example, suppose that you are mailing letters or flyers to customers to invite them to a private showing or exhibit for a new line of products to which the general public is not invited. Today is Wednesday. The exhibit will be held one week from today. You mail your letter or flyer on Friday, Monday is a holiday, and the letter or flyer arrives on Tuesday afternoon. How effective do you think such a mailing might be today, when people have tight schedules? The promotion would be far more effective if you allowed plenty of time for the flyer to be received so that the invitees could plan to attend.

As a rule of thumb, mail announcements early enough so that the invitees can make plans, and you do not look as though you forgot to allow adequate time. Depending on the situation, you may also want to send out a reminder notice.

Delivery Method

Keep in mind what you have read in other chapters about interpersonal communication. Usually, communicating in person or over the telephone is better than through written means if you want your message to be understood and you want to encourage feedback. Even so, you should follow up important telephone conversations with a written summary.

Based on the subject and the situation, however, you may decide that written communication is the best approach. If this is the case, you then have to decide on the best delivery method. Until recent years, the delivery options were limited—U.S. mail or couriers. That was then, and this is now. Today, in addition to the U.S. mail and couriers, the fax, priority and express mail through the U.S. Post Office, rapid delivery by various carriers (UPS, FedEx, RPS), e-mail, and interoffice mail are all available. Your choice will be affected by a number of factors:

How fast you need the document delivered.

The size and weight of the document.

Time constraints.

The image you wish to project.

Content (e.g., legal documents requiring an original signature).

Drafting Your Masterpiece

By taking the time to write your ideas on paper in the form of a draft, you can later spot grammar and syntax errors, see possible "political time bombs" (e.g., sexist language, offensive tone, or inappropriate words), or faulty organization. The drafting phase is *not* the time for editing. That comes in the third phase of preparing your correspondence. Editing as you go slows you down and can cause you to lose your train of thought, so that you might forget to include some important information that you intended to use. As you draft your document, use your planned comments or thoughts and write quickly. Don't get bogged down with grammar and spelling errors. Also, do not toil over getting the wording exactly right. You can correct these things when you edit. Your purpose in drafting is to capture the essence of your message.

Other options for drafting include taping your thoughts and later transcribing them, or jotting down key points on Post-It notes or index cards that you can reposition on a board or wall as you edit.

Editing Your Work

Try to catch your own errors, or have someone proofread your work, before sending your letter to a customer. This will help prevent a customer call arising from a misleading or incomplete letter. Also, keep in mind the image you want to send and make sure that your document supports that image.

Check your work to be sure you covered the following:

Did I include a date line?

Is the addressee (and any other recipient) clearly and appropriately identified?

Is my writing clear and concise?

Does each sentence and each paragraph contain only one thought or main idea?

Have I followed the structural formats (shown later in this chapter) for letters and memorandums?

Did I proofread each message carefully?

For e-mail, did I observe the etiquette outlined in Chapter 7?

Is there a call for action in the text of the document?

Have I included a signature?

If enclosures or attachments will be sent, did I indicate their existence on the document?

WRITING YOUR WAY TO BETTER SERVICE

▶ **CONCEPT:** Letters, memorandums, and e-mails have certain parts and are formatted in a particular style. The appearance of your written material often affects how the reader will respond.

In addition to the other tools that help you better serve your customers, a variety of written products can help you get your message across. These materials are probably familiar to you; however, when you are charged with using them, it sometimes helps to revisit some basic concepts and dos and don'ts, so that you present a professional image to customers. Many forms of written materials are used in businesses today (e.g., promotional materials, reports, proposals, policies, and other operational and informational documentation). The three types of written materials that a typical customer service representative, or someone dealing with customers, prospects (prospective customers), vendors, and others will use are letters, memorandums, and electronic mail (e-mail). Each has

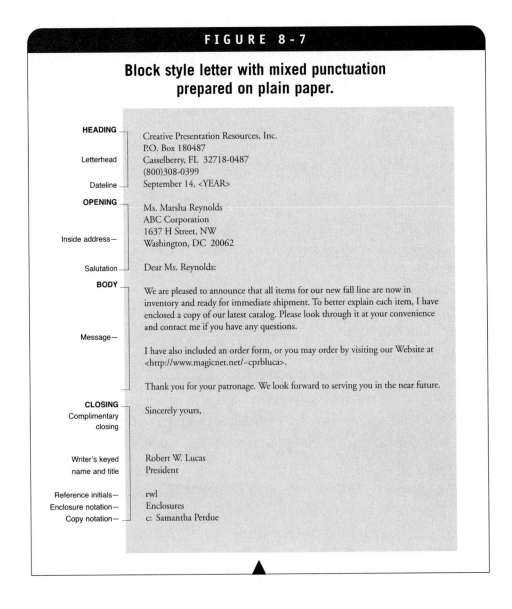

FIGURE 8-7

Block style letter with mixed punctuation prepared on plain paper.

HEADING

Letterhead

Creative Presentation Resources, Inc.
P.O. Box 180487
Casselberry, FL 32718-0487
(800)308-0399

Dateline — September 14, <YEAR>

OPENING

Inside address —

Ms. Marsha Reynolds
ABC Corporation
1637 H Street, NW
Washington, DC 20062

Salutation — Dear Ms. Reynolds:

BODY

Message —

We are pleased to announce that all items for our new fall line are now in inventory and ready for immediate shipment. To better explain each item, I have enclosed a copy of our latest catalog. Please look through it at your convenience and contact me if you have any questions.

I have also included an order form, or you may order by visiting our Website at <http://www.magicnet.net/~cprbluca>.

Thank you for your patronage. We look forward to serving you in the near future.

CLOSING
Complimentary closing

Sincerely yours,

Writer's keyed name and title

Robert W. Lucas
President

Reference initials —
Enclosure notation —
Copy notation —

rwl
Enclosures
c: Samantha Perdue

advantages when you are trying to communicate a specific type of message and image to someone.

Letters

Letters come in all types of formats and lengths. Your intended purpose, recipient, content, organizational style, and many other factors affect the final appearance of your letters. The key in all correspondence is to remain professional in tone and appearance. The way you word your letters, along with all the other factors you read about earlier in this chapter, will help determine the way in which the reader interprets what you have written. Before writing a business letter, find out whether your organization has a *style manual* that outlines the format to be used for outgoing letters. If there is no manual, use Figures 8–7 and 8–8 as guides.

Enhancing Appearance

Whether you are using preprinted letterhead with a logo at the top of the sheet, or you generate your own letterhead using a template available from your software, your letters might adhere to the following guidelines:

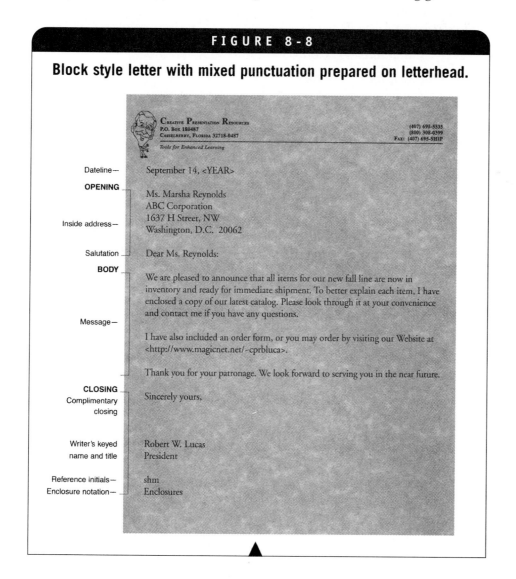

FIGURE 8-8

Block style letter with mixed punctuation prepared on letterhead.

CREATIVE PRESENTATION RESOURCES
P.O. BOX 180487
CASSELBERRY, FLORIDA 32718-0487
Tools for Enhanced Learning

(407) 695-5535
(800) 308-0399
FAX: (407) 695-SHIP

Dateline — September 14, <YEAR>

OPENING

Inside address — Ms. Marsha Reynolds
ABC Corporation
1637 H Street, NW
Washington, D.C. 20062

Salutation — Dear Ms. Reynolds:

BODY

We are pleased to announce that all items for our new fall line are now in inventory and ready for immediate shipment. To better explain each item, I have enclosed a copy of our latest catalog. Please look through it at your convenience and contact me if you have any questions.

Message —

I have also included an order form, or you may order by visiting our Website at <http://www.magicnet.net/~cprbluca>.

Thank you for your patronage. We look forward to serving you in the near future.

CLOSING
Complimentary
closing — Sincerely yours,

Writer's keyed
name and title — Robert W. Lucas
President

Reference initials — shm
Enclosure notation — Enclosures

Use a margin of 1 inch on the sides and bottom of the sheet.

Use a top margin of 2 inches, or use a ¹/₂-inch space between the letterhead and the first element in the letter.

Use a 12-point serif-style font such as Times New Roman or a sans serif font such as Arial.

Either left-justify (all lines align at the left margin) the text and leave the ends of the lines unjustified (ragged right) or fully justify all lines so that the text at the left and right margins is aligned.

Parts of a Letter

The four main parts of a letter are the heading, the opening, the body, and the closing.

- Heading. *An organization's logo, name, and address are normally included in a letterhead. If you are creating a letter on a blank sheet of paper, type this information either above the date or below the typed signature at the end of the letter. If you type the information, include the following items:*

  Organization name

  Street address

  City, state, and ZIP Code

  Country (if appropriate)

  Telephone and fax numbers and e-mail and Website addresses

The date is part of the heading section. Type the date in the form as *month, day, and year* (e.g., October 6, 2001). It may be necessary to use a different form for the date depending on your customer. For example, the military and European countries use the sequence *day, month, and year* (e.g., 6 October 2001). Note that, with this form, no comma is used after the month.

When typing your address or date line at the top of a blank sheet, start typing approximately 2 inches from the top of the sheet. Type the date on the next line (see Figures 8-7 and 8-8). If you are using letterhead stationery, type the date about ¹/₂ inch below the letterhead.

- Opening. *The opening of a letter contains the inside address and the salutation. Leave 3 blank lines under the date and begin typing the inside address, including the following information (see Figures 8-7 and 8-8):*

  Name of recipient

  Job title of recipient (if applicable)

  Name and address of the recipient's organization

  Room, suite, or apartment number

  Street address or post office box number

  City, state abbreviation (see Figure 8-9), and ZIP Code Country (in all-capital letters), if applicable

FIGURE 8-9

Abbreviations of states and territories of the United States.

AL	Alabama	Ala.	KY	Kentucky	Ky.	OH	Ohio	...
AK	Alaska	...	LA	Louisiana	La.	OK	Oklahoma	Okla.
AS	American Samoa	...	ME	Maine	...	OR	Oregon	Oreg.
AZ	Arizona	Ariz.	MH	Marshall Islands	...	PW	Palau	...
AR	Arkansas	Ark.	MD	Maryland	Md.	PA	Pennsylvania	Pa.
CA	California	Calif.	MA	Massachusetts	Mass.	PR	Puerto Rico	P.R.
CO	Colorado	Colo.	MI	Michigan	Mich.	RI	Rhode Island	R.I.
CT	Connecticut	Conn.	MN	Minnesota	Minn.	SC	South Carolina	S.C.
DE	Delaware	Del.	MS	Mississippi	Miss.	SD	South Dakota	S.Dak.
DC	District of Columbia	D.C.	MO	Missouri	Mo.	TN	Tennessee	Tenn.
FM	Federated States of		MT	Montana	Mont.	TX	Texas	Tex.
	Micronesia	...	NE	Nebraska	Nebr.	UT	Utah	...
FL	Florida	Fla.	NV	Nevada	Nev.	VT	Vermont	Vt.
GA	Georgia	Ga.	NH	New Hampshire	N.H.	VI	Virgin Islands	V.I.
GU	Guam	...	NJ	New Jersey	N.J.	VA	Virginia	Va.
HI	Hawaii	...	NM	New Mexico	N.Mex.	WA	Washington	Wash.
ID	Idaho	...	NY	New York	N.Y.	WV	West Virginia	W. Va.
IL	Illinois	Ill.	NC	North Carolina	N.C.	WI	Wisconsin	Wis.
IN	Indiana	Ind.	ND	North Dakota	N.Dak.	WY	Wyoming	Wyo.
IA	Iowa	...	MP	Northern Mariana				
KS	Kansas	Kans.		Islands	...			

Use the two-letter abbreviation on the left when abbreviating state names in addresses. In any other situation that calls for abbreviations of state names, use the abbreviations on the right: if no abbreviation is given, spell the name out.

Source: Marilyn Satterwaite and Judy Olson-Sutton, *Business Communication at Work*, Glencoe/McGraw-Hill, Columbus, Ohio, 2000.

Type the **salutation** on the second line under the inside address. The form of the salutation will be determined by the content, purpose for writing, whether you know the recipient, and the image you are trying to convey. When typing the title and name of your recipient:

Start at the left margin.

Leave 1 space above and below the salutation.

Abbreviate titles as such Mr., Mrs., Ms., *and* Dr.

Spell out titles of position or rank such as Sheriff, General, Mayor, Pastor, *or* Chairperson.

Follow the salutation with a colon for business letters (or a comma for informal correspondence.

Capitalize the first noun or title in a salutation:

Dear Ms. Harold

Dear Colonel Rushmore

Dear Mayor Linowski

My dear Mr. Freeman

Note: If you know the title or organization name only, but do not know the name of a recipient, or do not know the recipient's gender, you have some options:

Title only: *Dear Human Resources Director*

Organization only: *Dear National Geographic Society, Ladies and Gentlemen, or Dear Sir or Madam*

Unknown gender: *Dear J. P. Murphy*

- Body. *The body of a letter consists of the message—what you want to say to your recipient. In composing the body of a letter, apply all the guidelines related to parts of speech that were covered earlier in this chapter. As you create your message, think about the key points you wish to make and include them in the first one or two paragraphs. Many people will not read beyond that point if they do not feel a need to know what you have said. To get and hold the attention of your reader, word your opening statement in a way that gives the reader a reason to continue. Think about the way a great novel, speech, or movie begins. Each of these communication vehicles makes a powerful statement or provides a strong image to pique your interest and make you want to continue. The same is true of great letters. You will read later about words that make a positive and negative impact. The key is to start strong and avoid overused introductions. Do you recognize any of the following tired, old introductions?*

  As per our conversation ...

  Per your request ...

  In accordance with ...

  It was a pleasure speaking (or meeting) ...

How many of these statements make you want to know what's coming next? Too often, writers begin their correspondence with a trite statement and then go to the real message. Unfortunately, by the time they get to the "good stuff," the reader is no longer with them. Look again at the examples above. Do any of them really say anything? When you read the last one, do you really think someone would write a customer to say that it was *not* a pleasure to speak with him or her?

As you read earlier in this chapter, the key to successful correspondence is to plan, draft, and edit your message from your customer's perspective. Think of how you would feel if you received what you have written. Also, make sure that the document looks professional. As you develop your message, follow these guidelines:

  Start with a strong opening statement.

  Single-space each paragraph.

  Leave 1 blank line between paragraphs.

  Keep paragraphs short and concise. Limit the first and last paragraphs to four lines (not sentences). Limit other paragraphs to six to eight lines for maximum readability.

  Indent the first sentence (about $1/2$ inch) of each paragraph, if desired.

- Closing. *A typical letter ends with a complimentary closing (e.g., Respectfully yours, Sincerely yours, or Cordially) followed by a comma. The writer's name and title are placed under the complimentary closing, and reference initials (the initials of the person who prepared the document) appear below the writer's name and title.*

Enclosure and copy notations may also be added, along with a postscript. A typical closing might look as follows:

Respectfully yours,

Bob Lucas, President
Enclosure

Memorandums

To a great extent, memorandums (memos) have been replaced in many organizations by e-mail. Memorandums were originally designed to provide quick information in an informal format. They are intended mainly for use inside an organization (internal) and often serve as follow-up documentation to a conversation, meeting, or other encounter with a person.

Many people make the mistake of using memorandums when a more formal letter or approach would be appropriate (e.g., to a customer outside the organization or a vendor). Some people make their memorandums too complex, and some fail to follow some common formatting guidelines. A memorandum should normally address a *single* topic. If you need to cover other topics, have a meeting with the person, if possible, send separate memorandums for each topic, or write a detailed letter and attach enclosures.

When formatting your memorandums, decide who really needs a copy of the document. Many people get so much mail and e-mail these days, they do not have time to read all of it in detail. Make the lives of others easier by omitting from the address line the names of people who do not need to receive the information. Memos have two main parts, the heading and the body.

The *heading* includes the following:

The names of the intended receiver and the sender. There may be multiple recipients and senders. If this is the case, list their names from top to bottom based on rank (e.g., CEO first, followed by VPs, and so on). You can also list these names under the line Distribution after the sender's name at the bottom of the letter.

Names of people who will receive a courtesy copy.

The date that the memorandum was sent.

A short, concise subject line.

The *body* includes the following:

Plenty of white space to aid readability.

A purpose sentence (why you are writing).

Concise, short sentences that convey your primary message.

Paragraphs that are short, concise, and to the point.

Key points or ideas numbered or bulleted for easier reading, if appropriate.

A concluding sentence or paragraph that calls for action.

The initials of the originator of the message.

An enclosure notation, if appropriate.

Memo formats vary widely. Many organizations have style manuals that dictate how written correspondence should be formatted. Some companies even have computerized memorandum *templates* or printed forms for employees to use. If your organization does not have these tools, use the following formatting guidelines (see also Figure 8-10):

Set 1- to 1¼-inch margins on the sides.

Start typing 2 inches from the top of the sheet or about ½ inch under the organization's name, if your organization provides preprinted stationery.

Double-space the guide words in the heading (e.g., To, CC, From, Date, and Subject).

Use a colon after each heading guide word.

Tab after each guide word (clear the longest guide word by at least 2 spaces).

Use uppercase and lowercase letters for the addressee's name, sender's name, title and/or department, date, and subject.

Start the message body at the left margin. Use block style (all lines begin at the left margin). Use a ragged right margin (do not justify the right margin).

If you have enclosures (attachments to the memorandum), place an enclosure notation under the originator's initials. Reference initials, file name notations, and enclosure notations should all begin at the left margin.

E-Mail

As you read in Chapter 7, e-mail is an integral part of nearly all businesses in the twenty-first century. When using this tool for customer communication, you must remember all the things you read in Chapter 7 regarding e-mail etiquette.

Because of the informal nature of this medium of communication, use e-mail carefully and sparingly in interactions with customers. When you do use it, choose your words carefully, proofread, spell-check, and double-check your message before clicking on "Send."

The importance of your message is crucial in deciding whether to use e-mail or some other method of message delivery. For example, if you need a record of message delivery, e-mail may not be the best choice. Even though some systems give you a return receipt notification when a message is received, you do not know who received it. You only know that it got to a destination. Also, if someone changes his or her e-mail provider without informing you, the message may be lost in an electronic void. Or, if you are lucky, the undelivered message may be returned to you. E-mail is not like the U.S. Postal Service.

FIGURE 8-10

An example of a memorandum.

HEADING

MEMORANDUM

TO: Chris Sibling
Accounting Clerk
Accounting Department

Guide words—

CC: Danielle Clausen
Supervisor
Accounting Department

FROM: Tim Williams *TW*
Customer Service Representative
Customer Retention Department

DATE: February 20, <YEAR>

SUBJECT: Credit for Samantha O'Brien

BODY
Purpose—

I am following up to provide the details you requested concerning the subject customer, whom we discussed on the telephone today.

Message—

On January 19, Ms. O'Brien placed an order for office supplies. Because of an error at the warehouse, she failed to receive a printer cartridge (model E714) that she had requested. I am attaching a copy of her order for your reference.

Since then she has purchased the item from a competitor and is asking for a credit to her account.

Conclusion/Action—

Please process this request as quickly as possible, since Ms. O'Brien is a good customer and orders from us frequently.

Reference initials—
Enclosure notation—

tw
Enclosure

---

6 SETTING THE TONE OF YOUR CORRESPONDENCE

▶ **CONCEPT:** The tone that you set in your correspondence can influence your customer to do business with you or not.

Remember what you read about tone of voice in earlier chapters? Tone can send a very powerful message about your attitude, even when you write. Tone can convey your frame of mind—arrogant, angry, frustrated, sarcastic, friendly, hostile, and so on. Tone is conveyed through your word choice, sentence structure, and punctuation. For example, if you respond to a customer's voice message or e-mail with an abrupt e-mail that uses short sentences punctuated with exclamation points and negative words, you can send a negative message. Read the following examples to see how different messages can be transmitted. Assume that the customer has called twice during the week about a problem with a product shipment, and then e-mailed you today.

Here is one response to the customer:

As a means of communicating, e-mail facilitates the rapid exchange of ideas and views around the world in a matter of minutes. How do you decide whether to send an e-mail or a letter?

Dear Ms./Mr. _____

As I told you in our last telephone conversation, I am researching the problem you have called about twice before! I will contact you as soon as I have more information.

Thank you for writing.

Here is another response:

Dear Ms./Mr. _____

Thank you for writing concerning the problem you and I discussed on the telephone earlier this week. I apologize for the delay in resolving the issue. I am still researching the cause; however, I do not have an answer yet. I will contact you this coming Monday to update you, or sooner if I get the answer.

Thank you for your patience.

As a customer, which response would you react to more positively? Why?

One way to avoid sending a negative message when you are emotionally charged is to have someone else read what you have written before you send it to a customer. If this is not possible, write a draft, set it aside for a couple of hours or a day to give you time to cool off, and then reread it. Ask yourself the following questions and then modify the text as necessary:

What message is this correspondence supposed to convey? Did I convey that message?

Have I addressed the customer's questions or problems?

How would I react to this message?

Is there anything in the wording, punctuation, or sentence structure that could be misconstrued by the customer?

Did I use the active voice in structuring the sentences?

What do I need to add or take away?

Speak to Your Customer

People typically respond better to information that is directed at them. When you personalize what you write through use of words such as *you, your, I, ours, we,* and *mine,* you have established a mental link with your reader. Think of the way this book is written. Throughout, the words *you* and *your* have been used to make the text more conversational. Often, people do not consciously realize that you are using a personalized approach, but they react positively to the relaxed or friendly tone.

Use a Positive Tone

Even when you have to say no or deliver "bad news" to a customer, try to do so in a positive manner. Choose your words carefully so that you sound courteous and friendly, and yet assertive. To do so, keep the saying "It's not what you say, but how you say it" in mind. Use all the standard pleasantries such as *Please, May I,* and *Thank you* as you write in order to help make the customer feel appreciated and important to you and your organization (see Figure 8–11).

The most successful strategy for communicating a positive tone is through effective "reader management." By choosing the right words and style of writing, you can often guide your reader to a decision or in the direction in which you want them to go. To do this in correspondence that has good news or is advantageous to the customer, use the AVARFM principle. In other words, give the customer a reason to read on.

Here are some ways to get the reader's attention in a good-news letter.

Congratulations Mr. Hostler! You have won the grand prize ...

Greetings and congratulations! It is my pleasure to inform you ...

Today is your lucky day!

You are cordially invited ...

You have been selected ...

Good news!

FIGURE 8-11

Words that convey a positive tone.

The following words can help impact a positive tone to messages:

able	enriched	markedly	productive
absolutely	expanded	marvelous	progress
advantage	favorable	modern	promise
appreciation	free	monumental	recommended
approval	genuine	motivation	revolutionary
assist	grateful	multifaceted	reward
assure	great	necessary	satisfactory
bargain	guarantee	notable	save
benefit	happy	offer	security
complimentary	helpful	often	superior
comprehensive	honest	opportunity	terrific
congratulations	important	original	thank you
delighted	initiative	outstanding	timely
determine	invaluable	particular	total
easy	kind	patronage	unique
effective	lasting	perfect	unlimited
efficient	long-lasting	permanent	valued
enhanced	major	pleasure	wonderful

Delivering Bad News or Saying No Positively

Writing to a customer to say that you cannot satisfy his or her needs may not be an easy task for you. You may remember what you learned as a child: "If you can't say anything nice, don't say anything at all." Or, you may have compassion for the customer and realize how you might feel if you received such correspondence. Regardless of how you might feel, part of your job as a representative of your organization may be to deliver bad news to customers. Keep in mind that your customer does not want to hear what you cannot do. Instead, the customer wants to hear how you can assist him or her.

When you must say no, try to do so in a manner that protects the relationship between the customer and your organization. One way to accomplish this is to be considerate in your writing style and avoid words that convey a negative tone (see Figure 8-12). With letters that are likely not to be well received, and in which you must relay some negative information or news, start off with some pleasant information and lead up to the letdown or bad news. Here are three basic parts to use in such communications:

- Use a buffer. *This is a mild statement that communicates friendliness and comes across as neutral; for example, "We recently received your documentation and a request for reimbursement of expenditures resulting from the repair of the refrigerator you purchased from us three years ago. Thank you for bringing the issue to our attention."*
- State the reason for the refusal. *In this part, use an honest, open approach to explain why the customer's request cannot be fulfilled; for example, "Over the years, (company name) has wrestled with the issue of creating a reimbursement policy that is fair to our customers and ourselves. Last year, we decided to set a two-year cutoff for reimbursements except in unusual cases. That decision was based on the fact that if any problems are going to occur, they usually do so during that period. We have consistently found that the quality of our products typically prevents repair problems. After reviewing your documentation, and for these reasons I have just described, I must reject your request for repair reimbursement. If you have questions or comments about this matter, please contact me immediately."*
- Reaffirm the value to your organization of the customer and the relationship. *End the correspondence in a manner that maintains the customer-provider relationship and shows goodwill toward the customer; for example, "Mr. Moreno, although we could not assist you in this matter, we do value your business and want to continue to serve you in the future. To help demonstrate our sincerity, I am enclosing a certificate good for 25 percent off the price of any merchandise in our store (including sale items), good for 60 days ..."*

FIGURE 8-12

Words that convey a negative tone.

The following words and phrases might conjure up negative images:

abuse	complain	false	lose	sorry
angered	crisis	fault	mediocre	stubborn
anxious	damage	guilty	misinform	stupid
apology	deceive	harass	misrepresent	tardy
argue	delay	hardship	mistake	trouble
bad	delinquent	hate	neglect	unable to
blame	difficulty	helpless	negligence	unfair
broken	disappoint	ignorant	oversight	unfortunate
canceled	dispute	impossible	problem	unsuccessful
cannot	exaggerate	insist	regret	useless
careless	excuse	invalid	rude	victim
cheap	fail	irritate	shortsighted	wrong

Use the Active Voice When Writing

People writing in the business world sometimes take a low-key or passive approach to writing. This can confuse a reader. Use a direct or active approach when you write to customers. This is especially important when someone must take an action. If you use the **active voice,** you focus action on the subject of your sentence and help the reader understand who is taking action. The active voice helps define where, when, and why an action is taking place. It also livens up sentences by eliminating unnecessary words.

On the other hand, passive sentences make it hard to determine the focus of the action, for no responsibility is assigned in a sentence written in the passive voice. Look at the following examples to get a better idea of the effect of each type of sentence (active and passive):

Active voice:	*Next week, a third-party vendor will contact our customers.*
Passive voice:	*Our customers are being contacted by a third-party vendor next week.*
Active voice:	*Charlotte will handle the new account.*
Passive voice:	*The new account will be handled by Charlotte.*
Active Voice:	*Carl will change the customer's oil later.*
Passive Voice:	*The customer's oil will be changed later by Carl.*

Work It Out 8-2

Work It Out 8-2. Using the Active Voice

Convert the following passive sentences to the active voice. Be prepared to explain your responses to the class.

Passive voice	**Active voice**
Your request for a refund was received yesterday.	_____
Sometimes requests cannot be honored.	_____
Your request will be processed as promptly as possible.	_____
Your request will be processed by Chris.	_____
Customers are typically notified of the status of their requests within seven working days.	_____

Use Inclusive Language

Respect for others must be observed in the workplace. This is not only because there are laws saying that you must respect the rights of others, but because it is the right thing to do. The easiest way to accomplish this and send a positive tone at the same time is to choose appropriate words in addressing people in your writing.

Specifically, when you refer to individuals, groups, job positions, and other workplace-related topics, be sure that you use **inclusive language**. This means using appropriate nouns and pronouns that include people of all races, gender, religions, and ethnicities (see Figures 8-13 and 8-14).

FIGURE 8-13

Gender-specific and gender-neutral terms.

Avoid using the gender-specific terms listed below, and instead use the suggested gender-neutral terms.

Gender-Specific Terms	Gender-Neutral Terms
anchorman or anchorwoman	anchorperson
boss man or boss lady	supervisor or manager
businessman or businesswoman	businessperson
chairman or chairwoman	chair or chairperson
clergyman	member of the clergy
fireman	firefighter
foreman	foreperson or supervisor
guys or gals	men or women
mankind	human race or humanity
man-made	synthetic
policeman or policewoman	police officer
repairman	service technician
salesman or saleswoman	salesperson, sales associate, sales representative
spokesman or spokeswoman	spokesperson
stewardess or steward	flight attendant
waiter or waitress	server
weatherman or weather girl	meteorologist
workman or workmen	worker or workers

---

7 | STYLE AND WRITING SOURCES

▶ **CONCEPT:** Effective word choice and style are essential when you correspond. When you are in doubt about either, refer to a reference or style book.

Developing an effective writing style can take years of practice and review. This chapter has barely touched the surface of what you need to know. Depending on whether you are drafting a letter or memorandum, or developing a formal report or research paper, there are many sources that

Inclusive nouns.

Capitalize the proper names of peoples, races, tribes, religions, and so on. Use lowercase for common nouns describing groups of people.

Aryans	hill tribes
African Americans	Italians
Asian Americans	Jews
blacks	Native Americans
bush people	Navajo
Caucasians	Puerto Ricans
Catholics	whites

you can look to. In addition to books listed in the Bibliography, the following are standard references.

William A. Sabin, *The Gregg Reference Manual*, 9th ed., Glencoe/McGraw-Hill, Columbus, OH, 2001.

Joseph Gibaldi, *MLA Handbook for Writers of Research Papers*, 4th ed., Modern Language Association of America, New York, NY 1995.

The American Psychological Association, *Publication Manual of the American Psychological Association*, 4th ed. Washington, D.C., 1994.

The University of Chicago Press, *The Chicago Manual of Style*, 14th ed., Chicago, IL, 1993.

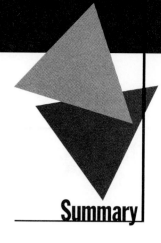

Summary

Chapter Summary

In this chapter, you have explored some of the basics of effective business writing, starting with the eight parts of speech and the use of the KISS principle in selecting just the right words for your message. You also read about the need to plan, draft, and edit anything you write before sending it to a customer. Failure to do so can lead to a reduced image of professionalism and customer confusion. Once you have organized your message, you must consider who will be receiving the message, your purpose for writing, the format and appearance, the appropriate time to deliver the message, and how you will send it (e.g., letter, memorandum, or e-mail).

In addition, you should consider the tone of what you write. Tone is influenced by the way you address your customer (e.g., *you* or *your*), the approach you use (positive or negative), and the voice (active or passive).

CHAPTER REVIEW QUESTIONS

1. How can the information provided in this chapter help you to better serve customers? _____

_____

_____

2. Why is it sometimes important to put communications to customers in written form? _____

_____

_____

3. What are some of the basics that are important to use effectively when writing to a customer? _____

_____

_____

4. How does word choice affect your customer's reaction to a written message? _____

_____

_____

5. What is the value in following a three-step process when preparing written material? _____

_____

_____

6. What are the role and importance of formatting when writing to a customer? _____

_____

_____

▼ SEARCH IT OUT

Search the Internet for Names and ZIP Codes

To practice obtaining names, addresses, and ZIP Codes to use with customer correspondence, log onto the Internet to search for information:

1. Go the U.S. Post Office site www.usps.com, click on "ZIP Codes/ Addresses," and search for the following:

   - *Type in* George Mason University *and the ZIP Code 22030 to get the complete mailing address and last four digits of the ZIP Code.*
   - *Type in* 1600 Pennsylvania Ave., NW, Washington, D.C., *to get the name of the resident and the ZIP Code.*
   - *Type in* 1331 F St., Washington, D.C., *to get the name of the organization and suite number for a group that works with disabled employees.*

2. Go to any search engine and type in *state senators* or *representatives*. Get the names of the senators or representatives from your state. Next, go to the <www.whowhere.com>, type in a senators or representative's name, and get his or her mailing address.

COLLABORATIVE *Learning Activity*

Writing Appropriate Correspondence

Select one of the following options to practice using the skills outlined in this chapter.

1. Your instructor will provide you with written materials (e.g., articles or promotional materials). Use them to practice identifying parts of speech in the sentences that make up the first paragraph of one of the selections.

2. Select one of the following scenarios and create either a letter or a memorandum to the customer based on the information provided and what you read in this chapter:

   - *A customer has failed to pay an invoice within the 30 days required. You must write to remind her of the tardiness and to request payment.*
   - *Write to a customer informing him or her that in order to receive a complimentary two-night resort stay, he or she must return an attached marketing survey by a specified date.*
   - *The owner of a small business wrote to inform you that the catalogs that were to be delivered earlier this week have not arrived and that she has a special mailing of the materials scheduled for next Wednesday.*

WRITTEN CORRESPONDENCE AT WILLIAM'S PEST CONTROL

Background

William's Pest Control services is a locally owned business in Charlotte, North Carolina. The company has a good customer base in and around the downtown Charlotte area. Most of its clients are businesses; however, there are also some residential customers.

William Mascot established the company after he was released from active duty in the Marine Corps in 1985. As a teenager, he had worked for another pest control business for three years, prior to spending seven years in the Corps. William's younger brother John and cousin Mark help with service calls. The service consists of basic rodent and pest control and an occasional call to deal with insect or rodent infestations.

Chris Mansfield, who has been with the company for over three years and runs the office, schedules appointments, dispatches service technicians, and handles administrative functions, including all incoming calls and correspondence. Everyone deals with routine customer service matters while on calls.

Your Role

You are Chris Mansfield. Three months ago, service was provided to a long-time client Stephanie's Convenience Mart. John and Mark went to the business site to spray for flying ants. This was done as a routine service call. Nothing has been heard from the client until a letter arrived in the mail today. According to the letter, the flying ants were actually termites, which have eaten away portions of the supporting beams in the roof and parts of the walls. Stephanie's got a repair estimate last week— $18,000. The letter demands that William's pay for the repair. You have conferred with William, who has asked you to write a letter to Stephanie's.

Critical Thinking Question

1. Write the letter to Stephanie. What do you think the reaction will be to your letter? _____

_____

_____

_____

_____

_____

_____

_____

_____

_____

FROM THE FRONTLINE
Interview

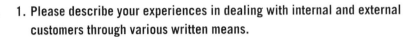

Peggy Isaacson
President
Peggy Isaacson
and Associates
The Portable
Personnel Office
Orlando, Florida

1. Please describe your experiences in dealing with internal and external customers through various written means.

When I was a corporate human resources manager, my external customers were job applicants and my internal customers were company staff and managers. Written communications (mainly letters and memos) could be characterized by the term *responsiveness*. Applicants needed to know that we had received their résumés and how they had fared in the selection process. Because of the volume of applications, we used acknowledgment postcards for résumés, "regrets" postcards for individuals who were not interviewed, and "regrets" letters for people who were interviewed but not selected. An extra "wrinkle" for us was that applicants were potential customers for our products. Hired or not, applicants were treated well so that they would continue to think well of the company and our products.

Company staff needed answers to questions. Responsiveness to their needs helped cement relationships so that we built and maintained a reputation for assisting and for being team players.

In my current business (human resources consultant and management trainer for small to midsize businesses, nonprofit organizations, and government agencies), written communication takes the form of marketing letters, proposals, documentation of consulting sessions, confirmation of training dates and details, and human resources documents and information. E-mail and fax communications have been added to the mix.

2. What are your general impressions of customer service in the United States? Why do you feel this way?

Good customer service in this country is the exception rather than the rule—it is so rare that, when I do encounter it, I am surprised. Companies talk a good line about the importance of good customer service (it is certainly one of my more popular training programs), but in the main, I think that companies fail to identify, and then teach their employees, the philosophy, techniques, and attitudes that will give customers a positive, pleasant experience. Also, I believe that companies get wrapped up in policy and procedure, forgetting that it is they who serve the customer, not the other way around.

3. **In your experience in working with customers, what are some of the most important things to remember related to providing quality service through written means? Please explain.**

Written customer communications should be timely, readable, and simple. Customers want answers and information quickly. If they are to believe that the vendor is interested in them and concerned about them, that belief will stem, in large part, from how promptly their needs are addressed. Written communications must be expressed in language that a customer understands. Industry jargon and complex technical terms don't inspire a customer's faith in the vendor's competence; they make a customer wonder what the vendor is hiding. Directions and procedures must be easy to follow; forms should have clear, simple instructions.

4. **What are some of the advantages in providing written information to customers?**

Written information provides both the vendor and the customer with documentation to back up oral communication, eliminating the potential for disputes about what was actually said, what was actually meant.

5. **What are some issues or pitfalls that service providers who correspond with customers should avoid?**

At the top of my list is poor use of the basics of writing (grammar, spelling, punctuation, sentence structure, proofreading). How we appear on paper is similar to how we appear in person. A sloppy, haphazard appearance sends customers several messages that damage the vendor's credibility: (1) The vendor doesn't think that details are important, (2) the vendor isn't competent, (3) the vendor doesn't respect the customer.

Assumptions made on the basis of appearance may not be fair, but they are made.

6. How does the way you and other employees deliver service via written means affect your organization and your customers?

Technology makes it easier to communicate with customers. Instead of playing telephone tag, my customers and I can talk with each other via fax and e-mail, saving both of us time. Also, in my line of work, I constantly urge clients to document conversations and actions taken. I am a role model for that behavior when I provide information in writing to my clients.

7. What advice, related to correspondence in a customer service environment, would you give someone who is entering the customer service profession?

To be a successful customer service provider, whatever your job title, take the time to do two things: (1) Learn how to see an issue or problem from the customer's perspective, so that the focus of your writing is to meet the customer's needs. (2) Take a course or get a good book on business writing, so that your writing inspires the customer's confidence in your professionalism and competence.

CRITICAL THINKING

What role do written communications play in customer? Do you agree with the advice given by Peggy Isaacson?

Chapter 9

Handling Difficult Customer Encounters

OBJECTIVES

After completing this chapter, you will be able to:

- *Recognize a variety of difficult personality types.*

- *Use the Emotion-Reducing Model to help keep difficult situations from escalating.*

- *Determine appropriate strategies for dealing with various types of customers.*

- *Exhibit confidence when involved in difficult customer interactions.*

- *Develop better relationships with internal customers.*

- *Use the five-step problem-solving model in handling difficult customer situations.*

> "Working with people is difficult, but not impossible."
>
> Peter Drucker
> Author and Management
> Consultant

Before reviewing the chapter content, respond to the following questions by placing a "T" for true or an "F" for false on the rules. Use any questions you miss as a checklist of material to which you will pay particular attention as you read through the chapter. For those you get right, congratulate yourself, but review the sections they address in order to learn additional details about the topic.

_____ 1. An important realization that will assist you in better serving customers is to acknowledge that they all have needs and expectations.

_____ 2. Customer needs are driven by internal motivators and can be broken down into five categories.

_____ 3. Behavioral style preferences do not affect customer needs or satisfaction levels.

_____ 4. An upset customer is usually annoyed with a specific person rather than the organization or system.

_____ 5. An effective strategy for dealing with angry customers is to let them know exactly what your company policy is.

_____ 6. When you cannot comply with the demands of an angry customer, you should try to negotiate an alternative solution.

_____ 7. In some cases, indecisive customers truly do not know what they need or want.

_____ 8. Demanding customers often act in a domineering manner because they are very self-confident. This is a function of behavioral style.

_____ 9. Rude customers need to be controlled or "put in their place" to prevent a repetition of the behavior.

_____ 10. Some service providers have difficulty handling talkative customers.

_____ 11. Adopting a "good neighbor policy" can help in dealings with internal customers.

_____ 12. As part of trying to help solve a customer problem, you should assess its seriousness.

1. T   7. T
2. T   8. T
3. F   9. F
4. F   10. T
5. F   11. T
6. T   12. T

1 | DIFFICULT CUSTOMERS

CONCEPT: Successful service will ultimately be delivered through effective communication skills, positive attitude, patience, and a willingness to help the customer.

You may think of difficult customer contacts as those in which you have to deal with negative, rude, angry, complaining, or aggressive people. These are just a few of the types of potentially difficult interactions. From

time to time, you will also be called upon to help customers who can be described in one or more of the following ways:

Lack knowledge about your product, service, or policies.

Dissatisfied with your service or products.

Demanding.

Talkative.

Internal customers with special requests.

Speak English as a second language (discussed in Chapter 10).

Elderly and need extra assistance (discussed in Chapter 10).

Have a disability (discussed in Chapter 10).

Each of the above categories can be difficult to handle, depending on your knowledge, experience, and abilities. A key to successfully serving all types of customers is to treat each person as an individual. Avoid stereotyping people according to their behavior. Do not mentally categorize people (put them into groups) according to the way they speak or act or look—and then treat everyone in a "group" the same way. If you stereotype people, you will damage the customer-provider relationship.

Ultimately, you will deliver successful service through your effective communication skills, positive attitude, patience, and willingness to help the customer. Your ability to focus on the situation or problem and not on the person will be a very important factor in your success. Making the distinction between the person and the problem is especially important when you are faced with difficult situations in the service environment. Although you may not understand or approve of a person's behavior, he or she is still your customer. Try to make the interaction a positive one, and if necessary ask for assistance from a coworker or refer the problem to an appropriate level in your operational chain of command.

Many difficult situations you will deal with as a service provider will be caused by your customer's needs, wants, and expectations. You will read about service challenges in this chapter, along with their causes and some strategies for effectively dealing with them.

2 WHY PEOPLE BUY

> **CONCEPT:** Understanding the drive behind customers' needs, wants, and emotional reactions will help you know why people buy. You will be able to give better customer service once you understand the customer better.

Factors such as needs, wants, and emotional reaction cause customers to buy things. Each of these factors provides a stimulus for the customer to shop, compare, and possibly purchase a product or service.

Needs are things that a customer feels compelled to address or believes are necessary. Needs are an individual matter and arise from internal sources or motivations that vary from one customer to the next according to their situation and background.

You will be helped in serving your customers if you understand that all people have needs. Since each person's needs are different, no two customers are going to like the same thing or buy the same product or service for the same reason. Therefore, although some of the basic customer service techniques discussed in earlier chapters will help you in determining and addressing customer needs, there will be times when these techniques will not help you at all. Customer diversity, which you will read about in Chapter 10, along with customer expectations and the various circumstances in which you and your customers find yourselves, also affects your success. Depending on the customer, situation, emotions, and other factors, you will find that some customer contacts are challenging or difficult. These situations are not hopeless if you plan ahead and mentally prepare yourself for them.

You should understand, too, that needs alone do not cause customers to make purchases. Research has shown that emotion often influences buying decisions. A classic example of this was demonstrated when the Coca-Cola Company decided to introduce the "New Coke." Company executives had become concerned about sales. They were losing ground to their major competitors, Pepsi and 7UP, and also to their own Diet Coke. Also, they had seen the price of sugar rise and were looking for ways to reduce costs and increase revenue. They decided that they would introduce a new product and gradually take the original Coca-Cola off the market. The decision was affected also by the fact that Pepsi and Diet Coke had a smoother, sweeter taste than Coca-Cola.

Before making such an important decision, Coca-Cola managers did all the right things. They experimented to find just the right combination of ingredients, and they market-tested their product through blind taste tests (in which consumers were blindfolded and asked to sample various products including the original Coke, Pepsi, and Diet Coke). During the tests, consumers overwhelmingly selected the "New Coke" as their product of choice. Coca-Cola then put together fancy advertisements and an advertising campaign to introduce the product with great fanfare.

Coca-Cola executives were sure that they had a huge success on their hands and believed that they would leave Pepsi far behind in the market ratings. Instead, they failed partly because Coca-Cola had kept secret its plan to remove the original Coke from the shelves the same week that the new product was released. The public was outraged. Coca-Cola had one of the greatest marketing fiascoes of the twentieth century on its hands. What Coca-Cola had failed to reckon with was the emotional reaction of the public. Even before people tasted the new product, they felt betrayed by a company they trusted. As a result, they rebelled. They wanted the original Coke back. After all, they had grown up with this product. The New Coke was introduced on April 23, 1985. Within days, Coca-Cola received thousands of calls and letters of complaint. On July 11, 1985, at a press conference, the chairman of Coca-Cola, Roberto Goizeuta, and president and CEO, Donald Keough, announced, "We have heard you." New Coke faded into oblivion and "Classic Coke," made with the original formula, was born. The public celebrated (with a Coke of course!).

The Basis of Customer Needs

To address customer needs, you must first understand the origin of needs and why people buy different products. As psychologist **Dr. Abraham Maslow** once stated, "The human being is a wanting animal and rarely reaches a state of complete satisfaction except for a short time. As one desire is satisfied, another pops up to take its place. When this is satisfied, still another comes to the foreground and so on. It is characteristic of human beings throughout their whole lives that they are practically always desiring something."[1]

Figure 9-1 illustrates **Maslow's hierarchy of needs** that also applies to customers' needs. **Needs** are often derived from internal motivators or things that make us happy and satisfy us. A classic study on human motivation conducted by Maslow after World War II might help you understand human needs. Although his work focused on the needs of employees in the workplace, it has application in many other environments.

In his research, Maslow found that people have specific needs starting at the basic or *physiological* level, at which they need items that will sustain life (e.g., food, shelter, clothing, water, and air). Once people have satisfied their basic needs, they can move up the hierarchy to other needs, such as the second level, *safety* or *security*. At that level, people focus on products and services that will help them feel protected (e.g., insurance,

---

[1] Maslow, p.7.

firearms, security devices, and fault-free electrical or mechanical products). The third level identified by Maslow was *social*, which concerns the need to feel accepted or loved. Products or services that can help people fulfill their social needs can go a long way toward making them feel successful (e.g., flowers, gifts, or other items that demonstrate love, affection, and caring). Anything that makes people feel as if they belong to a group or **subculture** will help fulfill this need. The fourth level of need is that of *esteem* or *ego*. Items that can help customers feel better about themselves (self-esteem), project status or prestige, or gain the respect of others are important (e.g., clothing, cars, furniture, jewelry, body adornments, or grooming products).

The highest level on Maslow's hierarchy is *self-actualization* or, in the words of a U.S. Army recruiting slogan, "Be all you can be." Anything that can help customers attain their highest potential addresses this final need category (e.g., educational software, professional development seminars, or tools that enhance effectiveness and efficiency).

To relate this theory to reasons why customers become dissatisfied and difficult to deal with, think about a situation like the following: A customer goes into a convenience store on the way home from work. He has a very stressful job. He earns minimum wage, and his wife is unemployed. Recently, he had to quit taking classes at a local college, where he was trying to get an associate degree in order to qualify for a higher-paying job, because he had to take a second job to help support the family. He has two sick toddlers at home and has stopped in at the store to get cough medicine. He specifically chose this store because he had seen a flyer in the morning

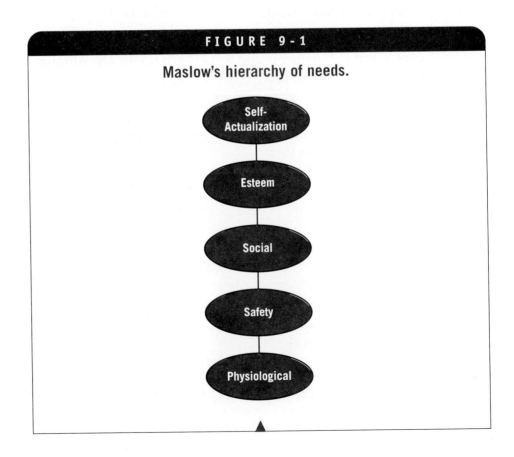

FIGURE 9-1

Maslow's hierarchy of needs.

paper indicating that cough syrup was on sale. When he checked the shelf, the product was out of stock. The customer is not happy!

A knowledge of Maslow's work can help you determine your customer's level of need. Try completing Worksheet 9-1 to see how well you can guess which level of need is being demonstrated.

Customer Expectations

As you have read in earlier chapters, today's customers are more discerning, better educated, have access to more up-to-date and accurate information, and are often more demanding than in the past. They have certain expectations about your products and services, and the way that you will provide them. Figure 9–2 shows some common expectations customers might have of a service organization. Failure to fulfill some or all of these expectations can lead to dissatisfaction and in some cases confrontation and/or loss of business.

WORKSHEET 9-1

Worksheet ▼
9-1

Determining Needs

Based on what you read about Maslow's hierarchy of needs, determine the primary needs being expressed by the following customer statements. (The answers are at the end of the worksheet.)

Customer Statement   **Need**

1. *I have a very important interview with a
   recruiter at a Fortune 500 company, so I'm
   looking for a new tie that will send just the
   right message.*   _____

2. *Can you point me in the direction of the
   rest room?*   _____

3. *I have a date with this really great guy,
   and I need a killer dress. Can you help?*   _____

4. *Do you think that this suit makes me look fat?*   _____

5. *What kind of warranty does this product carry?*   _____

Answers:
1. *Self-actualization*, from the standpoint of wanting to get a better job and reach a higher goal, and esteem, from the perspective of wanting the recruiter to be impressed.
2. *Physiological*, based on biological need.
3. *Social*, from the standpoint of wanting to be accepted and to fit in.
4. *Esteem*, based on concern for the opinion of others and self-esteem, because this person wants to think that he or she looks good.
5. *Safety*, based on concern that protection is needed if something goes wrong.

FIGURE 9-2

Typical customer expectations.

Customers come to you expecting that certain things will occur related to the products and services they obtain. Customers typically expect the following:

Expectations related to people

Friendly, knowledgeable service providers

Respect (they want to be treated as if they are intelligent)

Empathy (they want their feelings and emotions to be recognized)

Courtesy (they want to be recognized as "the customer" and as someone who is important to you and your organization)

Equitable treatment (they do not want to feel that one individual or group gets preferential benefits or treatment over another)

Expectations related to products and services

Easily accessible and available products and services (no lengthy delays)

Reasonable and competitive pricing

Products and services that adequately address needs

Quality (appropriate value for money and time invested)

Ease of use

Safe (warranty available and product free of defects that might cause physical injury)

State-of-the-art products and service delivery

Easy-to-understand instructions (and follow-up assistance availability)

Ease of return or exchange (flexible policies that provide alternatives depending on the situation)

Appropriate and expedient problem resolution

---

3 | THE ROLE OF BEHAVIORAL STYLE

▶ **CONCEPT:** Behavioral preferences have a major impact on the interactions of people. The more you know about style tendencies, the better you will understand your customers.

As you read in Chapter 6, behavioral style preferences play a major part in how people interact. Styles also affect the types of things people want and value. For example, people with high expressive tendencies will probably buy more colorful and people-oriented items than will people who have high decisive tendencies.

The more you know about style tendencies, the easier it becomes to deal with people in a variety of situations and to help match their needs with the products and services you and your organization can provide. Take a few minutes to review Figure 6-3 before going further in this chapter. The suggested strategies found there can assist you in dealing with customers who exhibit a specific behavioral style preference and are upset, irrational, or confrontational. Keep in mind that everyone possesses all four behavioral styles discussed in Chapter 6 and can display various types of behavior from time to time. Therefore, carefully observe your customer's behavior and use the information you learned about each style as an indicator of the type of person with whom you are dealing. Do not use such information as the definitive answer for resolving the situation. Human beings are complex and react to stimuli in various ways—so adapt your approach as necessary. In addition, learn to deal with your emotions so that you can prevent or resolve heated emotional situations.

Handling Emotions With the Emotion-Reducing Model

It is important to remember when dealing with people who are behaving emotionally (e.g., irritated, angry, upset, crying, or raising their voice) that they are typically upset with the structure, process, organization, or other factors over which you and/or they have no control. They are usually not upset with you (unless you have provoked them by exhibiting poor customer service skills or attitude).

Before you can get your customer to calm down, listen, and address the situation, you must first deal with her or his emotional state. Once you do this, you can proceed to use problem-solving strategies (discussed later in this chapter) to assist in solving the problem. Until you reduce the customer's emotional level, he or she will probably not listen to you or be receptive to what you are saying or your attempts to assist. In some cases, she or he may even become irritated because you seem nonempathetic or uncaring.

To help calm the customer down, you must send customer-focused verbal and nonverbal messages. You need to demonstrate patience and use all the positive communication skills you read about in Chapters 3 to 5. Most important among those skills are the ability and the willingness to listen calmly to what the customer has to say without interrupting or interjecting your views. This lesson is taught to many law enforcement officers to help them deal with crisis situations such as domestic disturbances. If your customer perceives that you are not attuned to his or her emotional needs or thinks that you are not working in his or her best interest, you become part of the problem, rather than part of the solution.

Keep in mind that a customer generally wants to be respected and **acknowledged** as an individual and as being important. As you interact with the customer, you can soften the situation and reduce emotion by providing customer-focused responses. Simple customer-focused messages can put you on a friendly (human) level while at the same time helping to calm the emotion.

Here's how the Emotion-Reducing Model works: As a customer approaches (or when you answer the telephone), greet him or her with "Good morning (or afternoon)," a smile, and open body language and gesturing (customer-focused message). Then, as the customer explains the problems (emotion), you can offer statements such as, "I see," "I can appreciate your concern, frustration, or anger," or "I understand how that can feel (customer-focused)." Such statements can help you connect psychologically with the customer. Continue to use positive reinforcement and communication throughout your interaction. Once the problem has been defined and resolved(problem resolution), take one more opportunity at the end of your interaction to send a customer-focused message by smiling and thanking the customer for allowing you to assist. Also, one last apology may be appropriate for inconvenience, frustration, mistreatment, and so on (customer-focused). Figure 9–3 provides a visual model of this process.

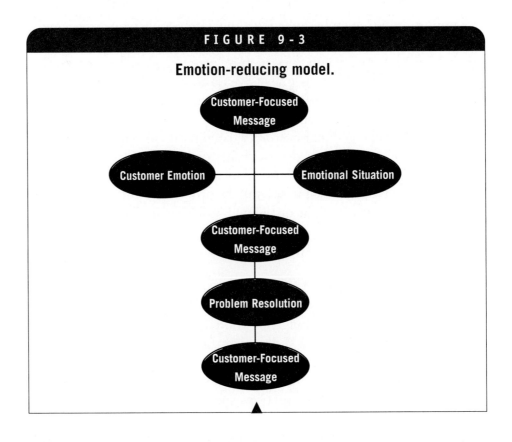

FIGURE 9-3

Emotion-reducing model.

Customer-Focused Message

Customer Emotion · Emotional Situation

Customer-Focused Message

Problem Resolution

Customer-Focused Message

4 | WORKING WITH DIFFICULT CUSTOMERS

CONCEPT: You will need to be calm and professional when dealing with difficult customers.

Most customers have a specific type of product or service in mind when they make contact with your organization. They are also willing to let you help them if you do so in a positive, pleasant, and professional manner. There are others who, because of their outlook on life, attitude, personal habits, or background, may cause you frustration and require additional effort. You should expect to encounter difficult people and try to serve them to the best of your ability. With difficult customers, you should remain calm and professional.

Angry Customers

Dealing with angry people requires a certain amount of caution. For you to effectively serve an angry customer, you must move beyond the emotions to discover the reason for his or her anger. Here are some possible tactics:

- Be positive. *Tell the customer what you can do, rather than what you cannot do. If you say, "Our policy won't permit us to give you a refund," you can expect an angry response. On the other hand, you might offer, "What I can do is issue a store credit that may be used at any of our 12 branch stores in the city."*

Note: Before dealing with customers, check with your supervisor to find out what your policies are and what level of authority you have in making decisions.

By having this information before a customer encounter, you will have the tools and knowledge necessary to handle your customers effectively and professionally.

- Acknowledge the customer's feelings or anger. *You cannot and should not try to deny the customer's anger. Doing so could result in a serious confrontation. Instead of saying, "You really don't have to be upset," try, "I can see you're upset. I want to help solve this problem, so could you please help me understand what's happened?"*

By taking this approach, you've acknowledged the customer's feelings, demonstrated a willingness to assist, and asked the customer to participate in solving the problem.

- Reassure. *Reassure the customer. Indicate that you understand why he or she is angry and that you will work to solve the problems. Statements such as these can help ease the frustration of your customers: "I'm going to do my best to help resolve this quickly," "I can assure you that this will be resolved by Monday," "You can rest assured that I am going to make this a priority."*
- Remain objective. *As mentioned earlier, becoming part of the problem is not the answer. Even if the customer raises his or her voice or uses profanity, remain calm. This may be difficult, but it will help keep the situation from escalating. If necessary, count to ten in your head and take a deep breath before responding. Remember, angry customers are usually angry at the organization, product, or service that you represent, not at you. If they do not settle down, calmly but assertively explain that although you want to assist, you cannot do so until they help by providing information. If possible, suggest moving to a private area away from other customers and ask for help from a supervisor or team leader, if appropriate.*

- Determine the cause. *Through a combination of asking questions, listening, feedback, and analyzing the information you receive, try to determine the cause of the problem. The customer may simply have misunderstood what was said. In such an instance, a clarification may be all that is required. Try something like, "There seems to be some confusion. May I explain?" or possibly, "It appears that I was unclear. May I explain?"*
- Listen actively. *When people are angry, they need a chance to vent their frustration and be heard. Avoid interrupting or offering "Yes, but . . ." types of remarks. This only fuels their anger. Suppose that a customer calls to make an appointment for an oil change and is told that the special sale ended yesterday. The customer then says that there was no indication in the newspaper advertisement that there was an expiration date. You respond with, "Yes, that's true, but we always run our sale ads for only one week. Everybody knows that." Naturally, the customer is now upset. A better response would be something like, "Although that sale ended yesterday, we will honor the coupon because the expiration date was inadvertently omitted from the advertisement." Whether the customer is "right" or "wrong" makes no difference in situations like these. You will build stronger customer relationships when you make this kind of concession, because you are bringing in money you might not have received if the customer got upset. Moreover, the customer is now satisfied, may tell others, and will likely return.*

(Do, however, inform your supervisor of the problems caused by the omission of expiration dates in ads.)

- Reduce frustrations. *Don't say or do anything that will create further tension. For instance, don't transfer a caller to another extension if the customer told you he or she has already been transferred several times, interrupt to serve another customer (especially for a telephone caller—unless your organization's policy requires that you do so), or put the person on hold repeatedly to handle other customers or tasks not related to serving the original customer.*
- Negotiate a solution. *Elicit ideas from the customer on how to solve the problem. If the customer's suggestions are realistic and feasible, implement them. Or negotiate an alternative. By using customers' suggestions, you are likely to gain their agreement. Also, if something goes wrong later, they may be less likely to complain again since it was their idea in the first place.*
- Conduct a follow-up. *Don't assume that the organization's system will work as designed. If there is a breakdown, the customer has your name and may complain to your supervisor. Or, the customer may not complain but instead go to a competitor. Either way, you lose.*

Once an agreed-upon solution has been implemented, take the time to follow up to ensure that all went well. This may involve personally calling the accounting department to ensure that proper credits were made, delivering an order or materials to shipping tem yourself, or calling or writing the customer after a period of time to make sure the customer is satisfied and to offer future assistance. Whatever it takes, do it to ensure customer satisfaction. As a rule of thumb, *under* promise and *over* deliver.

Work It Out 9.1. Dealing With Angry Customers

Work It Out
9-1

Work with a partner. Discuss situations in which you had to deal with an angry person. Think about what made the person angry and what seemed to reduce tension. On the lines provided, make a list of these factors and be prepared to share your list with the class.

Use the results of this discussion to develop strategies to help calm angry people in the future.

What Angered?	**What Calmed?**
_____	_____
_____	_____
_____	_____
_____	_____
_____	_____
_____	_____
_____	_____

Dissatisfied Customers

Occasionally, you will encounter customers who are **dissatisfied** or unhappy when you meet them. Possibly they have been improperly served by you or one of your peers, or by a competitor in the past. Even if you were not personally involved in their previous experience, you represent the organization or you may be considered "just like that last service employee." Unfair as this may be, you have to try to make these customers happy. To do so, try the following strategies:

- Listen. *Take the time to listen actively, as discussed in Chapter 4. Often, when people are upset, all they want to know is that you're willing to attend to their concerns.*
- Remain positive. *Even though angry customers drain your energy, don't get drawn into mirroring their anger or agreeing with their putdowns of your company, competitors, peers, products, or services. This only fuels the fire. If appropriate, smile and interject positive comments into the conversation as you listen, and try to determine an effective course of action.*

FIGURE 9-4

Positive wording.

When faced with a customer encounter that isn't going well, remain positive in language. This will help you avoid escalating the situation.

Negative Words or Phrases	Positive Alternatives
Problem	Situation, issue, concern, challenge
No	What I (or) we can do is ...
Cannot	What I (or) we can do is ...
It's not my job (or my fault)	Although I do not normally handle that, I'm happy to assist you.
You'll have to (or you must ...)	Would you mind ...? Can I get you to ...?
Our policy says ...	While I'm unable to ... What I can do is ...

▲

Keep in mind what you read about the power of positive language in Chapter 3. Figure 9–4 shows some examples of negative wording and some possible alternatives.

- Smile, give your name, and offer assistance. *Sometimes a typically cheerful greeting is not possible because a customer verbally attacks first (e.g., you pick up a ringing phone or a customer walks up as you are serving another customer or looking down or away). In such instances, listen to what the customer is saying, use positive nonverbal cues (e.g., nodding, open or nonthreatening body posture, and possibly smiling) and inject paralanguage (e.g., Uh-huh, Hmmmm, Ahhhh, or other vocalizations). By demonstrating positive nonverbal behaviors, you may be able to psychologically "bond" with the customer. People usually do not attack a "friend," someone they know, or someone who is trying to assist them. This is why many law enforcement officers are trained to introduce themselves and to use a person's name.*
- Don't make excuses. *Typically, customers are not interested in why they did not get the product or service they wanted or thought they paid for; they just want the problem solved (in their favor). Look for ways to correct a mistake rather than cover it up.* Remember: if you get defensive, you become part of the problem and not part of the solution.
- Be compassionate. *Try to remain warm, compassionate, empathetic while you are trying to uncover the cause of the problem. You can then attempt to service the customer properly and promptly. Many times this can be done by using statements such as:*

  I see.

  I can relate to that.

  I understand what you're saying.

I can appreciate your point.

I know how you feel. (Use caution with this statement if some one is very emotional. This type of comment could increase the customer's anger and escalate the situation).

- Ask open-ended questions. *By using specific open-ended questions, you can obtain the information you need to serve the customer. For example, "Mr. Washington, can you explain exactly what you expected from our service contract?"*
- Verify information. *To prevent misunderstandings or the possibility of escalating an uncomfortable situation, be sure that you received the correct message. Too often, we believe we understand the meaning of a message, only to find out later that we misinterpreted it. Test your interpretation of a customer's message by stating it in your own words. For example, "Mr. Rasheed, if I heard you correctly, you were told by the clerk who sold you this table that it would be assembled upon delivery, but the driver refused to do so. Is that correct?"*
- Take appropriate action. *After you have gathered all pertinent information you need to make a decision, work with the customer to satisfy his or her needs.*

Work It Out 9-2. Identifying Dissatisfiers

Take a few minutes to think about your organization or one with which you are familiar. Look for factors that might contribute to customer dissatisfaction. Make a list of them, and then list some strategies for eliminating or reducing them. As an alternative, you might want to work with someone else and compare lists.

Dissatisfiers	Strategies for Reducing
_____	_____
_____	_____
_____	_____
_____	_____
_____	_____
_____	_____

Indecisive Customers

You will encounter people who cannot or will not make a decision. They sometimes spend hours vacillating. In some cases, indecisive customers truly do not know what they want or need, as when they are looking for a gift for a special occasion. Sometimes such customers are afraid that they will choose incorrectly. In these situations, use all your communication skills. Otherwise, indecisive customers will occupy large amounts of your time and detract from your ability to do your job effectively or to assist other customers.

Be aware, however, that some people really *are* just looking as they check out sales, kill time between appointments, relax, or they may be lonely and want to be around others. Strategies for dealing with an indecisive person are given in the following sections.

- Be patient. *Keep in mind that, although indecisive people can be frustrating (especially if you have a high D behavioral style preference), they are still customers. Greet such customers just as you would any other customer and offer assistance. If the customer refuses your help or wants to browse, that's fine, but indicate where you will be and watch for the customer to signal for assistance.*

- Ask open-ended questions. *Just as you would do with a dissatisfied customer, try to get as much background information as possible. The more data you can gather, the better you can evaluate the situation, determine needs, and assist in the solution of any problems.*

- Listen actively. *Focus on verbal and nonverbal messages for clues to determine emotions, concerns, and interests.*

- *Suggest other options. Offer alternatives that will help in decision making and reduce the customer's anxiety. For example, "Ms. Sylvester, if you find that the color of the fabric doesn't match your wallpaper, you have 30 days to return it." This approach shows that you are informed and trying to assist, and it may help the person make up his or her mind. Suggesting a warranty or exchange possibility may make the customer more secure in the decision-making process.*

- Guide decision making. *By assertively, not aggressively, offering suggestions or ideas, you can help customers make a decision. Note that you are helping them, not making the decision for them. If you push your preferences on them, they may be dissatisfied and return the item. Then you, or someone else, will have to deal with an unhappy customer.*

▶ Think about a recent time when you were indecisive about purchasing a product or service, and then respond to the following questions:

1. What caused your indecisiveness? _____

_____

_____

2. What ultimately helped you to make a decision? _____

_____

_____

3. How can you use your own strategies to help satisfy an indecisive customer? _____

_____

_____

Demanding or Domineering Customers

Customers can be demanding for a number of reasons. Many times, domineering behavior is part of a personality style, as discussed in Chapter 6. In other instances, it could be a reaction to past customer service encounters. A demanding customer may feel a need to be or stay in control, especially if he or she has felt out of control in the past. Often, such people are insecure. Some strategies for effectively handling demanding customers are discussed in the following sections:

- Be professional. *Don't raise your voice or retaliate verbally. Children engage in name-calling, which often escalates into shoving matches. Unfortunately, some adults "regress" to childish behavior. Your customer may revert to negative behavior learned in the past. Both you and the customer lose when this happens.*

- Respect the customer. *Showing respect does not mean that you must accommodate your customer's every wish. It means that you should make positive eye contact (but not glare), remain calm, use the customer's name, apologize when appropriate and/or necessary, and let the customer know that he or she is important to you and your organization. Work positively toward a resolution of the problem.*

- Be firm and fair and focus on the customer's needs. *As you read in Chapter 3, assertive behavior is an appropriate response to a domineering or demanding person; aggression is not. Also, remember the importance of treating each customer as an individual.*

- Tell the customer what you can do. *Don't focus on negatives or what can't be done when dealing with your customers. Stick with what is possible and what you are willing to do. Be flexible and willing to listen to requests. If something suggested is possible and will help solve the problem, compliment the person on his or her idea (e.g., "Mr. Hollister, that's a good suggestion, and one that I think will work"), and then try to make it happen. Doing this will show that you are receptive to new ideas, are truly working to meet the customer's needs and expectations, and value the customer's opinion. Also, remember that if you can psychologically partner with a customer, he or she is less likely to attack. You do need to make sure that your willingness to assist and comply is not seen as giving in or backing down. If it is, the customer may make additional demands or return in the future with similar demands. To avoid this, you could add to the earlier statement by saying something like, "Mr. Hollister, that's a good suggestion, and although we cannot do this in every instance, I think that your suggestion is one that will work at this time." This puts the customer on alert that although he or she may get his or her way this time, it will not necessarily happen in the future. Another strategy is to make a counteroffer.*

If you are thoroughly familiar with your organization's policies and procedures and your limits of authority, you will be prepared to negotiate with demanding customers. If they want something you cannot provide, you might offer an alternative that will satisfy them. Remember that your goal is customer satisfaction.

Work It Out 9-4. Handling the Demanding Customer

▶ Survey customer service professionals in various professions to see how they handle demanding or domineering customers. Make a list for future reference and role-play a variety of scenarios involving demanding customers with a peer.

Rude or Inconsiderate Customers

Some people seem to go out of their way to be offensive or to get attention. Although they seem confident and self-assured outwardly, they are often insecure and defensive. Some behaviors they might exhibit are raising the voice, demanding to speak to a supervisor, using profanity, cutting in front of someone else in a line, being verbally abrupt (snapping back at you) even though you're trying to assist, calling you by your last name, which they see on your name tag (e.g., "Listen, Smith"), ignoring what you say, or otherwise going out of the way to be offensive or in control. Try the following strategies for dealing with such customers:

- Remain professional. *Just because the customer is exhibiting inappropriate behavior does not justify your reacting in kind. Remain calm, assertive, and in control of the situation. For example, if you are waiting on a customer and a rude person barges in or cuts off your conversation, pause, make direct eye contact, smile, and firmly say, "I'll be with you as soon as I finish with this customer, sir or madam." If he or she insists, repeat your comment and let the person know that the faster you serve the current customer, the faster you can get to the person waiting. Also, maintaining decorum may help win over the person or at least keep him or her in check.*

Before you can deal with a customer's business needs, you must first address the customer's emotional issues and try to calm him or her. What would you do to calm these customers?

- Don't resort to retaliation. *Retaliation will only infuriate this type of customer, especially if you have embarrassed him or her in the presence of others. Remember that such people are still customers, and if they or someone else perceives your actions as inappropriate, you could lose more than just the battle at hand.*

Work It Out 9-5. Responding to Rudeness

Working with a partner, develop a list of rude comments that a customer might make to you (e.g., "If you're not *too* busy, I'd like some assistance") along with responses you might give (e.g., "If you could please wait, I'll be happy to assist you as soon as I finish, sir (or madam). I want to be able to give you my full attention and don't want to be distracted.").

Rude Statements	Responses
_____	_____
_____	_____
_____	_____

Talkative Customers

Some people phone or approach you and then spend excessive amounts of time discussing irrelevant matters such as personal experiences, family, friends, schooling, accomplishments, other customer service situations, and the weather. The following tips might help:

- Remain warm and cordial, but focused. *Recognize that this person's personality style is probably mainly expressive and that his or her natural inclination is to connect with others. You can smile, acknowledge comments, and carry on a brief conversation as you are serving this customer. For example, if the person comments that your last name is spelled exactly like his or her great aunt's and then asks where your family is from, you could respond with "That's interesting. My family is from . . . but I don't believe we have any relatives outside that area." You have responded but possibly cut off the next question. Anything less would probably be viewed as rude by the customer. Anything more could invite additional discussion. Your next statement should then be business-related (e.g., "Is there anything else I can assist you with today?").*

- Ask specific open-ended questions. *These types of questions can assist in determining needs and addressing customer concerns.*
- Use closed-ended questions to control. *Once you have determined the customer's needs, switch to closed-ended questions to better control the situation and limit the opportunity for the customer to continue talking.*
- Manage the conversation. *Keep in mind that if you spend a lot of time with one customer, other customers may be neglected. You can manage a customer encounter through questioning and through statements that let the customer know your objective is to serve customers. You might say, "I know you said you have a lot of shopping to do, so I won't keep you any longer. Thanks for coming in. Please let me know if I can assist in the future." Imply that you are ending the interaction to benefit the* customer.

Work It Out 9-6. Building Your Skills

▶ Go on a field trip to a variety of businesses or stores (possibly a mall). As you visit these establishments, play the role of a customer and engage customer service professionals in lengthy conversation. Take note of the techniques they use to regain control of the conversation. Chances are, most, especially the more inexperienced, will allow you to talk and will respond to you rather than risk being rude. Remember the effective techniques described and jot them down below.

_____

_____

_____

_____

_____

_____

_____

_____

_____

_____

_____

WORKING WITH INTERNAL CUSTOMERS (COWORKERS)

CONCEPT: Relationships with your internal customers are important. You should meet your commitments and build a professional reputation.

As we discussed in earlier chapters, you have to deal with internal as well as external customers. Although your interactions with internal customers may not be difficult, they can often be more sensitive than your dealings with outsiders.

After all, you see peers and coworkers regularly, and because of your job, office politics, and protocol, your interactions with them are ongoing. Therefore, extend all the same courtesies to internal customers that you do to external ones—in some cases, more so. Some suggestions that might help you enhance your interactions with internal customers are given in the following sections.

Stay Connected

Since relationships within the organization are so important, go out of your way to make contact with internal customers periodically. You can do this by dropping by their work area to say hello, sending an e-mail, or leaving a voice mail message. This helps keep the door to communication open so that if service does break down someday, you will have a better chance of hearing about it and solving the problem amiably. You might describe your coworkers as your "normal" internal customers, but do not forget the importance of your relationships with the cleaning crew (they service your office and work area), security force (they protect you, your organization, and your vehicle), and the information technology people (they maintain computer equipment). All these groups and many others within the organization add value and can be a big help to you.

Meet All Commitments

Too often, service providers forget the importance of internal customers. Because of familiarity, they sometimes become lax and tend to not give the attention to internal customers that they would give to external customers. This can be a big mistake. For example, if you depend on someone else to obtain or send products or services to external customers, that relationship is as crucial as the ones you have with external customers. Don't forget that if you depend on internal suppliers for materials, products, or information, these people can negatively affect your ability to serve external customers by delaying or withholding the items you need. Such actions might be unintentional or intentional, depending on your relationship.

To prevent, or at least reduce the possibility of such breakdowns, honor all commitments you make to internal customers. If you promise to do something, do your best to deliver, and in the agreed-upon time. If you can't do something, say so when your customer asks. If something comes up that prevents you from fulfilling your commitment, let the internal customer know of the change in a timely manner.

Remember, it is better to *under* promise and *over* deliver than vice versa. If you beat a deadline, they will probably be pleasantly surprised and appreciative.

Don't Sit on Your Emotions

Some people hold on to anger, frustration, and other negative emotions rather than getting their feelings out into the open and dealing with them. Not only is this potentially damaging to your health, for it might cause stress-related illnesses, but it can also destroy working relationships. Whenever something goes wrong or you are troubled by something, go to the person and, using the feedback skills you learned in Chapter 3, talk about the situation. Failure to do so can result in disgruntled internal customers, damage to the customer-supplier relationship, and damage to your reputation. Don't forget that you will continue to rely on your customer in the future, so you cannot afford a relationship problem.

Build a Professional Reputation

Through your words and actions, go out of your way to let your customer and your boss know that you have a positive, can-do, customer-focused attitude. Let them know that you will do whatever it takes to create an environment in which internal and external customers are important. Also, regularly demonstrate your commitment to *proactive* service. This means gathering information, products, and other tools before coming into contact with a customer so that you are prepared to deal with a variety of situations and people. It also means doing the unexpected for customers and providing service that makes them excited about doing business with you and your organization.

Adopt a Good-Neighbor Policy

Take a proactive approach to building internal relationships so that you can head off negative situations. If your internal customers are in your department, act in a manner that preserves sound working relationships. You can accomplish this in part by avoiding the following negative work habits:

- Avoid gathering of friends and loud conversation in your work space. *This can be especially annoying if the office setup consists of cubicles as sound travels easily. Respect your coworkers' right to work in a professional environment. If you must hold meetings or gatherings, go to the cafeteria or some other place away from the work area.*
- Maintain sound grooming and hygiene habits. *Demonstrate professionalism in your dress and grooming. Avoid excessive amounts of colognes and perfumes.*

- Don't overdo call forwarding. *Sometimes you must be away from your work space. Company policy may require that you forward your calls. Do not overdo forwarding your calls. Your coworkers may be inconvenienced and resentful if you do.*
- Avoid unloading personal problems. *Everyone has personal problems now and then. Do not bring personal problems to the workplace and burden coworkers with them. If you have personal problems and need assistance, go to your supervisor or team leader or human resources department and ask for some suggestions. If you get a reputation for often having personal problems—and bringing them to the workplace—your career could suffer.*
- Avoid office politics and gossip. *Your purpose in the workplace is to serve the customer and do your job. If you have time to spread gossip and network often with others, you should approach your supervisor or team leader about job opportunities in which you can learn new skills. This can increase your effectiveness and marketability in the workplace.*
- Pitch in to help. *If you have spare time and your coworkers need assistance with a project, volunteer to help out. They may do the same at some point in the future when you are feeling overwhelmed with a project or assignment.*
- Be truthful. *One of the fastest ways for you to suffer a damaged relationship, or lose the trust and confidence of your coworkers and customers, is to be caught in a lie. Regard your word as your bond.*

6 THE PROBLEM-SOLVING PROCESS

> **CONCEPT:** To solve a problem, you need to first identify the problem and determine if the problem is one that should be solved. Once you decide to solve the problem, follow the five proven steps to problem solving.

When customers have a complaint or a problem to be solved, they want solutions, not excuses. To ensure that you address customer needs effectively in these situations, you need to be effective at problem solving. Figure 9-5 shows a concise five-step process of problem solving.

Before you begin to solve a customer's problem, consider the fact that he or she may not really want you to "solve the problem." In some cases, a person simply wants to vent frustration or be heard. This is where the empathetic listening you have read about will come in handy. In many cases, your customer will often have a solution in mind when he or she calls or comes in. Your role may be to simply listen and offer to facilitate the implementation of the suggested solution. In some situations, you may have to "plant a seed" by asking an open-ended question that suggests a solution. If the customer picks up on your "seed" and nourishes it, you end up with an outcome for which he or she feels ownership. For example, assume that a customer wants a product that you do not have in stock. Instead of saying, "I'm sorry, that item is out of stock," you could ask a question such as, "How do you think _____ would work as an alternative?" You have now subtly made a suggestion without saying, "You could use ____ instead. It does the same thing."

If you jointly solve a problem, the customer feels ownership—that he or she has made the decision. This customer is likely to be a satisfied customer. The following sections describe some key actions involved in this process.

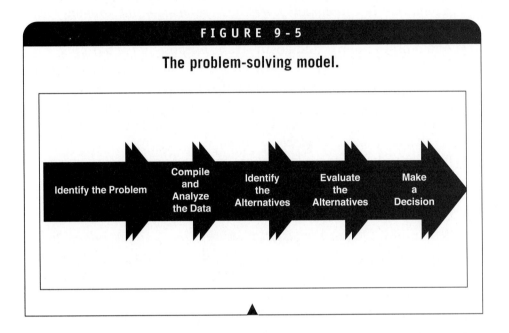

FIGURE 9-5

The problem-solving model.

Identify the Problem → Compile and Analyze the Data → Identify the Alternatives → Evaluate the Alternatives → Make a Decision

Step 1: Identify the Problem

Before you can decide on a course of action, you must first know the nature and scope of the problem you are facing. Often, a customer may not know how to explain his or her problem well, especially if he or she speaks English as a second language or has a communication-related disability. In such cases, it is up to you to do a little detective work and ask questions or review available information.

Begin your journey into problem solving by apologizing for any inconvenience you or your organization has caused. The customer probably wants someone to be responsible. A simple "I'm sorry you were inconvenienced. How may I assist you?" coupled with some of the other techniques covered in this book can go a long way toward mending the relationship. Take responsibility for the problem, even if you didn't actually cause it. Remember that, in the customer's eyes, you represent the organization. Therefore, you are "chosen" to be responsible. Don't point fingers at other employees, policies, or procedures. It is also important to let the customer know that you are sincerely regretful that the problem has occurred and will do whatever possible to quickly and effectively solve it.

To learn as much about the problem as you can, start by speaking directly to the customer, when possible. Collect any documentation or other background information available.

Ask Questions

Ask specific questions so that you can gather the information you need to help identify and solve a customer's problem. The only way to get the information you want is to ask the right questions. You might use a variety of question types. Here are some examples.

- Open-ended. *As discussed in Chapter 5, open-ended questions are good for defining issues, clarifying, gathering information, and getting involvement. When asking open-ended questions, phrase them in a manner that allows the customer to respond as he or she feels necessary. You are not making a decision or forcing a response, as you can do with other types of questions; you are providing a vehicle for sharing information. Help focus the customer's response by asking* specific *open-ended questions. Note the difference between the sample questions that follow.*
  Nonspecific: "How do you like this new product?"
  Specific: "What uses can you see for this new product?"

Although the first question may yield a useful response, you have not asked for a specific, focused piece of information. On the other hand, the second question will get the same bit of information but will also lead the customer to think of specific applications. You have thereby created a need (in the customer's mind) and she or he may now buy your product or service.

- Closed-ended questions. *As you also saw in Chapter 5, closed-ended questions are sometimes valuable for getting a quick response, gaining minimal involvement, controlling the conversation, verifying information, and clarifying or confirming points. For example:*

  Mr. Ho, didn't you say that your son would be the primary user of this product? (yes or no)

  Mrs. Lacata, how many times have you used our services? (a specific number)

  Ms. Hyland, do you prefer the blue or yellow one? (a choice between two items)

An important aspect of asking questions is to find out the customer's true concerns and solve his or her problems. For example, a customer may call and say that he or she wants to return a television set because it doesn't work. By asking questions, you may be able to help the person solve the problem without the added expense of shipping or having a service technician call on the customer. You may ask for background information about the television set and then ask some specific questions about the problem. Questions such as the following might be appropriate:

What model is it?

What, exactly, is wrong?

Does it have an antenna attached?

Is there a remote control?

Have you checked to see that the power cord is firmly attached?

Have you tried using a different electrical outlet?

Have you checked to make sure that the power strip is turned on?

Step 2: Compile and Analyze the Data

To be able to effectively determine a course of action, you need as much information as possible and a thorough understanding of what you are dealing with. To get that data requires active listening and a little investigative work. You may need to collect information from a variety of sources, such as sales receipts, correspondence, the customer, public records, the manufacturer, and files.

In gathering data, you should also do a quick assessment of how serious the problem is. You may hear about one instance of a defective product, or you may hear about a pattern of inefficient service.

Once you have collected information through questioning and from other sources, spend some time reviewing what you have found. If time permits and you think it necessary or helpful (e.g., the customer is not present or on the telephone), ask for the opinions of others (e.g., coworkers, team leader or supervisor, technical experts). Ultimately, what you are trying to do is determine the choices available to you that will help satisfy the customer and solve the problems.

Step 3: Identify Alternatives

Let customers know that you are willing to work with them to find an acceptable solution to the problem. Tell them what you can do, gain their agreement, and then set about taking action.

Since you are new to the situation when a customer notifies you of a problem or their dissatisfaction, you have an objective perspective. Use this perspective as a basis on which to offer suggestions or viewpoints that the customer may not see or has overlooked. Also, make sure that you consider various possibilities and alternatives when thinking about potential solutions. Look out for the best interests of your customer and your organization. To do this, be willing to listen to the customer's suggestions and to think creatively. Perhaps you will come up with ideas other than the ones that you and your organization typically use. Don't sacrifice customer satisfaction for convenience. If necessary, seek approval from higher authority to use creative solutions (e.g., to make a special purchase of an alternative item for the customer, or to give a refund even though the time frame for refunds has expired).

Step 4: Evaluate Alternatives

Once you have collected all the facts, examine your alternatives or options. Be careful not to let cost be the deciding factor. A little extra time and money spent to solve a problem could save a customer and prevent recurring problems. Consider the following factors in this evaluation process:

What is the most efficient way to solve this problem?

Which are the most effective options for solving this problem?

Which options are the most cost-effective?

Will the options being considered solve the problem and satisfy the customer?

Step 5: Make a Decision

Based on the factors in Step 4, and any others you wish to use in your evaluation process, make a decision on what your course of action will be. To do this ask the customer "Which option would you prefer?" This simple question puts the customer into the decision-making position and makes the customer feel empowered. The customer chooses. If the request is reasonable and practical, proceed and solve the problem. If not, negotiate a different alternative.

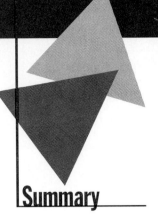

Summary

Chapter Summary

Dealing with various types of people can be frustrating, but it can also be very satisfying. Many times, you will have to deal with a variety of external and internal customers, including those who are angry, indecisive, dissatisfied, demanding, domineering, rude, or talkative. Your goal in all your efforts should be to work harmoniously with all customers. Whenever you can address customer needs in a variety of situations and find acceptable solutions, you, the customer, and the organization win. To assist customers effectively doesn't take magic; all it takes is a positive attitude, preparation, and a sincere desire to help others. If you use the techniques outlined in this chapter, and others in this book, you're on your way to providing stellar customer service and satisfying customer needs.

CHAPTER REVIEW QUESTIONS

1. What are the five levels of needs identified in Maslow's hierarchy of needs, and how do they affect customer service? _____

_____

_____

_____

_____

2. What causes customers to become dissatisfied? _____

_____

_____

_____

_____

3. What tactics can you use to deal with angry customers? _____

_____

_____

_____

_____

4. What can you do to assist indecisive people in coming to a decision?

_____

_____

_____

_____

5. Why might some customers feel they have to demand things from others?_____

_____

_____

_____

6. How can you effectively deal with rude or inconsiderate customers?

_____

_____

_____

_____

7. What are some steps to help regain control of a conversation with a talkative customer without causing offense? _____

_____

_____

_____

_____

8. What strategies can you use to build strong relationships with coworkers? _____

_____

_____

_____

_____

9. List the strategies for effective problem solving. _____

_____

_____

_____

_____

▼ SEARCH IT OUT

Search the Internet for Information on Problem Solving

Log onto the Internet and locate information on providing customer service to irate customers. Also look for information on the following topics:

Conflict resolution

Problem solving

Handling stressful situations

Be prepared to share what you find with your classmates at the next scheduled class.

Role-Playing Difficult Customer Situations

Work with a partner and role-play one or more of the following scenarios. Each of you should choose at least one scenario in which you will play the service provider role. The other person will play the customer. In each instance, discuss what type of difficult customer you are dealing with and how such an encounter might go. At the end of each role-play, both persons should answer the following questions and discuss ideas for improvement:

Questions

1. How well was service provided?

2. Were any negative or unclear messages, verbal or nonverbal, communicated? If so, discuss.

3. How can you incorporate the improvements you have identified into a real customer service encounter?

4. What open-ended questions were used to discover customer needs? What others could have been used?

Scenario 1: Terry Welch entered your shoe store over 30 minutes ago and seems to be having trouble deciding the style and color of shoes he wants.

Scenario 2: Chris Dulaney is back in your lawn mower repair shop. This is the third time in less than two weeks that she has been in for repairs on a riding mower. Chris is getting upset because the problem stems from a defective carburetor that has been repaired on each previous visit. She is beginning to raise her voice, and her frustration is becoming evident.

Scenario 3: You are a telephone service representative for a large retail catalog distribution center. You've been at work for about an hour when you receive a call from Pat Mason, who immediately starts making demands (e.g., "I've only got a few minutes for you to tell me how to order." "Look, I've read all the articles about the scams telemarketers pull. I'll tell you what I want, and you tell me how much it will cost." "Listen, what I want you to do is take my order and get me the products within the next two days. I need them for a conference."

Scenario 4: You are a cashier in the express lane at a supermarket. As you are ringing up a customer's order, a second customer approaches, squeezes past several people in line and says, "I'm in a hurry. All I have is a quart of milk. Can you just tell me how much it costs, and I'll leave the money right here on the register."

Scenario 5: You are a very busy switchboard operator for ComTech, a large corporation. A vendor whom you recognize from previous encounters has just called to speak with your purchasing manager. As in previous calls, the vendor starts a friendly conversation about the weather, how things are going, and other topics not related to business.

FACE TO FACE

Handling a Dissatisfied Customer at Newsome Furniture and Appliances

Background

Newsome Furniture and Appliances is a small family-owned store that has been in operation for 47 years in Billings, Montana. The store employs 16 employees in two locations. Most customers are local residents, but there is a steady flow of customers from nearby smaller towns and cities. Most customers shop at Newsome's store that is located in a large shopping mall outside of Billings.

On an average weekday, Newsome's two stores, combined, get 80 to 150 walk-through customers. On Saturdays several hundred customers patronize the two stores.

Of the frontline employees (sales, customer service, and credit staff), most have been with the company at least five years. No formal classroom training on effective customer service techniques is offered to the staff. However, each employee is encouraged to attend one professional development workshop or community college course each year. Mr. Newsome pays 75 percent of the cost of such courses. You were hired as a customer service assistant eight months ago after you graduated from high school. You report to the customer service supervisor, Ginny Hall. In school, you took a couple of business courses and have read numerous books on sales and customer service. You hope for career advancement in this field.

On Saturday morning Mr. and Mrs. Wyland Sommers came into your store. Both are senior citizens and longtime Billings residents. They have made numerous purchases at Newsome's over the past 18 years.

The Sommers bought a sofa bed last week, and it was delivered on Friday. The sofa had been a floor model, and the price had been reduced by 50 percent. The tag on the sofa said "as is" because there was a large tear in the mattress cover.

Your Role

When Mr. and Mrs. Sommers came into the store, they proceeded directly to the customer service department. As they approached, you smiled, said good morning, and offered to assist them. The following conversation occurred:

Mr. Sommers [without acknowledging your greeting]:	*Where's Ginny?*
You [smiling]:	*Ginny's off today, sir. May I help you?*
Mr. Sommers:	*Where's Tom Newsome?*

You [still smiling]:	He had to go to our other store. Can I help you?
Mrs. Sommers:	We bought a sofa bed here, and when they delivered it, I found a big hole in the mattress. My son and his wife will be here on Wednesday. I can't have them sleep on that old thing. I'd be too embarrassed.
Mr. Sommers:	I can't believe you'd sell something like that to a loyal customer. Do you have any idea how much money we've spent in this store over the past 18 years?
You:	Eighteen years is a long time to shop at a store. We appreciate your business. I'm terribly sorry that the sofa was damaged, I can't believe our warehouse would ship a damaged; piece of furniture.
Mr. Sommers [raising his voice]:	Well they sure did! I just told you they did! Don't you believe me?
You:	I'm sorry sir. I didn't mean that you weren't telling the truth. I meant that I was surprised that we'd do that. Do you have your sales receipt? I'll see if I can't help work this out.
Mrs. Sommers:	We've got to have a sofa by Wednesday. My daughter-in-law comes from a very nice family in Virginia. I'd die if she saw that old thing you sent.
You:	Yes, ma'am. I'm sure we can fix the problem.
Mr. Sommers:	I don't want anything fixed. I want a new sofa before Wednesday. The last time I bought something here, you people messed up the order too. I guess I should have learned my lesson then.
You:	I apologize for any inconvenience we've caused. I can assure you we'll get this worked out. If you'll just give me your receipt, I'll get started.
Mr. Sommers:	I'll have to go see if it's in the pickup. Hold on. Ma, you wait here.
You [Mr. Sommers has returned with the receipt):	I think I understand why your sofa has a damaged mattress. The sofa was a

	floor model discounted 50 percent and sold as is.
Mrs. Sommers [voice raised]:	What do you mean, "as is"? We paid a lot of money for that sofa!
You:	Yes, ma'am, I see you did. What I mean is that because the sofa had some damage, we reduced the price significantly to sell it.
Mr. Sommers:	Well, nobody told us the thing was damaged. I want to talk to Tom right now. You call him at the other store!
You:	I think I have an idea. We have another sofa exactly like yours that is on sale. Since you saved 50 percent off your sofa, if we could exchange mattresses for say, 50 extra dollars, you'd still be saving hundreds off the original price. You could have the mattress by Monday, and your daughter-in-law would never know. What do you think?
Mr. Sommers:	Well, I don't know. I didn't want to spend any more money.
Mrs. Sommers:	Lou, that young salesman did say that we were getting a really special price because of some minor damage.
Mr. Sommers:	Yeah, I guess maybe he might have mentioned the damage. We just didn't know the hole would be as big as it is.
You:	I am truly sorry for any misunderstanding, and I wouldn't want Mrs. Sommers to be embarrassed. That's why I suggested the exchange. What do you think, folks?
Mr. Sommers:	Okay. But you better have it there by Monday at the latest.
You [smiling]:	Yes, sir. You'll have it by 3 p.m., or I'll deliver it myself.
Mr. Sommers [smiling]:	Thanks, kid.

Questions

1. What were the needs of these customers?
2. What considerations about the customers did you have to take into account during this exchange?
3. What worked well here?

FROM THE FRONTLINE
Interview

Sandy Carson
Trainer/CMS
Performance
Development Team
FirstUSA Bank
Orlando, Florida

1. In one or two paragraphs, please describe your experience in dealing with external and internal customers.

Prior to my call center experience, I spent eight years in retail service. For six years, I checked telephone orders and shipping dates, and dealt with account questions from customers. I was employed by a small tool company, and the challenges were limited. I did learn how to determine customer needs, and I developed strategies to use when dealing with customers face-to-face. This interaction was more personal. I could see the smile, or know immediately whether the service we were providing was not enough. I could make customers happy by offering options. I enjoyed the creative aspect of customer service, and I especially enjoyed the people.

When I started working in the training department for a call center more than $2^1/_2$ years ago, the challenges increased. My "customer" was the customer service provider I was training. It was not enough to give information and teach or reinforce technical skills; I also had to infuse a strong desire in each person to want to help the customer. Just as each customer who calls us for service is an individual, so is each person we train to do the job. This industry provides tremendous challenges, but it also provides tremendous satisfaction when we are able to see the results.

2. What are your general impressions of customer service in the United States? Why do you feel this way?

My general impression is that, because of the growing number of people we serve, and the desire of each customer to be served efficiently and quickly, the customer service industry, specifically the call center industry, is facing a huge challenge. Voice response units can service simple calls in the call center. However, some customers have questions or problems that must be handled by an experienced representative, and some customers simply can't tolerate the impersonal service of an automated system.

Our biggest challenge is that, although we may feel overwhelmed by the sheer volume of customers, we must remember that each customer is an individual with individual needs and concerns. We *must* give each customer the same personalized service that we would expect ourselves.

3. **In your experience working with internal and external customers, what are some of the most helpful things to remember related to avoiding or reducing negative encounters?**

Of all the skills for dealing with customers, in my opinion the most important is listening. Our business lives are hectic, and we tend to rush through interactions with others. Stop and listen. This sounds much simpler than it really is because most of us are already thinking ahead, or we are on the way to another meeting. Take a breath and listen. You will save time and energy in the long run. You miss subtle things when you don't listen. Also people believe that you don't care about what they are saying.

We are taught to listen and acknowledge the external customer, but sometimes we forget those lessons when we deal with our internal customers. Our colleagues are our customers, too. We support each other, and we all need to share crucial information and have the respect for each other that listening involves.

4. **What are some pitfalls that service providers should avoid when dealing with customers in order to reduce problem encounters?**

Again, not listening to the customer. Our call center representatives are well trained in the problems that can arise with an account. Although most problems can be diagnosed and addressed quickly, often the challenge is to allow the customer to finish voicing his or her concerns or frustrations, before interjecting an explanation or answer. We must take the time to respect the customer's point of view, listen carefully, acknowledge his or her feelings, and then respond with an appropriate business solution.

5. How does the way you and other employees deliver service affect your organization and your customers?

Every time a customer talks to one of our call center representatives, that representative is our company. A customer may have called many times before and received excellent customer service, but if one call makes him or her feel unappreciated or not respected in any way, every positive interaction that has happened in the past can be negated. A representative who takes 80 to 100 calls a day must remember that to the customer on the telephone, this is the *only* call of the day—and that this call will determine that customer's opinion of our company in the future.

6. What advice, related to customer service, would you give someone entering the customer service profession?

A call center involves a unique set of challenges. When a customer reaches us, we are a voice at the other end of the telephone line. We don't have the advantage of speaking face-to-face with our customer. To anyone entering the call center service profession, or indeed any line of customer service, I would say that you must have a sincere respect for other people. We can train people about the product and the systems. We can teach the *technical*. The *caring* has to be there already.

CRITICAL THINKING

Why is it important to provide internal customers with patient and efficient service? How do you think customer service providers should treat external and internal customers?

Chapter 10

Customer Service in a Diverse World

OBJECTIVES

After completing this chapter, you will be able to:

- *Recognize that differences are not bad.*

- *Develop a sensitivity to the fact that we are all unique.*

- *Understand the need to treat customers as individuals.*

- *Determine actions for dealing with various types of people.*

- *Identify a variety of factors that make people diverse and that help better serve them.*

- *Comply with legal requirements in assisting customers with disabilities.*

- *Serve all customer groups effectively.*

"Generally, until human beings have the opportunity to learn otherwise, they assume that other people look at the world just as they do, everyone has similar values, and everyone is motivated for the same reasons."

Sally J. Walton
Cultural Diversity in the Workplace

Before reviewing the chapter content, respond to the following questions by placing a "T" for true or "F" for false on the rules. Use any questions you miss as a checklist of material to which you will pay particular attention as you read through the chapter. For those you get right, congratulate yourself, but review the sections they address in order to learn additional details about the topic.

_____ 1. Diversity is an important aspect of everyone's life that presents many negative challenges.

_____ 2. Many people associate the term *diversity* with the word *cultural*, which describes the differences between groups of people from various countries and with differing beliefs.

_____ 3. The diverse nature of your customer population requires you to be aware of the various ways people from different cultures interact in the business setting.

_____ 4. Values are the "rules" that people use to evaluate situations, make decisions, interact with others, and deal with conflict.

_____ 5. In some cultures, direct eye contact is often discouraged, for it suggests disrespect.

_____ 6. Today, many cultures use less formality in the business environment and do not stress the importance of using titles and family names as often as they did in the past.

_____ 7. When encountering someone who speaks English as a second language, you should avoid jokes, words, or acronyms that are uniquely American or tied to sports, historical events, or specific aspects of American culture.

_____ 8. In serving customers from other cultures, it is important to avoid the use of the word *no* because this word may cause the customer to become embarrassed or experience a "loss of face."

_____ 9. According to the U.S. Census Bureau, approximately 54 million Americans have some level of disability.

_____ 10. When a customer has a disability, the disability should be de-emphasized by thinking of the person first and the disability second.

_____ 11. When dealing with an elderly customer, you should always be respectful.

_____ 12. Young customers are as valuable as those in any other group and should be professionally served.

4. T   8. T   12. T
3. T   7. T   11. T
2. T   6. F   10. T
1. F   5. T   9. T

1 | THE IMPACT OF DIVERSITY

CONCEPT: Diversity is an important aspect of everyone's life. Encounters with others gives us an opportunity to expand our knowledge of others.

As the world grows smaller economically or otherwise (e.g., world trade, international travel, and technologically transmitted information exchange), the likelihood that you will have contact on the job with people from other cultures, or who are different from you, increases. This likelihood also carries over into your personal life. Diversity is encountered everywhere (supermarkets, churches, public transportation) and so is an important aspect of everyone's life. Although it presents challenges in making us think of differences and similarities, it also enriches our lives—each encounter we have with another person gives us an opportunity to expand our knowledge of others while growing personally.

WORKSHEET 10-1

Encountering Diversity

Take a few minutes to think about diversity and what it means to you. Write your own definition of diversity here:

_____

_____

_____

_____

During the past week, in what situations have you encountered someone from a different culture (someone whose values or beliefs differed from yours or who looked or dressed differently from you or your group)? List the diversity and the situations encountered here:

Diversity	Situation(s)

Worksheet ▼
10-1

---

2 | DEFINING DIVERSITY

CONCEPT: Diversity is not a simple matter; it is not difficult to deal with if you are fair to people and keep an open mind.

The word *diversity* encompasses a broad range of differences. Many people associate the term *diversity* with the word *cultural*, which has to do with the differences between groups of people depending on their country of origin and their beliefs. They fail to recognize that diversity is not just cultural. Certainly, diversity occurs within each cultural group; however, many other characteristics are involved. For example, within a group of Japanese people are subgroups such as males, females, children, the elderly, athletes, thin people, gay or lesbian people, Buddhists, Christians, married people, and unmarried people, to mention just a few of the possible characteristics, beliefs, and values.

Diversity is not a simple matter, yet it is not difficult to deal with, if you are fair to people and keep an open mind. In fact, when you look more closely at, and think about, diversity, it provides wonderful opportunities because people from varying groups bring with them special knowledge and value. This is because even though people have differences, they have many traits in common. Their similarities form a solid basis for successful interpersonal relationships if you are knowledgeable and think of people as unique individuals. If you cannot think of the person instead of the group, you may stereotype people—lump them together and treat them all the same. This is a recipe for interpersonal disaster.

The basic customer service techniques related to communication found in this book can be applied to many situations in which you encounter customers from various groups. Coupled with specific strategies for adapting to special customer needs, these techniques provide the tools you need to provide excellent customer service.

Some factors that make people different are innate, such as height, weight, hair color, gender, skin color, physical and mental condition, and sibling birth order. All these factors contribute to our uniqueness and help or inhibit us throughout our lives depending on the perceptions we and others have. Other factors that make us unique are learned or gained, for example, religion, **values**, **beliefs**, economic level, lifestyle choices, profession, marital status, education, and political affiliation. These factors are also used to assign people to categories. Caution must be used when considering any of these characteristics since grouping people can lead to stereotyping and possibly discrimination.

The bottom line is that all of these factors affect each customer encounter. Your awareness of differences and of your own preferences are crucial in determining the success you will have in each instance.

3 | CUSTOMER AWARENESS

> **CONCEPT:** Applying Western practices to a situation involving someone from another culture can result in frustration, anger, poor service, and lost business.

Aren't all customers alike? Emphatically, no! No two people are alike, no two generations are alike, and no two cultures are alike. In addition, as we discussed in Chapter 9, each customer has needs based on his or her own perceptions and situation.

In our highly mobile, technologically connected world, it is not unusual to encounter a wide variety of people with differing backgrounds, experiences, religions, modes of dress, values, and beliefs within the course of a single day. All these factors affect customer needs and create situations in which you must be alert to the verbal and nonverbal messages that indicate those needs. Moreover, the diverse nature of your customer population requires you to be aware of the various ways people from different cultures interact in the business setting. Applying Western practices to a situation involving someone from another culture can result in frustration, anger, poor service, and lost business.

Recognizing Your Unique Qualities

To help in relating to others, take a few minutes to discover or acknowledge things about yourself. How do you describe "you"?

Height (tall, short, average) _____

Weight (thin, stocky, overweight, underweight) _____

Age (old, young, middle age) _____

Place of birth _____

National and/or cultural origin of your ancestors _____

Gender _____

Color of skin (white, black, olive) _____

Sibling birth order (oldest, youngest, middle, only child) _____

Favorite type of pet (cat, dog, bird)_____

Religious affinity (Catholic, Protestant, atheist)_____

Values (what's important to you) _____

Lifestyle (eclectic, modest, extravagant) _____

Beliefs (what you trust or hold as true) _____

Economic status (affluent, middle-class, poor) _____

Profession (salesperson, mechanic, nurse) _____

Political affiliation (Republican, Democrat, Liberal)_____

Education (high school, college, trade school) _____

Marital status (single, married, divorced, separated)_____

Number of children _____

Review your answers. Could any of them create barriers to quality customer service? Which ones? _____

_____

---

4 THE IMPACT OF CULTURAL VALUES

▶ **CONCEPT:** Values often dictate which behaviors and practices are acceptable or unacceptable. These values may or may not have a direct bearing on serving the customer.

Although many cultures have similar values and beliefs, specific cultural values are often taught to members of particular groups starting at a very young age. This does not mean that a particular group's values and beliefs are better or worse than those of any other culture; they are simply important to that particular group. These values often dictate which behaviors and practices are acceptable or unacceptable. These values may or may not have a direct bearing on serving the customer, but they can have a very powerful influence on what the customer wants, needs, thinks

The mobility of modern-day society may put you in regular contact with customers from a variety of cultures. The more informed you are about similarities and differences, the greater the likelihood that you will provide quality service. How should you provide customer service to someone from another culture?

is important, and is willing to seek or accept. Being conscious of differences can lead to a better understanding of customers and potentially reduce conflict or misunderstandings in dealing with them.

Many service providers take values for granted. This is a mistake. Values are the "rules" that people use to evaluate issues or situations, make decisions, interact with others, and deal with conflict. As a whole, a person's value system often guides thinking and helps him or her determine right from wrong or good from bad. From a customer service perspective, values often strongly drive customer needs and influence the buying decision. Values also differ from one culture to another based on its views on ethics, morals, religion, and many other factors. For example, if customers perceive clothing as too sexy or too conservative, they may not purchase the items, depending on what need they are trying to meet. Or, they may not buy a house because it's in the "wrong" neighborhood.

Values are based on the deeply held beliefs of a culture or subculture. These beliefs might be founded in religion, politics, or group mores. They drive thinking and actions and are so powerful that they have served as the basis for arguments, conflicts, and even wars.

To be effective in dealing with others, service providers should not ignore the power of values and beliefs, nor should they think that their value system is better than that of someone else's. The key to success is to be open-minded and accept that someone else has a different belief system that determines his or her needs. With this in mind, you as a service provider should strive to use all the positive communication and needs identification you have read about thus far in order to satisfy the customer.

Cultural values can be openly expressed or subtly demonstrated through behavior. They can affect your interactions with your customers in a variety of ways. Figure 10-1 shows the results of one study that compared the top five personal values of Asian respondents to those of their American counterparts. In the next few pages, consider the connection of values with behavior, and how you can adjust your customer service to ensure a satisfactory experience for diverse customers.

The goal is to provide service to the customer. In order to achieve success in accomplishing this goal, service providers must be sensitive to, tolerant of, and empathetic toward customers. You do not need to adopt the beliefs of others, but you should adapt to them to the extent that you provide the best service possible to all of your customers.

FIGURE 10-1

Top five Asian and American personal values.

A survey of 101 Asians from eight countries and 28 Americans from U.S. foreign affairs offices in Washington and East Asia revealed the differences in values shown here, ranked from top to bottom.

Asian	American
Hard work	Self-reliance
Respect for learning	Hard work
Honesty	Achieving success in life
Self-discipline	Personal achievement
Self-reliance	Helping others

(Source: Hitchcock, pp. 21-22.)

Modesty

Modesty is exhibited in many ways. In some cultures (e.g., Muslim) conservative dress by women is one manifestation of modesty. For example, in many Arab cultures women demonstrate modesty and a dedication to traditional beliefs by wearing a veil. Such practices are tied to religious and cultural beliefs that originated hundreds of years ago. In other cultures, nonverbal communication cues send messages. For example, direct eye contact is viewed as an effective communication approach in the many Western cultures, and lack of eye contact could suggest dishonesty or lack of confidence to a Westerner. In some cultures (India and Japan), direct eye contact is often discouraged, in particular between men and women and between people who are of different social or business status, for it is considered disrespectful. Often a sense of modesty is instilled into people at an early age (more so in females). Modesty may be demonstrated by covering the mouth or part of the face with an open hand, or through avoiding direct eye contact in certain situations.

Impact on Service

When encountering such behavior, evaluate the situation for the true message being delivered. The person may really be exhibiting suspicious behavior. However, instead of assuming that the customer is being evasive or dishonest, consider the possible impact of culture. Don't force the issue or draw undue attention to a customer's nonverbal behavior, cultural dress, or beliefs being demonstrated. Instead, continue to verbally probe for customer needs and address them. In addition, provide the same quality of friendly service as you would to others who display behavior or cultural characteristics that differ from your own.

Expectations of Privacy

Based on your personality and prior life experiences, you may be more or less likely to disclose personal information, especially to people you do not know well. You should be aware that disclosing personal information about oneself is often a cultural factor. According to research, people who are British, German, Australian, Korean, or Japanese display a tendency to disclose less about themselves than Americans do.[1]

Impact on Service

If you tend to be gregarious and speak freely about virtually any topic, you should curtail this tendency in the customer service environment. Failure to do so could make your customer feel uneasy and uncomfortable. This is true in part because, in Western cultures, when someone asks a question or shares information, there is an expectation that the other party will reciprocate. Reluctance to do so is sometimes perceived as being unfriendly or even rude. A good rule of thumb is to stay focused on the business of serving your customer in an expeditious and professional manner. Keeping your conversations centered on satisfying the customers' needs can accomplish this.

Forms of Address

Although Americans often pride themselves on their informality, people from other countries see informality as rudeness, arrogance, or over-familiarity. Many cultures stress formality in the business environment and place importance on the use of titles and family names when addressing others (e.g., Argentina, European countries, China).

To further confuse the issue of how to address a customer, some cultures have differing rules on how family names are listed and used. For example, in China, each person is given a family name, a generational name (for the period during which they are born), and a personal name at birth. The generational and personal names might be separated by a hyphen or space (a female might be named Li Teng Jiang or Li Teng-Jiang). Women typically do not take their husband's surnames. When addressing someone from the Chinese culture, use an appropriate title such as *Mr.* or *Mrs.* followed by their family name (Mrs. Li) unless you are asked to use a different form of address. Many people adopt a Western first name when they immigrate to the United States (Amanda or Richard). In Argentina

---

[1] Dodd, pp. 243–244.

(and most Hispanic cultures), people have two surnames: one from their father (listed first) and one from their mother (Jose Ricardo Gutierrez Martinez). Usually, when addressing the person, use a title only with the father's surname (Mr. or Mrs. Gutierrez).[2]

Impact on Service

A customer's preference for a particular name or form of address has an impact upon your ability to effectively deal with him or her. If you start a conversation with someone and immediately alienate the person by incorrectly using his or her name, you may not be able to recover. Moreover, informality or improper use of family names could send a message of lack of knowledge or concern for the customer as an individual or as being important to you.

Respect for Elders

In most cultures, some level of respect is paid to older people. Often this respect is focused more on males (when older men are viewed as superior, as among Chinese).[3] This arises from a belief that, with age, come knowledge, authority, and higher status. Thus, respect for or deference to elders is normal. Also, in many cultures age brings with it unique privileges and rights (such as the right to rule or to be the leader). This is true in many Native American cultures.[4]

Impact on Service

You must be careful to pay appropriate respect when speaking to older customers. Further, you should be sensitive to the fact that if the customer demands to speak to a senior person or to the manager or owner, he or she may be simply exhibiting a customary expectation for his or her culture or generation.

If you can assist without creating conflict, do so; if not, honor the request when possible.

Importance of Relationships

In many Asian, Latin American, and Middle Eastern cultures, the building of a strong interpersonal relationship is extremely important before business is conducted. For example, in Malaysia, Indonesia, Myanmar, Korea, and Japan it is not unusual to have a number of meetings with people in an organization before coming to an agreement. Lunch, dinner, and office meetings often occur for weeks before an agreement is reached. Also, unless you reach the right level of management in the organization for these meetings, all your efforts may be wasted.

---

[2] Morrison, Conway, and Borden, pp. 5, 61.

[3] Chen and Starosta, p 47.

[4] Locke, p 67.

Impact on Service

Failure to establish support or an environment of trust could lead to a breakdown in service and/or lost customers. This does not mean that you should assume a quicker familiarity with customers from such cultures. This could also alienate them. Instead, when you will be having ongoing contact or be doing repeat business, follow the customers' lead. Get to know them and share information about your organization and yourself that can lead to mutual respect and trust. You may find that you have to take time at the beginning of each encounter with your established customer to reestablish the relationship. This may involve spending time in conversations related to nonbusiness topics (sports, hobbies, pets, or other topics in which the customer is interested).

Relationship building may also involve presenting gifts to persuade various people in the organization that you are a friend and have their interests at heart. Only then can you proceed to determine need(s) and provide service.

Gender Roles

Culturally, and individually, people view the role of men and women differently. And, although the roles of men and women are continually evolving throughout the world, decision making and authority are often clearly established as male prerogatives within a culture, subculture, or family.[5] For example, in many Middle Eastern, Asian, South American, and European countries, women have not gained the respect or credibility in the business environment that they have achieved in many parts of North America. In some countries it is not unusual for women to be expected to take a "be seen and not heard" role or to remain out of business transactions. In Korea and other Pacific Rim countries, it is rare for women to participate in business. Men still have higher social status than females. Among many Israelis, men are prohibited from touching a woman in the business environment. Thus Israeli women cannot shake hands and exchange business cards in the Western fashion. To exchange a business card, they often must place the card on a table so that a man can pick it up.[6]

You don't have to agree with this behavior, but you will need to take it into consideration when facing it in customer encounters. People leave a country, but they take their culture with them. Failure to consider alternative ways of dealing with people in certain instances might cause you to react negatively to a situation and nonverbally communicate your bias.

Impact on Service

If you are a female dealing with a male whose cultural background is like one of the ones just described, he may reject your assistance and ask for a male service provider. If you are a male dealing with a male and female from such a culture, don't be surprised if your conversation involves only

---

[5] Dodd, p. 43.

[6] Samovar, Porter, and Stefani, p. 191.

the male. Attempts to draw a woman into such a transaction may embarrass, offend, or even anger customers and their family members.

Attitude Toward Conflict

Conflict is possible when two people come together in a customer environment, but it does not have to happen. By recognizing your biases and preferences, and being familiar with those of people from other cultures, you can reduce the potential for disagreement. Certainly, there will be times when a customer initiates conflict. In this case all you can do is to use the positive communication techniques described throughout this book.

Many times, the way we deal with conflict is rooted in our culture or subculture and is based on our behavioral style preference (discussed in Chapter 6). Some cultures are individualistic (emphasis is placed on individuals' goals, as in Western countries), and some are collective (individuals are viewed as part of a group, as in Japan or in Native American cultures). See Figure 10-2. Members of individualistic cultures are likely to take a direct approach to conflict, whereas people whose culture is collective may address conflict indirectly, using an informal mediator in an effort to prevent loss of face or embarrassment for those involved. Even within subcultures of a society, there are differing styles of communication and dealing with conflict.[7] For example, cross-cultural studies have shown that many African Americans prefer a controlling (argumentative) **conflict resolution style**, but Americans of European ancestry prefer a solution-oriented (discussion) approach. Of course, regardless of culture or group, people choose different forms of conflict resolution on the basis of personality style preferences (see Chapter 6).

FIGURE 10-2

Ranking of 40 countries on individualism and collectivism.

Country	Ranking*	Country	Ranking*
Argentina	23	Japan	22
Australia	2	Mexico	29
Austria	18	Netherlands	5
Belgium	8	New Zealand	6
Brazil	25	Norway	13
Canada	4	Pakistan	38
Chile	3	Peru	37
Colombia	39	Philippines	28
Denmark	9	Portugal	30
Finland	17	Singapore	34
France	11	South Africa	16
Germany	15	Spain	20

---

[7] Gudykunst, pp. 246–268.

FIGURE 10-2 (Continued)

Country	Ranking*	Country	Ranking*
Great Britain	3	Sweden	10
Greece	27	Switzerland	14
Hong Kong	32	Taiwan	36
India	21	Thailand	35
Iran	24	Turkey	26
Ireland	12	U.S.A.	1
Israel	19	Venezuela	40
Italy	7	Yugoslavia	31

*A high score means the country can be classified as collective; a lower score is associated with cultures that promote individualism.

(Source: Hofstede, G., *Cultures and Organizations: Software of the Mind*, p. 53. Reproduced with permission.)

Impact on Service

Depending on the individuals you encounter and their cultural background, you and your customers may deal differently with conflict. If you use the wrong strategy, emotions could escalate and customer dissatisfaction could follow. The key is to listen and remain calm, especially if the customer becomes agitated.

The Concept of Time

Americans are typically very time-conscious. You often hear such phrases as "Time is money," "Faster than a New York minute," and "Time is of the essence." In Germany, punctuality is almost a religion, and being late is viewed as very unprofessional and rude. In most business settings in the United States, anyone over 5 minutes late for a meeting is often chastised. In many colleges and universities, etiquette dictates that students wait no longer than 15 to 20 minutes when an instructor (depending on whether he or she is a full or associate professor) is late. Americans tend to expect people from other cultures to be as time-conscious as they are. This is not the case, however. For example it is not unusual for people from Arab countries to be a half hour or more late for an appointment or for a person from Hispanic and some Asian cultures to be an hour late. A phrase used by some Asian Indians sums up the concept and justifies the lateness: "Indian standard time." Such tardiness is not viewed as disrespect for the time of others or rudeness; it is simply indicative of a cultural value or way of life. In fact, in some Latin American countries, one is expected to arrive late for an appointment as a show of respect.[8]

Impact on Service

In Western cultures you are expected to be punctual. This is a crucial factor in delivering effective service. Although others may not have the same beliefs and may be late for meetings, you must observe time rules in order to project an appropriate image and to satisfy the needs of your customers and organization.

---

[8] Samovar, Porter, and Stefani, p. 167.

Ownership of Property

In many cultures (e.g., Buddhist, certain African tribes, and the Chickasaw Indian nation) accumulation of worldly goods or wealth is frowned upon. In the case of the Chickasaw Indians, such things as the earth, nature, natural resources, possessions, and individual skills are shared among the tribal group. They are not to be owned or kept from others, for the Creator gave them.[9] Many devout Buddhists believe that giving away personal belongings to others can help them reach a higher spiritual state. Thus the amassing of material things is not at all important to them.

Impact on Service

People have differing levels of needs. Ask customers what their needs are and listen to their responses. Don't persist in upgrading a customer's request to a higher level or more expensive product if he or she declines your suggestion. You may offend and lose a customer. Of course, if you are in sales, you must make a judgment on whether an objection is one that you should attempt to overcome or whether it is culturally based and means no.

WORKSHEET 10-3

Identifying Your Biases

Worksheet ▼
10-3

We sometimes have biases that interfere with our interactions with others. Typically, these biases are based on learned behavior (something we have personally experienced or have been taught by others). By thinking of your biases and bringing them to a conscious level, you can better control or eliminate them in dealing with your customers and others.

Think about the qualities of other people that you do not like or prefer to avoid. List them, along with the basis (why you believe them to be true) for each.

Bias	Basis
_____	_____
_____	_____
_____	_____
_____	_____
_____	_____
_____	_____
_____	_____
_____	_____
_____	_____
_____	_____
_____	_____

---

[9] Chickasaw Nation home page.

PROVIDING QUALITY SERVICE TO DIVERSE CUSTOMER GROUPS

▶ **CONCEPT:** As a service provider, you should become proficient in working with customers with language differences and disabilities; you also need to work with young and elderly customers.

Given the potential diversity of your customer base, it may be impossible to establish a service strategy for each group. However, you should think of what you might do to address the needs of some of the larger categories of customer with whom you will probably come into contact. The next few sections provide some strategies for dealing effectively with people from four diverse groups: customers with language differences, customers with disabilities, elderly customers, and young customers.

Customers With Language Differences

According to U.S. Census Bureau figures, about 26 million foreign-born people live in the United States (9.7 percent of the population). Figure 10-3 gives an idea of how these numbers break down by country of origin. The key to effectively serving people from different cultures is flexibility. Since you are likely to encounter customers from virtually any country in the world, you need to be prepared. You need to have a way to use alternative methods or strategies for providing service. For example, you might identify people in your organization who speak languages other than English so that you can call upon them, if necessary. Or, you can do research on the Internet and at the library to learn about different cultures or countries. You might subscribe to publications that focus on cultural

---

FIGURE 10-3

Foreign-born population of the United States.

Based on census figures, the foreign-born population of the United States continues to grow.

Country of Birth	Number of Births
Europe	4,297,000
Asia	6,822,000
Africa	558,000
Oceania	176,000
Latin America	
Caribbean	2,777,000
Central America	8,769,000
South America	1,530,000
North America	550,000
Total	**25,479,000**

(Source: U.S. Bureau of the Census, March 1997 Current Population Survey (extracted from Table 1-1: Nativity, Place of Birth of the Native Population, and Region of Birth of the Foreign-Born Population.)

issues and a variety of countries, such as *National Geographic*.[10] If a customer speaks a little English or has a heavy accent, try the strategies described in the following sections.

Let Your Customer Guide the Conversation

When possible, let your customer take the lead in guiding the interaction. Some customers may want to spend time getting to know you, others may take a rigid or formal approach and get right down to business by taking the lead, and still others may choose to have someone else act as a mediator or an intermediary. Learn to recognize the cues and follow along when you can.

Be Flexible

Communicating with people from other cultures who do not speak English fluently can be frustrating and complicated. Even if you do not understand their culture or language, using the positive listening, non-verbal, and verbal techniques you read about in Chapters 3 to 5 can help. If you are having difficulties, try some of the specific ideas included in this section of the book. Part of being flexible is recognizing that your views are not the way of the world. Making the mistake of believing that everyone has the same experiences and sees things the way you do can lead to communication and relationship breakdown. It is probably wise to assume that people from other cultures with whom you come into contact do not have the same knowledge and experience that you have. You can then proceed to share information with each other openly and freely. Listen for points of agreement or commonality.

Listen Patiently

You may be frustrated, but so is the other person. Focus on what he or she is saying and try to understand the meaning of the message.

Speak Clearly and Slowly

Most adults in the United States speak at a rate of about 125 to 150 words a minute. Speak at a rate slow enough that allows understanding without being insulting.

Speak at a Normal Volume and Tone

Yelling or changing tone does nothing to enhance understanding. A customer who is unable to speak English is not deaf. You may naturally raise your voice if a customer cannot speak English, but if you do, the customer may become offended or think that you are hard of hearing and raise his or her voice also. This is not an effective way to communicate or provide effective customer service.

Use Open-Ended Questions

Open-ended questions encourage customers to share information. On the other hand, closed-ended questions do not allow you to accurately gauge a customer's viewpoint or understanding. Either because of embarrassment

---

[10] National Geographic

or to avoid saying no, some customers from other cultures may not admit that they do not agree, have an answer, or want to do something if you used a closed-ended question. This reluctance can lead to misunderstandings and possibly resentment if you do not recognize a customer's nonverbal signals.

Pause Frequently

Pausing allows your customer to translate what you have said into her or his language, comprehend, and then respond in English or ask questions.

Use Standard English

Avoid technical terms, contractions (e.g., *don't, can't*), slang (e.g., *like, you know, whoopee, rubberneck*), or broken English (e.g., sentences that fail to follow standard rules of grammar or syntax). Some people, when encountering non-English-speaking customers, revert to an insulting singsong, almost childish, form of English. This does nothing to aid communication, for it is offensive and any English the customer understands gets lost in translation. Remember, some people understand English though they may not be able to speak it well. Also, some people do not speak English because they are self-conscious about their ability or choose not to. Many cultures value and use silence as an important aspect to communication, something that people of Western cultures find difficult to understand. Westerners often believe that silence means that a person does not understand.

A scene in the movie *Rush Hour*, with Chris Tucker and Jackie Chan, was a perfect example of how some people make assumptions about people from other cultures and end up communicating ineffectively. Tucker (playing a Los Angeles police officer) is sent to the airport to pick up a Chinese police officer. Tucker immediately makes assumptions about Chan's ability to communicate in English:

> Tucker [upon meeting Chan]: "Please tell me you speak English."
>
> Chan [gives no response; just looks at a Chinese airline pilot standing next to him].
>
> Tucker [raises his voice]: "I'm Detective Carter. You speaka any English?"
>
> Chan [again looks at others and says nothing]
>
> Tucker [in a loud, exaggerated voice and gesturing toward his mouth]: "Do you understand the words coming out of my mouth?"
>
> Chan [smiles and says nothing]
>
> Later in the movie, as the two are riding in Tucker's car, Chan finally speaks in English.
>
> Tucker: "All of a sudden, you're speaking English now."
>
> Chan: "A little."
>
> Tucker: "You lied to me."
>
> Chan: "I didn't say I didn't speak English. You assumed I didn't. Not being able to speak is not the same as not speaking."

Avoid "Americanized" References

To reduce the risk of misunderstandings by people who speak English as a second language, stick with basic verbiage. Avoid jokes, words, or acronyms that are uniquely American or tied to sports, historical events, or American culture. For example, avoid these types of statements: "I'll need your John Hancock on this form," "If plan A fails, we'll drop back and punt," or "We scored a base hit with that proposal yesterday." These phrases might be understood by someone acculturated to American society but will likely make no sense to others.

Be Conscious of Nonverbal Cues

Continually monitor nonverbal reactions as you converse with a customer. If you sense confusion or lack of comprehension, stop and try to reestablish a bond. Also, be aware of the cues you send and make sure that they are in line with your verbal message.

Paraphrase the Customer's Message

After focusing on what you think is the customer's message, you may convey your understanding to the customer in your own words. When you think that you don't understand, either paraphrase the part of the customer's message up to the point at which you did understand or ask clarifying questions. For example, "Mr. Rasheed, I understand your complaint, but I'm not sure I understand what you expect us to do. How can I help make this better for you?"

WORKSHEET 10-4

Identifying Problem Language

Working with several other people, list Americanized sayings that you have heard or used and that might be a barrier to effective communication with someone who is not fluent in English.

_____

_____

_____

_____

_____

_____

Try Writing Your Message

Some people understand written English better than they speak it. If a customer seems to be having trouble understanding what you are saying, try printing your message (legibly) to see if they can understand your meaning. You might even try using recognizable symbols, if appropriate (e.g., a stop sign when you are giving directions or a picture of an object if you are describing something).

Try Another Language

If you speak a second language, try using it. Your non-English-speaking customers may understand. At the very least, they will appreciate your efforts to communicate with them.

Avoid Humor and Sarcasm

Humor and sarcasm do not work well with customers whose first language is not English. They could lead to customer confusion and embarrassment. Differing cultural values and beliefs result in different points of view about what is socially acceptable. Also, jokes and other types of humor are typically based on incidents or people connected to a specific culture. They do not "travel well" and may not be understood by someone not of that culture.

Avoid Saying No

Americans are very direct. They often use an abrupt *no* in response to a request they cannot fulfill. This behavior is viewed as rude, arrogant, and closed-minded in many cultures. Some countries do not even have a word in their language for *no* (e.g., Burmese). In many cases (e.g., parts of Asia) the response *no* in a conversation may cause a person embarrassment or loss of face (the esteem of others). Many people try to avoid such embarrassment at all costs. In some instances, people from certain parts of Asia may say yes to your proposal and then not follow through on your suggestion rather than tell you no. Such behavior is acceptable in some cultures.

If you are dealing with customers who might react to your saying no in these ways—and you must decline—smile, apologize, and then try something like, "I am not sure we can do this" or "That will be difficult to do." Then, offer an alternative.

Avoid Criticism

If a customer makes a mistake (e.g., improperly fills out a form or uses the wrong word), do not point out the mistake. Instead, take responsibility for correcting the error or clearing up the misunderstanding (e.g., "I am sorry that these forms are so confusing. I have trouble with them too)."

Use Questions Carefully

As mentioned earlier, phrase questions simply and avoid the use of closed-ended questions that require a yes or no. Watch your customer's nonverbal responses so that you will be able to gauge his or her reactions to your questions.

In some cultures, people believe that questioning someone is intrusive, and they therefore avoid it. This is especially true if the questions are personal (e.g., "How is your family?").

Use a Step-by-Step Approach

When explaining something, outline exactly what you will do or what will be expected of the customer. Write this information down for the customer's future reference in order to prevent misunderstandings. If the customer cannot read it, and does not want to admit this out of embarrassment, he or she now has something to take to someone else for translation.

Keep Your Message Brief

Avoid lengthy explanations or details that might frustrate or confuse your customer. Use simple one-syllable words and short sentences. But also avoid being too brisk.

Check Frequently for Understanding

In addition to using short words and sentences, pause often to verify the customer's understanding of your message before continuing. Avoid questions such as "Do you understand?" Not only can this be answered with a "yes" or "no" as you read earlier, but it can also offend someone who speaks and understands English reasonably well. The nonverbal message is that the person may not be smart enough to get your meaning. Instead, try tie-in questions such as "How do you think you will use this?" or others that will give you an indication of whether the customer understands the information you have provided. These types of questions help you and the customer visualize how the information will be put to use. They also give you a chance to find out if the person has misunderstood what you explained.

Keep Smiling

Smiling is a universal language. Speak it fluently!

Customers With Disabilities

According to the U.S. Census Bureau, approximately 54 million Americans have some level of disability.[11] It is also estimated that about 26 million people have what are defined as severe disabilities. These numbers are projected to continue to grow as the population ages.

"Attention to diversity" is more than a snappy phrase or industry trend. Every interpersonal interaction challenges you to discover and meet the individual needs of the people you serve. What steps should you take to be sure that you are comfortable working with customers with disabilities?

---

[11] McNeil, pp. 61–70.

From a customer service perspective, it is a certainty that you will at some point encounter someone who has a disability that requires your assistance in serving him or her. Some customer service professionals are uncomfortable working with people who have disabilities because they have had little prior exposure to people who have disabilities, they are uninformed about various disabilities, or they have unfounded fear or anxiety. Even though you may be unfamiliar with how people with disabilities adapt to life experiences, you should provide excellent service to them. In most cases, customers who have disabilities do not want to be treated differently; they want to be treated equally.

In addition to all the factors you have read about previously, to be effective in dealing with customers, you must be aware of the 1990 Americans with Disabilities Act (ADA) and other legislation passed by Congress to protect individuals and groups. You should also understand the court interpretations of these laws that require businesses to provide certain services to customers with disabilities and to make certain premises accessible to them. The laws also prohibit any form of discrimination or harassment.

Since the passage of the ADA, much has been published about the rights of and accommodations for people with disabilities. Figure 10-4 provides general strategies for working with customers and others with disabilities and complying with the ADA. In addition, the following sections discuss specific approaches you can take to work well with people with certain disabilities.

FIGURE 10-4

General strategies for servicing customers with disabilities.

In addition to the suggestions offered in this chapter for serving customers with specific disabilities, here are some general guidelines for success:

Be prepared and informed. You can find a lot of literature and information about disabilities. Do some reading to learn about the capabilities and needs of customers with disabilities.

Note: If you deal with customers who use computers (e.g., computer training or sales) a free video entitled *Enable* is available through the Internet at www.microsoft.com/enable/productions. The video helps increase awareness about the capabilities of people with various disabilities and how computers can help them compensate for lost abilities.

Don't patronize. Customers with disabilities aren't your children; don't talk down to them. Just because they have a physical or mental disability does not mean that they should be valued less as a customer or person.

Treat them equally, not differently. Just as you would other customers, work to discover their needs and then set about satisfying them.

Refer to the person, not the disability. For example, instead of referring to the *blind man*, refer to the *man with a sight loss* or *man who is blind*, or better yet, *the man*.

FIGURE 10-4 (Continued)

Offer assistance; do not rush to help without asking. Just as you would ask someone without a disability whether you might hold a door or carry a package, do the same for a person with a disability. Unsolicited assistance can be offensive and might even be dangerous, if it is unexpected and causes the person to lose his or her balance, for example.

Be respectful. The amount of respect you show to all customers should be at a consistently high level. This includes tone of voice (showing patience), gestures, eye contact, and all the other communication techniques you have learned about.

Customers With Hearing Disabilities

Customers who have hearing impairments have special needs, but they also have certain abilities. Do not assume that people who are hearing impaired are helpless. In interactions with such customers, you can do a variety of things to provide effective service:

- *Provide written information and instructions where appropriate and possible.*
- *Use pictures, objects, diagrams, or other such items to communicate more clearly.*
- *To get the person's attention, use nonverbal cues such as gesturing.*
- *Use facial expressions and gestures to emphasize key words or express thoughts.*
- *Face the person directly.*
- *Enunciate your words and speak slowly so that the customer can see your mouth form words.*
- *Use short sentences and words.*
- *Check for understanding frequently by using open-ended questions to which the customer must provide descriptive answers.*
- *Communicate in a well-lighted room when possible.*
- *Avoid backlighting, which may reduce visibility.*
- *Reduce background noise, if possible.*

Customers With Vision Disabilities

According to the National Eye Institute in Bethesda, Maryland, approximately 3 million Americans have low vision, almost 1 million are "legally blind," and another 220,000 are totally blind. This means that you are likely to encounter someone with a vision impairment. Like people who have hearing impairments, vision-impaired customers may need special assistance but are not helpless. Depending on your organization's product and service focus, you can do things to assist visually impaired customers. Be aware that, depending on the type of impairment, a person may have limited vision that can be used to advantage. Here are some strategies to use:

- *Talk to a visually impaired person the same way you would talk to anyone else.*

- *You do not have to raise your voice; the person is* visually *impaired.*

- *Do not feel embarrassed or change your vocabulary. It is okay to say things like "Do you see my point?" or "Do you get the picture?"*

- *Speak directly to the customer.*

- *If the customer uses a guide dog, do not pet, feed, or otherwise distract the animal without the owner's permission. A guide dog is especially trained to perform specific functions. If you interfere, the dog might become confused. The owner could possibly be injured as a result.*

- *Speak to the person as he or she enters the room or approach the person so that he or she knows where you are. Also, introduce others who are present, or at least inform the customer of their presence.*

- *If appropriate, ask how much sight he or she has and how you can best assist.*

- *Give very specific information and directions (e.g., "A chair is approximately ten feet ahead on your left").*

- *If you are seating the person, face him or her away from bright lights that might interfere with any limited vision he or she may have.*

- *When walking with someone who is blind, offer your arm. Do not take the person's arm without permission; this could startle him or her. Let the person take your elbow and walk slightly behind you.*

- *When helping a blind person to a chair, guide his or her hand to the back of the chair. Also, inform the person if a chair has arms to prevent him or her from overturning the chair by leaning or sitting on an arm.*

- *Leave doors either completely closed or open. Partially open doors pose a danger to visually impaired people.*

Customers With Mobility or Motion Impairments

Customers who have mobility or motion impairments often use specially designed equipment and have had extensive training in how to best use assistive devices to compensate for the loss of the use of some part of their body. You can best assist them by offering to help and then following their lead or instructions. Do not make the assumption that they need your assistance and then set about giving it. You can cause injury if you upset their balance or routine. Here are some strategies for better serving these customers:

Prior to a situation in which you may have to accommodate someone who uses a walker, wheelchair, crutches, or other device(s), do an environmental survey of your workplace. Note areas where space is inadequate to permit mobility (a minimum of 36 inches is needed for a standard wheelchair) or where hazards exist. If you can correct the situation, do so.

Otherwise, make suggestions for improvements to the proper people in your organization. Remind them that the ADA and state regulations require an organization to accommodate customers with such disabilities.

Do not assume that someone who has such an impairment cannot perform certain tasks. As mentioned earlier, people who have disabilities are often given extensive training. They have learned how to overcome obstacles and perform various tasks in different ways.

Make sure that you place information or materials at a level that makes it possible for the person to see without undue strain (e.g., eye level for someone in a wheelchair so that he or she does not have to look up).

Stand or sit so that you can make direct eye contact with a person in a wheelchair without forcing the person to look up at an uncomfortable angle for extended periods.

Do not push or lean on someone's wheelchair without his or her permission.

Work It Out 10-1. Identifying Resources

▶ Check with local advocacy groups or on the Internet for information on the types of accommodations you might make for people with various disabilities and how best to interact with people who have specific disabilities (e.g., sight, mobility, hearing impairment). Collect and read literature on the subject. Share the information with other students and/or coworkers (if you currently work in a customer service environment).

What to look for:

Definitions of various disabilities.

Strategies for better communication.

Accommodations necessary to allow customer access to products and services.

Resources available.

Bibliographic information.

Elderly Customers

Being elderly does not make a person or a customer less valuable. In fact, many older customers are in excellent physical and mental shape, are still employed, and have more time to be active now than when they were younger. Studies show that senior citizens have more disposable income now than at any other time in history. And, as the **baby boomer** population (people born between 1946 and 1964) ages, there are more senior citizens than ever. Moreover, as the population ages, there will be a greater need for services—and service providers—to care for people and allow them to enjoy a good quality of life. Figure 10-5 shows the projected increase in the number of people who will fall in the over-65 age group starting in the year 2000. Consider the following strategies when you are interacting with an elderly customer.

FIGURE 10-5

Projected increase in U.S. population above the age of 65.

Year	65–74 Male	65–74 Female	75–84 Male	75–84 Female	85+ Male	85+ Female
2000	8,180,000	9,956,000	4,938,000	7,378,000	1,229,000	3,031,000
2010	9,753,000	11,305,000	5,363,000	7,317,000	1,772,000	3,899,000
2030	17,878,000	19,529,000	10,818,000	12,699,000	3,021,000	5,434,000
2050	16,699,000	18,033,000	12,342,000	13,563,000	7,036,000	11,188,00

(Source: U.S. Bureau of Census, Projections of the Population, by Age and Sex, Race and Hispanic Origin: 1995 to 2050 (P25–1130), February 1996, Table 2.)

Be Respectful

As you would with any customer, be respectful. Even if the customer seems a bit arrogant, disoriented, or disrespectful, don't lose your professionalism. Recognize that sometimes these behaviors are a response to perceptions based on your cues. When this happens, quickly evaluate your behavior and make adjustments, if necessary. If an older customer seems abrupt in his or her response, think about whether you might have nonverbally signaled impatience because of your perception that he or she was slow in acting or responding.

Be Patient

Allow older customers the time to look around, respond, react, or ask questions. Value their decisions. Also, keep in mind that as some people age, their ability to process information lessens and their attention span becomes shorter. Do not assume that this is true of all older customers, but be patient when it does occur.

Answer Questions

Providing information to customers is crucial in order to help them make reasoned decisions. Even though you may have just explained something, listen to the customer's questions, respond, and restate. If it appears that the customer has misunderstood, try repeating the information, possibly using slightly different words.

Don't Patronize

If you appear to talk down to older customers, problems could arise or you could lose a customer. Customers who are elderly should not be treated as if they are senile! A condescending attitude will cause any customer, elderly or otherwise, to take his or her business elsewhere.

Avoid Overfamiliarity

Addressing senior citizens accompanied by their children or grandchildren with "Good morning, Grandma" because one of their family members used that language is inappropriate and rude.

Guard Against Biases

Be careful not to let biases about older people interfere with good service. Don't ignore or offend older customers by making statements such as "Hang on, old timer. I'll be with you in a minute."

Communicate Effectively

Even if an elderly customer does not exhibit the common symptoms of hearing loss (e.g., incorrect responses or facial expressions indicating that she or he is straining to hear or may have missed the message), use the following to help enhance communication:

- *Face the person.*
- *Talk slowly and enunciate words clearly.*
- *Keep your hands away from your mouth.*
- *Do not chew gum or eat food when talking.*
- *Observe the customer's nonverbal cues.*
- *Reword statements or ask questions again, if necessary.*
- *Be positive, patient, and practice the good listening skills covered in Chapter 5.*
- *Stand near good lighting, and keep background noise to a minimum, when possible.*
- *If an interpreter is with the customer, talk to the customer and not the interpreter. The interpreter will know what to do.*

Younger Customers

You have heard the various terms describing the "younger generation"—Generation Y, Nexters, MTV generation, millennial generation, cyberkids. Whatever the term, this group follows Generation X (born 1964–1977) and is now entering the workplace as employees and as consumers in great numbers. Financially, the group accounts for billions of dollars in business revenue for products such as clothes, music, videos, and electronic entertainment equipment. Generation Y is a spending force to be reckoned with, and marketers are going after them with a vengeance. If you don't believe this, pick up a magazine and look at the faces of the models, look at the products being sold, and watch the shows being added to television lineups each year. All of this affects the way you will provide service to this generation of customers. Depending on your own age, your attitude toward them will vary. If you are of Gen Y, you may make the mistake of being overly familiar with your age group in delivering service. If you are a baby boomer or older, you may feel paternalistic or maternalistic or might believe some of the stereotypical rhetoric about this group (e.g., low moral values, fragmented in focus, overprotected by legislation and programs). Although some of these descriptions are accurate, it is dangerous to pigeonhole any group or individual. This is especially true when providing service, for, as you have read, service is based on satisfying personal needs and wants.

Remember when you were young and felt that adults didn't understand or care about your wants or needs? Well, your younger customers probably feel the same way and will remember how you treat them. Their memories could prompt them to take their business elsewhere if their experience with you is negative. If you are older, you may be tempted to talk down to them or be flippant. Don't give in to the temptation. Keep in mind that they are customers. If they feel unwelcome, they will take their business and money elsewhere, and they will tell their friends of the poor treatment they received. Just as with older customers, avoid demeaning language and condescending forms of address (*kid*, *sonny*, *sweetie*, or *sugar*).

An additional point to remember when dealing with younger customers is that they may not have the product knowledge and sophistication in communicating that older customers do. You can decrease confusion and increase communication effectiveness by using words that are appropriate for their age group and by taking the time to explain and/or demonstrate technical points. Keep it simple without being patronizing.

Work It Out 10.2. Serving a Variety of Customers

▶ Pair up with a peer and use the following scenarios as the basis of role-plays to give you practice and feedback in dealing with various categories of customers. Before beginning, discuss how you might deal with each customer in a real-life situation. After the role-plays, both persons should answer the following questions and discuss any ideas for improvement.

Questions:

1. How well do you feel that service was provided?

2. Were any negative or unclear messages, verbal or nonverbal, communicated? If yes, discuss.

3. What open-ended questions were used to discover customer needs? What others could have been used?

4. How can identified areas for improvement be incorporated into a real customer service encounter?

Scenario 1: Farooq Khan was recently hired as a telecommunications specialist for a local telephone company. Your company is providing and installing equipment at a new relay station, and you will be working closely with Farooq, who is the project manager, over the next three months. On several occasions during the past week, you have spoken with Farooq over the phone and are now going to meet him in person for the first time. You are not impressed by him since, as you told a coworker, "He's an ignorant foreigner who doesn't even understand English." Your purpose for meeting with Farooq is to get to know him and discuss an implementation schedule for the project. You also want to find out his expectations for you and your company on the project.

Scenario 2: You are a shuttle driver for the airport and just received a call from your dispatcher to proceed to 8172 Dealy Lane to pick up Casandra Fenton. You were told that Ms. Fenton is blind and will need assistance getting her bags from the house to the bus. Upon arrival, you find Ms. Fenton waiting on her front porch with her bags.

Scenario 3: Mrs. Zagowski is 62 years old and is in the library where you are working at the circulation desk. As you observe her, you notice that she seems a bit frustrated and confused. You saw her browse through several aisles of books, then talk briefly with the reference librarian, and finally go to the computer containing the publication listings and their locations. You are going to try to assist her. Upon meeting her, you realize that she has a hearing deficit and has difficulty hearing what you are saying.

Scenario 4: You are the owner of a small hobby shop that specializes in coins, stamps, comics, and sports memorabilia. Tommy Chin, whom you recognize as a regular "browser," has come in while you are particularly busy. After looking through numerous racks of comic books and trading cards, he is now focused on autographed baseballs in a display case. You believe that he cannot afford them, although he is asking about prices and for other information.

6 COMMUNICATING WITH A DIVERSE AUDIENCE

▶ **CONCEPT:** Many considerations need to be taken into account when you are delivering service to a diverse customer base. Appropriate language usage is a meaningful tool that you should master for good customer service.

Given all this diversity, you must be wondering how to provide service that is acceptable to all of these customer groups. As you've seen, there are many considerations in delivering service to a diverse customer base. Therefore, consider the following basic guidelines for communicating; these tips are appropriate for dealing with all types of customers.

Avoid Remarks or Jokes That Discriminate or Offend

Comments that focus on any aspect of diversity (religion, sexual preference, weight, hair color, age) can be offensive and should not be made. Also, humor does not cross cultural boundaries well. Each culture has a different interpretation of what is humorous and socially acceptable.

Make Sure That Your Language Is "Inclusive"

When speaking, address or refer to the people from various groups that are present. If you are addressing a group of eight men and one woman, using the term *guys* or *fellows* excludes the woman and thus is not inclusive.

Respect Personal Preferences When Addressing People

As you read earlier, don't assume familiarity when addressing others. (Don't call someone by her or his first name unless he or she gives permission.) Don't use *Ms.* if a female customer prefers another form of address.

Also, avoid terms such as *honey*, *sugar*, and *sweetheart* or other overly familiar language.

Use General Terms

Instead of singling a customer out or focusing on exceptions in a group, describe people in general terms. That is, instead of referring to someone as a *female supervisor*, *black salesperson*, or *disabled secretary*, say *supervisor*, *salesperson*, or *secretary*.

Don't Use Terms That Demean

Keep in mind that certain words have a negative connotation and could insult or offend. Even if you do not intend to offend, the customer's perception is the deciding factor of your actions. For example, using the terms *handicapped* or *crippled*, *boy*, *girl*, *queer*, or *idiot* may conjure up a negative image to some groups.

FIGURE 10-6

Nonverbal cue meanings.

The following are symbols and gestures that are commonly used in the United States but have different—and negative or offensive—meanings in other parts of the world:

American Gesture or Symbol	Meaning in Other Cultures	Country
Beckoning by curling and uncurling index finger[1,2]	Used for calling animals or ladies of the evening	Hong Kong, Australia, Indonesia, Yugoslavia. Malaysia
V for victory sign (with palm facing you)[1,2]	Rude gesture	England
Sole of foot pointed toward a person[1,3]	You are lowly (the sole is lowest part of the body and contacts the ground)	Thailand, Saudi Arabia, Singapore, Egypt
"Halt" gesture with palm and extended fingers thrust toward someone[1,2,3]	Rude epithet	Greece
Thumb up (fingers curled) indicating *okay, good going*, or *everything is fine*[1,3]	The number 5 Rude gesture	Japan Nigeria, Australia
Thumb and forefinger forming an O, meaning *okay*[1,3]	Zero or worthless Money Rude gesture	France Japan Brazil, Malta, Greece, Tunisia, Turkey, Italy, Paraguay, Russia

---

FIGURE 10-6 (Continued)

American Gesture or Symbol	Meaning in Other Cultures	Country
Waving good-bye with fingers extended, palm down, and moving the fingers up and down toward yourself[1,3]	Come here	Parts of Europe, Myanmar, Colombia, Peru
Patting the head of a child	Insult; inviting evil spirits	Parts of the Far East
Using red ink for documents	Death; offensive	Parts of Korea, Mexico, and China
Passing things with left hand (especially food)	Socially unacceptable	India, Pakistan

[1] Axtell, R., *Gestures: The DO's and Taboos of Body Language Around the World*, John Wiley and Sons, NY, 1991.
[2] Wolfgang, A., *Everybody's Guide to People Watching*, International Press, Yarmouth, MA, 1995.
[3] Morris, D., *Bodytalk: The Meaning of Human Gestures*, Crown Trade Paperback, NY, 1994.

Use Care With Nonverbal Cues

The nonverbal cues that you are familiar with may carry different meanings in other cultures. Be care when you use symbols or gestures if you are not certain how your customer will receive them. Figure 10-6 lists some cues that are common in Western cultures but have negative meanings in other cultures.

WORKSHEET 10-5

Describing Groups

Worksheet ▼
10-5

Think about negative or unflattering terms you have used or heard others use to describe or refer to certain groups of people. List these terms along with possible positive alternatives for each of the following categories or groups.

	Negative Term(s)	Alternatives
People over age 50	_____	_____
	_____	_____
	_____	_____
People under age 18	_____	_____
	_____	_____
	_____	_____
Asian Americans	_____	_____
	_____	_____
	_____	_____

WORKSHEET 10.5 (Continued)

African Americans	______________	______________
	______________	______________
	______________	______________
Hispanics	______________	______________
	______________	______________
	______________	______________
Europeans	______________	______________
	______________	______________
	______________	______________
Middle Easterners	______________	______________
	______________	______________
	______________	______________
Gays or Lesbians	______________	______________
	______________	______________
	______________	______________
People with disabilities	______________	______________
	______________	______________
	______________	______________
Men	______________	______________
	______________	______________
	______________	______________
Women	______________	______________
	______________	______________
	______________	______________

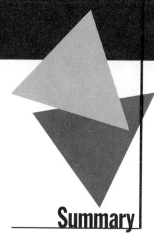

Chapter Summary

Opportunities to deal with a diverse customer base will increase as the global economy expands. With continuing immigrations, an aging U.S. population, changes in values, and increased ease of mobility, the only thing certain is that the next customer you speak with *will* be different from you. Remember, however, that he or she will also be similar to you in many ways and that both of you will have a basis for discussion.

The success you have in the area of dealing with others is totally dependent on your preparation and attitude toward providing quality service. Learn as much as you can about various groups of people in order to effectively evaluate situations, determine needs, and serve all customers on an equal basis.

Summary

CHAPTER REVIEW QUESTIONS

1. What are some innate qualities or characteristics that make people unique? _____

_____

_____

2. What external or societal factors affect the way members of a group are seen or perceived? _____

_____

_____

3. What are values? _____

_____

_____

4. Do beliefs differ from values? Explain. _____

_____

_____

5. Why would some people be reluctant to make eye contact with you?

_____

_____

6. When dealing with customers with a disability, how can you best help them? _____

_____

_____

7. How can recognition of the cultural value of "importance of family" be helpful in customer service?_____

_____

_____

8. What are some considerations for improving communication in a diverse environment? _____

_____

_____

9. How can you effectively communicate with someone who has difficulty with the English language?_____

_____

_____

10. What are some techniques for effectively providing service to older customers? _____

_____

_____

▼ SEARCH IT OUT

Search the Internet for Diversity Information

Log on to the Internet to locate information and articles related to topics covered in this chapter. Be prepared to share what you found at your next scheduled class or session. The following are some key words you might use in your search:

> *Diversity*
>
> *Cultural diversity*
>
> *Cultural values*
>
> *Beliefs*
>
> *Disabilities*
>
> *Disability advocacy*
>
> *Intercultural communication*
>
> *Intercultural dynamics*
>
> *Any country name (e.g., Australia, Canada, Sri Lanka)*
>
> *Elderly*
>
> *Generation X*
>
> *Generation Y*
>
> *Population projections*

COLLABORATIVE *Learning Activity*

Awareness of Diversity

To help raise your awareness related to diversity in the customer service environment, try the following activities:

1. Pair up with someone to role-play scenarios in which you are a service provider and have customers from the following groups:

An elderly person who has a hearing loss and wants directions on how to use some equipment (you choose the equipment and provide instruction).

Someone who speaks English as a second language (with a heavy accent) and needs to fill out a credit card application or some other form.

Someone with a sight impairment who wants to "see" several blouses or shirts or needs directions to another part of your store.

A ten-year-old who wants a new computer and has questions about various types, components, and how they work.

2. Interview a variety of people: from different cultures, from various age groups, with disabilities, male or female (opposite of your sex), or gay or lesbian. Find out whether they have preferences in the type of customer service they receive or in the kind of language used to refer to their group. Also, ask about ways you can better communicate with and understand them and people from their group.

3. Suggest to your supervisor, team leader, or work group peers that employees meet as a group to discuss situations in which all of you have encountered people from different cultures or groups. Exchange ideas on how to better serve such people in the future. Report the results of your efforts to your class members at the next scheduled meeting.

4. Working in teams assigned by your instructor, set up an appointment to visit a local advocacy group for the disabled or aging, or contact a national group (e.g., the National Society to Prevent Blindness, assisted-living facilities, World Federation of the Deaf, National Information Center on Deafness, National Eye Institute, National Institute on Aging). Focus on gathering information that will help you understand various disabilities and develop strategies for effectively communicating with and serving people who have disabilities. Write a brief summary of your experience and report back to your peers.

FACE TO FACE

Dealing with Difficult People on the Phone at MedMobile

Background

MedMobile is a medical supply business located in Los Angeles, California, employing 62 full-time and 11 part-time workers. The company specializes in equipment designed to improve patient mobility (walkers, motorized carts, wheelchairs, mechanized beds and chairs). Average yearly sales are in the area of $1.5 million.

The primary client base for the company is insurance companies that pay for rehabilitation following worker accidents or injuries. Medical professionals who conduct the patient medical case file reviews and recommend treatment programs are in regular contact with the account representatives for MedMobile.

Your Role

As an account representative with MedMobile, you have been with the company for about 18 months. Your main job is to help clients determine and obtain the correct equipment needed to assist their patients. To do this, you spend hours on the phone daily and often know clients by voice. In recent months you have become extremely frustrated, almost to the point of anger. A new claims adjuster works for one of your primary account companies, TrueCare Insurance Company. His name is Abeyola Pepukayi, and he has been with TrueCare eight weeks. He has been an adjuster for a little over a year.

You just got off the phone after a lengthy conversation with Abeyola and you are agitated. For over half an hour you tried unsuccessfully to explain why you felt the equipment being ordered by Abeyola was not the best for the patient's injury, as he described it to you.

Because this isn't the first time such an encounter has taken place, you are now in your supervisor's office venting. While discussing the situation with your boss, you note the following about Abeyola:

He doesn't listen. No matter what you say, he asks totally irrelevant questions about other equipment.

He usually has no idea what you're talking about.

He is rude and interrupts, often making statements such as "One moment, please. That makes no sense."

You have spent hours discussing equipment design and function because he doesn't know anything about it.

He spends endless amounts of time getting off track and trying to discuss other issues or topics.

After your conversation, your boss called a friend at TrueCare to see what he knew of the situation. The friend, David Helmstedter, supervises Abeyola. Apparently, Abeyola has been venting to David about you. From what David has been told:

You are rude and abrupt and aren't very friendly. Abeyola has tried to establish a relationship, but you have ignored his efforts.

Abeyola is trying hard to learn the terminology and equipment but you are unwilling to help.

You speak rapidly, using a lot of technical language that you don't explain.

QUESTIONS

1. What seems to be happening here? Does Abeyola have any legitimate complaints? If so, what are they?
2. What steps or process can you use to clarify understanding?
3. What cultural differences might be involved in this scenario?

FROM THE FRONTLINE
Interview

Judith A. Mosto
President
J.A. Mosto Strategic
Programs &
Development, Inc.
Winter Springs, Florida

1. **What are your general impressions of customer service in the United States? Why do you feel this way?**

"In the United States" is the key phrase. This question is really about customer service with regard to diversity. I think that we in this country have a tendency to view our customers through our own eyes and not from their perspective. We have a habit of viewing the general population as "American" and not adjusting our behavior to respect and honor different races and ethnic backgrounds.

2. **What is the biggest challenge you have witnessed related to delivering customer service in a business world where so much diversity is present?**

For many years we talked about "managing diversity," and we approached the subject from an analytical perspective. Only during the last few years of the twentieth century have we begun to acknowledge what diversity is and to focus on the commonalities (e.g., personal value systems). Also, we have begun to combine this approach with a respect for diversity.

3. **What are some pitfalls service providers should remember when dealing with people who might be different from them?**

Education is a wonderful thing; I would begin there. Far too many people don't attempt to educate themselves (with an open mind) about the entire subject called diversity. It's not just about race and ethnicity; it's about every aspect of what makes each of us unique. Along with shifting the focus to commonalities rather than differences, I would encourage everyone to begin with a humanistic approach. The ability to see the human being first allows you to move beyond the differences that separate you.

4. In your experience, what are some of the positive strategies and techniques that customer service providers can use to deal with diverse customers?

Effective listening techniques are powerful communication tools. Listening with your eyes allows you to listen with your heart. Customers are valued and respected when the provider acknowledges their expectations and tries to meet them. The other techniques mentioned in previous questions should be included as well: valuing and respecting the human being first, being open and receptive to one's own change and growth, and shifting the focus from the differences to the common threads that unite us—as one would view a finely woven tapestry. We should celebrate the diverse world we live in and set aside the obstacles of the past.

5. From your perspective, what is the most important thing to remember when dealing with various types of customers, both external and internal?

Don't make any assumptions! I am embarrassed to say that I have been guilty of this. Many students in Orlando are from the Caribbean. Being aware of the biases and racism that exist not only from one country or culture to another but also within specific races and cultures can prevent one from making embarrassing assumptions!

6. What advice related to diversity would you give someone entering the customer service profession?

Your success could depend on how well you relate to internal and external customers. Begin now to develop a plan of how you will develop and grow as a person. Personal development from a reflective perspective will increase your sensitivity. Only by beginning within yourself can you move beyond the obstacles that prevent you from changing your views about the world.

CRITICAL THINKING

How do you think customer service operates in this organization? Would you handle it the same? Do you agree with the advice given?

PART

III

Self-Help Skills

Chapter 11

Managing Your Stress

OBJECTIVES

After completing this chapter, you will be able to:

• *Identify leading causes of stress in the customer service environment.*

• *Describe personal stressors.*

• *Recognize potentially stressful situations.*

• *Avoid stressful situations.*

• *Develop techniques for reducing stress.*

"Learn calm to face what's pressing."

Horace, 65–8 B.C.
Roman poet and satirist
Odes

Before reviewing the chapter content, respond to the following questions by placing a "T" for true or an "F" for false on the rules. Use any questions you miss as a checklist of material to which you will pay particular attention as you read through the chapter. For those you get right, congratulate yourself, but review the sections they address in order to learn additional details about the topic.

_____ 1. Both positive and negative stress exist.

_____ 2. Studies do not substantiate employee claims that customer service is a stressful profession.

_____ 3. Stressors do not affect all people in the same manner.

_____ 4. Physical reactions caused by stress are observable.

_____ 5. Environmental factors such as lighting, temperature, and noise can be stress-inducing.

_____ 6. Unresolved personal issues can cause workplace stress.

_____ 7. The way a job is structured has little impact on stress levels.

_____ 8. A lack of time for oneself does not typically create stress.

_____ 9. The use of "I" language can help in reducing stressful situations.

_____ 10. Taking regularly scheduled breaks can add to your stress because you'll probably have work waiting for you when you return.

_____ 11. According to the Better Sleep Council, most people get enough sleep each night.

_____ 12. Each week, an average of 20 people are killed on the job as a result of workplace violence.

1. T   5. T   9. T
2. F   6. T   10. F
3. T   7. F   11. F
4. T   8. F   12. T

---

1 STRESS RESEARCH

> **CONCEPT:** Stress has been linked to all the leading causes of death, including heart disease, cancer, lung ailments, accidents, and suicide. Dealing with stress is a major health-related issue today.

Stress is a major contributor to loss of workplace efficiency. Each year, millions of dollars and countless worker-hours of productivity are lost because of stress-related illnesses (see Figure 11-1). In all stress-related statistics, customer service is rated among the top most stressful occupations. In fact, many studies have consistently listed customer service in the top ten most stressful occupations in the country. This is because the variety of people and situations you face on any given day require you to call on a multitude of skills and to think quickly. According to the American Institute of Stress, customer service representatives ranked fourth behind air traffic controllers, inner-city high school teachers, and police officers as having the most stressful job in the country. Additional studies conducted by Yale University ranked customer service as the eighth most stressful occupation.

The results of pressures that people are facing in the workplace have been staggering, financially and from a health standpoint (see Figure 11-2).[1] Thus, stress can be a problem, especially if you aren't prepared to handle it.

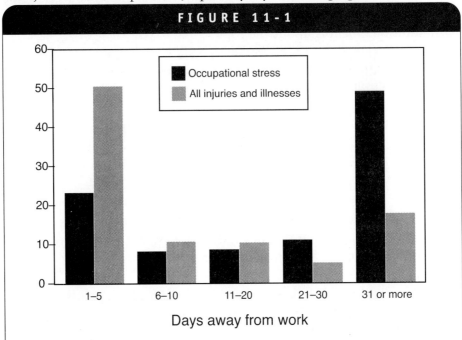

FIGURE 11-1

Figure 11-1 Percent of occupational stress and all nonfatal occupational injury and illnesses cases involving days away from work, 1997. (Source: U.S. Bureau of Labor Statistics, *Issues in Labor Statistics*, Summary 99-10: September 1999.)

FIGURE 11-2

The impact of stress.

- Stress is America's No. 1 health problem.
- Among adults, 43 percent suffer adverse health effects due to stress.
- Of all visits to primary care physicians, 75 to 90 percent are stress-related.
- Stress has been linked to all the leading causes of death, including heart disease, cancer, lung ailments, accidents, and suicide.
- An estimated 1 million workers are absent on an average workday because of stress-related complaints. Stress is said to be responsible for more than half of the 550 million workdays lost annually because of absenteeism.
- A three-year study conducted by a large corporation showed that 60 percent of employee absences were due to psychological problems such as stress.
- Nearly half of all American workers suffer from symptoms of **burnout**, a disabling reaction to stress on the job.
- The proportion of workers who reported feeling highly stressed more than doubled from 1985 to 1990.

[1] American Institute of Stress.

FIGURE 11-2 (Continued)

- Job stress is estimated to cost U.S. industry $300 billion annually, as measured by absenteeism, diminished productivity, employee turnover, and medical, legal, and insurance fees. Sixty to eighty percent of industrial accidents are due to stress.

- Workers' compensation awards for job stress, rare in the early 1980s, have sky-rocketed and threaten to bankrupt insurance systems in some states. Employers in California shelled out almost $1 billion for medical and legal fees alone. Nine of ten job stress lawsuits are successful, with an average payout more than four times that for regular injury claims.

- The cost of stress management programs, products, and services was $9.4 billion in 1995, and is projected to be $11.31 billion in 1999.

- It is estimated that 40 percent of worker turnover is due to job stress. The Xerox Corporation estimates that it costs approximately $1 million to $1.5 million to replace a top executive, and average employee turnover costs between $2,000 and $13,000 per individual.

- Workplace violence is rampant. Almost 2 million cases of homicide, aggravated assault, rape, or sexual assaults are reported each year. Homicide is the second leading cause of fatal occupational injury and the leading cause of death for working women.

2 WHAT IS JOB STRESS?

> **CONCEPT:** Nowadays many workers feel that their job is full of stress. Stress can create problems in the workplace. However, not all stress is bad stress.

Job stress can be defined as the harmful physical and emotional responses that occur when the requirements of a job do not match the capabilities, resources, or needs of the worker.[2] Bad stress, or *distress*, causes problems in dealing with customers and other people, reduces your effectiveness, dampens your motivation, makes your life miserable, and can lead to long-term mental and physical problems or death. Although some of the stress that you encounter in the workplace can be eliminated, some cannot; you simply have to work to minimize it as much as possible. Strategies and techniques for doing this are given in this chapter.

You are not alone in feeling stressed on the job. Nowadays, many workers believe that their jobs are stressful (see Figure 11-3).

Not all stress is bad, however. Dr. Hans Selye, a prominent psychologist, coined the term *eustress* a number of years ago to describe "good" stress. You would experience eustress if you set a goal for yourself and achieved that goal (e.g., running three miles in under 20 minutes, graduating from high school or college, delivering a successful presentation to clients). You would feel good about your accomplishment. You might also feel negative stress along the way toward your goal because of the tasks required to achieve your ultimate objective (e.g., the physical conditioning necessary to strengthen your body to run faster, staying up all night to study for an examination, or spending hours researching and rehearsing a presentation). With eustress,

---

[2] Center for Disease Control, National Institute for Occupational Safety and Health (NIDSH).

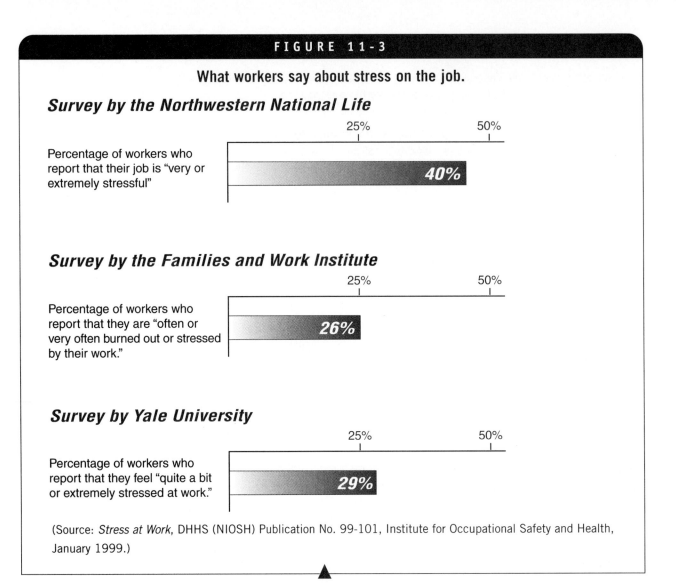

FIGURE 11-3

What workers say about stress on the job.

Survey by the Northwestern National Life

Percentage of workers who report that their job is "very or extremely stressful" — 40%

Survey by the Families and Work Institute

Percentage of workers who report that they are "often or very often burned out or stressed by their work." — 26%

Survey by Yale University

Percentage of workers who report that they feel "quite a bit or extremely stressed at work." — 29%

(Source: *Stress at Work*, DHHS (NIOSH) Publication No. 99-101, Institute for Occupational Safety and Health, January 1999.)

you may go through the same physiological stages that you would for negative situations, but at the end, when you reach your goal, you have a sense of accomplishment and a feeling of exhilaration.

3 WHAT CREATES STRESS?

CONCEPT: What you feel in the environment, on the job, and your personal factors are some of the things that create stress.

In a word, *life* creates stress. As you read in Chapter 7, the world moves at a much faster pace than it did decades ago. People's values, beliefs, and expectations have caused much of this acceleration. Customers have become conditioned to expect quality products and services at competitive prices and in time frames unheard of one or two decades ago. The speed of services is spoiling customers. You can see the impact of customer expectations when you recall a FedEx television advertisement of a few years back. Remember: "When your package absolutely, positively, has to get there overnight?" Customers are also becoming complacent. They assume that if they want something, service providers will provide it instantaneously. . . and in many cases they are right. Organizations realize the value of providing service on demand. Tasks that used to take hours, days, and even weeks are now done almost instantaneously, or certainly in a greatly reduced time frame. The idea of getting it now has so permeated the culture that failure to provide the quickest, most efficient delivery of products and services can be the kiss of death for an organization. As a result of this "get it now" mentality, each new generation has less memory of the long waiting times experienced by their forebears. Today, if customers cannot get what they want from you and your organization, when they want it, they go elsewhere. Increasing schedule pressures can add to stress for you and your coworkers.

It is important to remember that stress affects different people in different ways. You will likely handle an angry customer's response or a tight deadline in a different way than a coworker might. Psychological and physical reactions to stress vary from one person to another. The environmental, job, and personal factors you encounter throughout your day can have a major impact on your mental and physical state and can affect how you react to the stress you experience.

You are a product of evolution when it comes to your brain's reaction to stress. When your brain recognizes or perceives danger (or stress), it triggers a chain reaction of events, starting with the release of chemicals (adrenaline) into the nervous system. Your heart starts beating faster, sending more blood throughout the body. Your breathing accelerates so that you take in more oxygen so that you are ready to deal with the situation (fight), or perhaps to leave the area (flight). This reaction has been called the **fight** *or* **flight syndrome**. Typically, after spurts of excessive adrenaline and activity, the body needs to take a break to recoup. Think about times when you have worked very hard (studying all night for an exam or preparing for an interview or presentation). You were able to accomplish the task but subsequently required time to recuperate. You may have heard about how a small person was able to do extraordinary things (lift a car off someone who became trapped when a jack collapsed). Because of body chemistry changes brought on by stressful situations, you, and they, had the necessary tools to accomplish unusual tasks. These are examples of how the fight or flight syndrome works.

In the customer service environment increased levels of adrenaline can be helpful in solving customer problems, or it can cause problems if you lose control. On the positive side, getting excited about a project can work in your favor. This is especially true when deadlines are tight for extended periods. For example, assume that your organization just bought out a rival company and taken over a call center site. A new computer-based communication system will be installed to better handle customer calls and contacts. You have an eight-week window during which you can move into the new facility, hire and train additional staff, and install the communication system before going online to take calls. You and other employees will have to work overtime for the entire period. If eight weeks was a realistic estimate of the time needed, you will probably meet your deadline, but then, you and the others will need time to rest.

On the negative side of the fight or flight syndrome in the customer environment, increased levels of adrenaline can create problems in maintaining the customer-provider relationship. For example, assume that you encounter a very disagreeable customer who has experienced a problem. No matter what positive communication and customer service skills you try, the customer will accept nothing less than what he is demanding. In addition, he is yelling and using profanity directed at you and the organization. In such a situation, the added adrenaline may lead you to react inappropriately (fight). In such instances you must remain professional, maintain control, excuse yourself, and seek a supervisor or someone else to handle the situation (flight).

The speed at which customers expect product and service delivery in the twenty-first century will likely increase. Current systems efficiency is causing customers to keep demanding faster service. Some of the things that fuel such expectations are:

- *Almost instantaneous access to telephone numbers via directory information over the telephone or the Internet*
- *ATM banking*
- *E-mail*
- *Microwave ovens*
- *Fax machines*
- *One-hour photo processing*
- *Automobile oil changes in under a half hour*
- *Convenience stores open 24 hours a day*
- *Supermarkets with bank services, florists, pharmacies, and delis*
- *Express delivery by the U.S. Post Office and other carriers in less than 24 hours*
- *Cellular phones*
- *Beepers*
- *Electronic book publishing for out-of-print or out-of-stock books*
- *Drive-up laundry and dry cleaning services*
- *Twenty-four-hour automobile club towing services*
- *Credit approvals over the telephone, or in person, in less than an hour*
- *Electronic IRS filings*
- *Laser eye surgery in less than a half hour.*

Work It Out 11-1. Fight or Flight?

▶ Think of a time when you have experienced the fight or flight syndrome in a customer environment as either a provider or a customer. Answer and discuss the following:

1. What happened?. _____

_____

Work It Out
11-1

2. Was the situation handled professionally? Explain._____

_____

_____

3. If not, what was done wrong?. _____

_____

_____

4. What could have been done differently?. _____

_____

_____

4 RECOGNIZING STRESS

▶ **CONCEPT:** Stress has observable symptoms such as fatigue, aggressiveness, nail biting, and tardiness to name a few.

Stress has many observable symptoms, but some symptoms are difficult to pinpoint. The following are some typical indicators that stress is present:

- *Inability to focus or concentrate on a customer problem or workplace situation.*
- *Irritability in dealing with others in the workplace.*
- *Excessive fatigue, which causes you to daydream or "nod off" during the day. Fatigue also prevents you from operating at your full potential or exercising initiative.*
- *Intestinal irritation that can affect your appetite or cause you to be absent from work.*
- *Tardiness or absenteeism because of physical symptoms or the need to catch up on sleep.*
- *Being argumentative or aggressive with customers and others.*
- *Nail biting or other nervous habits (e.g., fidgeting, sighing, playing with hair, wringing hands, constantly tapping the feet or an object).*
- *Poor attitude, which manifests itself in phrases like "Who cares?," "It's not my problem," "Whatever," or "Tell someone who cares."*
- *Insomnia.*
- *Rapid or irregular heartbeat.*
- *Feelings of depression, crying spells, or feelings of uselessness and being underappreciated.*
- *Bingeing on food, alcohol, or tobacco.*
- *Pains in the stomach or head, neck or muscle pains, rapid pulse, high blood pressure, or irregular menstrual cycles.*

Such symptoms, left unchecked for long periods of time, can cause serious health problems and even death. They can also affect your relationships with others for they can prevent you from performing at peak efficiency. If any one of these symptoms occurs, you may not need to be concerned (unless it lasts for an extended period of time); however, the occurrence of multiple symptoms should raise a red flag that causes you to seek assistance. Such help might be in the form of going to your supervisor or team leader to request reassignment, additional training, or more tools to help you do your job. A trip to a medical professional may be required. The important thing is to take action—quickly. Taking the "ostrich approach" (hiding your head in the sand) will not solve a problem. Such behavior will only expose you to risk.

Environmental Factors

Many factors in the workplace can add to your stress level. Some are discussed in the following sections.

PEOPLE

People can be a major source of stress. This is because you cannot control other people and how they behave. Another person's behavioral style, emotional and mental state, and unwillingness to communicate appropriately and effectively, may make it stressful for you to do your job.

Physical factors. Physical factors such as noise, odors, bright or dim lighting, and heat or cold might affect you more than they affect others. Your ability to perform at peak efficiency may be inhibited by these factors. Such situations should be brought to the attention of a supervisor or team leader. In addition, depending on your job and what is permitted, you could take such actions as wearing earplugs or possibly having a radio on your desk that is tuned to an easy-listening or instrumental station. Such music is often subconsciously soothing. Depending on the tasks you are performing, you might be able to relocate to a quieter office, cubicle, or work area for short periods as you complete an assignment (e.g., assembling information packets, counting items, or filing).

Occupational hazards. Hazards that cause you to be concerned for your safety and that of others can be stressful. Such *stressors* (things that cause stress) are dangerous people or situations, heavy equipment or machinery, flammable, caustic, or explosive materials, or heavy lifting. It is important that you and other workers use caution in such environments.

If you are injured, you, the organization, and ultimately the customer suffer. Wear safety equipment, take your time when performing dangerous tasks, read instructions before using equipment, and point out any potentially dangerous situations to supervisors, team leaders, or other appropriate people.

Nonergonomic situations. Physical stress is created in environments in which chairs, tables, computer equipment, and other tools do not conform with industry standards related to employee protection, comfort, and safety. Back, eye, wrist, hand, arm, and leg strain, among other medical problems, can occur when such industry standards are not followed. When assigned a work area, make (or have others make) the necessary adjustments to the level of your desk surface, computer keyboard, computer monitor, telephone, and do anything else that would increase efficiency and reduce repetitive-motion injuries. If you must stand in one place for extended periods (e.g., manufacturing, cashier, or security staff), request a cushioned floor pad or chair as appropriate.

Organizational elements. The organization you work for can play a big role in increasing or decreasing your stress levels. This is especially true if the organization is undergoing various changes—in structure, product and/or service focus, technology, and so on. Employees often help reduce their stress levels in such situations by asking for information and by looking for opportunities to get involved in problem-solving and decision-making meetings. Having some degree of control over your environment can make a lot of difference in reducing stress.

Job Factors

In addition to the environmental aspects of a job that can lead to increased stress levels, other job-related factors can frustrate you and add tension to your day. For example, suppose that your organization provides only one microwave oven in the lunchroom. During the 45-minute lunch period, 30 to 40 people need to use the oven at the same time. Such situations are often not something you can control. You might choose to look for another job. In most instances, however, if you take the time to think of the situation and the interpersonal skills you have read about in this book, you can likely reduce your stress levels.

The key to improving your job and environment is often related to simple, effective interpersonal communication. Working with your team leader or supervisor, move toward changing the way you and your organization view your job and the way you perform it. Do this by openly discussing the following:

- *Your level of authority and decision making in dealing with customer situations.*
- *Realistic and mutually agreed-upon performance goals.*
- *Specific opportunities for personal and professional growth.*
- *Recognition and reward for job performance.*
- *Elimination of unnecessary and repetitive tasks, where possible.*
- *Increased open communication between all levels within the organization.*

Many aspects of your job and organization can affect your stress levels. Some of these include:

Job structures. Organizational structures that require you to work various shifts and/or overtime in order to complete assigned work can be stressful and can lead to physical and mental side effects. Also, whether you work in a hierarchical or team-based environment can have an impact. Both organizational structures have advantages and disadvantages, based on how they are designed, managed, and allowed to function.

To improve your chances for success, become aware of your job responsibilities quickly (especially when they change), try to focus on the positive side of change (e.g., new opportunities to learn, increased opportunity for promotion, and the possibility of streamlining job functions and becoming more effective and efficient), and take advantage of the changing situation. Victims rarely win in changing environments. As organizations try to cut overhead costs, make systems more efficient, and better serve customers, they want employees who can support their goals. Make yourself more marketable by continually gaining new knowledge and skills so that you will be better prepared for the inevitable change that will occur in your organization.

Job insecurity. Employees often go through a period of insecurity when major changes occur within an organization. Some of their insecurity can be attributed to the behavioral style preferences that you read about in Chapter 6, but much of it is simply human nature. Such insecurity is often the result of a lack of adequate and effective communication from upper management. It can also be caused by a volatile industry or job market, as in the case of technology-based organizations that depend on military or government contracts; when government spending is curtailed, employees may be laid off.

If you find yourself in such a situation, use a proactive approach of gathering information, asking questions of your employers, reading materials given to you by the organization, taking the opportunity to get involved on committees or projects, and generally becoming a "player" rather than an "observer" as change occurs.

Unreasonable goals. Goals are part of evaluating job performance in most organizations. There are personal and organizational goals. You will typically be held accountable for personal goals that can ultimately influence the attainment of the goals of the organization.

Unfortunately, many supervisors and team leaders set goals with little or no personal input from the employees who have to meet them. Employees are held accountable for unrealistic production (dollar volume) goals, and in some organizations their results are publicly displayed. This practice can cause disillusionment among employees, as well as low morale, resentment, and frustration.

Help yourself and your organization by jotting down personal and performance goals throughout the year, so that when the time to set your performance goals for the next evaluation period comes around, you can have some input. Your goal might be personal (you want to learn a new software program or skill to better prepare you for job openings that occur from time to time), or it might be job-related (you need additional knowledge or skills to better perform your job and serve customers). By being proactive and demonstrating to your supervisor that you care about the goals set for you, you might rise in the opinion of your supervisor, since most employees do not take such actions.

Conflicting demands. In today's competitive environment, most employees have multiple responsibilities. Naturally, these demands may sometimes conflict. Although most employees prevail and accomplish their job tasks, there may be times when you may not achieve the degree of success that you prefer and desire. This is often because your need and efforts to provide quality service might be hampered by policies and procedures or by other factors not within your control. In addition, personal demands can cause internal conflict while you are on the job. A good time management system is sometimes the answer. For other situations, you may have to use your interpersonal communication skills to negotiate a settlement or compromise. Remember that you cannot always eliminate sources of stress. Therefore, you must seek ways of dealing with them.

Repetitive tasks. Many positions require employees to do repetitive tasks (e.g., data entry, manufacturing, cashiering, and some call center positions) that provide little or no opportunity for initiative or change in routine. Such responsibilities can sometimes lead to boredom or to a lackadaisical attitude toward job performance and lowered morale. If you find yourself in such a position, you might volunteer for additional assignments, committees, or cross-training in order to break the monotony and better qualify you for other positions.

Limited authority. One of the most frustrating situations for service providers and customers occurs when the provider does not have the authority to make decisions or assist customers. Suppose, for example, that a customer calls or comes to your organization and wants a refund, but you do not have the authority because the cost of the item cost is over your authorization limit (say $100). This type of situation sets up potential customer confrontation and resentment and can ultimately cause lost business.

If you find yourself in this type of situation, try suggesting to your supervisor some alternative systems for dealing with customer returns. There may be reasons why a system cannot be changed, but you will never know unless you ask.

Limited opportunities for advancement. Another job factor that often creates challenges for employees and their organizations occurs when opportunities for professional development are limited. Such roadblocks to professional and personal goal achievement can dampen an employee's desire to excel, use creativity and initiative, or remain in the job. To deal with this problem, many organizations offer on-site as well as computer-based training opportunities. Taking advantage of such opportunities builds your current job efficiency and also prepares you for future situations.

Work It Out 11-2. Personal Job Stressors

▶ Think about all the elements of your workplace or one in which you would like to work. What are some of the factors that can lead to personal stress?

_____

_____

_____

_____

_____

_____

_____

_____

_____

Personal Factors

Many things people do in their lives outside the workplace carry over into the workplace. Habits, activities, and other aspects of their personal life can create stress. Some of these elements are discussed in the next section.

Relationships. If organizations could place a box at the entrance to their building with a sign saying "Leave your personal baggage here. Pick it up on your way out," it would be wonderful. In reality, this cannot be done. People are complex creatures. You cannot disassociate yourself from others very easily. As a result, you bring emotional "baggage" with you to work each day. For example, if you have an argument with a spouse or friend, that emotional encounter will stay with you when you report to work. Other aspects of relationships can create stress (for example, a spouse or roommate who does not do his or her part in helping with household chores, grocery shopping, or paying the bills). In such situations, communication skills that you learned earlier in this book can be a great help. Work to negotiate an equitable arrangement. If necessary, bring in an outside intermediary (counselor or financial planner). Such resources are often available through employee assistance programs.

From a positive perspective, your relationships with others outside the workplace can provide you with valuable tools for dealing with customers. In interacting with people outside of the workplace, you learn about behavioral styles, diversity, and human nature. The knowledge you gain outside the workplace can strengthen relationships in the workplace.

Physical condition and nutrition. How well you maintain your body can have a major impact on the way you feel, your energy level, your ability to think clearly and creatively, and ultimately how long you live. Recent reports of the "fattening" of Americans are alarming. After years of healthy eating and exercising, Americans are reverting to a less active lifestyle. If you are not monitoring your food intake and exercising, you could be setting yourself up for problems and lessening the chances that you will be ready to face the various customer service or workplace situations that surface.

Chemical use. Drinking, smoking, taking drugs, or using any other chemical substance can reduce your effectiveness on the job, and actually be deadly. Most health plans nowadays offer assistance in reducing substance dependency. If you use any of these substances, you may want to check with your supervisor to find out whether programs to help you change your behavior are available.

Financial problems. If you are like most people, you have financial problems from time to time. Perhaps you don't have enough money in your checking account to cover expenses or you don't have the cash to make a needed purchase. These problems can weigh heavily on your mind and lessen your effectiveness in dealing with customers. If you have financial problems, look for resources (books, classes, employee assistance programs) that can help you get on sound financial footing.

Lack of "alone" time. Taking time for yourself is crucial for good mental hygiene. Sometimes the pressures of work and family responsibilities cause extreme stress levels to build up. When this happens, you can become like a bomb with a short fuse waiting to be lit. And, if the match comes in the form of a difficult customer situation, problems for you, your organization, and your customer may be the result.

Build time into your schedule for you. Read a book, watch a movie, or do whatever you want to do. This sometimes takes negotiation with others in your personal and work life, but the dividends are worth the effort.

Overworking. Does the term *workaholic* apply to you? Because of competition in the workplace, concerns about job security, overextension of credit by banks, downsizing or "rightsizing" (or "capsizing") in many organizations, and numerous other factors, a lot of people spend more time at work than elsewhere. If you are such a person, the positive side is that you are doing more work and gaining new skills and knowledge while possibly moving up the career ladder. The downside is that other parts of your life may be suffering. The key to real long-term success is balance. You can obtain some balance through effective time usage (see Chapter 12). Here are some quick questions to help determine whether you fall into the workaholic category. If you answer yes to all or most of these questions, there is a good chance that you are a workaholic.

- *Do you arrive early for work, no matter how late you stayed the night before?*
- *Do you volunteer to take on new tasks, even if you already feel overwhelmed?*
- *Do you skip lunch and breaks (and sometimes dinner) in order to work on job-related tasks?*
- *Do you regularly volunteer for overtime or work on weekends and holidays?*
- *Do you find it difficult to be inactive or relax?*
- *Do you approach every activity as a competition or challenge (even leisure activities or hobbies)?*
- *Do you find it hard to take a vacation (and when you do, you take work along)?*
- *Can you not envision yourself ever retiring?*

Work It Out 11-3 Personal Factors That Create Stress

▶ Develop a list of stressors in your personal life that might carry over to and affect your workplace performance and/or your personal relationships.

_____

_____

_____

_____

_____

_____

_____

_____

_____

_____

_____

AVOIDING STRESS THROUGH EFFECTIVE COMMUNICATION

▶ **CONCEPT:** Effective communication techniques such as politeness, being assertive rather than aggressive, and expressing your feelings are a few ways that you can avoid stress.

As you have discovered in other chapters, your key tool for success when dealing with customers is your ability to communicate in a positive, effective manner. By practicing active listening, selecting words and nonverbal cues carefully, and then selecting the right time and place to deliver your message, you can significantly improve your relationships with customers and reduce stress levels (for you and your customers) at the same time. The following sections discuss specific strategies for communicating with customers.

Be Polite

Think of all the things you have been taught throughout your life related to courtesy. You may have heard statements such as "You can catch more flies with sugar," or you were reminded to always say please and thank-you. Whatever you learned, the concepts are the same—treat people well and with respect, and things will go much better. This is especially helpful in emotional or stressful encounters. By acknowledging customers as important people, you can sometimes get them to calm their own emotions and thus reduce stress levels for both of you. If nothing else, they will sometimes start to become embarrassed or feel bad about the way they are treating you and will calm down.

A customer may vent frustration by yelling at you. What can you do to avoid this type of sitaution?

Respond Appropriately to Messages Received

When a customer asks a question or makes a statement, it is crucial that you listen and respond in a suitable manner. Summarizing what was said is one technique to accomplish this. Failure to respond appropriately can frustrate and irritate a customer or lead to escalated emotion.

Recognize that your customers are just like you—they experience pressure and stress. They come to you and your organization to fulfill a need or obtain something they want, not to receive poor service or defective products or to add more stress to their lives. They also do not expect to find you in a nonreceptive mood. If you and the organization disappoint the customer, he or she will likely become irritated or upset. A key point to remember is that although the customer may or may not have a legitimate complaint, it is your job to listen and take action to solve the problem to the best of your ability, and in a manner that will satisfy the customer.

Speak Assuredly

As you learned in Chapter 3, there is a difference between assertive and aggressive language and voice tones. When a customer or someone else is upset, it is best to allow him or her to vent without responding immediately. This can take the edge off an otherwise stressful situation. When you do speak, do so clearly and with authority and confidence. Also, stay calm as you communicate.

Do not let the other person irritate you or draw you into an emotional exchange. This will only heat up the situation, and will not help you to lead the conversation toward resolution.

Use "I" Language

Remember what you have learned about word choice. The word *you* can sound accusatory and challenging, but "I" language sounds as if you are taking on responsibility and are trying to join the other person in solving a problem. For example, suppose that a customer comes into your store complaining that a power tool does not work properly, all the while repeating that he or she had a similar one before and has read the owner's manual. If you say something like, "You're incorrect . . . ," a confrontation is likely to occur. On the other hand, if you say something like, "I'm not sure, but I believe that if you do. . . it will work fine. May I please show you?" In the second example, you are working with the customer in a nonthreatening manner to solve the problem without posing a challenge. You are also asking permission when you use the word *please*.

Communicate Your Feelings

A big factor contributing to stress is caused by failing to give feedback or to express yourself effectively. If you are troubled by something or someone, think about how to address the matter and then tactfully and professionally approach the person. Keeping feelings or emotions bottled up inside can cause stress and ultimately lead to relationship breakdown and illness. Management consultant and author Ken Blanchard calls this storing of feelings *gunnysacking*. He equates carrying around built-up emotions to putting them in an imaginary sack that you carry with you. Whenever someone does something you object to, you (figuratively) put it into your sack. You collect your complaints. You may grumble (to yourself), "I hate it when he does that," or "There he goes again. One of these days, I'm going to talk to him about that." What often happens is that at some point a small thing sets you off and you begin to unpack your gunnysack. You say things to the other person like, "I hate it when you do such and such," or "And another thing you do that makes me crazy . . ." The recipient of your anger is dumbfounded because he had no idea you had stored all the feelings you are now releasing. The result: You may feel better, but your relationship may be irreparably damaged.

As you read in Chapter 3, it is far better to share your feelings in a low-key rational manner than to save them up and explode. The other person may also explode, and you could end up in a highly charged, emotional argument. Instead, when something occurs that bothers you, take the time to provide immediate (or as soon as possible) feedback to the person. Discuss the behavior, the impact it had, your feelings on the subject, and then listen to his or her side of the situation, offer suggestions where appropriate, and reaffirm the value of the relationship to you. These simple things can mean a lot in maintaining a strong relationship with a customer or someone else in your life.

6 | MAINTAINING YOUR SANITY

▸ **CONCEPT:** Maintaining your sanity means that you take active and positive steps to reduce your stressful situations. Managing your time effectively, setting realistic goals, and taking frequent breaks are just a few steps that will help.

You can probably identify many things that add stress to your personal life. With the added stress of dealing with difficult customers, how can you keep your sanity? To help cope with the day-to-day pressures brought on by dealing with difficult customers and workplace situations, try the tips given in Figure 11-4.

FIGURE 11-4

Stress-reduction strategies.

There are things you can do to reduce your stress level. Here are a few:

- Stay calm
- Manage your time effectively
- Avoid procrastination
- Prioritize tasks
- Set realistic goals
- Take frequent breaks
- Exercise regularly
- Eliminate vagueness
- Reduce personal tensions

- Use positive self-talk
- Vary your activities
- Get more sleep
- Find a hobby
- Take a humor break
- Be a realist
- Take a mental trip
- Smile

Stay Calm

Even though a customer or someone else does or says something that angers or upsets you, stay in control. When an incident occurs that makes you frustrated or emotional, keep smiling inside, politely excuse yourself, and take a quick break from the situation. Breathe deeply and think of something pleasant. Either return once you cool down or ask someone else to handle the person.

Manage Your Time Effectively

Chapter 12 will provide you with some ideas and specific tips for effectively managing your time. The key to successful customer service is to establish a system for managing your time. There are many good books, audiotapes, videos, and seminars that teach the skill of organization and task management. Learning and practicing these skills can help relieve stress. For example, taking care of difficult or unpleasant tasks first thing in the day means that you will not dread them all day long.

Avoid Procrastination

As you record tasks that need attention, take care of them. Putting them off only adds the stress of "one more thing to do." If your tasks seem overwhelming, break them into manageable chunks and work on one small piece at a time. For example, assume that you have been given the task of going through all correspondence files for the past year to identify recurring complaints. Try asking whether you can do a portion of the job at a time. If you are given permission to divide the work into chunks, you might work on three months of files each day until you have completed the review.

Prioritize Tasks

You will learn strategies for effective time management in Chapter 12. Specific techniques such as making a list of tasks to be accomplished at the end of each day or first thing in the morning and then following through on them can help reduce your stress level. With this technique, tasks not handled by the end of the day can become a high priority on your list for the following day.

Set Realistic Goals

Many people subject themselves to unnecessary stress by reacting as events occur. By setting attainable goals, you stay on track and feel a sense of accomplishment when you reach them. Also, get in the habit of rewarding yourself when you achieve goals. Do this by taking a short break or having a snack.

Take Frequent Breaks

Too many service providers develop the habit of skipping breaks and lunch or speaking to customers for hours at a time. This is a mistake. You need an occasional escape from the routine of dealing with customers and workplace activities. Taking time away from customers and job tasks can revitalize you mentally. If you also build in some exercise, as suggested in the next section of this chapter, you will double the benefit. Moreover, if you spend some time with coworkers occasionally during the day (e.g., breaks, lunch, or brief chats between customers), you will have an opportunity to strengthen workplace relationships while networking and sharing new ideas and information. All of this can be very valuable to your long-term health and success. Take opportunities during lunch or breaks to go outside the building to read, for fresh air, to walk, for a change of scenery, or to meet with friends. You'll return refreshed and ready to deal with customers again.

Exercise Regularly

Even though there are not enough hours in the day to accomplish everything that you have to do in your personal and work life, exercise is one thing that you should try to keep in your schedule. Exercise can provide many benefits, including prevention of emotional trauma brought on by stressful situations. Practices such as using the stairs instead of the elevator or escalator, walking at lunchtime, taking a brisk walk before or after work, and riding a bicycle to the convenience store rather than driving can add significantly to a feeling of good health. You may choose to park in a distant parking lot so that you have farther to walk. Walk in the mall at lunch or at night.

You can even exercise right on the job. Try using some simple isometric exercises (pushing against your chair seat or desk, grasping the edges of your chair seat and pulling firmly as you are seated, or keeping the feet flat on the floor while seated and pushing down against the floor). You can also do simple stretching activities (raising your arms above your head and reaching toward the ceiling, rolling your head slowly, and bending slowly to touch your toes).

Eliminate Vagueness

Much stress is due to uncertainty. To reduce uncertainty, research solutions, ask questions, or set up a system to deal with various situations that occur in your job or personal life. For example, suppose that a certain customer situation comes up periodically, and yet no policy or procedure exists to deal with it. You might check to see what other customer service professionals do in similar situations and then suggest to your team leader or supervisor that your organization implement a standard policy or procedure.

Reduce Personal Tensions

You cannot switch off your personal life while you're at work. Take the time to deal with problems in your personal life as they surface. Ignoring them will only frustrate you. Also, strive for balance in your personal and professional life (instead of spending all your waking hours working, develop a hobby, take a trip, spend time with friends and loved ones, or just relax). If you spend too much time and energy on either work or relaxation, you will neglect the other.

Use Positive Self-Talk

Give yourself a pep talk by saying positive things such as "I can handle this," "I won't let this get to me," or "This is only a temporary event, and a year from now, it will have no meaning." Too often, people get caught up in negative self-talk, which is unhealthy. They tell themselves things such as "I can't do this," "I can't do anything right," "Why can't I be more like . . . ?"

If you tell yourself these types of things often enough, they might become a reality, because initiative fades as defeat is accepted. This can lead to stress and depression.

Vary Your Activities

You may have heard the phrase "Variety is the spice of life." Variety is also crucial for preventing mental **burnout**. Your brain needs stimulation and challenge. If you follow the same routine day in and out, you have little opportunity to develop new ideas, explore other alternatives, and allow the brain to grow.

Be creative in your job and personal life. If you usually get up at 6:30 a.m., try getting up at 6 to read the paper, watch the news, or go for a walk or bicycle ride. If you always eat in the company cafeteria, try getting together with others to go off-site. If you usually follow one route to and from work, try an alternative. By varying routine and what you see or experience, you will gain a new perspective. This can lead to reduced stress, improved job performance, and increased satisfaction.

Making some of the minor routine changes shown in Figure 11-5 can often lead to enhanced creativity, different perspectives, and a feeling of being refreshed or renewed. The reason for this is that the brain is exercised by being exposed to new and different stimuli that cause it to adapt and learn. This can lead to more effective job performance and better interactions with customers and others in the workplace.

FIGURE 11-5

Mental stimulators.

- Take a shower instead of a bath, or vice versa.
- Get up earlier or later each day.
- Change your morning routine.
- Have something different for breakfast occasionally.
- Take a different route to work.
- Listen to a different radio station in the car.
- Watch a different television channel.
- Shop at different stores.
- Go to lunch or on breaks with different people.

Get More Sleep

According to the Better Sleep Council in Alexandria, Virginia, most people do not get enough sleep. Each person is different in the amount of sleep needed to be efficient. Typically, eight hours of sleep has been recommended for years by various experts. If you find yourself tying to "catch up" on your sleep during weekends, your body is telling you that it is sleep-deprived during the week. Instead of staying up to watch the late news, turn off the set and go to bed earlier. If you really want to see the program, videotape it for viewing later. Or, watch the early morning news offered on stations in most cities.

If you are a shift worker or work nights, try the following tips for a better sleep period:

- *Make sure that the room in which you sleep is dark and quiet. Use heavy window coverings to block out light.*

- *Make sure that the room is cool, approximately 65°F.*

- *Make sure that your mattress is comfortable and supportive, and is large enough so that you can move around comfortably.*

Find a Hobby

Most people who participate in a hobby that they enjoy (e.g., gardening, ceramics, painting, dancing, photography) find that it relaxes them by providing a mental diversion (as discussed earlier). Whether you look for an active or a sedentary activity depends on your time, desires, and capabilities. The key is to do what you want to do and like.

Take a Humor Break

Read, watch, or listen to something humorous. In the workplace, take a break with some of your peers and share humorous experiences that you have had in dealing with customers. You might even learn some new customer service strategies.

Be a Realist

You are not superwoman or superman, so don't try to act as if you are. Recognize that you cannot do everything yourself or take on all opportunities offered to you. Trying to do so can ultimately cause you to burn out mentally, can lead to serious health problems, and can reduce your effectiveness and efficiency in dealing with people and situations. Use some of the time-management strategies discussed in Chapter 12 to assist in improving your performance while decreasing your stress.

Take a Mental Trip

Close your eyes and relax as you think of pleasant events or locations. Instead of listening to loud, reverberating music, try something light, instrumental, or low-key as you relax.

Smile

The old adage "Laughter is the best medicine" has merit. Try to find something humorous about the situations you encounter at work and home. This can help reduce tensions. Lighten up. Don't take everything people say seriously or personally.

Looking for the reasons why you feel stressed may help you find ways to relieve the stress. Coping with stress is important if you are to remain healthy.

Coping With Stress

Think about ways you deal with stress that are not healthy, and then think of more positive, healthy approaches. List both the positive and the negative below. Some examples are provided.

NEGATIVE	POSITIVE
Yell at an angry or rude customer.	Count to ten. Take a deep breath and then respond professionally.
Ignore the feelings of pressure.	Find a quiet place to sit down and relax. Take a "mental vacation" to a pleasant location.

Work It Out 11-4. Stress-Reduction Activity

▶ Take a few minutes when you are feeling stressed to give yourself a mental break. To do this, follow the steps outlined below.

1. Find a straight-backed chair and sit comfortably, not rigidly (depending on where you are, you can lie on the floor).

2. Mentally prepare yourself by telling yourself that you are going to take the next few minutes out of your hectic schedule "for you."

3. Relax your whole body by settling into the chair and allowing it to support you.

4. Close your eyes in order to block out visual stimulation or other distractions.

5. Start breathing slowly and deeply. As you inhale, say to yourself, "I am . . ." and, as you exhale, ". . . relaxed."

6. Continue this slow, rhythmic breathing and repeating of the phrase for the duration of the activity.

Work It Out 11-4. Stress-Reduction Activity (Continued)

7. To conclude, discontinue the phrase *I am relaxed* but continue to breathe deeply for a few moments. As you end the activity, slowly and gently extend and stretch your legs, feet, arms, hands, and whole body.

8. Open your eyes slowly.

Note: Depending on your location and musical taste, you may want to play some mellow, instrumental relaxation music in the background.

7 WORKPLACE VIOLENCE

▶ **CONCEPT:** Since 1980, changes in the workplace as well as external factors such as substance abuse, shifting values and beliefs, violence on television and in the movies, and a general trend to lash out at others have made workplace violence a familiar phrase. You should learn to recognize the danger signals and how to address them.

No chapter on stress would be complete without a discussion of **workplace violence**. Prior to 1980, workplace violence was virtually unheard of. Since then, the culture of the workplace has changed dramatically because of many factors addressed in other parts of this book (e.g., diversity, organizational restructuring, downsizing, technology, and increased job demands). Other external factors are adding fuel to this smoldering fire (substance abuse, shifting societal values and beliefs, illegal drugs, violence on television and in movies, and a general trend for people to lash out at others in the form of verbal or physical assault, as in the case of so-called **road rage**).

Violence in the workplace is nearing epidemic proportions and is creating a true crisis. According to research by the National Institute for Occupational Safety and Health (NIOSH), "Violence is a substantial contributor to occupational injury and death, and homicide has become the second leading cause of occupational injury or death. Each week, an average of 20 workers are murdered and 18,000 assaulted while at work or on duty. Nonfatal assaults result in millions of lost workdays and cost workers millions of dollars in lost wages." Moreover, NIOSH found that "Workplace violence is clustered in certain occupational settings: For example, the retail trade and service industries account for more than half the workplace homicides (56%) and 85% of nonfatal workplace assaults. Of any occupational group, taxicab drivers are at the highest risk of being the victims of homicide. Workers in health care, community services, and retail settings are at increased risk of nonfatal assaults."[3] Statistically, the persons in greatest potential peril are employees whose jobs involve routine public contact and the exchange of money. Obviously, these figures indicate that this is an issue to be concerned about.

---

[3] U.S. Department of Health and Human Services, National Institute for Occupational Safety and Health, Current Intelligence Bulletin 57, Publication DHHS (NIOSH), Publication No. 97—100, July 1996.

Preventing Workplace Violence

Each employee must take a proactive role in dealing with and preventing workplace violence. A key to prevention is to conduct yourself in a professional manner at all times, keeping in mind the positive communication skills described in this book. By doing so, you are less likely to escalate a situation into an emotional confrontation or provoke a violent reaction from others. Also, it is important to educate yourself on strategies for recognizing danger signals and how to address them. At the very least, talk to your supervisor about the organization's approach to dealing with violence and plan an escape route from the work area, in case you ever need it.

Recognizing Potential Offenders

During the past few decades, many law enforcement and private organizations have sought to create a profile of potentially dangerous people in the workplace. The following characteristics are offered to aid your awareness, not to make you suspicious of someone who fits the profile. Also, keep in mind that many factors, such as problems in someone's life, could trigger violent behavior. Some general characteristics of offenders are:

- *White male who is between 35 and 45 years of age.*
- *Has a history of job changes.*
- *Takes constructive feedback or criticism poorly.*
- *Is interested in firearms and other weapons.*
- *Identifies with or talks about violence.*
- *Is a loner who has few friends and little family contact.*
- *Fails to take responsibility or blame when errors occur.*
- *May use drugs and/or alcohol.*

Identifying Warning Signs

Many people who are prone to violence exhibit telltale behaviors that, when viewed in their totality, should be a warning signal for you and those around you. By being vigilant, you can possibly head off trouble by changing your approach in dealing with a possible offender, or at least reporting the behavior that you observe to a supervisor, team leader, human resources, and/or security. The following are possible indicators that someone could become violent under the certain circumstances.

History of violence. If someone discloses to you that in the past he or she has been involved in violent criminal acts or domestic violence, or has had verbal or physical confrontations with others, you may want to be alert. Typically, past behavior is a good indicator of future behavior. This is especially true if the person seems to brag about the past negative or antisocial behavior. For example, suppose that you are in the cafeteria of your organization and a male coworker brags about the fact that over the weekend he got into an argument in a local nightclub. He says that he had to hit some guy for looking at his date. He then gives a gloating blow-by-blow description of the ensuing fight, which caused the other person to go to the hospital. It is wise to listen silently, excuse yourself at the earliest opportunity, and steer clear of this person as much as possible in the future.

Romantic obsession. Many stories are based on the theme of obsession. In such scenarios, the stalker pursues his or her prey relentlessly even when the other person hasn't the slightest interest. In these stories, often someone is hurt or killed as a result of the obsession. This is a strong message. If someone seems to have such an obsession with you or someone else in your workplace, seek assistance immediately by reporting it to your supervisor or team leader and your human resources department.

Alcohol or chemical abuse. Substance abuse can send someone over the edge. If a coworker shows signs of being under the influence of alcohol or drugs, confidentially report the matter to your supervisor or team leader immediately. In some serious situations when a coworker's activities off the job are negatively influencing his or her on-the-job performance, you may want to inform your supervisor or team leader. It is unfair to you, your customers, and the organization if your coworker cannot do his or her job because of outside activities. If a customer appears to be under the influence of alcohol or drugs, politely excuse yourself and seek assistance from your supervisor or team leader immediately.

Depression. Depression is a major contributor to suicides and workplace violence. Certainly, it can negatively affect job performance and the ability to deliver quality customer service. If someone you know seems to be depressed, it may be time to speak to this person confidentially and encourage him or her to seek assistance. Many times, depression can be brought on by personal problems (e.g., a relationship, financial, or legal problem) or by workplace issues (e.g., dissatisfaction, disciplinary actions, termination, or poor relationships with others). In extreme cases, you may also want to alert your supervisor or team leader.

When customers appear to be depressed, provide cordial, friendly service and get them out of the area as quickly as possible without provoking an emotional reaction.

Threatening behavior. Take all threats seriously. When someone becomes verbally and/or physically threatening, harassing, or belligerent, it is a cry for help and should not be ignored. Even if he or she apologizes, recognize that something is not right. If you receive a threat face-to-face, in writing, or over the telephone, report it immediately to your supervisor or team leader.

Mental conditions. Obviously, you are not a psychiatrist and should not try to act like one in diagnosing a person's behavior. However, if you deal with people day in and out in your job, you can probably recognize unusual behavior. For example, you should be concerned when you notice coworkers who stop paying attention to their hygiene or appearance, have serious mood swings, become withdrawn, complain about a supervisor, their job, customers, or the organization excessively and dramatically, and/or display empathy for people who commit violent acts. You should also closely monitor customers who send cues such as erratic gestures, talking to themselves, responding to or asking questions illogically, or referring to imaginary people or objects. Such people may be harmless, but you can never tell what is affecting their behavior. They might be mentally ill, or they might be under the influence of some substance. Keep your distance, and quietly seek assistance.

As you have discovered through experience and by your study of this chapter, stressors are possible and likely in everyone's life. Your task or goal will be to find ways to control the effects of stress so that you can work with your customers more efficiently and effectively.

Summary

Chapter Summary

Stress is costly and unproductive in the workplace and in your personal life. Throughout this chapter, you have explored what stress is, its causes and costs, the factors that contribute to increasing stress, the strategies for reducing or eliminating it, and the trend toward workplace violence. A key way to reduce stress and violence is through education. Using the material in this chapter can help make you more productive and possibly improve the quality of your life. By identifying and eliminating stressors in your life, you can enhance the enjoyment you receive from your job and deliver higher-quality service to your customers.

CHAPTER REVIEW QUESTIONS

1. How does stress benefit you? _____
   _____
   _____
   _____

2. Describe the fight or flight syndrome _____
   _____
   _____
   _____

3. What are some signs of stress? _____
   _____
   _____
   _____

4. What are five environmental factors that cause increased stress?
   _____
   _____
   _____

5. What job factors cause increased stress levels? _____
   _____
   _____
   _____

6. What are some personal factors that contribute to high stress levels?
   _____
   _____
   _____

7. What are some communication strategies that can help reduce stress?

_____

_____

_____

8. What are some strategies for maintaining your sanity in the workplace? _____

_____

_____

_____

9. What are some characteristics of the typical violent offender in the workplace? _____

_____

_____

_____

10. What are some warning signs that someone in the workplace might become violent? _____

_____

_____

_____

_____

⬇ SEARCH IT OUT

Search the Internet for Information on Stress or Workplace Violence
Log onto the Internet to search for sites that contain articles and/or information related to any of the following:

Causes of workplace stress

Strategies for reducing or eliminating workplace stress

Research on stress

Research on workplace violence

Identifying workplace violence

Strategies for preventing workplace violence

COLLABORATIVE *Learning Activity*

Oral Presentation on Stress or Workplace Violence
Based on the topics in this chapter, research and write a five- to ten- page paper on workplace stress or workplace violence. Prepare a 15- to 20- minute presentation based on the paper and using some form of visual aid (e.g., overhead projector, PowerPoint, slides, flip charts, pictures, charts).

Dealing with Stress at Southside Memorial Hospital

Background

Southside Memorial Hospital is a state-of-the-art medical facility located just inside the city limits of Houston, Texas. The hospital will soon be merging with a competitor, Houston General Hospital. Many of the patients who visit the hospital each day are Hispanic, Vietnamese, or Laotian. In addition to the new multimillion dollar cardiovascular care unit, the hospital provides typical inpatient and outpatient care to over 60,000 patients a year. On a normal day, the emergency room sees 90 to 100 patients with complaints of everything from colds and flu to lacerations, head trauma, and gunshot or knife wounds. The atmosphere in the emergency room is usually tense, with a steady stream of patents entering, being processed, diagnosed, and sent to appropriate areas of the hospital for further evaluation and diagnosis or treatment. For the past four hours, there has been a problem with the air-conditioning unit for the emergency room waiting area and the temperature is now above 90° F. There are 10 to 20 people in the waiting room.

Your Role

You are the triage nurse at the front desk in the emergency room. You have been with the hospital for eight years but have recently been thinking of leaving because you were passed over for a position as emergency room supervisor and because of the merger with Houston General. Your primary job is to oversee and orchestrate the processing of everyone who enters the emergency room. This includes the initial discussion of the patient's needs, providing and collecting registration and insurance forms, logging the patient in, and ensuring that he or she is seen by appropriate medical staff members as soon as possible. The position requires a high degree of medical knowledge, patience, interpersonal communication skills, and compassion.

You have worked a double shift today because of a flu epidemic. You are tired, your feet hurt, you haven't eaten in eight hours, your 13-year-old daughter (you are a single mother) called earlier to tell you that she came home from school because she was sick, and you believe that you are also coming down with the flu. Also, during the past hour, there has been an influx of people into the emergency room. You have had to deal with screaming children with colds, or with objects stuck up their nose, and with people who did not want to be in the emergency room. You have also screened a woman in labor, a teenage boy who cut his foot badly while using a lawnmower, a man with severe back strain, an elderly woman who appears to be senile (she imagines that people are coming to get her; you think that she has broken her hip), and a man who had an 11-inch spike driven through his forearm in an occupational accident.

At 8:42 p.m., you receive a radio message from an incoming ambulance informing you that a patient is being brought in who is highly agitated, belligerent, and possibly under the influence of alcohol or some other substance. He has lacerations to his forehead and shoulder from an automobile accident. As the vehicle arrives, you meet the paramedics at the emergency room door along with an orderly and a member of the security team. While you are attempting to assess the man's injury, he pushes your hand away saying he doesn't need any help from some overweight cow. He then tries to get off the gurney he is strapped to.

Questions

1. What are some of the stressful environmental factors in this scenario?

_____

_____

_____

_____

_____

2. What are some of the stressful job factors present in this scenario?

3. What are some of the stressful personal factors in this scenario?

_____

_____

4. How would you handle the situation with the patient who has just arrived? Explain.

_____

_____

_____

_____

5. What could go wrong in this situation?

_____

_____

_____

_____

FROM THE FRONTLINE
Interview

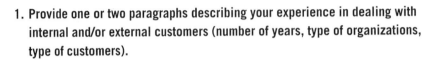

Catherine L. Jones
Postal Clerk
United States
Postal Service
Casselberry, Florida

1. Provide one or two paragraphs describing your experience in dealing with internal and/or external customers (number of years, type of organizations, type of customers).

I've been employed with the U.S. Postal Service for 14 years, serving the public daily. I approach situations with sincerity and concern for others to lessen some stress that comes with serving others. Additionally, I give a big smile and am polite to each customer because this is the way I want to be treated when going to other businesses. Customers come in with all kinds of problems, not just the mail. In dealing with them respectfully and knowing my duties very well, I am ready to give proper and accurate service.

2. What are your general impressions of the customer service in the United States? Why do you feel this way?

For the most part, customer service seems to be pretty good in the United States. I feel this way because most people are willing to be helpful and give good service. Once I went to an office supply store to get some name tags printed for an event we were having. I went a couple days prior to the event and the service person said it would take three to five working days for the printing process. Then she came up with the idea of using the computer to print the name tags. Thanks to her quick thinking I was saved from a predicament of not having the name tags in time.

3. What are some of the biggest contributors to stress in dealing with customers in your position?

Generally, the lack of patience that people exhibit seems to add the most stress in my job. In this day and time, everyone is a big rush and not going anywhere. Anger is another contributor. People seem to be so angry. I'm constantly trying to find out what their anger is all about and why they act that way. I try not to get angry with stressful people. Instead, I stay calm and listen to the customer. Additionally, when someone is upset, I respond with concern and if necessary, apologize—even if it is not my fault. It's also important to say "thank-you."

4. What are some strategies that you use to reduce or eliminate stress each day?

Customers often come in ready to scream at the first person that they see when they are upset. As a clerk working the front window at the post office, I have to be a good listener and help solve their problems.

My number one strategy is prayer. Other than that, I believe that you have to be considerate of others, be as efficient and speedy as possible when delivering service, and to smile and say hello to all customers.

An example of how this has helped me occurred when a customer came into the office to complain about not getting his mail. He said it was being forwarded to someone else's address, and he was upset. I asked him to remain calm while we figured out the problem. Apparently, someone had moved from his residence and had put in an address change for the entire family. We resolved the issue quickly.

5. How have you seen technology add to the stress level faced by employees in today's customer service environment?

Computers are good, but everyone does not know how to use them. Sometimes it is confusing, and you have to go through extra steps to perform or get information needed to get the job done. For example, at some post offices, customers can get a printout of each Zip code to which they send packages. First, I have to type in the information about the address. Some customers have lots of packages, so other customers have to wait in line longer than they want to. So while some customers only take a minute or two, others can take up to ten minutes to serve. Unfortunately, some customers are impatient, and this causes stress for them and me.

6. In your experience, what do service providers do to increase their own stress levels when dealing with customers?

Some service providers take everything personal. People should only deal with what they know and can do. If they cannot do something, or they don't know some information, they should find someone who can help them. Many people don't do this.

7. What advice related to stress and its reduction can you give to someone entering a customer service job today?

Everyone has some expertise in relating to others or in doing their job. Service providers should stick to what they know and can do well. For those customers and situations that they cannot handle, providers should refer them to others who can handle them. Doing this will ensure that the customer is happy or satisfied and that the service provider will be happy too. Also, by doing these things, stress levels for the customer and the service provider can be reduced.

For example, I recently referred a customer, who wanted specific stamps that we did not have, to another postal facility in the area. That facility almost always has the stamps the customer was looking for. Later the customer came back and thanked me for directing her to the other site. Being able to refer someone to another business or office is a way of properly serving customers.

CRITICAL THINKING

What steps or strategies are available for dealing with stress on the job? Do you think stress is a major problem on most jobs today?

Chapter 12

Managing Your Time

OBJECTIVES

After completing this chapter, you will be able to:

- *Realize how time reality and perceptions of time differ.*

- *Recognize the need for effective time management.*

- *Prioritize daily tasks.*

- *Apply techniques that save time while serving customers.*

- *Use time usage criteria to reclaim time.*

"There's never enough time to do it right, but there's always time to do it over."

Jack Bergman
Former VP, Jordache
Enterprises, Inc.
1987

Before reviewing the chapter content, respond to the following questions by placing a "T" for true or an "F" for false on the rules. Use any questions you miss as a checklist of material to which you will pay particular attention as you read through the chapter. For those you get right, congratulate yourself, but review the sections they address in order to learn additional details about the topic.

_____ 1. Increased self-satisfaction is one of the positive results of effective time management in the workplace.

_____ 2. The way you use time has little effect on your stress levels.

_____ 3. One technique for prioritizing your time is to schedule key events and then review the information regularly.

_____ 4. Time tends to pass more slowly when the mind is not actively engaged or proactively performing and being stimulated.

_____ 5. Tasks that could contribute to customer satisfaction and ultimately lead to improved performance should be a top priority, as should those regulated by law or established by policy or customer demand.

_____ 6. Being prepared by having information and materials available to help serve customers is one technique for saving time while serving customers.

_____ 7. You should look for opportunities to engage customers so that they will not become bored and dissatisfied and go to a competitor.

_____ 8. Using a "take a number" system for waiting customers is one way to stimulate your customers mentally.

_____ 9. When providing service by traveling to different locations or customer sites, you have virtually no control over your time because of unexpected delays.

_____ 10. You should always confirm appointments before leaving to attend them even though you spoke with the person with whom you are meeting when you scheduled the meeting.

_____ 11. To save time on the telephone, you should have a list of objectives before you call.

_____ 12. When calling someone, you should screen or identify the person who answers before you begin speaking.

_____ 13. Voice mail systems are a universally accepted tool for effective time management.

_____ 14. To better manage your e-mail, prevent messages from accumulating, and save time, you should answer e-mail messages as soon as they arrive.

_____ 15. Three criteria for examining time usage are necessity, appropriateness, and efficiency.

1. T   6. T   11. T
2. F   7. T   12. T
3. T   8. T   13. F
4. T   9. F   14. F
5. F   10. T   15. T

WHY THE NEED FOR EFFECTIVE TIME MANAGEMENT?

> **CONCEPT:** Time management is not just a workplace issue. Learning to apply skills that you use to manage your time away from the workplace to the workplace can make you more efficient.

This chapter focuses on increasing your awareness of the need for effective **time management**. By thinking about factors that inhibit effective productivity, and coming up with strategies for improving time usage, you can gain insights into ways to handle a variety of personal and workplace situations. Also, by better managing your time, you can improve your job performance and better serve your customers. One important thing to remember about time management is that it is not just a workplace issue. If you learn to manage your time outside the workplace, you can apply that skill to your job. On the other hand, if you mismanage your time outside the workplace, the problems will probably follow you to the job.

Four important positive results can come from effective time management in the workplace:

1. Elevated productivity through a more efficient approach to accomplishing tasks and dealing with customers.

2. Reduced stress levels, which can benefit you personally and can also make life easier for those around you since you will probably be calmer and seem more in control.

3. Increased self-satisfaction from confidence in your ability to get the job done professionally and in a more competent manner.

4. Improved quality of life, for good time management habits on the job can expedite the accomplishment of tasks and reduce the amount of overtime or extra hours needed to "catch up." This is time you can spend doing the things you enjoy in life either on or off the job.

As you read in Chapter 11, customer service is a very rewarding but stressful profession. With all the tasks and responsibilities that the average service provider must attend to, there are often not enough hours in a day to effectively balance work with personal life. Moreover, dealing with internal and external customers can be trying, to say the least. Many customers are a joy to serve; others are not. Even so, it is your job to smile, act professionally, and make a valiant effort to assist all of them to the best of your ability. Sometimes you are successful; sometimes you are not. Whatever the outcome, a key factor often influencing your actions (and inactions in some instances) is time. The amount of time you have or do not have has an important effect on your actions. In a workplace that has downsized, restructured, merged, and made all kinds of other adjustments, there never seems to be enough people or hours to get everything done. Add to this the fact that, in many cases, your customers are just as stressed and rushed as you are, and you have a formula for possible service breakdown. This potentially volatile combination can often lead to confrontation and customer dissatisfaction if you are not careful and cannot manage your time effectively. This is why your ability to manage time and tasks effectively is so crucial. If you can learn the skill of time management, you can squeeze out precious minutes throughout the day. Knowing how to manage your time can lead to fulfilling workplace experiences, satisfied customers, and self-satisfaction.

Worksheet ▼

12-1

Time Management Self-Assessment

Read and respond to the following questions. Do not dwell on and analyze the questions; simply respond as you believe appropriate. Once you answer the questions, score your results (see the section on scoring below). Use the results to focus on areas you indicated are weak (scores below 3).

KEY: Yes = 1   Often = 2   Sometimes = 3   Seldom = 4   No = 5

1. Do you use a structured time management system or tool? _____

2. Do you use clearly defined written objectives to accomplish tasks? _____

3. Do you prioritize your daily tasks? _____

4. Do you meet established deadlines? _____

5. Do you avoid non-customer-related tasks throughout the day? _____

6. Do you feel in control of your time? _____

7. Do you effectively use technology to assist with job tasks? _____

8. Do you effectively control interruptions and time wasters? _____

9. Do you have time in your schedule to take care of unplanned tasks? _____

10. Do you use available tools and resources to increase your effectiveness when possible? _____

11. Do you have adequate time to serve each customer appropriately? _____

12. Do you avoid procrastination? _____

TOTAL _____

Scoring: Add up your points for each question to determine your total. A lower score is better. For any item on which you rated yourself 4 or 5, start developing strategies for improvement. Use the concepts outlined in this chapter and also look for additional resources in books (see the Bibliography), magazines, and video or audio programs on time management, or search the Internet for such topics. Continually strive for improvement, and retest yourself periodically.

2 | WHERE DOES THE TIME GO?

▶ **CONCEPT:** Everyone has the same amount of time every day of the year. How you manage that time makes the difference.

As you saw from the opening quote for this chapter, there never seems to be enough time to get everything done that you have to do. As the workplace gets more chaotic and your responsibilities grow, you need as many tools as possible to gain control of your time and be more productive.

Time Reality

Everyone has the same amount of time each day (86,400 seconds, 1440 minutes, or 24 hours). Some people use their time more efficiently than others do. Depending on the type of work and home environments in which you find yourself, your stress may increase because of your difficulties in using time effectively. For example, if you work in production areas (e.g., sales, telemarketing, or call centers) where you are held accountable for production rates, have timed standards for productivity, or work at a hectic pace, time can seem like your enemy. Or, high levels of stress may be caused by too few people handling too many tasks. In these environments, employees often have to work extended amounts of overtime or on weekends in order to meet established goals or standards. The frequent result is that they have little time to think before they speak. This is why a good system for time management and effective time management strategies can come in handy. Even if you can squeeze out a few minutes here and there, those precious minutes can be very helpful in helping you to more effectively serve your customers or accomplish other tasks.

Time Perception

Time can move quickly or slowly, depending on the circumstances. Take a look at some of the following examples to see whether you agree.

Slow Time Passage	Fast Time Passage
Being on telephone hold (no music or announcements)	On a rollercoaster or amusement ride
In the dentist's chair	At an enjoyable lunch meeting
In the doctor's office	Taking a test (e.g., for a driver's license)
In a slow-moving bank line	Speaking with a service provider who bills by the hour (e.g., lawyer, consultant, plumber)
Waiting for popcorn to pop at a movie theater	

Notice in the situations in column 1, time seems to pass slowly when the mind is not actively engaged or proactively performing and being stimulated. Time seems to go quickly when the mind is involved in some sort of mental activity. The lesson to be learned is that you should try to engage your customers so that they will not become preoccupied with time. When people have time on their hands, the mind gets busy doing other things. In a customer situation, often the customer's mind starts focusing on the fact that it is bored or that it's taking you a lot of time to provide service. Also, an unusual thing starts happening in such situations: the customer's internal clock starts speeding up. Ten seconds can seem like minute. If you don't believe this, try an experiment. The next time you call a service provider and are put on hold before speaking with someone (e.g., a technical support line, bank or retail customer service, doctor's office,) have a stopwatch handy. Start the stopwatch the moment you are put on hold. Without looking at the stopwatch, mentally track time until someone answers. Then stop the watch, but don't look at it. Have a pencil ready and make a note of how long you thought you were on hold. Now look at the stopwatch. If you are like most people, you will have perceived that you were on hold longer than you actually were. This is usually the result of boredom.

This phenomenon is one of the reasons organizations put music or announcements on the telephone hold function. They are engaging the customer's mind. Some companies even play occasional messages such as "Your approximate wait time is . . . ." Many times, if you check the time, you will find that the wait time is much longer than the message indicates.

Work It Out
12-1

Work It Out 12-1. Time Passages

Working with your group, add to the list of slow and fast time passages given earlier. Try to think of specific customer service situations, possibly ones that you have experienced as a customer. Be prepared to discuss your answers.

_____   _____
_____   _____
_____   _____
_____   _____

3 PRIORITIZING YOUR TIME

CONCEPT: Use a system to prioritize your time.

Being able to prioritize is an important skill. Planning events, activities, and tasks on a yearly, monthly, weekly, and daily basis can be rewarding from the standpoint of allowing you to be more proactive in preparing to deal with situations. Such planning can reduce your need to be a **crisis manager**.

It is important on and off the job because, if you do not manage your personal life well, you may carry over the personal stress into the workplace. This is not only inefficient; it is also unfair to your employer, peers, and customers.

After you have scheduled key events and tasks using some type of scheduling system (e.g., time management software, written planning system or calendar, or electronic scheduling device that can download information into your computer), review the information regularly to avoid forgetting something.

One way to manage events, rather than having them manage you, is to create a list of activities each day and assign a value to each based on importance. The key is to be consistent and prioritize each day. Some people make planning the last activity of their workday. When they arrive in the morning, they are ready to begin rather than spending time preparing.

Guidelines for Setting Priorities

Three guidelines can help you in determining what tasks to do first. That is, they can help you create a realistic and achievable list of daily tasks. As you learned when you read about goal setting in other chapters, goals must be attainable. Use the following standards to guide your list of priorities.

Judgment. You are the best judge of what you can accomplish in any given day. You know your strengths and what has to be done. When selecting priorities, remember that the ones having the most impact on customers and others should be placed high on your list. On the other hand, do not put so many priorities on a daily list that you will not get them done. If this happens, you might become discouraged and give up. When you find that you have more high priorities than you have time, you may need to ask for help or guidance from your boss. Many times, simply asking helps develop your relationship with others. They feel respected and trusted by your gesture, as long as you don't appear to be unloading your tasks onto them. Also, consider other resources that you might use to accomplish tasks (e.g., technology, outside vendors, customers).

Relativity. Assigning priorities is a matter of relativity. Some tasks and projects are readily rated higher than others are rated. You should be guided by the question "What is the best use of my time?"

Many people fill their daily schedule with frivolous or easy tasks and with tasks that they like to do. This produces a hollow feeling of accomplishment, for they may get a lot done and enjoy doing it, but they have not added a lot of value to customer service or the organizational goals. Keep in mind when setting priorities that your No. 1 focus should be your customers and activities that support them.

Timing. Reality and deadlines have a way of dictating priorities. The starting time of a project or task also may establish priorities. Once you begin a task, there must be enough time to finish it. If this is not possible, you may have to reprioritize or seek assistance.

Be realistic about the time it will take to complete a task. Make sure that you schedule that much time, plus a little extra, on your daily planning sheet. Also, consider your peak time period for performance (your circadian rhythm, which you read about in Chapter 5). Each person typically has a period of the day in which he or she has more energy and can get more done. Capitalize on your peak period and schedule high-priority tasks during that time, if possible.

Prioritizing System

To set up your own priority system, list all your pending activities and then group them according to their level of importance. How you assign value to a task is not as important as long as you use the same format each day. Many people use an A, B, C system, and others use a 1, 2, 3 format. Here are suggested criteria for assignment:

Priority A—Must do or critical items. Some things must be done because of management directives, local, state, or federal regulations, importance to customers or clients, deadlines, or opportunities they provide for your success or advancement (e.g., state tax reports, actions requested by a customer, application for a position in the organization with a specific cutoff date for submission).

Priority B—Should do. Items in this category are of "medium" value. Although they may contribute to customer satisfaction and improved performance, they are not essential or do not have critical deadlines (e.g., mailing an unsolicited information kit to a customer about a new product or developing a proposal for changing an existing system or process).

Priority C—Nice to do. This is the lowest category and includes tasks that are not a direct link to customer satisfaction. They may even be fun or interesting but could be omitted or left undone. Postponing or scheduling such priorities until a slower time period will likely have little or no impact on customer service (e.g., meeting with team members to brainstorm ideas for a more efficient layout of cubicles, cleaning old e-mail files, or neatly lining up the products on a shelf).

Note: As you go through your e-mail and voice mail messages at the times you have scheduled throughout the day, prioritize them, and add them to your list of things to do.

4 | SAVING TIME WHILE YOU SERVE

▶ **CONCEPT:** Prepare your daily schedule to make your calls or other appointments a priority. Use your time to good advantage between appointments.

In addition to prioritizing, many strategies can save time and result in a better quality of customer service. A key to effective service is to allocate enough time to handle customer issues. With experience, you will get better at doing this and at estimating how much time you need for various situations. Until then, talk to other, experienced service professionals, your boss, and your customers to find out how long a task should normally take. Also, observe other service providers as they serve you. Make mental notes of the efficient and effective things you hear and see, and avoid those things you perceive as ineffective time management techniques.

Finally, be prepared to serve by having available the information and materials you need (e.g., know your company's policies and procedures, know the products and services offered, be familiar with the various forms, and have a pencil or pen handy) so that you do not have to search for something. Failure to be ready to serve wastes your time and that of your customers.

In addition to the tips you have just read, you can do some specific things in various situations to provide service while managing time effectively. As you read through the following sections, think of how you might apply the techniques described and what other ones you might use.

Time Management in Face-to-Face Situations

Time is an important element in a service provider's daily life. Whether you deal with complaints, counter service (e.g., post office, bank, supermarket), sales (e.g., car dealership, insurance agency, electronics store, department store), or are in any type of job in which you sell or assist customers after a sale, time management comes into play. All the interpersonal communication skills described in this text are crucial in the delivery of professional service. By building effective relationships, you have a better chance of ensuring that interactions between customers and others in the workplace will be positive. Thus you will need your conflict-resolution skills less.

Some time-saving techniques that you may want to consider are:

Recognize the value of a customer's time and show a service orientation. Recognize the customer's presence nonverbally by smiling, and gesture with an index finger to indicate that you will be available in about a minute.

Get the customer busy. If you need to do other things or wait on other customers, try to get a waiting customer actively involved in doing some task. For example, if a customer will need to fill out a form (e.g., a new patient in a doctor's or dentist's office, someone returning or exchanging a product at customer service, or an applicant for a job or license), give the customer a pen and form and let him or her get started while you serve another customer. This occupies the customer while you handle another customer—and the form gets filled out.

Give the customer something to read. Depending on the situation and the type of organization, you might give the customer new product brochures to read while he or she waits. This not only occupies the customer's mind but may answer questions that you won't have to answer later.

Have the customer take a number. Many organizations with high customer walk-up traffic volume (e.g., fast-food establishments, discount stores, motor vehicle offices, utility companies) use tear-off number dispensers to alert customers when it is their turn to be served. These ticket systems are also helpful during peak sales and service seasons (e.g., back to school, Christmas, going out-of-business or clearance sales). Such systems were designed to let customers know where they are in the line for service, keep customers moving, and save service providers the unpleasant and time-consuming task of having to deal with angry customers who think that other customers have been served out of turn.

Taking a number also gives customers some mental stimulation (unless service is really slow and they must wait for an unacceptable length of time to be served). Taking a number gives them something to do—watch the numbers of other customers get called until their own turn arrives.

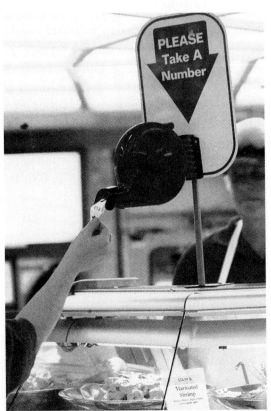

Having customers take a number organizes the wait time for service. How would you organize the wait time in a retail business?

If your organization has such a system, be sure that you are alert to people entering. Notify new customers to take a number for better service and to prevent confusion later over whose turn it is for service. Also, with such a system, be careful not to fall into the practice of thinking of your customers only as numbers. Instead of shouting out "Number _____," a more appropriate approach would be to say something like, "May I help number_____?" Then, as the person approaches, try to make eye contact, smile, and offer a greeting such as "Good morning. How may I assist you?"

Time Management on the Run

You have probably heard the saying "There just aren't enough hours in the day." This is especially true if your job involves traveling to a client's site or if you work at or travel between remote locations (e.g., branch offices). Transit time can take a big chunk out of your day. In such situations it is important to recognize how to best use your time. Here are a few tips:

Prepare in advance. Make sure that you schedule your appointments far enough in advance to allow for emergencies. Gather the materials and information you will need well before the scheduled date and time. Waiting until the last minute could cause trouble, especially if something you need is not readily available.

Plan visits during non-rush-hour traffic. If possible, schedule client or customer visits when traffic is not snarled and transit times can be reduced. Often, when you drive to other locations, something will slow you down (e.g., malfunctioning traffic lights, accidents, trains, vehicle breakdowns). You can grumble and accept lost productivity time, or you can be prepared by having alternative routes in mind and making sure that your vehicle is well maintained. Also, you can use the last tip in this section—listen to audiotapes to make the most of your downtime.

Group appointments. Setting up more than one appointment in the same geographic area can save you and your customers time, effort, and frustration while reducing your travel miles. You can use the "group" approach when customers or vendors come to your site for meetings. Also, try to schedule meetings for one part of a day (e.g., the morning). If you get all your meetings taken care of in the morning, you can then focus on other customer-related activities during the rest of the day without being interrupted.

Confirm your appointments. Take the time to e-mail or call your customer or client before leaving for an appointment. You will thus avoid an unnecessary trip if there was a change of plans and you were not notified, or someone forgot to note the meeting on his or her calendar. Your time, and the customer's, is precious; treat it as such.

Listen to audiotapes. Travel time is a great opportunity to catch up on the latest books on tape that you never seem to have time to read. You can also listen to taped notes from customers or meetings while you are traveling. You can also record information about various regular clients (ones you see or speak with periodically) and play them back on your way to appointments with them (e.g., past products or service used, organizational facts and statistics, names of key people in the organization).

Time Management and Technology

As you read in Chapter 7, there is much to consider in a workplace full of changing technology. As a result of technology, you may need to learn how to use all the technical tools available to help you better serve your customers. You may also have to struggle just to keep up with all the changes and upgrades; this is one of the big **time wasters** facing many organizations and service providers. The technology is needed to stay competitive, but it takes valuable time to install and maintain the equipment and software and to train employees to use it effectively.

Telephone Management

In addition to the interpersonal skills discussed in Chapters 3 to 5 and the basic guidelines for using the telephone that were covered in Chapter 7, effectively managing telephone time takes planning and skill. Additional strategies for increasing effectiveness and better managing your time when using the telephone are described below.

Establish objectives before making your calls. If you are in sales, your objectives might have to do with total number of sales per hour or gross or net sales volume. If you work in an outbound call center that sets up appointments or qualifies credit prospects, you might also have a specific number to attain. Representatives handling inbound customer service calls might have time limits per call. Whatever measure the organization or you use, it should be decided before you start making calls.

If you are simply calling a customer or vendor or returning a call, you should have a clear goal in mind related to your reason for calling and what you want to get from the call.

Prepare for the call by making a list of topics you wish to address. This involves knowing to whom you want to speak and having a clear understanding of the reason for your call. Further, have any support materials (e.g., letters, files, materials, statistics) right by the phone for easy access during the conversation. If you need answers to specific questions, write them down and leave space on the page for the responses. Also, put your questions or comments in the order of importance to you in case your conversation is cut short; at least you will get the most important information from your call recipient. If you are making a formal sales call, you may even have a structured script that you use with each customer. By having such things written down, you are less likely to forget to ask a question, give information, or fail to meet your objectives.

Screen your call recipient as soon as someone answers the telephone, unless he or she gives a name right away. Do not assume that you have the correct party on the telephone and immediately start talking or selling. You are wasting time (yours and that of the person on the telephone) if it is the wrong person. This is especially important if you are making a business-to-business call in which you phone another company to get or give information or to resolve a complaint. If you do not briefly define your reason for calling and then ask with whom you should speak, you may waste valuable time explaining everything to the wrong person, who will say, "I'm sorry, you'll need to speak to . . . " or transfer you and have you repeat the conversation to another person.

If your main job is to receive customer calls, use an efficient and customer-focused telephone technique. For example, get the name of the person and other pertinent information you will need to answer his or her questions, access customer records, and move the call along early in the conversation. However, try not to sound impersonal. It is best to get account information after you greet your caller. Keep in mind what you have learned about personalizing a call by using a salutation (e.g., "Good morning"), giving the name of your organization and your name, and then offering to assist. Many providers use a somewhat impersonal greeting that can sound mechanical and uncaring to a customer (e.g., "ABC Company, may I have your account number?"). This approach does not recognize the customer as a person, and it implies "I only care about getting through this call as quickly as possible." In many organizations, you may not have a choice on what greeting you use since you are held accountable for "talk time" or time spent on each call. If you do have flexibility, go for the personalization. It can pay off by avoiding negative situations that take time to resolve.

Measure your activity periodically to determine how well you are doing at meeting your objectives. Most call centers have software that tracks such activity.

Keep the customer informed by returning to the call every 20 to 30 seconds if you have placed someone on hold. If appropriate, offer to call the customer later. This approach saves the customer time and keeps you from having to continually come back on the line for an update.

Be efficient and service-oriented by avoiding transferring customers numerous times to different people. Use the standards of your organization related to transfers. If none exist, use two transfers as your maximum number before you personally assume responsibility for a call and handle a customer situation. Transferring a customer more than twice is not efficient and frustrates the customer while sending an unprofessional message about the organization and its employees.

Voice Mail Management

Voice mail systems and telephone answering machines were developed to increase efficiency by helping callers and call recipients save time. Unfortunately, owing to abuses on both sides, many people detest these inventions.

This is really a shame because, when used properly, they really are effective. Not only do they help organizations reduce staff costs and save time by using technology for simple information collection and dissemination, but they also assist service providers by gathering valuable customer information that allows the provider to do research and better assist customers.

The abuse part comes when call service providers decide to send all their calls to voice mail even though they are sitting at their desks working next to the telephone. The systems were not designed to replace you or take all your calls. You may have legitimate reasons to let the machine answer your calls even though you are at your workstation (e.g., you are in a meeting with a customer or discussing some business-related matter with a coworker, you are working on a project that has a tight deadline, or you are preparing for an upcoming meeting or other function). In general, though, these systems should be a backup, not a replacement, for you.

Callers also abuse the systems by either hanging up when they realize that they have reached a machine or leaving inadequate information. As you read in Chapter 7, at a minimum when you call someone and reach a voice mail, you should leave your name, the time and date of the call, your phone number (including area code if appropriate), and a *brief* message. If you fail to leave a message, you have wasted your time and will have to call again; moreover, the service provider cannot return your call or help you.

These systems were not designed to allow you to deliver a sales presentation. In some cases, the memory or tape length for recording messages is limited. If you leave long, drawn-out messages, you could irritate and offend your recipient by tying up all the recording space with your message. In that case you may never hear from the recipient, or you may receive a very terse response. Review Chapter 7 for information on leaving messages on voicemail and setting up your outgoing message for maximum efficiency.

E-Mail Efficiency

E-mail is a very quick and inexpensive way to get in touch with others inside and outside your organization. However, as you read in Chapter 7, you should observe e-mail etiquette. To use e-mail efficiently, you should respond to messages in a timely manner. This does not mean that you must stop what you are doing to respond every time a message arrives. That would be a poor time management strategy, for you will probably lose your train of thought by stopping continually. Instead, check and return e-mails at scheduled times throughout the day.

All the techniques described in this section and in Chapter 7 can help show your customers that you are a professional, are organized, and know how to use technology to help you manage time well. The techniques can also save you time because you will not have to go searching for people, information, or items before you can serve a customer. In addition, you will avoid spending time in dealing with an emotional or dissatisfied customer who reacts negatively to your lack of organization or inability to provide service in a timely manner.

Work It Out 12-2. Eliminating Time Wasters

Work It Out

12-2

Take ten minutes to develop a list of typical time wasters for service providers.

_____

_____

_____

_____

_____

_____

_____

_____

_____

_____

WORKSHEET 12-2

Worksheet ▼

12-2

Eliminating Time Wasters

Develop some strategies for eliminating or reducing the time wasters that your instructor has assigned to your group. Be prepared to discuss each.

TIME WASTER	STRATEGIES FOR ELIMINATION OR REDUCTION
_____	_____
	_____
	_____
	_____
_____	_____
	_____
	_____
_____	_____
	_____

5 | STRATEGIES FOR RECLAIMING TIME

▶ **CONCEPT:** Examine each of your activities according to the following criteria: necessity, appropriateness, and efficiency.

Before you can reclaim some of the time that is typically wasted during the day, you must evaluate how you use time. After you have measured the time you spend on tasks, you can begin evaluating how well you use your time. To do this evaluation, use copies of Figure 12-1 to track your daily activities for a week. Once you have done so, examine your time usage based on the following three criteria:

Necessity. Scrutinize each activity to be sure that it is necessary and contributes in some way to better customer service. Sometimes people go on using material that has outlived its usefulness (e.g., monthly reports—because they have always been done in a certain manner or format). If the activities you perform serve a useful purpose, continue doing them; just try to streamline and make them as efficient as possible (e.g., developing a form letter for regularly occurring messages, automating a process or file and otherwise using some of the technology discussed in Chapter 7). Doing this type of self-evaluation will help you reduce your tasks to only those that are essential.

Appropriateness. Once you have identified essential functions, determine who should be doing them (e.g., what person or department) and adjust your workload accordingly. Sometimes, you might do this by simply asking a peer to switch duties (with team leader or supervisory approval). In other instances, you might want to prepare a formal recommendation for your supervisor, asking that your job description be changed and listing the reasons such a change is warranted.

Efficiency. The third criterion in examining your tasks is to consider how efficiently you are currently performing. If you feel that things are going well, step back and look again—objectively. Ask yourself, "Is there a better way of doing this?" You may even want to ask some of your peers for input. You should continually improve in carving out more saved time during your day.

Think about how you use your time during the day and at night. Do you spend it as effectively and efficiently as you could? Evaluate your record in Figure 12-1. How can you improve your use of time?

TIME RECORD SHEET

Date _____

To better determine how you use your time throughout the day, make five copies of this form. For the next five days, record your daily tasks in 15-minute increments (e.g. met with client, spoke to customer on telephone, responded to e-mails, lunch, drove to customer site). At the end of each day, list the types of activities on a separate sheet of paper and total the minutes spent for each.

Start and End Times		Activity	Comments
____	____	_____	_____
____	____	_____	_____
____	____	_____	_____
____	____	_____	_____
____	____	_____	_____
____	____	_____	_____
____	____	_____	_____
____	____	_____	_____
____	____	_____	_____
____	____	_____	_____
____	____	_____	_____
____	____	_____	_____
____	____	_____	_____
____	____	_____	_____
____	____	_____	_____
____	____	_____	_____
____	____	_____	_____
____	____	_____	_____
____	____	_____	_____

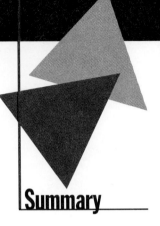

Summary

Chapter Summary

As you know from experience, and have read in this chapter, time management is a valuable skill to acquire and use. With so many things to do each day, it seems that our lives become more chaotic and less productive. Using the skills described in this chapter can help. The personal time record sheet, shown in Figure 12-1, will help you become more aware of how you use your time. By developing a prioritization system and using it regularly, recognizing the importance of good time usage strategies in face-to-face encounters, over the telephone, and when using technology, and then using the techniques described outlined in this chapter, you will regain and control more of your time. To be successful, you must continually search for ways to improve efficiency in your work area, master the available technology to deliver customer service, and enhance the systems you use to gather information and deliver it to others in a variety of settings.

CHAPTER REVIEW QUESTIONS

1. What are some reasons for practicing good time management? _____
   _____
   _____
   _____

2. What are four major positive results of good time management in the workplace? _____
   _____
   _____
   _____

3. What are three standards for prioritizing activities? _____
   _____
   _____
   _____

4. What are the three priority levels for daily activities? _____
   _____
   _____
   _____

5. What can you do to save time while serving a customer? _____
   _____
   _____
   _____

6. What are some time management techniques you can use in face-to-face service situations? _____

_____

_____

_____

7. How can you increase time efficiency when providing service "on the run"? _____

_____

_____

_____

8. What telephone time management techniques can assist in providing better service? _____

_____

_____

_____

9. What techniques for voice mail usage can help save time? _____

_____

_____

_____

10. How can e-mail be used effectively to add to, not detract from, available time? _____

_____

_____

_____

11. What are three criteria for measuring time usage and reclaiming time?

_____

_____

_____

▼ SEARCH IT OUT

Search the Internet for Information on Time Management Skills

Option 1: Log onto the Internet to research products, training programs, publications, and articles related to improving time management skills. Create a bibliographic list, make copies of the list, and share it with your peers and instructor in class.

Option 2: Research articles and Websites related to time management. Try to develop a list of at least ten different time-saving strategies other than the ones described in the text. Also, develop a list of time wasters in your personal life that ultimately can affect your ability to perform effective customer service.

Researching Wait Times

As a class, come up with a list of businesses in which customer wait times are typical (e.g., supermarkets, retail stores, call center support lines, doctors' offices, amusement parks, barber shops or hair salons, banks, car washes). Each person can select a business category, or teams can do research. Your research can be done in one of three ways:

- Personal experience
- Second-hand experience (observing or interviewing others)
- A combination of both personal and second-hand experience

During a two-week period, contact (or observe) people in your selected industry type and answer the following questions about each experience:

- What was the average wait time?
- What were you or other customers typically doing during the wait time?
- Was the wait time similar in the various organizations?
- What strategies did organizations use to reduce or minimize wait times?
- What were the actions or emotional levels of customers during their wait? (e.g., exhibiting impatience, fidgeting, complaining to service providers or other customers, showing signs of frustration, sighing, looking at watch)

At the end of two weeks, be prepared to discuss your observations and experiences with other students.

FACE TO FACE

Handling Change at a Call Center

Background

You are the team leader of a call center team made up of six customer service representatives. The team members have an average experience level of about one year. Your organization provides support to customers who purchase small electronic appliances and devices through retail stores and catalogs. The company also has a Website where customers can view product descriptions, place orders, e-mail your center with questions and comments, and request catalogs and other information through an online information fulfillment system. A unit within the call center provides third-party service support for companies that contract with your organization. Your facility is also equipped with a TTY system to assist the hearing-impaired, fax-on-demand, and other typical call center technology (e.g., e-mail, voice mail). A typical day for a representative in your unit involves answering customer calls directed from the ACD system, responding to e-mails and voice mails, handling routine administrative functions (e.g., completing and filing forms, attending team meetings, dealing with last-minute assignments, fulfilling internal customer requests for information).

Things have been hectic in the call center for the last three months. Rumor of a merger is spreading. Several employees have resigned, and you have not been able to find suitable replacements. Your manager transferred to another unit last month (you have heard that her decision to leave was based on her concern that her position would be eliminated if the merger went through). A senior team leader is now running the center until management decides how to proceed.

Also, for the past two weeks, your team has been beta-testing a new customer information tracking telephony system (trying it out to discover whether the functions work as designed and whether it meets current organizational needs, learning the applications, and so on). Representatives from the company that designed the software for your organization are on site. During the last few days, on a number of occasions the system has disconnected customers, wiped out information on computer screens as representatives were talking to clients, and blocked representatives from entry into certain areas of the program. The problem has not been resolved, and there have been numerous complaints by irritated customers. One customer even telephoned the CEO's office because he had been unable to resolve a problem after three attempts. A memorandum has arrived requesting an explanation and asking you to take immediate action to rectify the situation.

Your Role

Your name is Pat Wilson, and you have been working in the call center for almost 2 1/2 years. Earlier, you worked in the mailroom for your organization, in the customer care center (call center) for another organization, and in a fast-food restaurant for about a year. You are also a part-time student at the local community college, taking courses dealing primarily with customer service. You enjoy your work and interactions with customers and hope someday to become a call center manager. Therefore, you are reluctant to say no when someone asks you to take on a new assignment.

Because of all the changes, team members are getting anxious and coming to you with questions and concerns. You are responsible for employee training and working with the software representatives to overcome the glitches. You have also played a key role in preparing and delivering presentations to update senior management on the progress of the telephony system testing. In the last meeting the senior vice president responsible for the call center took you aside and stressed the importance of the project to the organization. She did not say so, but she implied that the success of the testing could have a serious impact on the merger.

On top of all this, you handle phone calls and perform the typical representative duties outlined above, must write performance appraisals for three team members this week, have examinations in your college courses in a week, are working on a proposal for streamlining voice mail responses, and have decided to set up a new filing system in your work area.

Questions

1. From a time management standpoint, what issues are you dealing with?

   _____

   _____

   _____

   _____

   _____

2. How should you prioritize the tasks you must handle?

   _____

   _____

   _____

   _____

   _____

   _____

   _____

   _____

3. Why did you prioritize the tasks in Problem 2 the way you did?

   _____

   _____

   _____

   _____

   _____

FROM THE FRONTLINE
Interview

Lauri Hopton
Training Administrator
The McGraw-Hill
Companies, Inc.
Columbus, Ohio

1. What is your experience in dealing with internal and/or external customers?

I have over 12 years of experience in dealing with both internal and external customers. I have held positions as an assistant manager in retail, manager at fitness centers, and customer service representative and customer service supervisor. Currently, I am a trainer.

2. What are your general impressions of customer service in the United States? Why do you feel this way?

In my estimation, customer service in the United States has declined tremendously. This seems odd because in recent years companies have switched their emphasis from a production and "bottom-line" approach to a "customer-focused" approach. But the focus on the customer does not seem to be trickling down to the front line. I am reminded of this every day, when I am checking out at the supermarket, calling to inquire about a product, or even calling to request service. I am struck by the lack of attentiveness to detail, poor listening skills, and an overall attitude of indifference.

3. What are some of the biggest time wasters you face each day in dealing with customers?

• **Lack of organization and planning.** In my current position, most of my customers are internal. One of the biggest time wasters I experience is lack of organization and/or poor preparation by an internal customer seeking my assistance or advice. Oftentimes, the preparation stage, as opposed to the problem-solving or defining stage, takes too much time because of this lack of preparation. Therefore, what should be a 15- to 20-minute meeting ends up taking an hour or more.

• **Distractions.** The phone or noise, in particular.

• **Rapidly changing environment.** Being a planner by nature, I am continually planning training events, activities, and agendas for my internal customers. Our environment changes so rapidly that priorities must also change to meet needs of the environment. Therefore, we have to spend more time regrouping and replanning to meet the current needs.

- **Procrastination of customers.** My work often depends on the activities of internal customers. When customers procrastinate on their part of the work, I spend my time trying to track down and complete their work so that I can continue with my part of the job.

  - *Customers changing plans without notice.*
  - *Customers not following through with decisions.*
  - *Customers not keeping appropriate records. This can result in duplication of my own work.*

4. **What are some strategies that you use to reduce the amount of time you lose each day?**

   - *I schedule and preplan my day to the best of my ability.*
   - *I remain flexible and willing to "zig" when I had planned to "zag."*
   - *I avoid distractions. If the need becomes critical, I put the phone on voice mail. I try to tune out the audible distractions, and I ask "visitors" to come back at another time.*
   - *Another tip: I try to be as specific as possible in giving directions and to make sure that my expectations are clear. This helps to avoid confusion and saves time right from the start.*

5. **How have you seen technology assist and/or detract from efficiency of time usage?**

Initially, technology was a time deterrent. The learning curve was formidable, and the newness of the technology generated feelings of inadequacy. Now, the newness has worn off, and the technology has become comfortable; the efficiency of time has improved greatly. A computer can now do tasks that used to be done on paper. This not only increases efficiency but also prevents a million pieces of paper from being lost. Technology has helped me to better serve both internal and external customers. For example, I am able to go to the

Internet and track packages immediately for our external customers. E-mail also allows for quick communication with both internal and external customers. Also, many other software programs make our lives easier—word processing and spreadsheet programs, just to name a few.

6. **In your experience, what can service providers do better to utilize their time when dealing with customers?**

   - *The first is to be ready to listen. When dealing with either internal or external customers, we must utilize active listening skills to ensure successful communication.*
   - *Make sure that all follow-up steps are taken and confirmed with the customer to prevent repeat visits or calls.*
   - *Try to accomplish as much as possible in an efficient manner while the customer is still either on the phone or standing next to you. This helps to ensure that there are no gaps or oversights.*

7. **What advice related to time management can you give to someone entering a customer service job today?**

   - *The most important skill is to be able to efficiently and effectively multitask. Many things go on at one time, and a successful customer service representative must be able to juggle these many tasks in a professional and time-sensitive manner.*
   - *Develop strong communication skills. These include active listening, probing, and writing skills.*
   - *Learn to express empathy by putting yourself in your customers' shoes, especially when it comes to time and efficiency.*
   - *Take the extra step to follow up with your customers. Following up will save time in the long run by enhancing relationships and preventing future misunderstandings.*

CRITICAL THINKING

How is customer service performed for internal customers? Do you agree with the advice given regarding time management?

Enhancing Customer Relationships

Chapter 13

Encouraging Customer Loyalty

OBJECTIVES

After completing this chapter, you will be able to:

- *Establish and maintain trust with customers.*

- *Develop the characteristics that will enhance customer loyalty.*

- *Recognize the provider's responsibility for establishing and maintaining positive customer relations.*

- *Help customers feel important.*

- *Select strategies to enhance customer satisfaction and build loyalty.*

"Every great business is built on friendship."

J. C. Penney

417

Before reviewing the chapter content, respond to the following questions by placing a "T" for true or an "F" for false on the rules. Use any questions you miss as a checklist of material to which you will pay particular attention as you read through the chapter. For those you get right, congratulate yourself, but review the sections they address in order to learn additional details about the topic.

_____ **1.** Customer satisfaction and loyalty are the result of effective product and service delivery, resolution of problems, and elimination of dissatisfiers.

_____ **2.** The number of customers with major problems who continue to do business with an organization if their complaint is resolved is about 9 percent.

_____ **3.** One way to take responsibility for customer relationships is to personalize your approach when dealing with customers.

_____ **4.** Customers usually decide to purchase or repurchase from a supplier based on the quality and performance of the products and services.

_____ **5.** Many customers return to organizations because of relationships established with employees even though comparable products and services are available elsewhere.

_____ **6.** As customers develop long-term relationships with an organization, they tend to become more tolerant of poor service.

_____ **7.** Projecting an enthusiastic "I'm happy to serve you attitude" is one way to have a positive effect on customer relationships.

_____ **8.** Customers usually exhibit six common needs that must be addressed by service providers in order to ensure customer loyalty.

_____ **9.** Using a customer's name is a good way to personalize your relationship with a customer.

_____ **10.** Trust is not a major concern for most customers.

_____ **11.** Handling complaints quickly and effectively is a good strategy for aiding customer retention.

_____ **12.** An important step often overlooked in dealing with customers is follow-up.

1. T   5. T   9. T
2. F   6. F   10. F
3. T   7. T   11. T
4. T   8. T   12. T

1 THE ROLE OF TRUST

> **CONCEPT:** Trust is the most important criteria for a relationship. Trust depends on many factors; communicating effectively, keeping your word, caring, and trusting your customers are some of these factors.

Relationships are built on trust! The most important thing to remember about trust is that, without it, you have no relationship. This applies to all human situations, not just the customer service environment. For customers to continue doing business with you, they must trust you and your organization. Trust has to be earned, and it does not happen overnight. Only through continued positive efforts on the part of everyone in your organization can you demonstrate to customers that you are worthy of their trust. Through actions and deeds, you must deliver quality products, services, and information that satisfy the needs of your customers. Even when you win trust, it is very fragile. An inappropriate tone, a missed appointment, failure to follow through on a promise, a lie, or a misleading statement to a customer are just some of the ways you can destroy trust quickly.

To gain and maintain trust, you and the organization must actively work toward incorporating the values and beliefs you read about in other chapters into daily actions. Failure to do so can send a message that you are not trustworthy or that you act according to a double standard of saying one thing but doing another. You must exhibit trustworthiness in words and actions, for although it takes a long time to gain trust, it can be lost in seconds. Once trust is gone, if you do not react quickly to correct the situation, you may never regain total customer confidence. Here are some basic strategies to gain and develop customer trust:

Communicate Effectively and Convincingly

If you cannot articulate or explain clearly (verbally and in writing) information customers can comprehend and act upon, they will not believe in you. You must provide more than facts and figures; you must send a message of sincerity, knowledge, and honesty.

As you communicate, project your feelings and emotions by being positive and enthusiastic. Let customers know that you are human and approachable. Also, communicate frequently and keep customers informed. This is especially important when they are awaiting a product or service that has been delayed. If you fail to update them regularly, they may become frustrated and could cancel their order, complain, take their business elsewhere, and tell others about their disappointing experience.

Display Caring

Emphasize to your customers that you have their best interests at heart. Work to demonstrate that you are willing to assist in satisfying their needs. Asking questions that uncover their needs and then taking positive action to satisfy them can do this. It can also be accomplished through passionate efforts to solve problems. Remember that their problem is your problem. Too often, service providers send a message that customers are not really that important. This can happen when service providers adopt a "next" mentality and treat customers as if they were numbers, not people. For example, think about the difference wording can make. Which of the following sends a more caring message to a group of customers standing in line as they wait for service?

1. A provider calls out "Next."
2. A provider looks over to the next person in line, smiles, and motions the person over with a waving hand gesture while saying, "May I help the next person in line?"

If you chose No. 2, you are on your way to providing caring service.

Be Fair

Make sure that you treat all customers with respect and consistency. If you give special discounts to established or return customers, do so discreetly. Failure to exercise discretion in these cases could cause other customers to be offended and take their business elsewhere. People like to feel that they are special. If a customer believes that another customer is getting special treatment, you could have problems. Such perceptions might even lead to legal action, if customers perceive they are being discriminated against.

Admit Errors or Lack of Knowledge

You are human and are expected to make mistakes. The key is to recover from errors by apologizing, accepting responsibility, and then quickly and appropriately solving the problem or getting the necessary information. One of the biggest mistakes a service provider can make is to deny accountability in dealing with a customer. When you or your organization or the products or services it sells cause customer inconvenience or dissatisfaction, take responsibility and work toward an acceptable resolution with the customer. To do otherwise is courting disaster. In some cases, even if a customer incorrectly perceives that you contributed to his or her dissatisfaction, it may be wise to take responsibility.

A story about the power of such action has been circulated for years. It involves the highly successful department store Nordstrom. As the story goes, a disgruntled customer brought a used car tire into a Nordstrom's store and complained that it was defective. After some discussion, the manager cheerfully accepted the tire and refunded the customer's money. This may not seem too unusual, except that Nordstrom does not sell automobile tires! So, why would the manager take such an extreme action? Think about the word-of-mouth publicity (how many people in your class now know this story from just reading it?) and the customer loyalty that likely resulted from it. Whether the event actually took place or someone made it up is irrelevant. The point is that taking unusual actions to solve ordinary customer problems can pay dividends long into the future.

In another classic example of taking responsibility for a problem, in 1982 an unknown person or group contaminated bottles of Extra-Strength Tylenol with cyanide. Seven people used the product and died. Upon finding out about the situation, the parent company (Johnson and Johnson) immediately called a press conference to announce the total recall of the product from store shelves (approximately 264,000 bottles). Johnson & Johnson started a major media campaign to reassure the public that its other products were safe. The company also helped lead the way in developing tamper-resistant packaging. The cost—millions. The result— walk into any store that sells over-the-counter drug products and look for Extra-Strength Tylenol. Tylenol is right there with all its competitors and is a strong seller. How did Johnson & Johnson pull this off? The actions of the company in taking responsibility for a situation that was not of its making communicated strong values and concern for public safety, and the public remained loyal as a result.

Other companies have not fared so well in the face of adversity. For example, think about the Exxon oil tanker *Valdez*, which spilled more than 200,000 gallons of crude oil along the Alaska coastline in 1989. This disaster caused major environmental as well as financial losses into the millions of dollars. This does not include the almost $3 billion Exxon has spent cleaning up the environmental damage and paying legal settlements. The company was slow to react, however, and did not, at first, take responsibility. As a result, it is still the object of litigation and jokes. From a trust standpoint, people harbor resentment over the incident, and, in protest, many people will not patronize Exxon gas stations.

Trust Your Customers

Most customers are not out to cheat or "rip you (or your organization) off." They do want the best value and service for their money and expect you to provide it. Make a good-faith effort to accomplish this and deal openly by communicating openly, listening objectively to their questions and concerns, providing service to the best of your ability, showing compassion for their needs, and demonstrating that you are their advocate when things go wrong (if appropriate).

One of the most common mistakes service providers make in dealing with customers who have a complaint or problem is to verbally acknowledge and agree but nonverbally send a message of skepticism. For example, suppose a customer comes in to complain about a defective product she purchased. As she is describing the symptoms of the problem, you use some of the paralanguage discussed in earlier chapters (e.g., "Uh huh," "I see," "Hmm"); however, the inflection you use or your tone of voice communicates questioning or doubt (e.g., "I seeee?" or "Hmmm?"). How do you think the customer might feel or perceive you at that point?

If you seek trust; communicate it.

Keep Your Word

Customers have many choices in selecting a service provider. If they feel you cannot be depended upon to take action, they simply leave, often without complaint or comment. When you tell customers you will do something, do it. Do not promise what you cannot deliver; many people take your word as your bond. Break the bond, and you risk destroying the relationship.

If feasible following service, contact your customer to make sure that he or she was satisfied and that your service met expectations. This follow-up can be an informal call or a more formal questionnaire. Always strive to *under*-promise and *over*-deliver. Suppose that a customer drops off film to be processed at your store on Tuesday. The store guarantees that the photos will be ready on Saturday. If possible, develop the film before Saturday, and call to tell the customer it's ready. When he or she comes to pick it up, give a coupon for a discount on the next roll of film.

Provide Peace of Mind

Be positive and assertive. Assure customers through your words and actions that you are confident, have their best interests at heart, and are in control of the situation. Let them know that their calls or messages, questions, and needs will be addressed professionally and in a timely manner. Reassure them that what they purchase is the best quality, has a solid warranty, will be backed by the organization, and will address their needs while providing many benefits. Also, assure them that their requests and information will be processed rapidly and promises will be met. All of these things can lead them to the belief that they made the right decision in selecting you and your organization and that you will take care of their needs.

2 THE IMPORTANCE OF CUSTOMER RELATIONSHIPS

CONCEPT: Long-term relationships are the ones that sustain organizations.

Why bother building relationships with customers? The answer would seem obvious—so that you can stay in business. However, when you examine the question further, you may find that there are more reasons than you think.

At one point in history, business owners knew their customers personally. They knew their customers' families, what their religious affiliation was, and what was happening in their lives. That was then, and this is now. The society is more mobile; people live in large metropolitan areas where relationships are distant. Large multinational organizations provide the products and services once provided by the neighborhood store. All this does not mean, however, that the customer-provider relationships can no longer exist.

Typically, many service providers look at customer interactions from a short-term perspective. They figure that a customer calls or comes in, they provide service, and then the customer goes away. This is a short-sighted viewpoint in that it does not consider the long-term implications. This is not the way to gain and sustain customer loyalty.

A more customer-focused approach is to view customers from a relationship standpoint. That does not mean that you have to become intimate friends with all your customers; it simply means that you should strive to employ as many of the positive relationship-building skills that you have learned as possible. By treating both internal and external customers in a manner that leads them to believe that you care for them and have their best interests at heart, you can start to generate reciprocal feelings. Using the interpersonal communication skills you have learned throughout this book is a great way to begin doing this. People usually gravitate toward organizations and people with whom they have developed rapport, respect, and trust, and who treat them as if they are valued as a person. Relationships are developed and enhanced through one-on-one human interaction. This does not mean that people who provide service via technology cannot develop relationships. Those relationships develop on a different level, using the nonverbal and written communication skills addressed in Chapters 4, 7, and 8.

Remember that long-term customer relationships are the ones that sustain organizations. Seeking out new or replacement customers through advertising and other means is a very costly proposition. This is because, in addition to having to find new customers, you and your organization have to educate and win them over. You have to prove yourself to newly acquired customers. More than likely, new customers are also going to be more apprehensive, skeptical, and critical than customers who have previous experience with your organization. For these reasons, it is imperative that you and every other member of your organization work to develop loyalty on the part of those customers with whom you have an existing relationship.

By providing excellent customer service and dealing with dissatisfaction as soon it is identified, you can help ensure that customers remain loyal and keep coming back. The following equation conveys this idea:

> **Effective product/service delivery**
> + **Proactive relationship building**
> + **Elimination of dissatisfiers**
> + **Resolution of problems**
> = **Customer satisfaction and loyalty.**

Traditionally, customers will remain loyal to a product, service, or organization that they believe meets their needs. Even when there is an actual or perceived breakdown in quality, many customers will return to an organization that they believe sincerely attempts to solve a problem or make restitution for an error. According to the **Technical Assistance Research Program (TARP)**, many organizations have found that, when complaints were acted upon and resolved quickly, most customers returned to the organization (see Figures 13-1 and 13-2).

The bottom line is that you and other employees must realize that customer service is everyone's business and that relationships are the basis of that business.

FIGURE 13-1

The importance of customer loyalty.

For almost three decades, the research firm TARP has conducted various studies to determine the impact of customer service. The research has revealed the following:

- It will cost an organization at least five times more to acquire a new customer as it will to keep an existing one.

- On average, 50 percent of consumers will complain about a problem to a frontline person. In business-to-business environments, this figure jumps to 75 percent.

- For small-ticket items, 96 percent of consumers do not complain or they complain to the retailer from whom they bought an item. For large-ticket items, 50 percent complain to frontline employees, and 5 to 10 percent escalate the problem to local managers or corporate headquarters.

- At least 50 percent of your customers who experience problems will not complain or contact your organization for help; they will simply go elsewhere.

- Customers who are dissatisfied will tell as many as 16 friends about a negative experience with your organization.

- The average business loses 10 to 15 percent of its customers per year because of bad service.

Source: Technical Assistance Research Program, or TARP, 1300 Wilson Boulevard, Suite 950, Arlington, Virginia 22209.)

FIGURE 13-2

The value of resolving customer problems.

How many of your unhappy customers will buy from you again?

Category	Percent of customers who will buy from you again
Noncomplainers	9% (Major problems — over $100)
	37% (Minor problems — $1 to $5 in losses)
Complainers	
Complaints not resolved	19% (Major problems — over $100)
	46% (Minor problems — $1 to $5 in losses)
Complaints resolved	54% (Major problems — over $100)
	70% (Minor problems — $1 to $5 in losses)
Complaints resolved quickly	82% (Major problems — over $100)
	95% (Minor problems — $1 to $5 in losses)

Source: National Consumer Survey, Technical Assistance Research Program (TARP), Arlington, Virginia, 1986.

Note: These figures are an update on an original Customer Satisfaction Survey conducted by TARP for the U.S. Office of Consumer Affairs from 1974–1979. Since the 1986 study, numerous other studies have been conducted by TARP, in a variety of industries, with similar findings.

Work It Out 13-1. Personal Customer Relationship Experiences

▶ Think about a service provider with whom you deal frequently and with whom you have established a better-than-average customer-provider relationship. Perhaps you have been dealing with the organization for a long period of time or visit frequently.

Reflect on the relationship and, on the rules below, make a list of positive customer service behaviors exhibited by this person. Then review the list and make it a personal goal to replicate as many of these behaviors as possible when dealing with your own customers.

_____

_____

_____

_____

_____

_____

_____

Work It Out 13-2. Personal Service Expectations

▶ Think of how you would expect to be treated if you were a customer of the company you work for currently. List behaviors that you would expect to encounter from customer service employees.

_____

_____

_____

_____

_____

_____

_____

3 PROVIDER CHARACTERISTICS AFFECTING CUSTOMER LOYALTY

CONCEPT: Personal characteristics of a service provider may affect customer loyalty, positively or negatively.

Many of your personal characteristics affect your relationships with customers. In customer service, some circumstances are beyond your control; however, your personal characteristics are not. Some of the most common qualities of service providers that affect customers are described in the next sections.

Responsiveness

Customers typically like to feel that they are the most important person in the world when they come in contact with an organization (see Figure 13-3). This is a human need (remember Maslow's hierarchy and the need for esteem?). If customers feel that they are not appreciated or not welcome by you or another service provider, they will likely take their business elsewhere. However, they will often first complain to management and will tell anyone who will listen about the poor quality of service they received.

A simple way to demonstrate responsiveness is to attend to the customer's needs promptly. If you get an e-mail or voice mail message, respond to it immediately, if possible. If that is not possible, try to respond within 4 hours, or certainly within 24 hours. If you have face-to-face customer contact, greet customers quickly (within 10 to 15 seconds), even if you are busy with someone else. If nothing else, smile and gesture that you will be with them momentarily.

Once you do get to serve the customer, and before getting to the business at hand, greet the customer with a smile and start the interaction on a friendly note in one or more of the following ways:

> **Be enthusiastic:** Use open body language, vocal cues, and gestures that you have read about previously in this book, coupled with some of the techniques described below to let your customers know that you are glad they have chosen you and/or your organization.

> **Use the customer's title and name:** If you know the customer's name, use it. Remember, though, not to assume familiarity and start using the customer's first name unless you are given permission to do so.

> **Show appreciation:** "Thank you for coming to _____." "It's nice to see you this morning." "You have been very patient while I assisted that other customer. Thank you."

> **Engage in small talk:** "Isn't this weather terrible?" "Is this your first visit to our store?" "Didn't I see you in here last week?" (Say this only if you recognize the customer. If he or she answers yes, thank the person for returning to the store.)

> **Compliment:** "You look like you're having a good day" (assuming the customer is smiling and does look happy). "That color really looks nice on you." "That's a beautiful necktie."

Work It Out 13-3. Passing Time

▶ To better realize how customers and service providers perceive time differently, partner with someone and try this experiment. When your instructor says "Go," mentally try to determine when 30 seconds have elapsed. When you believe 30 seconds has elapsed, say "Now." Afterward, you will participate in a discussion led by your instructor.

FIGURE 13-3

Addressing customer needs.

Everyone has needs that must be met in some fashion. Here are six common customer needs, along with strategies to satisfy them.

Need	Strategies for Satisfying the Need
To feel welcome	Use an enthusiastic greeting, smile, use the customer's name, thank the customer, be positive
To be understood	Listen actively, paraphrase, ask key questions, give positive feedback, empathize
To feel comfortable	Use an enthusiastic welcome, relieve anxiety through friendly communication, explain your actions calmly, ensure physical comfort (e.g., seats, refreshments)
To feel appreciated	Thank the customer, follow up, go beyond service expectations, provide "special" offers, remember special details about the customer (e.g., birthdays, favorite colors, facts about their families)
To feel important	Use the customer's name, personalize service, give special treatment when possible, elicit opinions, remember details about him or her (e.g., last purchase made, last visit, preferred styles or foods)
To be respected	Listen, don't interrupt, acknowledge the customer's emotions and concerns, take time to serve, ask advice, elicit feedback

WORKSHEET 13-1

Needs Identification

To identify your customers' needs, indicate below what customers might say or do to signal that they have a need that requires your attention.

What a Customer Might Say or Do to Signal a Need   *Message*

_____ *I need to feel welcome.*

_____ *I need to be understood.*

_____ *I need to feel comfortable.*

_____ *I need to be appreciated.*

_____ *I need to feel important.*

_____ *I need to be respected.*

Adaptability

In a continually evolving world, you will undoubtedly have many opportunities to deal with customers who have different beliefs, values, perceptions, needs, and expectations. You will also encounter people whose personality styles differ from yours. Each of these meetings will provide an opportunity for you to adapt your approach in dealing with others. By doing so, you increase the likelihood of a successful interaction as well as a satisfied customer emerging from the encounter. Taking measures to adapt your personality style to that of your customers in order to communicate with and serve them effectively is a smart move. Keep in mind that you cannot change the customers; however, you can adapt to them and their approach to a situation.

Another, more subtle way to show your ability to adapt relates to technology. By quickly learning and mastering new technology systems provided to you by the organization, you can respond faster and more efficiently to customer needs. This is especially true, for many of your customers will likely be very technology-literate. If you cannot match their expectations, or at least demonstrate knowledge and effectiveness in using technology, you might frustrate them and drive them away.

Communication Skills

As you have read earlier in this book, your ability to obtain and give information, listen, write, and speak effectively, as well as deal with emotional situations are keys to successful customer service. By using a variety of effective interpersonal techniques, you can determine customer needs. The most successful service providers are the ones who have learned to interact positively with and build rapport with customers. To help ensure the most effective service possible, you should continually strive to improve your ability to interact and communicate with a variety of people. The better your skills are, the more likely you will be able to address different situations that arise in the workplace.

Decisiveness

Decisiveness relates to being able and willing to make a decision and take necessary actions to fulfill customer needs. Taking a wait-and-see approach to customer service often leads to customer dissatisfaction. Just as you probably do, customers value their time. By keeping them waiting while you run to someone else for a decision or answer can be frustrating. Granted, such a situation is sometimes created by a management style that makes it necessary to get certain approvals (e.g., for checks, returns or refunds, or discounts). However, these are internal issues that should be resolved *before* the customer encounters them. If you face such barriers, think of alternative ways of handling them, and then approach your supervisor with suggestions for improvement. Your ideas may make your life easier by reducing the chances of a frustrating and unproductive service encounter.

Once you have supportive systems in place, gather information effectively by using the listening techniques discussed in Chapter 5, carefully and quickly analyze the situation, and then make a decision on how to solve the problem.

Enthusiasm

As discussed earlier, attaining and maintaining a level of excitement about your customers, products, services, organization, and job that says "I'm happy to help you" is an important step toward establishing a relationship.

If you are enthusiastic about serving your customers, they will often respond by loyally supporting you and the organization. People typically react positively to enthusiastic employees who appear to be enjoying themselves as they work. This should not be interpreted as meaning that providers should act unprofessionally or create an environment in which they have fun at the expense of customer service or attention to their customers.

The long-term benefit is that if you and your organization can generate return customers through enthusiasm, the potential for organizational growth and prosperity exists. This in turn sets the stage for better benefits, salary, and workplace modifications that lead to higher employee enthusiasm. So, all the elements are connected, and all contribute to successful customer service.

As a side note, many employees and employers are trying to find ways to make the workplace less stressful and more enjoyable for themselves and customers. Several resources listed in the Bibliography will help in this quest.

Ethical Behavior

Establishing and maintaining high legal, social, and ethical standards in all interactions with customers are imperative. Failure to do so can lead to loss of reputation and business, and/or legal liability. Some positive examples of ethical behavior are the following:

- *A company that voluntarily recalls a product that it discovered was defective or potentially dangerous.*
- *A manager who notifies a customer when he or she finds out that an employee has lied to or deceived the customer.*
- *An employee who reports a theft carried out by another employee.*
- *A cab driver who finds a wallet in his taxi and turns it in.*

Some negative examples are:

- *Providing or substituting an inferior product for an advertised name brand item.*
- *Providing inferior products or repairs on a service call.*
- *Lying to a customer about a warranty.*
- *Failing to adhere to local, state, or federal regulations (e.g., dumping hazardous waste, such as petroleum or pesticide products, in unauthorized areas or collecting sales taxes but failing to report the taxes).*

Initiative

Taking an action related to your job or customer service without having to receive instructions from others is a sign of initiative. Such actions also help to ensure that your customer's needs are identified and met. Too many service providers take the "It's not my job" or "I can't do that" approach to dealing with customer situations. This can lead to customer dissatisfaction because the provider seems to be lazy or uncaring. To counter such impressions, you should take responsibility when a problem arises. By building a strong knowledge base (as described in the next section) and using the skills discussed in this book, you will have the tools you need to deal effectively with various situations without having to turn to others for assistance. This can expedite service and enhance your reputation in the eyes of your customers, peers, and supervisors.

Worksheet ▼
13-2

WORKSHEET 13-2

Taking Initiative

Think about your own workplace, or one in which you have worked in the past, or one in which you might want to work in the future. What are some of the ways you can demonstrate initiative and better serve customers?

_____

_____

_____

_____

_____

_____

_____

Knowledge

Your customers expect you to know what business your organization is in. With all the products and service variations available to customers, the high level of technology, deregulation of industries, and innovations coming on the market daily, customers depend on service providers to educate and guide them in making purchases and decisions. Taking time to learn about policies, procedures, resources, products, services, and other information can help you provide total customer satisfaction in an efficient and timely manner.

Many organizations provide training and literature to help employees become more knowledgeable and to stay current. Take advantage of such resources, if they are available in your organization. If the organization you work for does not provide training or resources, take the initiative to ask supervisors or team leaders for materials and information. Also, develop a network with other employees throughout the organization and

Training is usually provided by most organizations to increase employee knowledge and effectiveness with customers. What training do you think would be useful to you in a new position in customer service?

use that network to gain access to information. You, your organization, and your customers will ultimately benefit from your initiatives.

Perceptiveness

Recognizing the need to pay close attention to verbal and nonverbal clues, cultural factors, and the feelings or concerns of others is important. If necessary, you may want to review these topics in Chapters 4 and 10. By staying focused on customers and the signals they send, you can often recognize hesitancy, interest in a product or adamant rejection, irritation, anxiety, and a multitude of other unspoken messages. Once you have identified customers' signals, you can react appropriately and address their needs.

One way you can address customer needs is to anticipate them. Suppose that a customer makes a comment like "Man, is it hot outside. My lips are parched." You might offer a cold drink or direct the customer to a cafeteria or soft drink machine. Or, you might offer a chair to someone who is accompanying a customer while he or she shops and tries on clothing. Such small gestures show that you are astute in noticing their needs and nonverbal cues. Remember, sometimes the little things mean a lot. Moreover, in both of these examples, by taking care of the customer's basic needs, you might encourage him or her to shop longer.

Planning Ability

Planning is a crucial skill to possess when operating in today's fast-paced, changing customer service environment, especially in technology-based environments. To prepare for all types of customer situations, you and your organization must have a strategy. This often involves assessing various factors related to your organization, industry, products, services, policies and procedures, resources, and customer base. By being proactive and in thinking about such factors, you will be able to provide better service to your customers.

Also, you should consider alternative strategies for dealing with unusual situations (contingency plans). Such alternatives are helpful when things do not go as originally planned (e.g., a computer database fails, service is not delivered as promised, or products that were ordered from another organization for a customer do not arrive as promised).

The following are some basic steps in planning (see also Figure 13-4).

Set a goal. In a customer service situation, the obvious goal is to prevent problems from occurring. You also want to successfully address customers' needs, have them leave the service experience satisfied, spread positive word-of-mouth advertising, and return in the future.

Examine and evaluate the situation. In this phase of planning, you should look at all possible factors that could affect a customer interaction (e.g., the environment, policies, procedures, your skills and authority level, management support, and the customer). With these factors in mind, work with your peers and supervisor or team leader to establish criteria for selecting acceptable actions. For example, it might be acceptable to use voice mail if you are dealing with a customer; however, it is not all right to forward incoming messages to voice mail so that you can meet with a peer on a non-work-related issue.

Identify alternatives. Meet with peers and supervisors or team leaders to develop a list of alternatives for dealing with various customer situations. Consider the advantages and disadvantages of each option.

Select the best alternative. After reviewing all the options, select the one (or more) that best addresses the targeted goal of providing quality service to customers. Do not forget to measure this choice against the criteria you established earlier.

Create an implementation plan. Working with peers and supervisors or team leaders, decide which resources (human and otherwise) will be needed to deliver effective service. Also, develop a system for evaluating success. For example, a customer wants two items, but you have only one in stock. You apologize for not being able to fulfill the customer's needs. Is this "success"? Or, would you be successful if, in addition to the apology, you called other stores, located another item, and had it delivered to the customer's house at no cost?

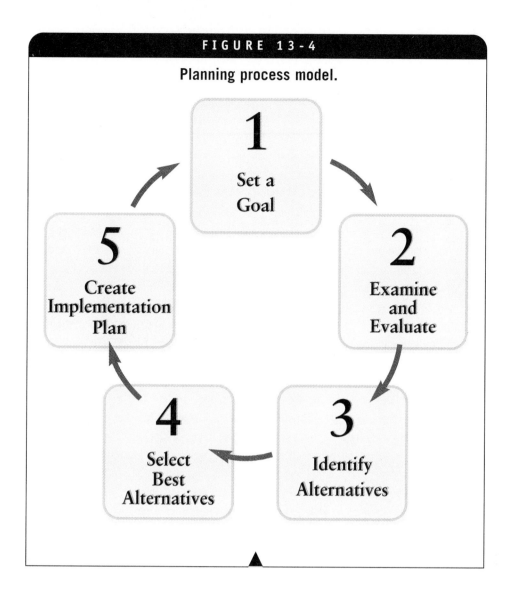

FIGURE 13-4

Planning process model.

1 Set a Goal

2 Examine and Evaluate

3 Identify Alternatives

4 Select Best Alternatives

5 Create Implementation Plan

Problem-Solving Ability

If a customer has a problem, you have a problem. Remembering this simple concept can go a long way in reminding you of your purpose for being a service provider. You exist (in your job position) to address the needs of your customer. To do this when a customer is dissatisfied or has a concern, you should take responsibility for the problem instead of trying to place blame. What or who created the problem (e.g., the weather, you, the customer, the manufacturer) doesn't matter. Your goal is to identify and implement appropriate solutions to the extent that you are authorized to do so. Otherwise, you should seek assistance from the appropriate person based on your organization's policy. To accomplish sound problem solving, you will need a process for gathering and analyzing information. As with the planning process discussed earlier, you should take some specific steps in finding a solution to a customer problem. These steps are described in the following sections. You learned a model for problem solving in Chapter 9 that can also be applied when you are trying to encourage and maintain customer loyalty (see Figure 13-5).

FIGURE 13-5

Problem-solving model.

- **Identify the problem.** Common sense dictates that before you can fix something, you have to find out in what way it is broken. However, many service providers do not seem to recognize this fact. Instead, they plunge into applying a standard solution because the problem resembles another one that the provider handled for another customer. Not only does this potentially waste time and other organizational resources, but it can also frustrate and anger the customer. This is especially true if the customer's problem is not adequately resolved.

  To effectively identify a problem, you must listen actively, ask questions to determine what did and did not work, and to determine the customer's expectation, paraphrase to the customer your understanding of the issue, and then go to the next step.

- **Analyze the problem.** In the second step of problem resolution, you should carefully evaluate what the customer has told you and get any additional information that will help you in understanding contributing factors and customer expectations for resolution of the problem.

- **Identify alternatives.** This step can significantly reduce the chance that you will provide a solution that does not satisfy your customer. Reflect on what you learned from the customer when you were identifying the problem and then determine what product and/or service options you have available to offer. For example, did the customer specify a certain brand, feature, color, or size? If so, providing an alternative may not be an acceptable option. However, if the customer was not specific, offering a compatible product or service might work.

- **Evaluate alternatives.** This step involves having a thorough knowledge of available products and services as well as knowing the warranty information, features, and benefits of each product and service. This knowledge can help you decide which of the alternatives available, if any, might be appropriate to offer.

  If the customer is with you or on the telephone, trying to determine an alternative may simply be a mental process of selecting possible solutions or options. With your goal being to meet customer needs and expectations, the more alternatives you can come up with, the better your chances for a successful resolution of the problem.

- **Make a decision.** Having identified the best alternatives, you can now offer specific suggestions to your customer. In some cases, this might result in a compromise. For example, assume that you are a host in a restaurant where reservations are required. A customer calls and wants a dinner reservation at 8 p.m., but no tables are available because a large party is being served at that time. So, you offer 7:30 as a compromise and offer free cocktails or wine. In offering this alternative, you may be able to satisfy the customer's desire to have dinner around 8 o'clock, and you have done a quick service recovery by offering the drinks.

Problem resolution is not difficult if it is approached systematically. If you have done the planning described earlier and know what options are available and what authority you have, it becomes much easier.

▶ Working in teams of three or four members, decide on a course of action to resolve the problem posed in the following scenario:

A customer comes into your gift shop and wants to return a lamp that she says she purchased from your store as a gift. Apparently, she discovered later that the recipient already had a lamp exactly like the one she bought. She has no receipt, and you do not recognize the product as one that your store sells. You are empowered to make exchanges and give refunds up to a product value of $50. The customer says the lamp was $49.95 before tax. Store policy says that the customer must have a receipt if a refund is to be made. What questions would you ask to clarify the situation? How would you handle the problem?

_____

_____

_____

_____

_____

_____

_____

Professionalism

As you have read in previous chapters, projecting a positive personal image, through manner of dress, knowledge, appearance of your work area, and your mental attitude, is a crucial element in communicating an "I care" image to customers and potential customers. By paying close attention to such factors, you better position yourself to establish and maintain a strong customer relationship. This is especially true where attitude is concerned. Attitude can mean success or failure when dealing with customers and can be communicated through the various verbal and nonverbal cues you have read about in other chapters.

4 BE RESPONSIBLE FOR YOUR CUSTOMER RELATIONSHIPS

▶ **CONCEPT:** Take responsibility for building good customer relationships by personalizing your service, listening, keeping an open mind, and respecting your customers. Ask for input from your customers.

Taking a concerned, one-on-one approach to working with customers helps satisfy immediate needs while building a basis for long-lasting relationships. Customers tend to enjoy dealing more with people who they believe are caring and have their best interests at heart. To interact with someone they like is a pleasant experience. Take the time to personalize your customer interactions and to make each customer feel special. This can lead to enhanced trust and helps ensure that the customer returns.

You have reviewed some of the following points in other chapters. They are solid skills and go a long way toward building customer loyalty and, ultimately, customer retention. Take the actions described in the next sections to make your customers feel special.

Personalize Your Approach

Think of the theme song for the television show *Cheers*. The idea of the theme song was that *Cheers* was a great place to go because "everyone knows your name." Do you remember the social need in Maslow's hierarchy of needs? For the most part, people are a sociable species and need to be around others to grow and flourish. Helping your customers feel accepted can create a bond that will keep them coming back.

To create a social bond with customers, you will need to take time to get to know your regular customers and serve them individually. Recognizing them and using their name while interacting goes a long way toward creating that bond. For new customers, immediately start using the positive interpersonal communication skills you have learned. Treating customers as individuals and not as a number or one in a series is a very important step in building rapport and loyalty.

Listen Actively

In Chapter 5 you learned specific strategies for effective listening. By practicing active listening skills and avoiding distractions while determining customer needs and providing service, you can send the "I care" message discussed earlier. At the same time, you can discover the customer's needs and work toward satisfying them.

Keep an Open Mind

To develop and maintain an open mind, make it a habit to assess your attitude about your job, customers, products, and services before making contact with your customers. Make sure that you are positive, objective, prepared, and focused. Don't let negative attitudes block good service. Many service providers, even the more seasoned ones, go through slumps during which they feel down about themselves, their job, supervisors, organizations, customers, and so on. This is normal. Customer service is a stressful job, and external and internal factors (e.g., Circadian Rhythm, workload, and personal problems) influence one's perceptions of people and the world in general.

If you are facing personal problems that seem overwhelming, contact your supervisor, human resources or personnel department, or any other appropriate resource to help you sort out your problems. Failure to do so could lead to poor customer service or a less than professional image.

Individualize Service

Each customer is unique and has his or her own desires and needs. For that reason, every situation you handle will be slightly different. As you read in Chapter 10, you should view each person as an individual and not deal with customers based on preconceived ideas. By addressing a customer as an individual, listening so that you can discover his or her needs and problems, and then working to satisfy the needs or solve the problems, you potentially create a loyal customer. A simple way of accomplishing individualized service is to ask what else the customer would like. For example, in the case of a restaurant server who uses such a question, a customer might respond, "Do you have any____?" If the item is available, the server could cheerfully reply, "We certainly do. I'll get it for you right away." If the item is not available, the server might reply, "I'm sorry we do not have ____. However, we do have____. Would that be acceptable?"

Remember: Tell the customer what you can do, not what you cannot do.

Show Respect

Even if you don't agree with a customer, respect his or her point of view or need and provide the best possible service. In return, the customer will probably respect and appreciate you and your efforts. A variation of an old adage may help put this concept into perspective: *"The customer may not always be right, but he or she is still the customer."*

If you lose sight of the fact that it is the customer who supports the organization, pays your salary, provides for your benefits, and gives you a job, you may want to examine why you are working in your current position. By acknowledging the value of your customers and affording them the respect and service that they deserve, you can greatly improve your chances of having a satisfied customer. Some easy ways to show respect to customers include: When addressing the customer, use his or her last name and title. (If you are on the telephone, you write down the customer's name along with other pertinent information.)

- *Stop talking when the customer begins to speak.*
- *Take time to address the customer's questions or concerns.*
- *Return calls or e-mail messages within reasonable amounts of time.*
- *Show up on time for scheduled meetings.*
- *Do what you promised to do, and do it right the first time, within the agreed-upon time frame.*

▶ Take a few minutes to think of other ways that you can show respect for a variety of customers (e.g., older, younger, people with disabilities, or of various cultural backgrounds).

_____

_____

_____

_____

_____

Elicit Input

Many times, service providers do not take the time to ask for feedback because they are afraid that it may not be good. In other instances, they simply do not think of asking or care to do so. To increase your own effectiveness and that of your organization, actively and regularly seek input from your customers. No one knows better than the customer what he or she likes or needs. Take the time to ask the customer, and then listen and act upon what you are told. By asking customers questions, you give them an opportunity to express interest, concerns, emotion, and even complaints. There are many ways of gathering this information (e.g., customer satisfaction cards, written surveys, and service follow-up telephone calls). The key is to somehow ask the customer "How well did we do in meeting your needs?" or "What do you think?"

Some people actually encourage rewarding customers who complain. In their 1996 book, Janelle Barlow and Claus Moller focused on the concept that "a complaint is a gift." The authors stressed that complaints provide feedback that can enable service providers and organizations to rapidly shift resources to fix things that are not working well in an effort to satisfy the customer. If you think about it, that makes sense.

Use Effective Closing Statements

Just as you would likely part company with a friend by saying good-bye, you should leave on a positive note with customers. After all, this is your final opportunity to convey your appreciation and show that you value the relationship you have established with them. Some typical approaches to accomplishing this are: "May I assist you with something else?" "If we may assist in the future, please let us know." "Please come again." "I look forward to serving you again, Ms. Ramirez. I'll see you at your next appointment."

▶ Reflect on a recent interaction you had with an internal or external customer as a provider (over the telephone, in person, via e-mail, or through any other means). Immediately after that interaction, if someone had handed the customer a piece of paper and asked her to write down her impressions of the treatment received from you, what would she likely have said? Why do you believe the customer would have said this?

Note: If you do not deal with customers, think of a situation that you recently experienced as a customer and answer the questions based on your experience. On the rules, record your perspective of what your customer's comments would have been, along with anything you could have done differently to improve the situation. Be as objective as you can.

_____

_____

_____

_____

_____

_____

_____

_____

_____

_____

_____

WORKSHEET 13-3

Building Relationships

Take a few minutes to review the actions discussed in the preceding sections that can lead to a positive relationship. List the qualities that you feel you exhibit in dealing with others. What other people-oriented characteristics do you have that can help build strong customer relationships?

_____

_____

_____

_____

_____

_____

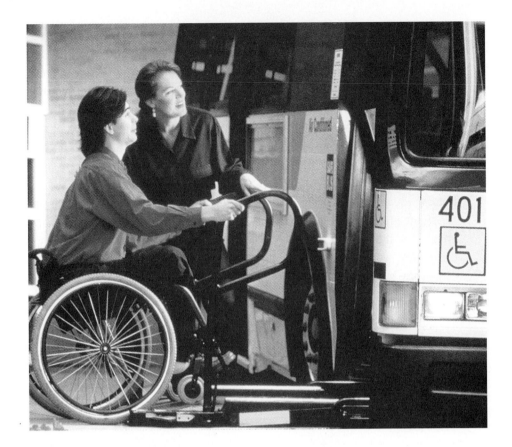

Customer loyalty is won by providing extra service for the customer. Organizations must assess individual needs and determine how to meet those needs better than the competition does. In this case, customers who have mobility impairments or limitations will keep coming back to this establishment because they have provided transportation for those with disabilities. How can you provide extra service for customers with special needs?

5 MAKING THE CUSTOMER NUMBER ONE

> **CONCEPT:** Make a good first impression by establishing rapport; then identify and satisfy your customers' needs. Follow up to obtain repeat business.

Most people like to feel that they are important and valued. By recognizing and acting on that fact, you can go a long way toward providing solid customer service and building a strong relationship with customers. By being an "I care" person, you can generate much goodwill while meeting customer needs.

Every time you encounter a customer in person or over the phone, you have an opportunity to provide excellent service. Some companies call a service encounter the **moment of truth,** in which the customer comes into contact with some facet of the organization. At this point you and other service providers have an opportunity to deliver "knock your socks off" service, as Kristin Anderson and Ron Zemke discuss in several of their books on customer service. Each customer encounter moves through the following stages, although sometimes the order varies. At each step, you have another opportunity to provide excellent customer service.

Make Positive Initial Contact

First impressions are crucial and often lasting. To ensure that you put your best effort forward, remember the basics of positive verbal and non-verbal communication—giving a professional salutation, projecting a positive attitude, and sincerely offering to assist. This is crucial because the average customer will come into an initial contact with certain expectations. If the expectations are not met, you and your organization can lose **relationship-rating points** that can ultimately cost the organization a customer. Such points are like the ones on performance appraisals used in many organizations to evaluate and rate employee performance (see Figure 13-6.) Use this scale frequently to evaluate your rating as you deal with various customers.

FIGURE 13-6

Relationship-rating point scale.

Exemplary (4) Service that is out of the ordinary and unexpected falls into this category. Examples: An auto repair shop details a customer's car after replacing a transmission. A beauty salon owner provides a free Swedish massage to a regular patron on her birthday. A restaurant server provides a complimentary meal and a coupon for a discount on a future visit to a customer who had to send her steak back twice to be cooked properly.

Above Average (3) Service in this category goes beyond the normal and may pleasantly surprise the customer, but does not dazzle or surprise the customer. Example: A regular customer at a bar gets a free second drink from the bartender. A clerk at a bank gives a customer a free wall calendar at the end of the transaction. A customer's son, who just received his first haircut, is given a lollypop by the barber.

Average (2) Service at this level is what is expected by a customer. Examples: A customer drops off laundry and when it is picked up, his shirts are starched as requested, on hangers, and in a plastic garment bag. A grocery store bagger asks, "Paper or plastic?" and then proceeds to comply with the customer's request. An accountant finishes a client's tax return on time, as promised.

Below Average (1) Service provided at this level is not as expected and disappoints customers. Examples: A newspaper deliverer brings a replacement paper after a customer calls to complain, leaves it on the doorstep, rings the bell, and departs without apologizing. A patient waits in a doctor's waiting room 15 minutes or longer beyond her scheduled appointment, and when she is finally seen, no one apologizes. A call center representative gives a customer a $15 credit on service because the customer had to call back three times to have a problem resolved.

Unsatisfactory (0) Service at this level is unacceptable and typically leads to a breakdown in the customer-provider relationship. (Examples: A customer's cat is neutered by a veterinarian when taken in for a flea dip. A plumbing company that advertises "immediate emergency service" takes over four hours to send a repairperson to fix a leaking pipe in a wall; all carpeting in the living room is being saturated, and one wall is crumbling. A contracted tree-trimming worker cuts a large section from a tree that crashes through the garage roof and onto a brand-new car.

Establish Rapport

Customers react to and deal effectively with employees who they perceive as likable, helpful, and effective. Throughout your interaction, continue to be helpful, smile, listen, use the customer's name frequently, and attend to the customer's needs or concerns. Also, look for opportunities to generate small talk about non-business-related matters. When something goes wrong, people who feel a kinship with service providers typically give higher ratings on the relationship-rating point scale than people who do not feel this connection.

Identify and Satisfy Customer Needs Quickly

Use the questioning, listening, observing, and feedback skills outlined in this book to focus on issues of concern to the customer. By effectively gathering information, you can then move to the next phase of customer service.

Exceed Expectations

As you can see on the relationship-rating point scale, customers typically expect that, if they pay a certain price for a product or service, they will receive a specific quality and quantity in return. This is not an unusual expectation. The average customer looks for value. As you read in earlier chapters, today's customers tend to be better-educated consumers who recognize that if they cannot fulfill their needs in one place, they can easily access the same or similar products and services on the Internet or by visiting a competitor. Therefore, you need to exceed a customer's expectations. Many terms are used to describe the concept of exceeding expectations—knock their socks off service, positive memorable customer experiences, E-plus service, customer delight, dazzling service, fabled service, and Five Diamond or Five Star service. All these phrases have in common the concept of going above and beyond customer expectations—*under* promise and *over* deliver. By going out of your way not only to satisfy a customer but also to "wow" them by doing, saying, or offering the unexpected related to high-quality service delivery, you can exceed expectations. The result could be the reward of continuing patronage by the customer.

An example of unexpected service or going the extra mile follows. A customer bought flooring tiles from a home product warehouse and took them home. Upon opening the box, he discovered that several tiles were broken. After the customer called the store, an employee delivered the replacement tiles and assisted the customer in laying them.

Follow Up

Service professionals regrettably often overlook this step although it can be one of the most crucial in establishing long-term relationships. Follow-through is a major key in obtaining repeat business. After you have satisfied a customer's needs, follow up with the customer on his or her next visit or via mail, e-mail, or telephone to ensure that he or she was satisfied. For external customers, this follow-up can be coupled with a small thank-you card, coupons for discounts on future purchases, small presents, or any other incentive to reward their patronage. You can follow up with internal customers by using voice mail or e-mail messages, leaving Post-It notes on their desks, inviting them for coffee in the cafeteria, or any other of a number of ways. The prime objective is to let them know that you have not forgotten them and appreciate their business and support.

Encourage Customers to Return

Just as with your initial impression, you need to close on a high note. Smile, remind the customer you are available to help in the future, give an opportunity for last-minute questions, and invite the customer to return.

Work It Out 13-7. Strategies for Making Customers Number One

▶ On a sheet of paper, list each of the initiatives for making customers No. 1 that you just read about. Then, develop an action plan for addressing each of them in your customer contacts. Be specific about exactly what you will do or say to address each strategy. Use the following setup as a sample format:

Initiative	Action(s)	Expected Customer Response
Make positive initial contact	_____	_____
	_____	_____
	_____	_____
	_____	_____
	_____	_____
Establish rapport	_____	_____
	_____	_____
	_____	_____
	_____	_____
	_____	_____
Identify and satisfy customer needs quickly	_____	_____
	_____	_____
	_____	_____
Exceed expectations	_____	_____
	_____	_____
	_____	_____
	_____	_____
	_____	_____

Follow up _____ _____

_____ _____

_____ _____

_____ _____

Encourage customers to _____ _____
return

_____ _____

_____ _____

_____ _____

---

6 | ENHANCING CUSTOMER SATISFACTION AS A STRATEGY FOR RETAINING CUSTOMERS

▶ **CONCEPT:** Do the unexpected; deal with one customer at a time; handle complaints efficiently. These are just some of the things you can do to enhance customer satisfaction.

Building good relationships in order to increase customer satisfaction is valuable because it can lead to repeat business—the key to keeping a business productive and profitable.

Satisfaction is a big factor for many customers in remaining loyal. Interestingly, a recent review of customer satisfaction in the United States shows a slight rise in the level of general customer satisfaction after a steady decline that began in 1994, when the numbers were first tracked. According to a news release by the University of Michigan, the average customer satisfaction level (including retail and finance and insurance sectors) was 72.6 percent in 1999 but is still lower than the 1994 high of 74.5 percent.

An example of the importance of customer satisfaction in the automotive industry was reported in The J. D. Power and Associates 1998 Customer Satisfaction Index Study. The study found that a customer who has a very satisfying customer experience with dealership service is three times as willing to purchase another vehicle from the same manufacturer compared to someone who had just an adequate experience. The downside of the Power's study is that only about 45 percent of those surveyed said they had excellent service experiences.

Based on the Power and University of Michigan studies, there is definitely room for improvement in delivering customer service. In your own organization, your efforts could be a deciding factor in customer ratings for the quality of service rendered.

Keeping customers can be difficult in a competitive, global marketplace because so many companies have joined in the race for customers. By providing a personal, professional strategy, you can help ensure that customers return. Some tips that can help provide quality service to customers are given in the following sections.

Pay Attention

As you listen, focus all your attention on the customer so that you can identify and address his or her needs. If you are serving in person, use positive nonverbal cues (e.g., face the customer, smile, use open gestures, make eye contact, stop doing other things, and focus attention on the customer) and language. Ask open-ended questions to determine the customer's needs. Also, use the active listening techniques discussed in Chapter 4 to ensure that you get all the information you need to properly address the customer's needs or concerns.

Deal With One Customer at a Time

You cannot effectively handle two people (on the phone or in person) simultaneously. When more than one call or customer comes in at the same time, seek assistance or ask one customer to wait (or ask whether you can get back to him or her at a later time). Then, give personalized attention to the other customer.

Know Your Customers

This is crucial with long-term customers, but it is also important with everyone. You may see or talk to hundreds of customers a week; however, each customer has only one or two contacts with you. Although you might not recall the name of everyone you speak with during a day, your customers will remember what was said or agreed upon previously, and expect you to do the same. For that reason, use notes or your computer to keep a record of conversations with customers. You can review or refer to these notes in subsequent encounters. This avoids having customers repeat themselves, and they will feel "special" because you remembered them.

Give Customers Special Treatment

As you read earlier, you should try to take the time for a little small talk once in a while. This will help you learn about your customers and what's important to them (potential needs). Occasionally, paying them compliments also helps (e.g., "That's an attractive tie," or "That perfume is very pleasing").

Service Each Customer at Least Adequately

Take the necessary time to handle your customer's questions, complaints, or needs. If you have a number of customers on the phone or in person, service one at a time and either ask to get back to the others or get help from a coworker, if possible. You might also suggest alternative information resources to customers, such as fax on demand or your Website, on-line information system, or interactive voice response. This may satisfy them and help reduce the calls or visits from customers, because they can now get the information they need from alternative sources.

Do the Unexpected

Do not just provide service; provide exceptional service. Provide additional information, offer suggestions that will aid the customer, send articles that may be of interest, follow up transactions with calls or letters to make sure that needs were met, or send cards for special occasions and to thank customers. These are the little things that mean a lot and can mean the difference between a rating of Average or Exemplary on the relationship-rating point scale. Read the article in the following box quickly to see an example of this concept in action.

Give 'Em the Extra Pickle!

An example of doing the unexpected came when Bob Farrell, founder of Farrell's Ice Cream Parlor restaurants, responded to a customer complaint a number of years ago. Farrell received a letter from a regular customer of many years. The customer had been ordering hamburgers with an extra pickle since he started patronizing Farrell's. At some point, the man went to Farrell's and ordered a hamburger but was told by a new server that the extra pickle would cost an additional 25 cents. When the man protested, the server conferred with her manager and happily reported that the extra pickle would cost only 5 cents. At that point the man left and wrote Farrell, who wrote back enclosing a free coupon, apologizing, and inviting the customer back.

The lesson to be learned here is that when you have a loyal customer whom you might lose because of enforcement of a trivial policy, you should be flexible. When policies inhibit good service and negatively affect customer relationships, they should be pointed out to management and examined for possible modification or elimination.

Handle Complaints Effectively

Treat complaints as opportunities to redeem missed service expectations, and handle them effectively. Acknowledge any error on your part, and do everything possible to resolve the problem quickly and to the customer's satisfaction. Thank the customer for bringing his or her concerns to your attention.

Sell Benefits

Show each customer how your product, service, or information addresses his or her needs. What benefit will result? Stress that although other organizations may offer similar products and services, yours fits their needs best (if they do). If your product or service doesn't fit their needs, admit it, and offer any available alternatives (such as referral to a competitor). Your customers will appreciate your honesty, and even if you can't help them, they will probably return in the future because you are trusted.

Know Your Competition

Stay abreast of what other, similar organizations are offering in order to counter comments about them. This does not mean that you should criticize or belittle your competitors or their products and services. Such behavior is unprofessional and will likely cause the customer to lose respect for you. And when respect goes, trust goes.

Staying aware of the competition has the additional benefit of helping you be sure that you can describe and offer the products, services, and features of your organization that are comparable to those being offered by others.

7 STRIVE FOR QUALITY

CONCEPT: A customer's perception of quality service is often one of the prime reasons for his or her return.

A final strategy for helping to increase customer loyalty relates to the quality of service you and your organization provide. So much is written these days about quality—how to measure it and its significance—that there is a temptation to think of it as a fad. In the areas of customer service and customer retention, thinking this way could be disastrous. A customer's perception of quality service is often one of the prime reasons for his or her return.

Terms such as **total quality management** (TQM) and *continuous quality improvement* (CQI) are often used in many industries to label the goal of improvement. Basically, quality service involves efforts and activities that are done well and that meet or exceed customer needs and expectations. In an effort to achieve quality service, many organizations go to great lengths to test and measure the level of service provided to customers.

On a personal level, you can strive for quality service by working to achieve an Exemplary rating on the relationship-rating point scale. Your organization's ability to deliver quality service depends on you and the others who provide frontline service to customers. If you do not adopt a professional attitude and continually strive to improve your knowledge, skills, and efforts in dealing with customers, failure and customer dissatisfaction can result.

A number of years ago, Texas A&M researchers developed a five-dimensional model, called *RATER* (for reliability, assurance, tangibles, empathy, and responsiveness), to describe quality service. The model, along with strategies for its implementation, is described below:

Reliability. The ability to provide what was promised, dependably and accurately.
IMPLEMENTATION STRATEGY: Make sure that you correctly identify customer needs, promise only what you can deliver, and follow through to ensure that the product or service was received as promised.

Assurance. The knowledge and courtesy of employees, and their ability to convey trust and confidence.

IMPLEMENTATION STRATEGY: Take the time to serve customers one at a time. Provide service assertively by using positive communication techniques and describing products and services accurately.

Tangibles. The physical facilities and equipment and the appearance of personnel.

IMPLEMENTATION STRATEGY: Maintain workspaces in a neat, orderly manner, dress professionally, and maintain excellent grooming and hygiene standards.

Empathy. The degree of caring and individual attention provided to customers.

IMPLEMENTATION STRATEGY: Listen for emotions in your customers' messages. Put yourself in their place and respond compassionately by offering service to address their needs.

Responsiveness. The willingness to help customers and provide prompt service.

IMPLEMENTATION STRATEGY: Project a positive, can-do attitude. Take immediate steps to help customers and satisfy needs.

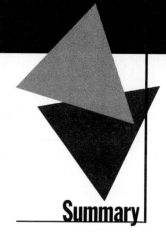

Summary

Chapter Summary

Build enduring, strong customer relationships based on the principles of trust, responsibility, loyalty, and satisfying customer needs. These are all crucial elements of success in an increasingly competitive business world. Retaining current customers is less expensive and more effective than finding and developing new ones. The key is to provide courteous, professional service that addresses customer needs. Although many factors potentially affect your ability to deliver quality service, you can apply specific methods and strategies to keep your customers coming back.

Too often, service providers lose sight of the fact that they are the organization and that their actions determine the outcome of any customer-provider encounter. By employing the strategies outlined in this chapter, and those you read about previously, you can do much to ensure customer satisfaction and organizational success.

CHAPTER REVIEW QUESTIONS

1. How can you build customer trust? _____

_____

_____

_____

_____

2. What are some key reasons why customers remain loyal to a product, a service, or an organization? _____

_____

_____

_____

_____

3. What are some of the provider characteristics that affect customer loyalty? _____

_____

_____

_____

_____

4. Describe the steps in the planning process model. _____

_____

_____

_____

_____

5. What are six common customer needs? _____

_____

_____

_____

_____

6. What are ways for service providers to take responsibility for customer relations? _____

_____

_____

_____

_____

7. What are some techniques for making the customer feel that he or she is No. 1? _____

_____

_____

_____

_____

8. What was the purpose of the RATER model developed at Texas A&M? _____

_____

_____

_____

_____

▼ SEARCH IT OUT

Search the Web for Information on Loyalty

Log on to the Internet to search for additional information related to customer loyalty. Select one of the following projects:

Go to the Websites of organizations that deal with customers and service. Identify research data, articles, bibliographies, and other reference sources (e.g., videotapes) related to customer loyalty and create a bibliography similar to the one at the end of this book. Here are a few sites to get you started:

<ICSA.com>

<SOCAP.com>

<CSR.com>

<e-satisfy.com>

<Amazon.com>

<Barnes&Noble.com>

<Borders.com>

Go to various search engines to locate information and articles on *customer loyalty*. To find information, enter terms related to concepts covered in this chapter or locate Websites dealing with such issues. Here are a few to get you started:

> *Customer loyalty*
>
> *Customer satisfaction*
>
> *Customer retention*
>
> *Customer Service Review magazine*
>
> *Total quality management in customer service*
>
> *Cost of customer service*
>
> *<www.customercare.com>*
>
> *<www.kestnbaum.com>*

COLLABORATIVE *Learning Activity*

Building Loyalty

Here are two options for activities that you and others can use to reinforce the concepts of building loyalty that you read about in this chapter.

1. Working with a partner, think of times when you have both been frustrated or dissatisfied with service received from a provider. Make a list of characteristics the service provider(s) exhibited that had a negative impact on you. Once you have a list, discuss the items on the list, and then honestly say whether either (or both) of you exhibit any of these negative behaviors when dealing with others. For the ones you answered yes, jointly develop a list of strategies to improve each behavior.

Behaviors Experienced	Improvement Strategy

2. Take a field trip around your town. Walk through and/or past as many establishments as possible. Look for examples of actions that organizations are doing to encourage and discourage customer loyalty. List the examples on a sheet of paper and be prepared to discuss them in groups assigned by your instructor when you return to class. Some examples of encouragement might be free samples of

a product being distributed at a food court, discount coupons, acceptance of competitor coupons, or free refills on drinks. Negative examples might be signs that say "Rest rooms for customers only" or "No change given," and policies that allow discounts only on certain days and no refunds on purchases (exchanges only).

FACE TO FACE

Assessing the Need for Reorganization at Get Away

Background

After over nine years in business, the Get Away travel agency in Des Moines, Iowa, is feeling the pinch of competition. During the past 14 months, the owners, Marsha Henry and Consuela (Connie) Gomez, have seen business profits dwindle by 18 percent. Neither Marsha nor Connie can figure out what has happened. Although travel reservationists have had to deal with airline fee caps, customers making more reservations on the Internet, and the fact that many industry travel providers are cutting back, competing agencies don't seem to be suffering as much as Get Away. The problem is especially worrisome because Marsha and Connie recently took out a second mortgage on their office building so that they could put more money into promotion and customer acquisition efforts. The more efforts they make at gaining exposure, the more customers they lose, it seems. Recently, they lost a major corporate client that accounted for over $100,000 in business a year. Out of desperation, they have decided to hire you, a seasoned travel agency manager, to try to stop their descent and turn the operation around.

Your Role

As the new manager at Get Away, you have been given the authority to do whatever is necessary to salvage the agency. By agreement with Marsha and Connie, they are delaying the announcement of your hiring to other agency employees. Your objective is to objectively assess the operation by acting as a customer.

Your first contact with the agency came on Thursday, when you placed a phone call to the office, posing as a customer. The phone rang 12 times and was curtly answered with "Hello. Please hold (click)." After nearly five minutes, an agent, Sue, came on the line and stated, "Sorry for the wait, we're swamped. Can I get your name and number and call you right back?" Two-and-a-half hours later, you got a call from Tom. He said that Sue had gone home for the day, and he was doing her callbacks. Sue would follow up when she came in the next day. You asked a friend to make a similar call on Wednesday, and she met with similar results.

On Thursday, you stopped by the office at 2:55 p.m. Of three agents who should have been there, only Claudia was present. Apparently Tom and Sue were still at lunch. Two customers were waiting as you arrived. Claudia greeted you with a small smile and asked you to "Take a number and have a seat." You looked around the office and saw desks piled high with materials, an overflowing trash can, and an empty coffeepot in the waiting area bearing the sign "Please have a cup on us." In talking to your fellow "customers," you learned that one had been there for over 45 minutes. Both were irritated at having to wait, and eventually, one left. You left after 30 minutes and passed Tom and Sue, who came in laughing. You thought you detected an odor of alcohol on Tom. Neither acknowledged you. From the office, you proceeded to a meeting with Marsha and Connie.

Questions

1. What impressions of the travel agency did you have as a result of your initial phone call? _____

_____

_____

_____

2. How did your office visit affect you? _____

_____

_____

_____

3. What will you tell Marsha and Connie about employee professionalism? _____

_____

_____

_____

4. What customer needs are being overlooked in this scenario? _____

_____

_____

_____

5. In what ways can this situation be improved? _____

_____

_____

_____

FROM THE FRONTLINE
Interview

Patricia A. Scott
Assistant Vice President
Manager of Credit Card
Customer Service
Huntington National Bank
Columbus, Ohio

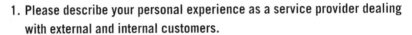

1. Please describe your personal experience as a service provider dealing with external and internal customers.

I have worked in Customer Service at Huntington National Bank for the past 20 years, focusing primarily on credit card and personal credit line products. The department I directly manage handles approximately 35,000 "live" customer calls a month. Our Customer Service Voice Response Unit, which I helped develop, handles an additional 100,000 calls a month. We answer approximately 8000 customer letters per month and act as the third-party mediator in disputes between our cardholders and merchants. In addition, we field inquiries from outside credit card processors, merchants, banking offices, and various internal Huntington National Bank departments.

2. What are your general impressions of customer service in the United States? Why do you feel this way?

I think that personal customer service has declined in the United States during the last 10 years. We have advanced our customer service technology by leaps and bounds during this same time frame. This has been a definite plus for customers and service providers alike. We have developed voice response units that provide automated account information; we also have automated order-taking systems, contact-management software, computerized troubleshooting, electronic newsletters, Websites, hyperlinks, and cyber feedback. With all this emphasis on technology, we sometimes forget that we are dealing with people, just like ourselves. And as people we want and deserve personal service. In order to give personal service, we sometimes have to listen to complaints. Complaints should be considered opportunities to fix problems and keep customers. According to Joel Marks, the Golden Rule tells you to treat customers the way you want to be treated; the Platinum Rule says to treat them the way they want to be treated. In order to do that, you need to listen to the customer.

3. Do you believe that there is such a thing as customer loyalty?

I not only believe it, I can prove it. Over the years I have received letter after letter and call after call from customers who tell me they are still with us because of the personal service they received from someone in a banking office or one of our call centers. Financial institutions are in the business of making money by providing financial benefits to their clients that (1) give them money, (2) make them money, (3) save them money, (4) protect their money, or (5) save them time or provide convenience. In order to be successful at all of these things, we must also provide personal service. In 1984 I took an address change request from one of our customers. I didn't think much of it at the time, but he thanked me profusely, going on to say that the Huntington was the only company that was able to handle this simple request in an efficient manner (he had spent the day on the phone informing various companies of his change of address). To this day, this customer continues to bank at Huntington even though he lives in Denmark. And his reason for staying is the experience he had in 1984, when changing his address. This is not an isolated incident. I hear comments like this from customers quite often.

4. What do you believe to be the biggest challenge for service providers in building customer loyalty?

Maintaining a healthy balance between technology, products, and personal service is probably the biggest challenge. This includes creating an environment that makes customers want to do business with you. By using service, products, and technology as tools that complement each other, you can build loyalty. This includes having business hours that are convenient for the customer, making sure that your voice response unit is truly user-friendly, giving the customer choices (payment preferences, shipping options), providing toll-free numbers, offering rewards programs, and making sure that the products and the service are top quality—to mention only a few ways to build loyalty.

5. What techniques or strategies do you believe to be the most effective in establishing and holding customer loyalty? Why?

I would say everything mentioned above, plus much more. Recently, someone gave me an outline of a crash course for customer service. I don't know the author, but it comes to my mind when I think about this question and goes like this:

The **10** most important words:
> *I apologize for our mistake. Let me make it right.*

The **9** most important words:
> *Thank you for your business. Please come back again.*

The **8** most important words:
> *I am not sure, but I'll find out.*

The **7** most important words:
> *What else can I do for you?*

The **6** most important words:
> *What is most convenient for you?*

The **5** most important words:
> *How may I serve you?*

The **4** most important words:
> *How did we do?*

The **3** most important words:
> *Glad you're here!*

The **2** most important words:
> *Thank you.*

The **1** most important word:
> *Yes.*

6. What are some behaviors of service providers that discourage customer loyalty?

- Not honoring commitments. Do what you say you'll do and follow up. If the customer can't depend on you, he or she can't depend on your products.

- Telling a customer you *can't* do something without offering what you *can* do.
- Not getting back to customers with answers to their questions. Don't know? Find out! Don't end a conversation with "I don't know" or "I'm not sure." Find out and get back to the customer as soon as possible.
- Spend less time talking and more time listening.
- Quoting "company policy." Customers aren't interested in excuses or policies. They want answers and solutions that reflect a "can-do" attitude. Bending the rules a little to satisfy a customer is better than losing the customer.

7. From your perspective, what is the most important thing to remember when dealing with a customer?

This is a tough question, because there are so many things to keep in mind—from basic customer service skills to advanced technology. If I had to choose one thing, I'd have to say focusing on customers' needs. Find out what they need, and deliver it. Customer service doesn't come from a manual; it comes from the heart—from realizing that we are all someone's customers, and each of us knows how we would like to be treated. You can never do too much.

8. What advice related to building customer loyalty would you give someone just entering the customer service profession?

If you have chosen to be a customer service professional, you need to master the basics, keep learning, obtain customer feedback to assist in developing products that they want and need, and take advantage of technology. And, finally: listen, listen, listen.

> ### CRITICAL THINKING
> How does customer service for providers in a bank differ from other providers? How would you serve banking customers?

Chapter 14

Service Recovery

OBJECTIVES

After completing this chapter, you will be able to:

- *Define what a service breakdown is.*

- *Discuss the causes of service breakdowns.*

- *Determine why customers leave following a service breakdown.*

- *Identify strategies for preventing customer dissatisfaction.*

- *Implement a frontline service recovery strategy.*

- *Spot roadblocks to service recovery.*

"Recovery is transforming a dissatisfied customer into a satisfied one."

Stephen C. Broydrick, 1994
How May I Help You?

Before reviewing the chapter content, respond to the following questions by placing a "T" for true or an "F" for false on the rules. Use any questions you miss as a checklist of material to which you will pay particular attention as you read through the chapter. For those you get right, congratulate yourself, but review the sections they address in order to learn additional details about the topic.

_____ 1. Service recovery occurs when a provider is able to make restitution, solve a problem, or regain customer trust after service breakdown.

_____ 2. Service breakdowns are rare in most organizations.

_____ 3. Thirteen percent of customers who have service problems tell three to five other people.

_____ 4. Organizational factors related to policies or procedures are rarely the basis for service breakdowns.

_____ 5. A good strategy for organizational success is to focus on the "average" customer.

_____ 6. Competency in communicating can eliminate the need for service recovery.

_____ 7. To effectively serve your customers, you need a strong knowledge of products, services, organizational structure, and organizational goals.

_____ 8. Service breakdowns always occur as a result of service provider error.

_____ 9. In the follow-through phase of recovery, negotiations take place when the organization and customer make a commitment to take specific actions.

_____ 10. One key strategy for preventing dissatisfaction is to learn to think like a customer.

_____ 11. The primary purpose of any good service recovery program should be to return the organization-customer relationship to a normal status.

1. T   5. F   9. T
2. F   6. T   10. T
3. T   7. T   11. T
4. F   8. F

1 WHAT IS SERVICE RECOVERY?

CONCEPT: When service breaks down, the customer expects that customer service representatives will take action to solve the customer's problem.

Effective **service recovery** occurs when an organization or service provider is able to solve a customer problem, make restitution, or regain trust following a breakdown in service delivery. Many times your customers have expectations that they will receive products, services, or other deliverables at a certain level. When they get something else, they can become frustrated, angry, and/or dissatisfied.

The challenge is to recognize that some customers will not tell you they are dissatisfied. That is where the ability to read their nonverbal cues and ask effective questions, as you read in Chapters 3 and 4, is paramount to your success. If you do not identify a customer's problem and take immediate steps to recover or make amends, you could lose a valuable customer, who may then tell others who might also defect or, if they are potential customers, stay away.

So in a way, you sometimes have to be part fortune teller, part detective, and part problem solver in order to deliver effective customer service. And, if you become really good at the service recovery technique, you may even be able to turn a negative situation into an additional sale or upgrade in products and services.

2 | WHAT IS A SERVICE BREAKDOWN?

▶ **CONCEPT:** Service breakdowns occur whenever any product or service fails to meet the customer's expectations.

Service breakdowns occur daily in many organizations. They happen whenever the product or service delivered fails to meet customer expectations. In some cases the product or service delivered may function exactly as it was designed, but if the customer perceived that it should work another way, a breakdown occurs. Here are some possible breakdowns:

- *A waiter serves a meal containing an ingredient not expected by the customer, or one that the customer specified should not be added. A note of caution: If you are in food service, be vigilant in monitoring orders when customers ask that certain ingredients not be used. Check food and drinks before you deliver them to your customer to be sure that the staff did not forget the special request. Also, do not simply remove a food item if it was placed on a plate inadvertently. Some people have severe allergies to certain foods that could cause serious illness and even death— and a huge liability for you and your organization.*
- *A hotel room is not available when the customer arrives. (In some cases a stated check-in time may exist and the customer may be early. Make every effort to accommodate the customer if this happens.)*
- *A car repair is not completed at the time promised, or is done incorrectly.*
- *An additional cash register is not opened even though there are eight to ten customers waiting in a line and cashier staff are available in the store. (Some companies have signs stating that they will open another register if more than a certain number of customers are waiting).*

- *According to the customer, room service food was cold when delivered (e.g., not at the degree of warmth desired or expected).*
- *A coworker expects your assistance in providing information needed for a monthly report, but you failed to get it to her on time or as agreed.*
- *A manufacturer does not receive a parts delivery as you promised, and an assembly line has to be shut down.*
- *A garment you needed for a meeting returns from the laundry with broken buttons and cannot be worn.*

In any of the situations described, customers may have not received what they were promised, or at least they perceived that they did not. When such incidents occur, there is a breakdown. Unfortunately, most such situations go unreported by customers. Moreover, when they are reported, often they are not effectively handled by businesses. TARP, a customer service research and consulting firm in Arlington, Virginia, has published numerous surveys on the topic of complaint handling in the United States. A landmark study commissioned by the U.S. Office of Consumer Affairs in 1979 and updated in 1986 demonstrated the value of effective customer complaint resolution. These findings have been validated since 1986 throughout various industries (see Figures 14-1, 14-2, and 14-3).

FIGURE 14-1

What complaint research shows.

The median number of people customers who have a small problem will tell is 5, if the problem is appropriately resolved, and 10 if they are not satisfied.

The median number of people customers who have a large problem will tell is 8, if the problem is appropriately resolved, and 16 if they are not satisfied.

In 1000 companies surveyed, on average, 50 percent of consumers and 25 percent of business customers who have problems never complain.

Three principal reasons why people do not complain:

(1) Complaining wasn't worth their time and effort.

(2) They believed that complaining wouldn't do any good; no one wanted to hear about their problems.

(3) They didn't know how or where to complain.

(Source: TARP, 1300 Wilson Blvd., Suite 950, Arlington, VA 22209)

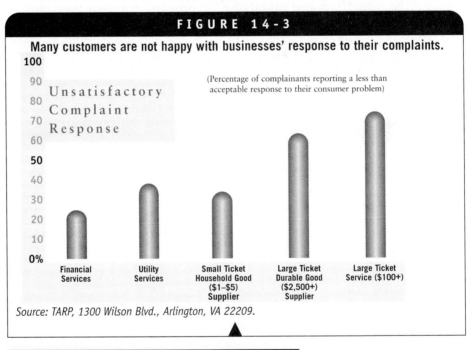

FIGURE 14-2

Many customers do not complain.

Percent of Unarticulated Complaints

(Percentage of customers experiencing problems with selected products/services who did not complain)

100
90
80
70
60
50
40
30
20
10
0%

| A Large Ticket Durable Good Supplier | A Medium Ticket Durable Good Supplier | A Large Ticket Service Supplier | A Small Ticket Service Supplier |

Source: TARP, 1300 Wilson Blvd., Arlington, VA 22209.

FIGURE 14-3

Many customers are not happy with businesses' response to their complaints.

Unsatisfactory Complaint Response

(Percentage of complainants reporting a less than acceptable response to their consumer problem)

100
90
80
70
60
50
40
30
20
10
0%

| Financial Services | Utility Services | Small Ticket Household Good ($1–$5) Supplier | Large Ticket Durable Good ($2,500+) Supplier | Large Ticket Service ($100+) |

Source: TARP, 1300 Wilson Blvd., Arlington, VA 22209.

Work It Out 14-1

Work It Out 14-1. Service Breakdown Examples

▶ What other examples of service breakdown have you have experienced or can think of? List them here:

_____

_____

_____

_____

_____

_____

3 CAUSES OF SERVICE BREAKDOWNS

CONCEPT: Service breakdowns can occur for a number of reasons. For the customer, however, the customer service provider is the organization when the service breaks down. The provider must identify the cause and remedy the situation to the customer's satisfaction.

Human beings make mistakes; this is a fact. Mistakes are often glaring to customers, who can be very unforgiving at times. The best you can hope for when something goes wrong is that you can identify the cause and remedy the problem quickly to your customer's satisfaction. By accomplishing this, you may maintain the customer loyalty as discussed in Chapter 13.

Many reasons exist for you and your organization to take action to remedy a situation that has gone wrong. Some typical events necessitating service recovery action are:

- *A product or service did not do what it was expected to do.*
- *A promise was not kept.*
- *A deadline was missed.*
- *Customer service was not adequately provided (the customer had to wait too long or was ignored).*
- *A service provider lacked adequate knowledge or skills to handle a situation.*
- *Your actions or those of the organization inconvenienced the customer (e.g., a lab technician took blood during a patient's visit, but the sample was mishandled, requiring the patient to return for a retest).*
- *A customer was given the "runaround" (was transferred to various employees or departments and required to explain the situation to each individual).*
- *The customer was treated unprofessionally or in a rude manner (or perceived that this was the treatment).*

Numerous factors in the service process can lead to a failure to meet customer expectations, and they can all influence service recovery. Generally, these factors fall into three categories—organizational, employee, or customer.

Organizational Factors

Organizational factors relate to processes, procedures, policies, and structures that, when not functioning effectively, can detract from service quality. As a frontline provider, you play a crucial role in implementing many of these practices. As such, you become the organization in the eyes of a customer. When a customer yells at you because he or she perceives that something did not go as promised or expected, he or she is usually yelling at the organization through you. That is why you must control the tendency to take the anger personally. Instead, continue to listen objectively to what he or she has to say in order to get the information needed to solve the problems. Even so, there are some factors over which you have no direct control but that affect you and your customers. These include the following.

Human Resources

The screening, selection, training, performance appraisal, and compensation of employees who interact with customers are crucial. Managers should take care to develop a job description that focuses on the competencies required for the position. This will help ensure that the right person is hired for a job.

You can help in this regard by openly discussing your regular job tasks with your supervisor. Often, over time, employees take on tasks because it is easier for them to do so than to ask someone else, or because job responsibilities evolve when changes are made in procedures. Your supervisor is usually aware of these modifications, but since they are minor, no change is made to your job description. Over time, your responsibilities may evolve far beyond the written job description. This is why you need to know what your job description defines as your duties and bring major changes to the attention of your supervisor. This is important because your performance is typically evaluated based on established goals and your job description.

Moreover, job descriptions are used to recruit and hire additional staff. It is to your advantage for your supervisor to have an accurate picture of the skills required so that he or she can adequately screen applicants and choose the best-qualified person to do the job. This is to your advantage since, if a person is hired based on an outdated job description, you may end up training this person on the job.

From a training standpoint, most large organizations spend millions of dollars each year training and updating employee knowledge and skills. Such efforts help companies stay competitive. Also, many organizations continually evaluate and modify compensation and benefit packages. They do this because all these factors affect employee morale and ultimately can create customer satisfaction, or dissatisfaction, depending on how they are handled.

Organization and Structure

Relationships between members of departments or cross-functional teams are typically clearly defined. Reporting structure, levels of empowerment (what employees are authorized to do and what decisions they are allowed to make) and integration of functions are examples. This may not be true in your organization. If necessary, go to your supervisor and ask for an explanation of the reporting hierarchy, as well as the customer-provider chain (people or groups to whom you supply and from which you receive products, information, and services). A thorough understanding of these relationships is important in making it possible for you to provide the best service possible to your customers. Such knowledge also allows you to follow up in cases of service breakdown and to recognize the limits of what you can and cannot do to satisfy customer needs or complaints.

Processes and Programs

The way complaints are handled, sales or promotional tools are used, products and services are delivered, and billing, advertising, and consumer-customer communications work falls into this category.

As a frontline provider, you must have a thorough knowledge of special sales and promotions and how all these systems function in service delivery. This allows you to respond consistently and correctly to customer questions or complaints. Failure to understand these processes can lead to miscommunication and customer dissatisfaction.

Product and Service Design and Delivery

Factors in this category are quality levels, available options, variety of offerings, performance, and availability. These factors often determine whether customers get what they perceive they deserve or need.

To effectively promote, sell, or service products or provide quality service levels, you need a comprehensive knowledge of what your organization offers. You must have a knowledge of processes related to these areas and also be able to discuss them clearly. Remember that you represent the organization, and your customers expect you to have answers.

Service breakdowns are sometimes related to a customer's frustration in getting accurate product information from a customer service representative. What information should a service provider know in order to help a customer?

Internal Communications

Internal communications involve the means for communicating within the organization to share information, elicit support, offer guidance, and train employees. Communication can be achieved through newsletters, meetings, bulletin boards, e-mail, voice mail, and various publications.

Since communication among members of your organization is crucial to your success, you need to be able to freely and regularly exchange product and service information, and to network with others through a variety of methods. The more access you have to data, the better informed you become, so that you are more capable of handling a variety of customer encounters.

Technological Support Systems

As you read in Chapter 7, computers, software, telecommunications, and other technology, along with the technical support staff to maintain the processes, are crucial in today's service environment. All of these resources play an integral role in allowing the exchange of information, problem solving, effective customer service, and keeping your organization competitive. In the age of the **information highway,** you need to be competent in using technology-based information systems, in order to gain and provide information to deliver quality service effectively and efficiently.

Customers don't want to hear "I'm sorry. I can't bring up your file. My computer is down." You need to know how to access information or quickly find someone who can. In addition, educating yourself on alternative information sources is helpful. Speak with your supervisor or team leader and peers to find out whether other ways exist for accessing information when technology fails. If such files or systems exist, learn to use them. If not, suggest them if appropriate.

Standards and Values

Standards are tenets or guidelines that affect the way employees view the organization and how they behave. They also influence the way people outside the organization perceive you and the organization. For example, do you and your company truly value customers? Do systems, products, and services support efforts to satisfy the most demanding customer? If you answered "yes," then you are on your way to flourishing in a competitive service market. If not, start analyzing what might need improvement and make recommendations for change to your supervisor or team leader. By focusing on the average customer, the organization is saying "We're happy to just get by with average service and results." Customer perception could be that your organization and/or you don't really care about satisfaction, but just profit and survival.

Preventing Organizational Breakdowns

Reflect on the organizational factors just discussed. Consider each factor and how you might create a strategy to reduce negative impact. List them below.

FACTOR	STRATEGIES FOR REDUCING NEGATIVE IMPACT
_____	_____
_____	_____
_____	_____
_____	_____
_____	_____
_____	_____

Employee Factors

These elements relate to your own abilities, competencies, knowledge levels, and expertise in dealing with others:

Communication Skills

Your verbal, nonverbal, and written communication and listening skills will often determine whether you'll have to initiate a service recovery strategy. For example, if you effectively communicate usage instructions for a piece of equipment you sell, a customer may not have difficulties once he or she gets home. This avoids customer frustration and reduces complaints. It can also result in time and effort saved for you and the customer, as well as in money saved and good customer rapport maintained.

Knowledge

To effectively serve your customers, you need a strong knowledge of products, services, organizational structure and goals, processes, procedures, and how to effectively provide service. Also, a sound understanding of some of the issues discussed in Part 2 of this book (e.g., interpersonal and written communication skills, diversity, and technology) is very helpful in gaining and maintaining a solid customer-provider relationship.

Through your knowledge, you will be able to quickly and effectively identify needs and offer the right solution to address customer needs and concerns.

Attitude

The way you perceive your organization, self, job, and customers determines much about the quality of service you provide. For example, an upbeat, positive focus will allow you to look forward to and enjoy each customer encounter (positive and negative). Your positive attitude will help you make a sincere effort to identify and satisfy customer needs.

Technical Skills

Your ability to safely and efficiently use equipment and systems that support service (e.g., computer, telephones, facsimile machines, photocopiers, and other job-related machinery and equipment) is important from an efficiency and safety standpoint and also from a service perspective. As you have read, technology can greatly enhance your ability to provide quality service to more customers, and to do it more quickly. Since technology is so commonplace, your customer expects that you will have access to and know how to operate various types of equipment. You may depend on heavy equipment to do your job and provide products or services to customers (e.g., construction equipment, power tools, electric pumps). Through knowledge and expertise in using such equipment, you will be able to provide products and services to your customers promptly and without service breakdowns.

Worksheet ▼

14-2

WORKSHEET 14-2

Reducing the Negative Impact of Employee Factors

Think about the employee factors you have just reviewed. Which ones have you witnessed from a personal standpoint as either a customer or an employee? What can be done to reduce the negative impacts from each of the factors? List your observations and strategies for reducing negative impact below:

FACTOR	STRATEGIES FOR REDUCING NEGATIVE IMPACT
_____	_____
_____	_____
_____	_____
	_____

Customer Factors

There are times when customer actions or inactions can lead to a service breakdown, as described in the following sections.

Failure to Use Product or Service Information Correctly

No matter how meticulous your explanations are, customers sometimes fail to listen to or follow instructions for proper product or service usage. By disregarding or missing key information relayed verbally or in writing, they increase the likelihood of improper use, and therefore dissatisfaction. They also increase the possibility of damage or injury. Subsequently, they may lodge a complaint of defective product or ineffective service.

Your objective in providing exceptional service, while raising your rating on the **Relationship-Rating Point Scale**, should be to practice active listening and read your customer's nonverbal cues in order to determine his or her level of understanding. Use effective open-ended questions, as were discussed in previous chapters. Only through your vigilant efforts can problems and misunderstandings be identified and corrected before the customer develops a problem or becomes dissatisfied.

Failure to Follow Through

Sometimes a customer buys a product or service and has a problem that necessitates recovery efforts. In these instances, negotiations often take place in which the customer and organization agree to take specific actions. Sometimes, the customer may not live up to his or her part of the bargain. For example, suppose a customer buys a new computer from your organization, has trouble getting it to function properly, and calls to complain. He talks to a technical support representative who informs him that the company stands behind its product warranty. The representative also asks the customer to write down error messages that appear on his computer monitor for the next two days so the problem can be better diagnosed, and then bring the unit to the store for repair. Two days later the customer shows up at the store with the computer but has forgotten to write down the error messages. This type of customer behavior and failure to follow through can be frustrating, but it may be unavoidable in some instances. When such events occur, the customer may still become dissatisfied and may even blame the organization or you. Either way, everyone loses. About the only thing you can do before and after such an event occurs is to practice effective communication skills and try to emphasize the importance of the customer following through with instructions and requests.

Work It Out 14-2. Helping Customers

▶ With a partner, discuss strategies or actions you can take that will aid customers and reduce the possibility that they will become dissatisfied by their own actions or failures. Write them down for future reference.

_____

_____

_____

_____

_____

_____

4 | REASONS FOR CUSTOMER DEFECTION

▶ **CONCEPT:** Failing to meet the customer's needs, handling problems inefficiently, treating the customer unfairly, and using inadequate systems are reasons for the customer to leave you and go elsewhere.

Following a service breakdown, there is often a possibility that you may never see the customer again. This is potentially disastrous to your organization, because it costs five to six times as much to win a new customer as it costs to retain a current one. And, as we saw earlier in this chapter, a dissatisfied customer is also likely to tell other people about the bad experience. For these reasons, you and others in your organization must be especially careful to identify and remedy potential and actual problems before they negatively affect the customer.

Poor service and complacency. If customers perceive that you and/or your organization do not sincerely care about them or about solving their problems, they may go elsewhere. If a concern is important enough for the customer to verbalize (formally or informally) or to write down, it is important enough for you to take seriously. You should immediately address the problem by listening, gathering information, and taking appropriate action. Customer comments might be casual, for example, "You know, I sure wish you folks stocked a wider variety of rose bushes. I love shopping here, but your selection is so limited." In this instance, you might write down the customer's name, phone number, and address and then follow up with your manager or buyers about it. Also, practice your questioning skills by asking, "What color did you have in mind?" or "What is your favorite color?" If the customer has a specific request, you could pass that along. You or someone else should try to obtain the item and then contact the customer to discuss your efforts and findings. Sometimes the obvious solutions are the ones that are overlooked, so be perceptive when dealing with customers and look for little clues such as these. It could mean the difference in continued business and word-of-mouth advertising by your customer.

Inappropriate complaint resolution. The key to remember about complaint resolution is that it is the *customer's* perception of the situation, not yours, that counts. If customers believe that they were not treated fairly, honestly, in a timely manner, and in an appropriate fashion, or if they are still dissatisfied, your efforts failed. Remember that only a small percentage of your customers complain. Second attempts at resolution by customers are almost unheard of.

Unmet needs. As stated in Chapter 13, customers have very specific needs to which you must attend. When these needs are not addressed or are unsatisfactorily met, the customer is likely to seek an alternative source of fulfillment.

So often, service providers make the mistake of trying to project their personal needs onto others. Their feeling is that "I like it, so everybody should like it." However, as you read in Chapter 10, today's diverse world requires you to be more knowledgeable and accepting of the ideas, values, beliefs, and needs of others. Failure to be sensitive to diversity may set you, your organization, and your customers on a collision course. Remember what you have read about trust and how quickly it can be destroyed in relationships.

Unfair treatment. When customers *perceive* that they have been treated unfairly or, worse—dishonestly—they are likely to leave. They may do so angrily and follow up with formal complaints or retaliation (e.g., in the form of letters to advocacy groups, senior management, or local news media, or even a lawsuit).

Inadequate systems. When breakdowns occur at crucial points of the service chain, you can expect customer dissatisfaction and desertion. Typical failures occur in order taking, billing, shipping, 800 numbers, e-mail, Internet response, inventory control, and customer service. To help reduce or eliminate such failures, look for potential problem areas and work with others in the organization to fix them before the customer comes into contact with them.

STRATEGIES FOR PREVENTING DISSATISFACTION

> **CONCEPT:** Focusing on the customers' needs and seeking ways to satisfy their needs quickly while exceeding customer expectations are ways to prevent dissatisfaction.

The best way to deal with a service breakdown is to prevent it from occurring. Here are some specific tactics that can help.

Think Like the Customer

Learn to use the interactive communication techniques described in this book. Once you've mastered them, set out to discover what customers want by observing nonverbal behavior, asking specific questions, and listening to their comments and responses. Learn to listen for their unspoken as well as verbalized needs, concerns, and questions. Think about how you would like to be served under the conditions you are dealing with and act accordingly.

Pamper the Customer

Make customers feel special and important. Treat them as if they are the center of your attention and that you are there for no other purpose than to serve them. Do the unexpected, and take any extra effort necessary to meet and exceed their needs. Even if you can't satisfy all their wishes, if you are positive, enthusiastic, and show initiative, customers can walk away feeling good about the encounter.

Respect the Customer

Before you begin focusing on customers' problems, take time to listen and show that you support them and their viewpoint. By using a people-centered approach to problem analysis and problem solving, you can win the customer over. With both of you working together, you can define the problem and jointly reach an acceptable solution.

Focus on the Customer

When a customer takes the time to share a concern, complaint, or question, take the following actions:

> **React to remarks or actions.** Let customers know that you heard what they said or received their written message. If the information is given in person, remember to use the verbal, nonverbal, and listening skills discussed earlier in this book. Smile and acknowledge their presence and comments. If you can't deal with them at that moment because you are serving another customer, let them

know when you will be available. If customer comments are in writing, respond quickly. If a phone number is available, try calling to speed up the response and then follow up in writing.

Empathize. Let customers know that you are concerned, that you do appreciate their views, feelings, or concerns, and that you'll do your best to serve them.

Take action. Once you've gathered enough information to determine an appropriate response, get agreement from your customer and then act. The faster you act, the more important the customer will feel.

Reassure or reaffirm. Take measures to let customers know that you and the organization have their best interests at heart. Stress their value to you and your commitment to resolving their complaint. Part of this is providing your name and phone number, and telling them what actions you will take; for example, "Mrs. Lupe, I appreciate your concern about not receiving the package on time. My name is Bob Lucas, my number is 407 555-6134, and I will research the problem. Once I've discovered what happened, I'll call you back. If it looks as though it will take more than a day, I'll call you by 4 p.m. tomorrow to update you. Is that acceptable?"

Follow up. Once a customer transaction is completed, make sure that any necessary follow-up actions are begun. For example, if appropriate, make an additional phone call to customers to be sure that they received their order, they are satisfied with your actions, or simply to reassure them and provide a opportunity for questions. If you promised to take some action, do so and coordinate with others who need to be involved.

Work It Out 14-3. Focusing on the Customer

▶ Think about the techniques described in this book for focusing on the customer. What additional strategies can you think of?

_____

_____

_____

_____

Exceed Expectations

Go the extra mile by giving your customers the exemplary service you read about in Chapter 13. Strive to get the highest rating possible on the Relationship-Rating Point Scale. To do so, work hard to understand what the customer wants and expects. Observe customers, monitor trends, and talk to customers. Constantly look for ways to go beyond the expected or what the competition provides. Provide it faster, better, and more efficiently than others, and exceed customer expectations. Do things for your

customer that set your service attitude apart from that of other providers. Some things cost little or nothing and return your "investment" many times over through goodwill and positive word-of-mouth publicity. To raise your rating and please your customers, try some of these simple strategies:

Clothing salesperson: "While you try on that outfit, I'll go pick out a couple of other blouses that would suit you perfectly."

Bank customer service representative: "While you are waiting for a loan officer, can I get you a cup of coffee?"

Hotel operator: "Along with your wake-up call, I'll have some coffee or tea brought up. Which would you prefer?"

Restaurant host: "The wait for a table is approximately thirty minutes. Can I get you a complimentary glass of wine or soft drink from the bar?"

Travel agent: "Since this is your honeymoon cruise, I've arranged for a complimentary bottle of champagne to be delivered to your room along with a book of discount coupons for onboard services."

Call center representative: "Because you were on hold so long to place your order, I'm taking 10 percent off your order."

Dentist: "For referring your friend to us, I've told my receptionist to take $25 off your next fee."

Plumber: "While I was fixing your toilet stopper, I noticed that the lift arm was almost rusted through, so I changed it too, at no charge."

6 | IMPLEMENTING A SERVICE RECOVERY STRATEGY

CONCEPT: The job of a service provider is to return the customer to a satisfied state. Not listening, poor communication, and lack of respect are roadblocks to service recovery.

The primary purpose of any good service recovery program should be to return the customer-provider relationship to its normal state. When this is done well, a disgruntled customer can become one who is very loyal and who acts as a publicist for the organization.

Typically there are five phases to the service recovery process:

1. **Apologize, apologize, apologize.** Showing sincere remorse throughout the recovery cycle is crucial. *Listen* carefully. Empathize with the customer as he or she explains and *do not* make excuses, interrupt, or otherwise indicate (verbally or nonverbally) that you do not have time for the customer. You want to retain the customer and have an opportunity for recovery. You must demonstrate that you care for the customer and that he or she is *very* important to you and your organization. Interestingly, many service providers do not accept responsibility and/or apologize when customers become

dissatisfied. Such an apology should come immediately after the discovery of the customer's dissatisfaction and should be delivered in person, if possible. The phone is a second option. Written apologies are the last choice.

2. **Take immediate action.** As soon as your customer has identified a problem, you must set about positively resolving it. As you proceed, it is crucial that you keep the customer informed of actions, barriers encountered, or successful efforts. Even if you are unable to make a quick resolution, the customer may be satisfied if he or she perceives your efforts as sincere and ongoing. You must convince customers through your actions and words that you are doing your best to solve the problem in a timely manner. Also, do not forget what you read earlier in the book about avoiding having to say no without offering **service options**. Remember that your customers want to hear what you *can* do for them, not what you cannot.

Certainly, there may be times when even though you want to give customers exactly what they want, you will not be able to do so because of regulations or **prohibitions** (e.g., local, state, or federal laws or regulations). In such cases, it is important to use all the interpersonal skills discussed throughout this book (e.g., active listening, empathizing, and providing feedback) to let customers know that you are prohibited from fulfilling their needs. It is also important to explain the why in such situations rather than just saying, "I'm sorry, the law won't let me do that." This type of response sounds as if you are not being truthful, do not want to assist, and are hiding behind an invisible barrier.

An example of a prohibition would be when the sister of a patient goes to a doctor's office to get a copy of her brother's medical records. Without specific permission, this would be against the law, because of a patient's right to privacy and confidentiality between patient and doctor. If you were the receptionist in a doctor's office and someone made such a request, your response might be: "Ms. Ramsey, I apologize for your inconvenience in coming in for nothing. I know it's frustrating. However, although I would love to assist you, I cannot because of state regulations that protect a patient's privacy and confidentiality. If you can bring me a signed medical release from your brother, I would be happy to copy his file for you. Can you do that?" In this instance, you have empathized with the customer, stated what you cannot do, explained why, and offered a way to resolve the problem.

In another situation, you may want to help a customer but cannot because your abilities, time constraints, resources, or the customer's timing of a request prevent fulfillment. Here are some examples of such situations, along with possible responses to your customer:

Your abilities. You work in a pet supply store, you are the only person in the store, and you have a severe back injury that prevents you from lifting anything over 25 pounds. A customer comes in and buys 50 bags of chicken feed, each weighing 100 pounds. She asks that you help her load the bags onto her truck.

YOUR RESPONSE: "Ms. Saunders, we appreciate your business. I know your time is valuable and I'd love to help you. However, I have a back injury and the doctor told me not to lift anything over 25 pounds. I'm the only person working here during the lunch hour. If you can come back in half an hour, I'll have two guys who will load bags for you in no time. Would that be possible?"

Time constraints. You work in a bakery and a distraught customer comes in at 3 p.m. Apparently he had forgotten that he was supposed to stop by on the way to work this morning to order a chocolate cake for his daughter's first birthday party, which is at 5 p.m. He wants you to make him a two-layer chocolate cake.

YOUR RESPONSE: "Mr. Simon, that first birthday party sounds exciting, and I want to help you make it a success. However, realistically, it just cannot be done. We sold our last chocolate cake half an hour ago, and if I bake a new one, it will still have to cool before I can decorate it. You will never make it by five o'clock. I know it's frustrating not to get exactly what you want. However, since your daughter is only 1 year old and won't know the difference in the type of cake, can I suggest an alternative? We have virtually any other kind of cake you could want, and I can decorate it for you in less than 15 minutes. Would that work?"

Available resources. You are in North Carolina, near the coastline. A customer comes into your lumberyard in search of plywood to board up his house a day before a major hurricane is predicted to hit the area. Since the impending hurricane was announced on the news, you have been overwhelmed with purchases of plywood and sold out two hours ago.

YOUR RESPONSE: "Mr. Rasheed, I can appreciate the urgency of your need. Unfortunately, as you know, everyone in town is buying plywood and we sold out two hours ago. However, I do have a couple of options for you. I can call our store in Jacksonville to find out whether any plywood is left. If there is some, I can have it held if you want to drive over there. The other option is that we have a shipment on the way that should arrive sometime around 3 a.m. I'll be here and can hold some for you if you want to come back at that time. Would either of those options work for you?"

Timing. It is April 13th and you are an accountant. With the federal tax filing deadline two days away, you and the entire staff of your firm have been working 12- to 14-hour days for weeks. A regular customer calls and wants to come in the next couple of days to discuss incorporating her business and to get some information on the tax advantages for doing so.

YOUR RESPONSE: "Ruth, it's great that you are ready to move forward with the incorporation. I think you will find that it will be very beneficial for you. However, with tax deadlines two days away, we are swamped and there is just no way I can take on anything else. Since your incorporation is not under a deadline, can we set up our meeting some time around the first of next week? That will give me time to wrap up taxes, take a breather, and then give you the full attention you deserve."

In all of these instances, you show a willingness to assist and meet the customers' requests even though you are prevented from doing so. You also partner with them and offer alternatives for consideration. This is important, since you do not want to close the door on customer opportunities. Doing so will surely send customers to a competitor.

There might be other occasions when you or your organization do not meet a customer's request even though it is possible to do so. In such cases, company restrictions keep you from fulfilling the customers' request. In this type of situation, you sometimes hear service providers hide behind a phrase such as "Policy says." The reality is that someone in the organization has decided for business reasons that certain actions cannot or should not be taken. If you encounter such "policies" that prohibit you from delivering service to customers, bring them to the attention of your team leader or management for discussion. These restrictions will most likely cost your organization some customers and result in bad word-of-mouth publicity. Some examples of such situations, along with possible responses, are described below:

> **Situation.** You work in a gas station in a major tourist area that has a policy that prohibits accepting out-of-town checks. A tourist from another state fills her car with gas and then comes to you to pay for her purchase. She tells you that she has only personal checks and $2 in cash with her. She is leaving town to return home at this time.
>
> YOUR RESPONSE: "I know that this is an inconvenience, and I apologize. However, because of problems we've had in the past, we do not accept checks from banks out of this area. We will gladly accept major credit cards, travelers' checks, or cash."

3. **Show compassion.** To help the customer see that your remorse and desire to solve a problem are genuine, you must demonstrate empathy. Expressions such as "I can appreciate your trust," "I understand how we have inconvenienced you," or "I can imagine how you must feel" can go a long way in soothing and winning the customer over. Before you can truly address the customers' problem, however, you must deal with their emotions or feelings. If you disregard their feelings, customers may not give you a chance to help resolve the breakdown. Also, keep in mind what you read about trust in an earlier chapter: you must give it to receive it.

4. **Provide compensation.** Prove to customers that they are valuable and that you are trying to make up for their inconvenience or loss. This penance or symbolic self-punishment should be significant enough that the customer feels that you and your organization have suffered an equal loss. The value or degree of your atonement should

equal the customer's loss in time, money, energy, or frustration. For example, if a customer's meal was cooked improperly and the customer and others in the party had to wait, you might give the customer a free meal. If you forgot a vegetable that was ordered and it came much later, a free dessert might suffice. The key is to make the offer without the customer having to suggest or demand it.

Not only must the recovery compensate original loss, it should give additional value. For example, if a customer had an oil change done on his or her car and oil was spilled on the carpet, an appropriate gesture might be to give the oil change free and have the carpet cleaned at your company's expense.

5. **Conduct follow-up.** The only way to find out whether you were successful in your recovery efforts or whether the customer is truly satisfied is to follow up. The preferable methods are face-to-face questioning or a phone call. This contact should come within a few days after the complaint was resolved. It could take the form of a few simple statements or questions (e.g., "I am following up in case you had any additional questions" or "I'm calling to make sure that _____ is now working as it should be. Is there anything else we can do to assist you?").

This last step in the recovery process can be the deciding factor in whether the customer returns to you or your organization. It is the phase that reemphasizes, the message "We truly care."

7 | ROADBLOCKS TO SERVICE RECOVERY

> **CONCEPT:** Service recovery depends on the provider recognizing a roadblock and taking steps to remove it so that recovery steps can begin.

From time to time, you may find your recovery efforts blocked by your own actions or inactions or those of others in your organization. Some of the obstacles that commonly derail recovery attempts are described in the next sections:

Not listening. As we discussed in the chapter on listening, you must take an active role to listen effectively. Not only must you receive data, but you must also analyze and act upon it. Many service providers go through the motions of listening, but they fail to do so accurately or actively. This can send the message, "I really don't care about you."

Lack of respect. Closely tied to listening is the matter of customer respect. Your actions or inactions related to customers and their problems can lead to a perception that you are being rude or disrespectful. Either way, you and the organization lose as customers desert to a competitor.

Poor or inadequate communication. The quality and amount of communication between you and your customer can be the determining success factor. You should make every effort to constantly update and consult with the customers. If they feel neglected or left out, further dissatisfaction and loss of business loyalty could follow.

Inadequate or outdated materials or equipment. Trying to provide service excellence without the necessary tools is frustrating and almost impossible. It also can destroy a customer relationship and trust. For example, you may be calling a customer from a list provided by the marketing department in order to update an address or to sell the customer new services or products. You may be unaware that others have already called the customer, that the customer has already made a purchase from another service representative, or that the customer had received a mail-order solicitation that had a different (and better) offer for the same products and services. Your frustration goes up and your credibility goes down in such a situation.

Lack of training. It's very difficult to perform at exceptional levels when you do not have the knowledge and skills required. Whenever you identify gaps in your knowledge or skill, you should approach your boss with a request for training. This training might be informal (e.g., audiotapes, self-study courses, Internet courses, or written materials) or formal (e.g., classrooms, one-on-one coaching, or conferences). The format is not as important as the results—you improve your skills to better interact with and serve your customers.

Work conflicts. No matter how much you care and want to provide quality service, you may fail if you overcommit or if your organization overextends its human resources. It's impossible to be everything to everyone. When work scheduling causes employees to be pulled in too many directions, failure is probable. To avoid this breakdown, constant monitoring of workload is required. Recommendations to your team leader or supervisor for schedule changes, job sharing, or reapportionment of workload might be appropriate.

Summary

Chapter Summary

Whenever a customer experiences an actual or perceived breakdown in service, prompt, appropriate recovery efforts may be your only hope of retaining the customer. In a profession that has seen major strides in quality and technology as well as increased domestic and global competition, service is often the deciding factor. Customers expect and often demand their rights and to be treated in an exemplary fashion. When they are disappointed, they simply go elsewhere. Your role in the process is to remain vigilant, recognize customer needs, and provide service levels that will keep them coming back.

CHAPTER REVIEW QUESTIONS

1. What is service recovery? _____
   _____
   _____

2. Define what is meant by the term service breakdown. _____
   _____
   _____

3. What are some of the organizational factors that can lead to service breakdown? _____
   _____
   _____

4. List the employee-related factors can contribute to service breakdown. _____
   _____
   _____

5. Why do customers defect? _____
   _____
   _____

6. List some strategies for preventing customer dissatisfaction. _____
   _____
   _____

7. When a service recovery strategy is implemented, what are the five steps that should be taken?_____
   _____
   _____

8. What are some of the roadblocks to service recovery? _____
   _____
   _____

Search the Internet for Service Recovery Information

Visit a variety of Websites in order to locate additional information on service recovery. Look for articles, books, research studies, or specific organizational strategies for handling service recovery. To locate the information, select some of the key terms mentioned in this chapter to prompt various search engines. Here are some of the terms you may want to try:

Service recovery

Customer satisfaction

Customer retention

Service breakdowns

Customer dissatisfaction

Customer defection

Also, try these sites as a starter:

www.tarp.com

www.ICSA.com

www.SOCAP.com

COLLABORATIVE *Learning Activity*

Role-Playing Failure to Address Needs

To give you some practical experience in using the techniques described in this chapter, you will interact with others in your group. Your instructor will assign one or more of the following activities.

Option 1: Pair up with another student and develop several scenarios in which a customer's needs or concerns have not been addressed. Role-play these scenarios, with each of you alternately taking the role of service provider and customer. Be sure to incorporate tips and strategies discussed throughout this book.

Option 2: Working with your classmates, develop a list of open-ended questions based on information related to service recovery that was covered in this chapter (similar to the type of questions in the From the Frontline interview at the end of this chapter). Use the questions to conduct an informal survey of friends, peers, and relatives. Try to determine what works and what does not work in service breakdown situations. Discuss your thoughts with other members of the class and then use this information to improve your own service efforts.

FACE TO FACE

Handling Service Breakdowns at AAA Landscaping

Background

You are the owner of AAA Landscaping, a small company in Orlando, Florida, that specializes in resodding and maintenance of lawns. Much of your business is through word-of-mouth advertising. Once a contract is negotiated, portions of it are subcontracted out to other companies (e.g., sprinkler system repair and pesticide services). Recently, you went to the home of Stu Murphy to bid on resodding Stu's lawn. Several other bids were obtained, but yours was the lowest. You arranged for work to begin to remove old grass and replace it with St. Augustine grass sod.

As part of the contract, Stu had asked that some basic maintenance be done (e.g., hedge and tree trimming, hauling away of old decorative wooden logs from around flower beds, and general sprucing up of the front area of the house). Also, fertilizer and pesticide were to be applied within two weeks. The contract was signed on Wednesday, and the work was to be completed by Saturday, when Stu had planned a party.

Your Role

You were pleased to get the contract worth over $1200. This is actually the third or fourth contract in the same subdivision because of word-of-mouth advertising. The initial sod removal and replacement, weeding, and pruning were completed on Saturday, and you received full payment on Monday.

Later in the week you received a call from Stu stating that several trees were not trimmed to his satisfaction, debris covering decorative rocks along hedges was not removed as agreed, and bags of clippings had been left behind. Because of other commitments, it was several days before you sent someone out to finish the job. A day later, Stu left another message on your answering machine stating that there was still an untrimmed tree, the debris remained, and the clippings were still in the garage. You didn't get around to returning his call. Over a week later Stu called again, repeating the message he'd left before and reminding you that the contract called for pesticide and fertilizer to be applied to the lawn. You called back and said that someone would be out later in the week. Again, other commitments kept you from following through. Stu called on Saturday and left a fourth message on your answering machine. He said that he was getting irritated at not getting callbacks and action on his needs. Without returning Stu's call, you responded by sending someone out on Tuesday to take care of the outstanding work.

It's been several days since the work was completed, and you assume that Stu is now satisfied since you have heard nothing else from him.

Questions

1. Based on information in this chapter, how have you done on providing service to Stu? Explain.

   _____

   _____

   _____

   _____

   _____

2. What were Stu's needs in this case?

   _____

   _____

   _____

3. Could you have done anything differently?

   _____

   _____

   _____

   _____

4. Are you sure that Stu will give a good recommendation to neighbors or friends in the future? Why or why not?

   _____

   _____

   _____

FROM THE FRONTLINE
Interview

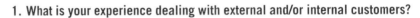

**Julio Fernandez
Senior Service
Representative
AAA, Heathrow,
Florida**

1. What is your experience dealing with external and/or internal customers?

Most of my customer service experience can be divided in two categories—the retail customer, and the rental car industry (corporate and leisure customers). In all, I have over 19 years of experience. The return customers were usually looking for a product and getting a good price. They were typically in a relaxed frame of mind. They needed accurate information, competitive pricing, and an appealing and durable product. On the other hand, the rental car customers were "on alert." They needed immediate service so that they could get on their way as quickly as possible.

While working in the rental car agency, I supervised several team members (internal customers). During that time I learned the importance of the internal customer.

I also learned the four most important factors in maintaining happy and loyal team members: make them feel valued, show appreciation, reward and recognize a job well done or a "wow" example of customer service, and make work fun. I've always heard that happy team members make for happy customers, and I have found that to be true.

2. What are your general impressions of customer service in the United States? Why do you feel this way?

My general impression of customer service in the United States is that good customer service is becoming extinct. People seem to be more interested in making a profit without really satisfying the needs of the customer. Service after the sale is very important, and many service providers fail to follow-up and listen to the customers.

3. **In your experience in working with customers who are dissatisfied, what are some of the most important things to remember related to solving their problem and maintaining the relationship?**

I call them the four essentials: listen, empathize, apologize, and resolve. By listening, you show respect—that the customers and their business is important to you—and, of course, listening helps you determine the actual problem. Empathizing shows that you understand and genuinely care about the customer's situation. Apologizing indicates humility and extends proper courtesies. Finally, by resolving, you've taken action to change their situation and hopefully ultimately restored their confidence and maintained the relationship.

4. **In your experience, what are some issues or pitfalls that service providers encounter related to recovering from situations with dissatisfied customers?**

Here are only a few examples that happen too often:

- The service provider lacks the proper training, lacks the product or service knowledge, and is unable to answer questions.

- The service provider is not empowered to make decisions. Providing a complimentary dessert or a bottle of wine, an upgrade, or some other extra when something goes wrong can make a great impression on a customer.

- The service provider does not effectively follow-up with customers. Follow-up is an easy way to show you care.

- The service provider does not ask questions or does not ask enough questions. Probing or asking questions is important in obtaining the information needed to improve or remedy a situation before things get worse; customers always appreciate a quick solution.

- The service provider does not listen well to a dissatisfied customer. Listening is a key factor in getting to the root of the customer's dissatisfaction.

- The service provider fails to "go the extra mile." That little extra can make a big impact on customers.

5. **How does the way you and other employees deal with service recovery affect your organization and your customers?**

In today's market, competition is fierce. Customers have knowledge, they have ample selection, and plenty of product. They even have the option of obtaining products through the Internet. The only tool we have in our arsenal to keep customers loyal and happy is exceptional, "wow" customer service.

Our business depends on this. Excellent customer service is the single most essential ingredient in the success of our business. It's quite simple: without the customer, we have no business.

6. **What advice, related to customer service in dealing with dissatisfied customers and regaining their confidence and support, would you give someone entering the customer service profession?**

My advice is to learn as much as possible about good customer service through seminars and educational tools. Always remember the Golden Rule—"Treat your customers the way you would want to be treated." Also, deliver what you promise. If you are honest, follow-up, and smile, you will find loyal customers. It's really a recipe for success.

CRITICAL THINKING
How can you resolve problems that contribute to dissatisfaction for your customers? Do you agree with the advice given?

Customer Service for the Twenty-First Century

Chapter 15

Focusing on the Future

OBJECTIVES

After completing this chapter, you will be able to:

- *Identify service challenges of the future.*

- *Use your knowledge of the changing demographics in the United States to be better prepared to provide service.*

- *Realize the impact of global competition on business.*

- *Build skills for future career growth.*

- *Plan to meet the challenges of the future.*

"From now on, any definition of a successful life must include serving others."

George Bush
Forty-First President of the
United States

Before reviewing the chapter content, respond to the following questions by placing a "T" for true or an "F" for false on the rules. Use any questions you miss as a checklist of material to which you will pay particular attention as you read through the chapter. For those you get right, congratulate yourself, but review the sections they address in order to learn additional details about the topic.

_____ 1. A longer life expectancy and a decline in the birthrate will contribute to a shortage of entry-level employees in the future.

_____ 2. The downside of an aging society is that customers will require fewer personal services.

_____ 3. Technological changes are occurring so rapidly that continual training, retraining, and education on software and delivery systems are needed.

_____ 4. Evolving technology has changed the roles and needs of customers.

_____ 5. During the past three decades, little has changed from a legal standpoint with respect to customer service.

_____ 6. Global competition has provided new career opportunities in customer service.

_____ 7. To meet today's business challenges, schools are improving programming and keeping pace with changes.

_____ 8. To keep up with competition, a leading-edge company might spend over $4 million dollars a year on employee training.

_____ 9. Some of the minimum skills for success in the customer service field are communication, creative thinking, and interpersonal skills.

_____ 10. Even though organizations are changing, the responsibility for leadership still rests with managers.

1. T 4. T 7. F 10. F
2. F 5. F 8. T
3. T 6. T 9. T

1 | FUTURE CHALLENGES

CONCEPT: By being aware of changes, you can better prepare yourself to serve your customers in the future.

Although no one can predict the future with any degree of certainty, economists, **futurists**, and business analysts can spot trends and make fairly accurate projections. Bookshelves are lined with publications containing insights and research on industry, economic, business, and demographic changes over recent decades. Some consistent patterns of change that have surfaced and that will directly affect your job and the customer service field are outlined in this chapter. By recognizing and understanding these trends, you can better prepare yourself for the inevitable changes. You can also build skills to better serve your customers.

2 | SHIFTS IN DEMOGRAPHICS

▶ **CONCEPT:** Society has changed dramatically over the last decade. Many changes that involve the population are related to its age, gender, ethnic background, and wants and needs, as well as income level, and will affect customer service.

For several decades, analysts have been tracking changes in the societal makeup of the United States and other countries. According to one study, people are living longer; the average life expectancy for men is 72 years of age; and for women 79 years. By the year 2050, it is projected that life expectance will be over 79 years for men and 84 for women[1]. Births will decline as a result of the "baby bust" (people born to baby boomers after 1964). The United States is facing an acute shortage of entry-level employees. On the one hand, the number of older people is increasing; on the other hand, fewer people are being born to take their place. The number of people in the 18- to 24-year age group peaked at around 30 million in the mid-1980s and since then has declined to approximately 25 million (in 1995). This age group is projected to slowly grow back to the 30 million mark around the year 2010 (see Figure 15-1).

FIGURE 15-1

Population by age: 1990-2050, in percent of resident population as of July1.

Year	Under 5 years	5–13 years	14–17 years	18–24 years	25–34 years	35–44 years	45–64 years	65+ years	85+ years	100+ years	Totals
1990	7.6	12.8	5.3	10.8	17.3	15.1	18.6	12.5	1.2	0.0	100.0
1995	7.5	13.1	5.6	9.5	15.5	16.2	19.9	12.8	1.4	0.0	100.0
2000	6.9	13.1	5.7	9.6	13.6	16.3	22.2	12.6	1.6	0.0	100.0
2005	6.7	12.5	5.9	9.9	12.7	14.7	24.9	12.6	1.7	0.0	100.0
2010	6.7	12.0	5.7	10.1	12.9	12.9	26.5	13.2	1.9	0.0	100.0
2020	6.8	12.0	5.3	9.3	13.3	12.3	24.6	16.5	2.0	0.1	100.0
2030	6.6	12.0	5.4	9.2	12.3	12.8	21.7	20.0	2.4	0.1	100.0
2040	6.8	11.9	5.4	9.3	12.4	11.9	22.0	20.3	3.7	0.1	100.0
2050	6.9	12.1	5.4	9.2	12.5	12.0	21.8	20.0	4.6	0.2	100.0

Source: U.S. Department of Commerce, Economics and Statistics Administration, Current Population Reports, Population Projections: States, 1990-2050 by Paul Campbell, P25–1131, May 1997, p. 10.

One impact of these numbers is that there are fewer younger entry-level people who traditionally begin their careers in the workforce in service jobs at theaters, fast-food restaurants, car washes, department and

---

[1] U.S. Bureau of Census, Current Population Reports, P25-1130, *Population Projections of the United States by Age, Sex, Race, and Hispanic Origin: 1990–2050*, U.S. Government Printing Office, 1996, Appendix B-2.

grocery stores, and similar businesses. To compensate, organizations are moving toward recruiting older workers who have retired or are using technology to handle many functions (e.g., telemarketing calls, information collection, ticket sales).

Another impact of the aging of Americans is that you'll be serving more people who are older. The number of people 65 years and older is expected to grow by almost 40 million in 2010 and by 69 million by 2030 (when baby boomers become 65 plus). At that point, approximately 20 percent of the U.S. population will be over the age of 65. Also, the fastest-growing age group is the 85-plus population. As a group, they are expected

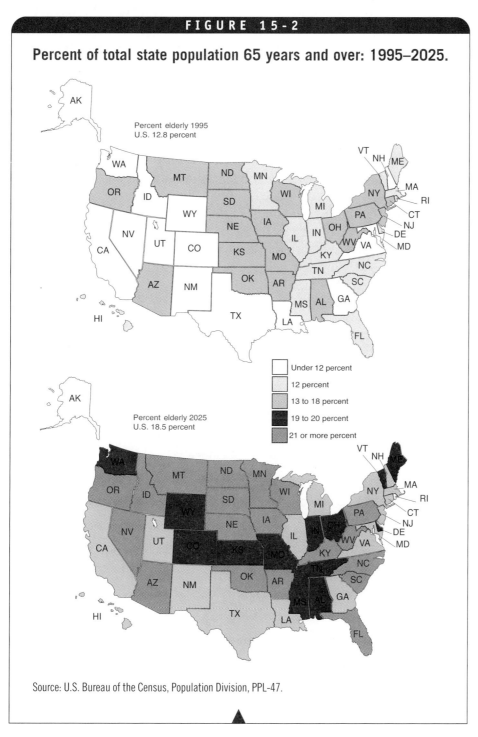

FIGURE 15-2

Percent of total state population 65 years and over: 1995–2025.

Percent elderly 1995
U.S. 12.8 percent

Percent elderly 2025
U.S. 18.5 percent

Under 12 percent
12 percent
13 to 18 percent
19 to 20 percent
21 or more percent

Source: U.S. Bureau of the Census, Population Division, PPL-47.

to grow fivefold by the year 2050.[2] That's where the skills discussed in Chapter 10, related to dealing with diverse individuals, will come into play for those in the service sector. In many cases older customers will want and need more services to ease their life (e.g., laundry, yard care, car maintenance, assisted-living, and personal shopping), and many will also seek employment to offset their medical and living expenses. Some will return to work simply to fulfill a need to interact with others in the workplace and feel productive. As this older group grows, their members will have a significant impact on commerce and the workforce, depending on where they are located. Figure 15-2 shows the anticipated dispersion of persons 65 years and older throughout the United States between 1995 and 2025. This distribution will take a toll on business, from the standpoint of the number of customers and of eligible workers, as well as on society through the need for social services (e.g., health care and human services). The need for support services will particularly apply to people in the aging group who believed that the Social Security system would be there as a retirement base or who did not adequately save for retirement, as well as for those who are less well educated.

An additional factor related to income and retirement readiness is that, statistically, men who have a high school diploma or who lack high school diploma have experienced a loss of income in the years between 1963 and 1997. Those with a high school diploma have seen their salary shrink from $28,914 in 1963 to $25,453. On the other hand, women who have the same educational level have seen their salary grow from 11,028 to $13,407 during the same period.[3] On the upside, more members of the graying population of baby boomers are college educated than their predecessors were, and as a result many earn more income. Since

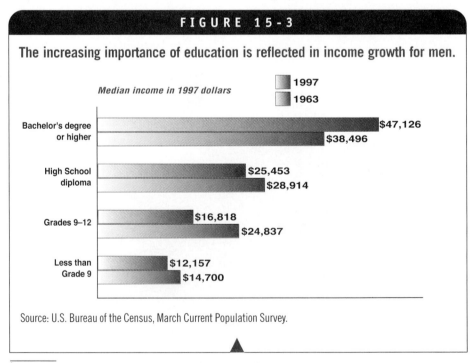

FIGURE 15-3

The increasing importance of education is reflected in income growth for men.

Median income in 1997 dollars

1997
1963

Bachelor's degree or higher	$47,126 / $38,496
High School diploma	$25,453 / $28,914
Grades 9–12	$16,818 / $24,837
Less than Grade 9	$12,157 / $14,700

Source: U.S. Bureau of the Census, March Current Population Survey.

[2] U.S. Department of Commerce, Economics and Statistics Administration, Bureau of Census, *Population Projections of the United States by Age, Sex, Race and Hispanic Origin: 1995–2050* (P25–1130) February 1996, p.1.

[3] U.S. Bureau of the Census, Current Population Reports, P60–20, *Measuring 50 Years of Economic Change Using the March Current Population Survey,* U.S. Government Printing Office, Washington DC, 1998

1963, the median income levels have risen for men and women who have a bachelor's degree or higher. For men, the figure in 1997 was $47,126 (up from the 1963 level of $34,494), and for women $29,781 (up from $19,443 in 1963). Figures 15-3 and 15-4 provide more information on the relationship between salary and education. This means that the college-educated group will have more disposable income than in the past and will likely use it for a variety of services that allow them to enjoy more free time and/or retirement.

An additional demographic shift affecting customer service professionals is the increase in the number of women, people of color, and immigrants entering the workplace. The total workforce makeup will continue to shift as the birthrate, which decreased slightly at the end of the twentieth century, gradually increases until around 2011, when it is expected to exceed the highest number of births experienced in the twentieth century, much of which is the result of the children of baby boomers beginning to have their own families. As a result of increased births and immigration, the U.S. population is expected to grow by about 29 million through 2020 and by 80 million by 2050. Of that portion of population growth due to immigration, census projections are that each year four of ten people will be Hispanic, three of ten Asian and Pacific Islander, two of ten non-Hispanic white, and one of ten black. Births would account for two of five people being non-Hispanic white, with the remainder being equally distributed among Hispanic, black, and Asian, and Pacific Islanders.[4]

These changes will mean that you will not only be serving but will also be working with a larger diverse group. The ability to speak a second language (e.g., Spanish) and a sound knowledge of the cultural differences described in earlier chapters of this book will be extremely important to your success and that of your organization.

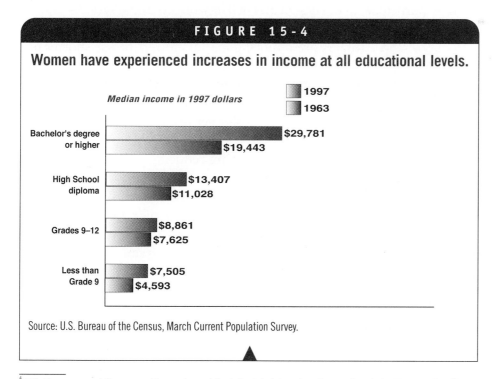

FIGURE 15-4

Women have experienced increases in income at all educational levels.

Median income in 1997 dollars

■ 1997
■ 1963

Bachelor's degree or higher: $29,781 / $19,443

High School diploma: $13,407 / $11,028

Grades 9–12: $8,861 / $7,625

Less than Grade 9: $7,505 / $4,593

Source: U.S. Bureau of the Census, March Current Population Survey.

[4] U.S. Department of Commerce, Economics and Statistics Administration, *Current Population Reports, Population Projections: States, 1995–2025 by Paul Campbell*, P25–1131, May 1997, p.2.

▶ Think about the advertisements you have seen on television and heard on the radio in the last couple of years.

What types of background songs are the advertisements using? (Give specific examples of songs.) _____

_____

What population group do you think they are targeting? Why? _____

_____

Do you believe that this is a smart marketing strategy? Why or why not? _____

_____

3 | TECHNOLOGY IMPLICATIONS

▶ **CONCEPT:** Technology has and will continue to affect customer service. Being aware of the latest technology and how to use it efficiently can help you become a more effective service provider.

For many customer service jobs, skill in using technology will increase your value as a source of information for current and future customers. How can you keep abreast of changes in technology?

As you read in Chapter 7, at no time in history has technology been more prominent in businesses or more complex. Changes are occurring so rapidly that you will have a continual need to train, retrain and educate yourself on software and delivery systems including computer hardware, telephone systems, fax machines, and other business and industrial equipment.

Technology has changed the roles and needs of customers. Often they actively participate in the design and delivery of goods and services tailored to fit their needs and preferences. For example, customers are requiring manufacturers to use shorter and more tailored production runs that produce merchandise in a more timely manner and will be customized to the needs of the individual rather than aimed at a mass market. Customers are also getting actively involved in such activities as the design of their own homes and insurance packages. They are reducing wait times and service effectiveness by accessing such innovations as iris-reading technology, which can scan the customer's eye to verify identification (much like a password does).

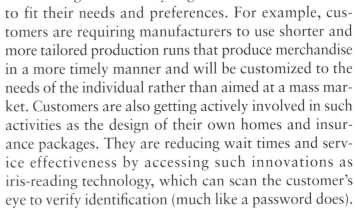

Future customer service will also involve a broader use of telecommunications. As you saw in Chapter 7, by tapping into the technological capabilities of many PC systems, organizations will be able to reach many more customers. Through other PC capabilities, such as enhanced information storage capabilities, catalogs and product service information will become more readily available to consumers. The Internet will drive e-commerce to new heights and will change the face of the economy in the United States and the world. Since

Internet commerce involves both consumer-based retail transactions and business-to-business transactions (e.g., Internet access services, financial services, client and support operations), the potential revenue is enormous. For example, during 1996 and 1997 the Internet economy more than doubled, from $15.5 billion to $38.8 billion. By the early part of the twenty-first century, the figures are projected to rise to over $350 billion[5] (see Figure 15-5).

Other sources of revenue generation that will likely continue to be popular and expand are the television shopping networks and infomercials. Through these sources, viewers see products and services displayed and described and then call in to order or obtain information. Certainly, as technology continues to be developed and refined, other options for delivery will evolve.

FIGURE 15-5

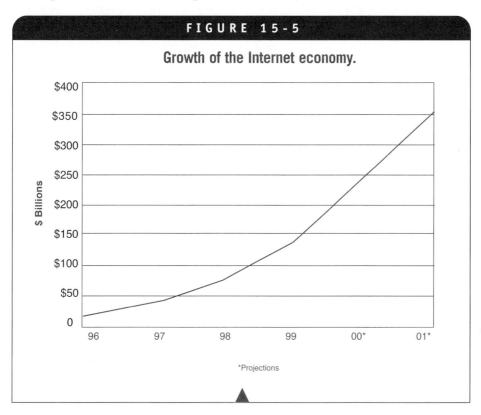

Growth of the Internet economy.

*Projections

Work It Out 15-2. Analyzing New Business Trends

Work It Out
15-2

▶ Think about new types of businesses that you have seen open in your community in the past couple of years and that focus on personal customer service.

What products and/or services do they provide? _____

_____

_____

What population group is most likely to use these products and/or services?

_____

_____

[5] The Progressive Policy Institute, *Technology, Innovation, and the New Economy Project,* Washington DC, http://www.dicppi.org, pp. 75–80.

4 | A CHANGING LEGAL ENVIRONMENT

> **CONCEPT:** Many laws have been enacted to protect consumers to ensure that they are treated well. Knowing these laws will enable you to serve your customers well and within the law.

The face of American business changed dramatically during the last part of the twentieth century. Consumer protection has become increasingly important. Legislators as well as advocacy groups have paraded before Congress and the public to demand that customers be treated well. Also, organizations that seek to cheat, defraud, or violate consumer rights and the law are dealt with harshly, often paying millions of dollars in reparation. Examples are the actions taken against the tobacco industry and producers of silicon breast implants by various states and individuals. Not only are the litigants seeking to stem the production and distribution of products viewed as hazardous, they are also seeking financial reparation for those harmed by such products.

Starting with enactment of legislation such as the Civil Rights Act of 1964 (which prohibited discrimination based on race, color, gender, religion, or national origin), the Americans With Disabilities Act of 1990 (which ensured access by disabled people to telecommunications, transportation, the workplace), and consumer protection laws that protect against telephone, mail, and Internet fraud, changes in customer service have occurred. Ignorance of the law is not an acceptable defense; therefore, many companies that might otherwise have discriminated or abused consumer rights have been forced to change their operating practices.

As you read in Chapter 10, some groups have special needs. Effectively serving those needs and complying with the laws affecting these groups require an increased awareness and improved skill level. Many organizations now make awareness training for laws affecting customer service part of the orientation of new employees. If your employer doesn't provide such training, you would be wise to check with your local library, the Internet, and/or publications that deal with workplace issues and consumer rights and read about pertinent laws.

5 | THE ROLE OF EDUCATION

> **CONCEPT:** Through the advancement of skills and knowledge as well as the reshaping of attitudes and opinions, organizations are realizing that training pays off in increased revenues and lower expenditures per customer.

In past decades, hard work and sweat often led to career advancement, sometimes into the executive office, but that isn't necessarily the case today. Because of the continued competitiveness of business on a global level, the increased use of technology, and the need for solid people skills, a solid education is now the best ticket upward. As you read earlier in this chapter, there is a direct correlation between education and income. If you want to excel, you'll need to invest in yourself (time and money) to gain needed skills. The other alternative is to find an employer who will make a commitment to your knowledge growth and provide regular training or educational opportunities.

Many employers realize that workers coming into the workforce today are not adequately prepared for the tasks that face them. In some cases, the educational system is failing to provide the skills and training necessary to meet today's business challenges. The result is a decrease in job and promotion opportunities and an increased pressure for training to be the responsibility of the individual and the organization.

Many organizations are starting to recognize the importance of investing in their most important resource—employees. As a result, millions of dollars are being spent to upgrade skills and prepare customer service representatives and others to create and maintain a customer-focused environment. Through the enhancement of knowledge and skills and efforts to reshape attitudes and opinions related to the "correct" way to serve customers, organizations are realizing a huge return on investment in the form of higher revenue and lower expenditures per customer. According to a 1998 study, typical leading-edge companies (fewer than 2250 employees and an annual payroll of $114 million) spent approximately $4.1 million on employee training in 1997, which was up from the 1996 figure of $3.4 million. The 1998 figure was approximately $4.7 million dollars[6].

Why are employers investing so heavily in this type of training? Quite simply, it's good business; if they don't do it, their competitors are likely to overtake them in the marketplace. A better-trained staff can more effectively and efficiently use systems and equipment while providing quality customer service.

Why should you care about additional training and learning? Studies consistently show a correlation between education and job security and salary.

Training employees to improve their knowledge and skills is important to the success of an organization. What skills do you need to improve, and how can you get this training?

---

[6] Laurie J. Bassie and Mark E. Van Buren, *The 1999 ASTD State of the Industry Report*, American Society for Training and Development, Alexandria, VA, pp. 3–5.

6 | SKILLS FOR SUCCESS

> **CONCEPT:** Among the skills for success that you need to acquire and perfect are reading, writing, computation, communication, the ability to work with others, and the ability to solve problems.

Change will continue to be the workplace norm. To get ahead of others today and in the future, you'll need specific abilities and skills. Skills that work today may not work tomorrow. Today's consumer does not accept the status quo or minimal standards. You must be versatile enough to handle the unusual, tailor product and service delivery to the individual customer, and interact with a variety of customers in many situations. The following skills are the minimum you'll need to be successful in the future.

Basic Skills (Reading, Writing, and Computation)

Service employees spend much of their working day reading forms, correspondence, directions, and technological support materials. They also answer memorandums and letters and share information in writing with others. Failure to communicate concisely creates misunderstandings and projects a negative image of you and your organization. This is why Chapter 8 is dedicated to written communication.

Computation skills are also crucial for many service workers, who need to do basic math computation (addition, subtraction, multiplication, and division) and compute measurements and distances. The following strategies can help you strengthen your skills in these areas.

Strategies for Improvement

- *Spend one hour a day reading a book, magazine, newspaper, or other publication.*
- *Attend a speed-reading workshop or course.*
- *Attend a basic grammar and/or business writing and proofreading course.*
- *Ask someone whom you believe to be a skilled writer to coach you and provide feedback on your writing.*
- *Review Chapter 8 from time to time.*
- *When faced with a problem, analyze the pros and cons before making a decision.*
- *Attend a refresher math course.*
- *Purchase books on mathematical problem-solving activities and practice doing the exercises.*

Communication Skills

As you read in Chapters 3 to 5, the ability to ask questions correctly, provide feedback, listen, read nonverbal cues, and share ideas effectively is a key to successful customer service. Since these are "life" skills, you can practice them anywhere and gain in your personal as well as professional relationships. Preview the following strategies and select a few to work on.

Strategies for Improvement

- *Regularly elicit feedback and ideas for improvement from others on your communication style and effectiveness.*
- *Identify at least five people whom you believe to have excellent communication skills. Have lunch with or network with them, and informally interview them about how they got to be such good communicators. This will enhance your knowledge, strengthen your relationships with these people, and make them feel good about their skills.*
- *Read books and articles on effective interpersonal communication.*
- *Attend a course on interpersonal communication at a local school or college.*
- *Develop a list of ways that you can provide feedback to others.*
- *Practice these skills regularly in a variety of situations.*

Creative Thinking Skills

To become a valued asset, you need to be able to go beyond normal paradigms (the way you typically view things). By breaking out of the traditional way of thinking, looking for new ways of doing things, and focusing on excellence, you move ahead of many coworkers who satisfy themselves with the status quo. Try the following tips for improvement.

Strategies for Improvement

- *Look at everything with which you come into contact (e.g., processes, procedures, policies, forms, products, services) from the standpoint of how it can be improved. Make recommendations to your supervisor.*
- *Read books or articles on creativity.*
- *Attend seminars or college courses on the topic.*
- *Develop an "idea file." Write down and keep ideas for future development or action.*
- *Network with others to share ideas for improvement.*
- *Challenge yourself with puzzles and exercises that stretch your mind.*

Interpersonal Skills

At no time in the history of business in the United States has the skill of working effectively with others, especially those who are different from yourself, been more important. Many companies have now adopted a team environment—employees work together on projects or tasks as a group, are accountable for results as a group, and are rewarded as a group. An inability to function in such an environment can lead to personal, team, and organizational failure while also alienating customers.

In the customer service arena, your ability to deal with others in a variety of situations can determine whether you succeed. You must be able to communicate and relate with a variety of personality and cultural styles, be willing to share information and interact with others, and deal with changing situations. Some ways to accomplish these things follow.

Strategies for Success

- *Volunteer to serve on a cross-functional team or committee in order to practice your communication and networking skills.*

- *Read books and articles on interpersonal skill building.*

- *Join a professional organization and get involved on committees or a board of directors.*

- *Actively participate in workplace group activities and committees.*

- *Attend after-work functions to get to know coworkers in a different environment.*

- *Target one knowledgeable, experienced person to serve as your career mentor (someone who can guide and coach you). Meet with your mentor and ask for tips on success and advancement.*

Leadership Skills

As organizations continue to change, employees will be required to assume new roles and exercise leadership not normally associated with their jobs. At some point, you will need to assume control of a situation or project in order to bring about a resolution or satisfy a customer. Often, you will be expected to do this in the absence of guidelines or directives from supervisors. Preview the following strategies and select ones that will assist your growth.

Strategies for Success

- *Before approaching others with an idea or proposal, list advantages on a piece of paper. Use them to defend your idea.*

- *Identify prominent historical leaders. Read their autobiographies and use their successful behaviors.*

- *Take the time to build relationships and gain influence.*

- *Read literature on leadership.*

- *Attend workshops or courses on the topic.*
- *Get actively involved in professional organizations by volunteering to chair committees or serve on a board of directors. You gain leadership experience and exposure by doing so.*

Negotiation Skills

Many of the daily encounters you'll have with customers, vendors, coworkers, and bosses will test your ability to compromise, collaborate, accommodate, and work toward a situation both parties can live with (win-win problem solving).

Strategies for Success

- *Practice compromise and sharing skills with others rather than always trying to win or be right.*
- *Read articles or books on the topic.*
- *Attend negotiation workshops or courses.*
- *Observe others in sales or negotiation situations. Make mental notes of their positive and negative actions. Use their positive techniques when you perform similar tasks or encounter similar situations.*

Problem-Solving Skills

As the workplace evolves, employees are being asked to do more with less (e.g., less money, fewer resources) while maintaining quality service. Your employer will likely look to you to recognize problems, develop resolution strategies, and implement them. How well you can do this is crucial. The following suggestions, coupled with what you read in Chapter 9, can get you started in developing or honing your problem-solving skills.

Strategies for Success

- *Volunteer to participate on committees that are established to solve problems or develop or redesign new products or processes.*
- *For every problem or challenge you encounter, try to come up with at least two possible solutions.*
- *Attend courses or workshops on problem solving.*
- *Read books, articles, or other publications on problem solving.*
- *Find information on organizations that have overcome adversity to regain market share after a loss of prestige or customer trust or respect (e.g., Coca-Cola after the failed 1985 introduction of the New Coke product, Tylenol after the 1982 tampering incident). Study how the decisions made turned the situations around.*

Technical Skills

Since so much of the customer service function is tied to various aspects of technology, you'll need to adapt to and master a variety of technical skills. In order to process information and serve the customer, you'll access various sources of information stored in computers. You will also need to operate a variety of machinery, equipment, and technology in order to be successful.

Strategies for Success

- *Read magazine articles, books, and other publications about the latest changes or inventions in the technology used in your profession.*
- *Attend courses that teach the operation and use of technology related to your job.*
- *Take courses on various software programs to expand your knowledge about the capabilities of the software products and to enhance your skills.*
- *Spend time surfing the Internet just to gain experience on navigating and on locating data.*
- *Practice, practice, practice.*

A Final Thought About Customer Service

Throughout this book, we've reviewed problems and strategies related to better serving the customer. We've looked at trends and how they do or will affect you as a customer service provider. Knowledge of all of those topics is crucial for the delivery of service excellence. However, the key component of the process is the customer. Never lose sight of the fact that the customer is your reason for existence in the workplace. Focus all your energies on understanding and responding to the customer and his or her needs. A good summary of what customer service is can be found on walls of offices all over the country. It is reprinted here. You may want to make a copy of it and post it on your work area wall as a reminder of your purpose.

> **The customer** is the most important person in any business.
>
> **The customer** is not dependent on us—we are dependent on the customer.
>
> **The customer** is not an interruption of our work—the customer is the reason for our work.
>
> **The customer** does us a favor when he or she calls—we are not doing the customer a favor by serving.
>
> **The customer** is part of our business—not an outsider.

The customer is not a cold statistic—he or she is a flesh-and-blood human being with feelings and emotions like our own.

The customer is not someone to argue with or match wits with.

The customer is a person who brings us his or her wants—it is our job to fill those wants.

The customer is deserving of the most courteous and attentive treatment we can provide.

The customer is the lifeblood of every business.

Like this operational motto, this book contains only words aimed at expressing concepts and ideas. It is up to you to decide whether the strategies and techniques you've read about are valuable. If you decide that they are, you'll then have to develop an action plan for implementation. This book is not the crucial link with your customer—you are!

7 | BUILDING FOR TOMORROW

> **CONCEPT:** Developing a plan for action to improve customer service is a goal worthy of your consideration.

Reflect on what you've experienced throughout this book and then turn to the Personal Action Plan at the end of this book and develop your own action plan. Refer to it regularly and share it with others so that they can encourage you to achieve your goals.

Summary

Chapter Summary

For years, some American organizations took a relaxed approach to doing business in which they disregarded the rise of their competitors. In recent decades, as competition from Asia, Europe, and elsewhere has gained momentum, companies in the United States that were previously satisfied with status quo began to pay attention. Recent decades have brought about the realization that traditional product and service leaders won't remain leaders in the face of strong competition. This awareness has served as a wake-up call to those organizations. Is it too late for those companies to regain their competitive edge? Time will tell, but the fact that awareness and focus are now centered on creating true customer-focused cultures is a good indication that there is a strong chance of success in the future.

CHAPTER REVIEW QUESTIONS

1. What are some of the major challenges that lie ahead for customer service professionals? _____

_____

_____

2. How will projected changes in the demographic makeup of society affect the customer service profession from the perspective of the customer? From the perspective of the customer service professional?

_____

_____

_____

3. How will technology affect the way service is delivered in the future?

_____

_____

_____

4. In what ways have you seen laws affect the delivery of service in the United States?_____

_____

_____

5. How might the economy affect service delivery?_____

_____

_____

6. What are some of the key projections for growth in the service economy? _____

_____

_____

7. How important will education and training be in the future?

_____

_____

8. What global factors have affected and will continue to affect customer needs and service delivery? _____

_____

_____

9. What are some of the key skills you'll need to be successful as a customer service professional in the future? _____

_____

_____

10. What are some steps you can take to prepare for the customer service job of tomorrow? _____

_____

_____

▼ SEARCH IT OUT

Search the Internet for Customer Service Articles

Log on to the Internet and search for information on trends related to customer service. Be prepared to discuss your findings in class. Search for some of the following topics:

Consumer rights

Legal environment related to customer service

Employee training and education

Technology in customer service

Changing demographics

Economic shifts

Product tampering

COLLABORATIVE _Learning Activity_

Emphasizing Education

Team up with several other people to form a discussion group. Spend some time talking about what you believe the role of schools is today and how well the schools are preparing young people for the work world. Share specific personal examples from your own educational background or that of someone you know.

During the next three to four weeks, I will work on _____

_____

_____.

My goal(s) in addressing this issue is to:

1. _____.

2. _____.

3. _____.

To accomplish my goal(s), I will need the following resources or reference materials:

_____

_____

_____.

I will enlist help to coach, guide, and/or encourage me from _____

_____

My target date for completion and improvement is _____.

I will know I have reached my goal(s) when _____.

_____.

Name _____

Title _____

Organization/School _____

Address _____

City/State/ZIP _____

Phone (___) _____

Customer feedback is crucial for delivering effective service and addressing specific needs. For us to make necessary additions, deletions, or corrections to this book, we need your help. Please take a few minutes to provide feedback in the following areas and return this questionnaire to the address at the end of the survey. In exchange for your thoughts and time, we'll send you a free booklet on effective interpersonal communication techniques.

(Photocopy the questionnaire if you prefer.)

Thank you.

1. Describe yourself in terms of customer contact experience:

   _____ Entry level (up to 1 year)   _____ Midlevel (2–5 years)   _____ Senior (5 + years)

2. Are you currently working in a frontline customer contact position?

   Yes _____   No _____

3. The information provided in this book was clearly written and easy to read.

   1_____ 2_____ 3_____ 4_____ 5_____ 6_____ 7_____
   Strongly   Neutral   Strongly
   Disagree   Agree

4. The techniques outlined in this book are realistic and useful.

   1_____ 2_____ 3_____ 4_____ 5_____ 6_____ 7_____
   Strongly   Neutral   Strongly
   Disagree   Agree

5. The supplemental materials (figures, role-play activities, questions, references) added value to the text.

   1_____ 2_____ 3_____ 4_____ 5_____ 6_____ 7_____
   Strongly   Neutral   Strongly
   Disagree   Agree

6. The design of this book was logical, efficient, effective, and easy to follow.

   1_____ 2_____ 3_____ 4_____ 5_____ 6_____ 7_____
   Strongly   Neutral   Strongly
   Disagree   Agree

7. The level of information was well targeted to entry-level to midlevel customer contact personnel.

1_____ 2_____ 3_____ 4_____ 5_____ 6_____ 7_____
Strongly   Neutral   Strongly
Disagree   Agree

8. The text included real-world examples and scenarios to which I could relate.

1_____ 2_____ 3_____ 4_____ 5_____ 6_____ 7_____
Strongly   Neutral   Strongly
Disagree   Agree

9. I can apply information or ideas learned directly to my current or future job.

1_____ 2_____ 3_____ 4_____ 5_____ 6_____ 7_____
Strongly   Neutral   Strongly
Disagree   Agree

10. I plan to use this book as a reference in the future.

1_____ 2_____ 3_____ 4_____ 5_____ 6_____ 7_____
Strongly   Neutral   Strongly
Disagree   Agree

11. This book met my overall needs and expectations.

1_____ 2_____ 3_____ 4_____ 5_____ 6_____ 7_____
Strongly   Neutral   Strongly
Disagree   Agree

12. I will recommend this book to others.

1_____ 2_____ 3_____ 4_____ 5_____ 6_____ 7_____
Strongly   Neutral   Strongly
Disagree   Agree

13. What chapter was most valuable to you? Why?

14. Please tell us one thing related to customer service that you would like to have seen added to this book.

15. In your mind, what is the most critical issue facing customer service professionals today?

16. What other topics related to customer service are of interest to you?

17. Were there any typographical or other errors noted in the text?

   Send to: Bob Lucas, President
   Creative Presentation Resources, Inc.
   P.O. Box 180487
   Casselberry, Florida 32718-0487
   (800) 308-0399/(407) 695-5535
   FAX: (407) 695-7447
   Email: **blucas@presentationresources.net**

A

Acknowledgment A communication technique for use with customers who have a complaint or are upset. It involves recognizing the customer's level of emotion before moving on to help solve their problem.

Active voice A verb form that directs action to the reader. This helps ensure that the reader quickly gets the essence of a message because it is clear who or what will receive the action and when, where, or why the action will take place.

Added Value And Results For Me (AVAR-FM) The concept of showing someone what can be gained from taking a certain action or buying in to an idea. The concept helps reinforce why someone should accept what is being offered or proposed.

Articulation The manner or clarity in which verbal messages are delivered. Synonyms include *pronunciation* and *enunciation*.

Assertiveness The projection of a presence that is assured, confident, and capable without seeming to be aggressive or arrogant.

Assigning meaning The phase of the listening process in which the brain attempts to match a received sound or message with other information stored in the brain in order to recognize or extract meaning. (See also *Comprehension*.)

Attending The phase of the listening process during which a listener focuses attention on a specific sound or message being received from the environment.

Attitudes Emotional responses to people, ideas, and objects. Attitudes are based on values, they differ between individuals and cultures, and they affect the way people deal with various problems and situations. (See also *Values*.)

B

Beliefs Perceptions or assumptions that individuals or cultures maintain. Beliefs are based on past experiences, memories, and interpretations, and they influence how people act and interact with certain individuals or groups.

Burnout A category of stress that encompasses exhaustion, lack of enthusiasm, reduced productivity, and apathy toward the job and customers.

C

Circadian rhythm The physiological 24-hour cycle associated with the earth's rotation that affects metabolic and sleep patterns in human beings.

Clauses Related groups of words that contain a subject and a verb.

Closed-ended questions These questions typically start with a verb and elicit short one-syllable answers (e.g., yes, no, or a number). They can be used to clarify, verify information already given, control conversation, or affirm something.

Clusters Groupings of nonverbal behaviors indicating intent (positive or negative). For example, crossed arms, closed body posture, frowning, or turning away could indicate negative intent, and smiling, open gestures, and friendly touching could indicate positive intent.

Comprehension The phase of the listening process in which the brain attempts to match a received sound or message with other information stored in the brain in order to recognize or extract meaning. (See also *Assigning Meaning*.)

Conflict resolution style The manner in which a person handles conflict. People typically use one of five approaches to resolving conflict—avoidance, compromise, competition, accommodation, or collaboration.

Congruence In communication, congruence relates to ensuring that verbal messages match or are in agreement with the accompanying nonverbal cues.

Crisis managers People who wait until the last minute to address a problem or take an action. The result is that others are then inconvenienced and have to shift their priorities to help solve the problem.

Cues See *Nonverbal messages*.

Cultural diversity The differences and similarities attributed to various groups of people within a culture.

Culture A set of fundamental beliefs, ideas, practices, attitudes, and norms for a group that guide behaviors within the group.

Customer-focused organizations Organizations that spend energy and effort on satisfying internal and external customers by first identifying customer needs and then establishing policies, procedures, management, and reward systems to support excellence in service delivery.

Customer needs Motivators that cause customers to seek out specific types of products or services. These may be market driven, based on advertising customers have seen, or they may tie directly to Maslow's hierarchy of needs. (See also *Maslow's hierarchy*.)

Customer service The ability of knowledgeable, capable, and enthusiastic employees to deliver products and services to their internal and external customers in a manner that satisfies identified and unidentified needs and ultimately results in positive word-of-mouth publicity and return business.

Customers See *External customers; Internal customers*.

D

Demonstrative pronouns These pronouns point directly to a noun (e.g., *this* book or *your* contract).

Deregulation The removal by governments of legislative or regulatory guidelines that inhibit and control an industry (e.g., transportation, natural gas, and telecommunications).

Dissatisfiers Elements of the service environment that inhibit satisfaction of customer needs and ultimately can result in reduced customer loyalty.

E

E-commerce The entire spectrum of companies that market products and service on the Internet and through other technology; and the process of accessing these products and services on the Internet by consumers.

Empowerment The possession of decision-making and problem-solving authority by lower-level employees in an organization. Empowerment means that permission need not be obtained from higher levels to take an action or serve a customer.

Etiquette The rules, manners, and practices of an organization, profession, or society.

Eustress A term coined by psychologist Hans Selye to describe positive stress that people sometimes experience when they set goals or objectives for themselves. Eustress provides the stimulation and exhilaration that are essential for personal expansion and growth.

External customers People outside the organization who purchase or lease products and services. This group includes vendors, suppliers, and so on. (See also *Internal customers*.)

F

Father of Listening Name sometimes applied to Ralph C. Nichols. It arose from the extensive amount of research he conducted and his contributions to understanding how human beings listen.

Faulty assumptions Service provider projections made about the underlying meanings of customer messages based on past experiences.

Fight or flight syndrome A term used by scientists to describe the body's reaction to stressors, when the heart starts pumping adrenaline into the blood-stream and the lungs start taking in more oxygen. This provides the fuel needed to deal with the situation. (See also *Stressors*.)

G

Gender The classification of pronouns that indicates whether the item is masculine, feminine, or neuter.

Global terms Potentially inflammatory words or phrases. They tend to reflect the user's inappropriate generalizing about people (e.g., *always, never, everyone, everything, all the time*).

Globalization The term applied to an ongoing trend of information, knowledge, and resource sharing around the world. The increased mobility of society and the easier access to transportation and technology have made it possible for more people to travel and obtain products and services from international sources than ever before.

H

Hearing The passive physiological process of gathering sound waves and transmitting them to the brain for analysis. It is the first phase of the listening process.

Hierarchy of needs See *Maslow's hierarchy*.

Hostile work environment A phrase legally defining a work environment in which offensive behaviors occur (e.g., ethnic, racial, or other acts such as offensive jokes are told, inappropriate and/or unwanted touching occurs, or certain groups are denied opportunities).

Hygiene The maintenance of a healthy body through practices such as regular bathing, washing of hair, brushing of teeth, cleaning of fingernails, and using commercial products to eliminate or mask body odor.

I

Inclusive Term referring to the concept of ensuring that people of all races, genders, religious, and ethnic backgrounds are included in activities in the workplace and elsewhere.

Inflection The change in tone of voice as one speaks. This quality is also called *pitch* and adds vocal variety and punctuation to verbal messages.

Internal customers People within an organization who either require support and service or provide information, products, and services. Such customers include peers, coworkers, bosses, subordinates, or people from other areas of an organization. (See also *External customers*.)

Internet Service Providers Technology companies that provide relay services for customers by linking their computers through a company's server. Customers can then access the Internet system in order to receive and transmit information.

J

Jargon (See also *Slang*.) A form of slang that is unique to a group, for example, an industry or a profession.

K

KISS principle The practice of Keeping It Short and Sweet when performing a task.

L

Lag time (or listening gap) The term applied to the difference between the rate at which the human brain can receive and process information and that at which most adults speak.

Learning organizations A term used by Peter Senge in his book *The Fifth Discipline* to describe organizations that value knowledge, education, and employee training. They also learn from their competition, industry trends, and other sources, and they develop systems to support continued growth and development in order to remain competitive.

Listening An active, learned process consisting of four phases—receiving or hearing the message, attending, comprehending or assigning meaning, and responding.

Listening gap See *lag time*.

M

Maslow's hierarchy A theory developed by Abraham Maslow, a psychologist, author, and educator. In extensive studies during the post-World War II era, Maslow identified five levels of human needs: physiological (basic), safety, social, esteem, and self-actualization. His work contributed to the understanding of employee motivation.

Mentees The recipients of the efforts of mentors.

Mentors Individuals who dedicate time and effort to befriend and assist others. In an organization, they are typically people who have a lot of knowledge, experience, skills, and initiative and a large personal and professional network.

Moment of truth A phrase popularized by Scandinavian Airlines President Jan Carlzon in his popular 1987 book of the same title. A *moment of truth* is defined as any situation in which a customer comes into contact with a representative of an organization.

N

Nichols, Ralph G. See *Father of Listening*.

Nonverbal messages (cues) Movements, gestures, body positions, vocal qualities, and a variety of unspoken signals sent by people, often in conjunction with verbal messages.

North American Free Trade Agreement (NAFTA) A trade agreement entered into by the United States, Canada, and Mexico to help eliminate barriers to trade, promote fair trade across borders, increase investment opportunities, and promote and protect intellectual property rights.

O

Objections Reasons given by customers during an interaction with a salesperson or service provider for not wanting to purchase a product or service (e.g., "I don't need one," "I can't afford it").

Open-ended questions These questions typically start with words like *who, when, what, how,* and *why* and are used to engage others in conversation or gain input and ideas.

P

Paralanguage Voice qualities (e.g., pitch, rate, tone) or noises and vocalizations (e.g., "Hmmm" or "Ahhh"), made as someone speaks, that let a speaker know that his or her message is being listened to and followed.

Parts of speech The elements of the English language. Words are categorized into seven primary groupings—nouns, pronouns, verbs, adverbs, adjectives, prepositions, and conjunctions. Some linguists also include interjections and articles as categories.

Perception checking The process of clarifying a nonverbal cue that was received by stating what behavior was observed, giving one or two possible interpretations, and then asking the message sender for clarification.

Phrases Groups of two or more words that lack a subject and a verb. Phrases usually act as modifiers.

Pitch See *Inflection.*

Prohibitions Local, state, or federal regulations that prevent a service provider from satisfying a customer's request even though the provider would normally do so. (See also *Service options.*)

R

Rapport The silent bond formed between two people as a result of their having interests in common.

Rate of speech The number of words spoken per minute. Some research studies have found that the average rate of speech for adults in Western cultures is approximately 125 to 150 words per minute (wpm).

Relationship-Rating Point Scale The mental rating system that customers apply to service and service providers. Ratings range from *Exemplary* to *Unsatisfactory,* with *Average* being assigned when service occurs as expected. The points are based on a number of factors, starting with initial impressions and including the quality and level of service provided.

RUMBA An acronym for the five criteria (**R**ealistic, **U**nderstandable, **M**easurable, **B**elievable, and **A**ttainable) used to establish and measure employee performance goals.

S

Salutation The greeting included in written communications (e.g., *Dear Dr., Dear Sir,* or *Dear Human Resources Director*).

Semantics The scientific study of relationships between signs, symbols, and words and their meaning. The way that words are used or stressed often affects their perceived meaning.

Service breakdowns Situations when customers have expectations of a certain type or level of service that are not met by a service provider.

Service culture The values, beliefs, norms, rituals, and practices of a group or organization.

Service economy A term describing the trend in which businesses have shifted emphasis from production and manufacturing to service delivery. As part of this evolution, many organizations have developed specifically to provide services to customers.

Service industry A term describing businesses engaged primarily in service delivery. *Service sector* is a more accurate term because many organizations provide some form of service to their customers even though they are primarily engaged in research, development, and manufacturing of products.

Service options Alternatives offered by service providers when an original request by a customer cannot be honored because of restrictions such as governmental statutory regulations, nonavailability of products, or inability to perform as requested. (See also *Prohibitions.*)

Service philosophy The approach that an organization takes to providing service and addressing the needs of customers.

Service providers Technology companies that provide relay services for customers by linking their computer through the company's server. Customers can then access the Inernet system in order to receive and transmit information.

Service recovery The process of righting a wrong or correcting something that has gone wrong involving the provision of a product or service to a customer. The concept involves not only replacing defective products but also going the extra step of providing compensation for the customer's inconvenience.

Service strategy A combination of systems and practices coordinated to help an organization determine how it will conduct business and remain competitive.

Slang Informal language or words developed by adapting existing words or creating new ones, usually without regard for contemporary rules of grammar.

Spatial cues The various culturally acceptable physical distances between people when they are engaged in interactions.

Stereotypes Generalizations made about an individual or group and not based on reality. Similar people are often grouped together for ease in categorizing them.

Stressors Factors in people's lives that cause them to react positively or negatively to a situation that caused pressure. (See also *Fight or Flight syndrome.*)

Style manuals Written guidelines produced by some organizations that outline how correspondence and presentation materials will be organized and how they should look. This is done to ensure a consistent, professional image in all written materials used to conduct business.

Subcultures Groups within a cultural group. Behavioral characteristics, language patterns, mode of dress, beliefs, or other tangible and intangible factors often identify such groups (e.g., within the United States are a variety of ethnic, religious, and other groups). (See also *Culture.*)

Subjects Words or phrases that identify or name the person, place, idea, quality, thing, or activity about which something is being said. A subject describes the focus of discussion (who or what). (See also *Clauses; Phrases*).

Syntax The way words (parts of speech) are arranged in a sentence and their relationships to one another.

T

TARP (Technical Assistance Research Program) An Arlington, Virginia–based research firm specializing in customer service research studies.

Telecommuting A trend seen in many congested metropolitan areas and government offices. To reduce traffic and pollution and to conserve resources (e.g., rent, telephone, and technology systems) many organizations allow employees to set up home offices and electronically communicate with and forward information to their corporate offices.

Telephone device for the disabled (TTY) Also known as Telephone Device for the Disabled (TDD) A teletypewriter used by people with hearing disabilities for typing messages back and forth via telephone lines.

Templates Formatted style sheets that can be used to prepare letters, forms, memorandums, or other such routine documentation. Many computer software programs come with such features programmed into them for quick reference.

Time management The systematic practice of categorizing daily activities, identifying and eliminating factors that interfere with efficiency, and developing effective strategies for getting the most out of the time available.

Time wasters Events, people, and other factors that create unnecessary loss of time.

Total Quality Management (TQM) A systematic approach to identifying and quantifying best practices in an organization and/or industry in order to make improvements in effectiveness and efficiency. Leading proponents of TQM are W. Edwards Deming, Joseph Juran, and Philip Crosby.

Total Quality Service (TQS) The service industry equivalent to total quality management (TQM), used in manufacturing firms. A main difference between the two is that TQS focuses on customers rather than systems and processes.

Two-way communication An active process in which two individuals apply all the elements of interpersonal communication (e.g., listening, feedback, positive language) in order to bring about the effective exchange of information and ideas.

V

Values A set of beliefs about the worth of an idea, person, place, thing, or practice as perceived by individuals, groups, or cultures. Values affect attitudes and behavior.

Voice quality The sound of one's voice. Some terms attributed to voice quality are *raspy, nasal, hoarse,* and *gravelly*.

Volume Loudness or softness of the voice when speaking.

W

Welfare to Work Partnership A national, nonpartisan, not-for-profit organization established by small, medium, and large businesses to help employ people formerly in federal assistance programs.

Workforce Investment Act of 1998 A law signed by President William Jefferson Clinton to replace the Job Training Partnership Act of 1982. It provides resources to job seekers, including skill assessment, counseling, and job skills training.

Workplace violence A trend that has developed and escalated during the 1990s. Spawned by changes in the workplace, shifting societal values and beliefs, and a variety of other factors, violence in the workplace continues to grow.

Abromovitz, Hedy G.. and Abromovitz, Les, *Bringing TQM on the QT to Your Organization*, SPC Press, Knoxville, Tenn., 1993.

Aguilar, Leslie, and Stokes, Linda, *Multicultural Customer Service: Providing Outstanding Service Across Cultures*, Irwin/McGraw-Hill, Burr Ridge, Ill., 1996.

Anderson, Kristin, *Great Customer Service on the Telephone*, AMACOM, New York, 1992.

Anderson, Kristin, and Zemke, Ron, *Knock Their Socks Off Answers*, AMACOM, New York, 1995.

Axtell, Roger E., *Gestures: The Do's and Taboos of Body Language Around the World*, Wiley, New York, 1991.

Barlow, Janelle, and Miller, Claus, *A Complaint Is a Gift: Using Customer Feedback as a Strategic Tool*, Barrett-Koehler, San Francisco, 1996.

Bayan, Richard, *Words That Sell*, Contemporary Books, Chicago, 1984.

Berko, Roy M., Rosenfeld, Lawrence B., and Samovar, Larry A., *Connecting: A Culture-Sensitive Approach to Interpersonal Communication Competency*, 2nd ed., Harcourt Brace, Fort Worth, Tex., 1997.

Blanchard, Ken, and Bowles, Sheldon, *Raving Fans: A Revolutionary Approach to Customer Service*, William Morrow, New York, 1993.

Broydrick, Stephen C., *How May I Help You?: Providing Personal Service in an Impersonal World*, Irwin/McGraw-Hill, Burr Ridge, Ill., 1994.

Carr, Clay, *Front-Line Customer Service: 15 Keys to Customer Satisfaction*, Wiley, New York, 1990.

Chen, Guo-Ming, and Starosta, William J., *Foundations of Intercultural Communication*, Allyn and Bacon, Needham Heights, Mass., 1998.

Cohen, R., *Negotiating Across Cultures: Intercultural Communication in an Interdependent World*, U.S. Institute of Peace, 1997.

Coscia, Stephen, *Customer Service Over the Phone*, Telecom Books, New York, 1998.

Coscia, Stephen, *TELE-Stress: Relief for Call Center Stress*, Telecom Books, New York, 1998.

Currie, Marilyn, *Achieving Customer Loyalty: A Retailer's Guide to Creating and Sustaining a Service Strategy*, Retail Learning Initiative, Toronto, Canada, 1996.

Davidson, Jeff, *The Complete Idiot's Guide to Managing Stress*, Alpha Books, New York, 1997.

Dee, David, *The Extra Mile: Building Profitable Customer Relations Every Time*, Dartnell Corporation, Chicago, Ill., 1994.

Dee, David, *Stand-Out Service: Talk Straight, Think Positive, and Smile!* The Dartnell Corporation, Chicago, Ill., 1994.

De Vries, Mary A., *The Complete Word Book: The Practical Guide to Anything and Everything You Need to Know About Words and How to Use Them*, Barnes & Noble, New York, 1999.

Dodd, Carley H., *Dynamics of Intercultural Communication*, 4th ed., Brown & Benchmark, Madison, Wisc., 1995.

Edstrom, K.R.S., *Conquering Stress*, Barron's, Hauppauge, NY, 1993.

Fast, Julius, *Body Language*, Pocket Books, New York, NY, 1960.

Finch, Lloyd C., *Telephone Courtesy & Customer Service*, Crisp Publications, Los Altos, Calif., 1987.

Finch, Lloyd C., *Twenty Ways to Improve Customer Service*, Crisp Publications, Los Altos, Calif., 1994.

Finch, Lloyd C., *Success as a CSR*, Crisp Publications, Los Altos, Calif., 1998.

Fisher, Donna, and Vilas, Sandy, Power Networking: *55 Secrets for Personal and Professional Success*, MountainHarbour Publications, Austin, 1992.

Fisher, Judith E., *Telephone Skills at Work*, Irwin/McGraw-Hill, Burr Ridge, Ill., 1994.

Fisher, Judith E., *The Phone Book: Telephone Skills for Business Success*, Irwin/McGraw-Hill, Chicago, Ill., 1996.

Glanz, Barbara, *The Creative Communicator*, Irwin/McGraw-Hill, Homewood, Ill., 1993.

Gorman, Tom, *The Complete Idiot's Almanac of Business Letters and Memos*, Alpha Books, New York, 1997.

Green, Michael, and Ripley, Jonathon G., *Communicating for Future Business Professionals*, Prentice Hall, Upper Saddle River, N.J., 1998.

Grey, John, *Men Are From Mars, Women Are From Venus*, HarperCollins, New York, 1992.

Griffin, Jill, *Customer Loyalty: How to Earn It How to Keep It,* Jossey-Bass, San Francisco, 1995.

Hanna, Michael S., and Wilson, Gerald, *Communicating in Business and Professional Settings,* 4th ed., McGraw-Hill, New York, 1998.

Hanson, Peter G., *Stress for Success: Thriving on Stress at Work,* Collins Publishers, Toronto, Canada, 1989.

Hargrave, Jan, *Let Me See Your Body Talk,* Kendall/Hunt, Dubuque, Iowa, 1995.

Harris, Elaine K., *Customer Service: A Practical Approach,* 2nd ed., Prentice Hall, Upper Saddle River, N.J., 2000.

Harvey, Eric, and The Walk the Talk Team, *180 Ways to Walk the Customer Service Talk: The How-To Handbook for Everyone in Your Organization,* Performance Systems, Dallas, 1999.

Hathaway, Patti, *Giving and Receiving Criticism: Your Key to Interpersonal Success,* Crisp Publications, Menlo Park, Calif., 1990.

Hecht, Michael L., Collier, Mary J., and Ribeau, Sidney A., *African American Communication; Ethnic Identity and Cultural Interpretation,* Sage Publications, Thousand Oaks, Calif., 1993.

Helmstetter, Shad, *What You Say When You Talk to Yourself,* Pocket Books, New York, 1986.

Hemsath, Dave, and Yerkes, Leslie, *301 Ways to Have Fun at Work,* Berrett-Koehler, San Francisco, 1997.

Hill, Norman C., *Improving Peer Relationships: Achieving Results Informally,* Crisp Publications, Menlo Park, Calif., 1996.

Hitchcock, David J., *Asian Values and the United States: How Much Conflict?,* The Center for Strategic and International Studies, Washington, D.C., 1994.

Ivy, Dianna K., and Backlund, Phil, *Exploring GenderSpeak: Personal Effectiveness in Gender Communication,* McGraw-Hill, New York, 1994.

Jandt, Fred, *The Customer Is Usually Wrong!,* Park Avenue Publications, Indianapolis, Ind., 1995.

Karr, Ron, and Blohowiak, Don, *The Complete Idiot's Guide to Great Customer Service,* Alpha Books, New York, 1997.

Kenton, Sherron, and Valentine, Deborah, *Crosstalk: Communicating in a Multicultural Workplace,* Prentice Hall, Upper Saddle River, N.J., 1997.

Kindler, Herbert S., *Managing Disagreement Constructively,* Crisp Publications, Menlo Park, Calif., 1996.

Knouse, Stephen B., Rosenfeld, Paul, and Culbertson, Amy L., *Hispanics in the Workplace,* Sage Publications, Newbury Park, Calif., 1992.

Leathers, David G., *Successful Nonverbal Communication,* 3rd ed., Allyn and Bacon, Boston, 1997.

Leland, Karen, and Bailey, Keith, *Customer Service for Dummies,* IDG Books, Foster City, Calif., 1995.

Lickson, Charles P., *Ironing It Out: Seven Simple Steps to Resolving Conflict,* Crisp Publications, Menlo Park, Calif., 1996.

Lindsekk-Roberts, Sheryl, *Business Writing for Dummies,* IDG Books, Foster City, Calif., 1999.

Lloyd, Sam R., *Developing Positive Assertiveness: Practical Techniques for Personal Success,* Crisp Publications, Menlo Park, Calif., 1995.

Lucas, Robert W., *Effective Interpersonal Relationships,* Mirror Press, Burr Ridge, Ill., 1999.

Lucas, Robert W., *Job Strategies for New Employees,* American Media, West Des Moines, Iowa, 1996.

Luhn, Rebecca R., *Managing Anger: Methods for a Happier and Healthier Life,* Crisp Publications, Menlo Park, Calif., 1992.

MacNeill, Dedra J., *Customer Service Excellence,* American Media, West Des Moines, Iowa, 1994.

Mallory, Charles, *How to Get Everything Done (and Still Have a Life),* American Media, West Des Moines, Iowa, 1997.

Mayer, Jeffrey J., *Time Management for Dummies,* 2nd ed., IDG Books, Foster City, Calif., 1999.

Mehrabian, Albert, *Silent Messages: Implicit Communication of Emotions and Attitudes,* 2nd Ed., Wadsworth Publishing Co., Blemont, CA, 1981.

Morris, Desmond, *Bodytalk: The Meaning of Human Gestures,* Crown, New York, 1994.

Morrison, Terri, Conaway, Wayne A., and Borden, George A., *Kiss, Bow, or Shake Hands: How to Do Business in Sixty Countries,* Adams Media Corporation, Holbrook, Mass., 1994.

Neher, William, and Waite, David H., *The Business and Professional Communicator,* Allyn and Bacon, Needham Heights, Mass., 1993.

Nelson, Bob, *1001 Ways to Energize Employees,* Workman Publishing, New York, 1994.

Nierenberg, Gerald I., and Calero, Henry H., *How to Read a Person Like a Book,* Barnes & Noble, New York, 1993.

Pepper, Gerald L., *Communicating in Organizations: A Cultural Approach,* McGraw-Hill, New York, 1995.

Potter, Beverly A., *Preventing Job Burnout: Transforming Work Pressure Into Productivity,* Crisp Publications, Menlo Park, Calif., 1996.

Quinlan, Kathryn A., *Customer Service Representative,* Capstone Press, Mankoto, 1999.

Raines, Claire, *Beyond Generation X: A Practical Guide for Managers,* Crisp Publications, Menlo Park, Calif., 1997.

Reardon, Kathleen K., *They Don't Get It Do They?: Communication in the Workplace—Closing the Gap Between Women and Men,* Little, Brown, Boston, 1995.

Reynolds, Larry, *The Trust Effect: Creating the High Trust High Performance Organization,* Nicholas Brealey, London, 1997.

Samovar, Larry A., Porter, Richard E., and Stefani, Lisa A., *Communication Between Cultures,* Wadsworth, Belmont, Calif., 1998.

Sanders, Betsy, *Fabled Service: Ordinary Acts, Extraordinary Outcomes,* Pfeiffer, San Diego, Calif., 1995.

Satterwhite, Marilyn and Olson-Sutton, Judith, *Business Communication at Work,* Glencoe/McGraw-Hill, Columbus, Ohio, 2000.

Senge, Peter M., *The Fifth Discipline: The Art and Practice of the Learning Organization,* Doubleday, New York, 1994.

Shelton, Nelda, and Burton, Sharon, *Assertiveness Skills,* Irwin/Mc-Graw-Hill, Burr Ridge, Ill., 1994.

Simons, George, with Zuckerman, Amy J., *Working Together: Succeeding in a Multicultural Organization,* Crisp Publications, Menlo Park, Calif., 1994.

Simons, George, and Weissman, G. Deborah, *Men and Women: Partners at Work,* Crisp Publications, Menlo Park, Calif., 1990.

Sterne, Jim, *Customer Service on the Internet: Building Relationships, Increasing Loyalty, and Staying Competitive,* Wiley, New York, 1996.

Tannen, Deborah, *You Just Don't Understand: Women and Men in Conversations,* Ballantine Books, New York, 1990.

Timm, Paul R., *Customer Service: Career Success Through Customer Satisfaction,* Prentice Hall, Upper Saddle River, N.J., 1998.

Whiteley, Richard C., *The Customer Driven Company: Moving From Talk to Action,* Addison-Wesley, Reading, Mass., 1991.

Willingham, Ron, Hey, *I'm the Customer,* Prentice Hall, Englewood Cliffs, N.J., 1992.

Wolvin, Andrew, and Coakley, Carolyn G., *Listening,* 5th ed., Brown & Benchmark, Madison, Wisc., 1996.

Woods, Donald R., and Ornerod, Shirley D., *Networking: How to Enrich Your Life and Get Things Done,* Pfeiffer, San Diego, 1993.

Zemke, Ron, *Service Recovery: Fixing Broken Customers,* Productivity Press, Portland, Oreg., 1995.

Zemke, Ron, Raines, Claire, and Filipczak, Bob, *Generations at Work: Managing the Clash of Veterans, Boomers, Xers, and Nexters in Your Workplace,* AMACOM, New York, 2000.

Psychological distractors, in listening, 147

Public distance, 113

Purpose, of written communication, 258

Q

Quality
  expectations of, 18
  striving for, 447–448

Questions
  careful use of, 336
  closed-ended, 159, 162–163, 307
  direct, 164–165
  as interruptions, 155–156
  in listening, 159–163, 232
  open-ended, 45, 159, 160–162, 297, 298, 302, 307, 333–334
  positive phrasing of, 79–80, 164
  in problem-solving process, 307–308
  specific answers to, 77, 342

R

Rapport, establishing, 442

Rate of speech, 110, 226–227, 333

RATER model, 447–448

Rational behavioral style, 182–183, 185, 191, 192, 193, 194, 201

Reaffirmation, 473

Realism, 378, 395, 398

Reassurance, 473

Receiver in verbal communication, 72

Receiving messages, 142

Recognition, 142

Refreshments, 128

Refusals, 273

Relationship Rating Point Scale, 441, 469, 473–474

Relationships
  customer, 422–424, 435–438
  importance of, 327–328
  and stress, 368–369

Relativity, in prioritizing tasks, 397

Repetitive tasks, and stress, 367

Reply to all function, 223

Respect, 342, 371, 420, 437, 472, 478

Responding in listening, 143

Responsiveness, 426

Return policies, 41–43

Rewards, 34, 44

Romantic obsession, 382

Rude customers, 300–301

RUMBA, 37–39

S

Samovar, 328n., 330n.

Sarcasm, 336

Satterwaite, Marilyn, 265

Screen pop-ups, 215

Self-assessment questionnaires, 178

Selye, Hans, 359

Semantics, 111

Sender in verbal communication, 72

Senge, Peter, 11–12

Senior customer service (CS) representative/member counselor, 24

Service, 27

Service breakdowns
  causes of, 463–469
  defined, 460
  nature of, 460–461

Service culture
  average versus excellent companies, 58
  customer expectations and, 59–60
  defined, 33–34
  elements of, 34, 35–47
  establishing service strategy, 48
  service delivery systems, 50–52
  strategies for promoting, 54–58
  system components, 49–50
  tools for service measurement, 53–54

Service follow-up, 58, 116, 442–443, 469, 473, 478

Service industry, concept of, 3–4

Service information, 469

Vision, 54, 55

Vision impairments, 339–340

Vocal cues, 93, 109–111, 120

Voice mail, 234–237, 403–404

Voice quality, 110

Voice recognition, 216

Voice response unit (VRU), 215

Volume of voice, 109–110, 226, 333

W

Walk-in traffic, 400–401

Warranties, 422

"We" messages, 78

Website, 217, 218, 220

Welfare to Work Partnership, 15

White-collar workers, 15

Win-win situations, 188

Women. See also Gender
   entering workforce, 16, 493

Word choice, 254–256

Word-of-mouth publicity, 129, 420–421

Wordiness, 256

Workaholism, 369–370

Workforce Investment Act of 1998, 15–16

Workplace
   demographic trends in, 10, 11, 16–17, 490–491
   violence in, 380–383

Written communication
   appearance of, 259–260, 263–264
   basic components of, 250–256
   e-mail, 214, 220–223, 268, 404–405
   importance of, 248–249
   improving customer service through, 262–276
   language differences and, 335
   letters, 263–267
   memorandums (memos), 267–268, 269
   reasons for using, 247–248
   setting tone for, 269–275
   style and writing sources, 275–276
   three-step process for, 257–261

Y

Yale University, 359, 360

Yeltsin, Boris, 14

"You" messages, 78, 84

Younger people
   customer service for, 343–344
   in workforce, 490–491

Z

Zemke, Ron, 21, 440

Photo Credits: